The Effects of U.S. Trade Protection and Promotion Policies

A National Bureau
of Economic Research
Project Report

The Effects of U.S. Trade Protection and Promotion Policies

Edited by Robert C. Feenstra

The University of Chicago Press

Chicago and London

Robert C. Feenstra is professor of economics at the University of California, Davis, and director of the International Trade and Investment Program at the National Bureau of Economic Research. He is also the editor of the *Journal of International Economics*.

The University of Chicago Press, Chicago 60637
The University of Chicago Press, Ltd., London
© 1997 by the National Bureau of Economic Research
All rights reserved. Published 1997
Printed in the United States of America
06 05 04 03 02 01 00 99 98 97   1 2 3 4 5
ISBN: 0-226-23951-9 (cloth)

Library of Congress Cataloging-in-Publication Data

The effects of U.S. trade protection and promotion policies / edited by Robert C. Feenstra.
    p.   cm.—(A National Bureau of Economic Research project report)
    Papers presented at a National Bureau of Economic Research conference held in Richmond, VA, on Oct. 6–7, 1995.
    Includes bibliographical references and index.
    ISBN 0-226-23951-9 (cloth : alk. paper)
    1. United States—Commercial policy—Congresses. 2. United States—Commercial treaties—Congresses. 3. Foreign trade promotion—United States—Congresses. 4. Protectionism—United States—Congresses. 5. Free trade—United States—Congresses. 6. Investments, Foreign—United States—Congresses. 7. Investments, American—Congresses. 8. United States—Foreign economic relations—Japan—Congresses. 9. Japan—Foreign economic relations—United States—Congresses. I. Feenstra, Robert C. II. National Bureau of Economic Research. III. Series.
HF1455.E43 1997
382′.3′0973—dc20   96-38174
                                                CIP

Relation of the Directors to the
Work and Publications of the
National Bureau of Economic Research

1. The object of the National Bureau of Economic Research is to ascertain and to present to the public important economic facts and their interpretation in a scientific and impartial manner. The board of Directors is charged with the responsibility of ensuring that the work of the National Bureau is carried on in strict conformity with this object.

2. The President of the National Bureau shall submit to the Board of Directors, or to its Executive Committee, for their formal adoption all specific proposals for research to be instituted.

3. No research report shall be published by the National Bureau until the President has sent each member of the Board a notice that a manuscript is recommended for publication and that in the President's opinion it is suitable for publication in accordance with the principles of the National Bureau. Such notification will include an abstract or summary of the manuscript's content and a response form for use by those Directors who desire a copy of the manuscript for review. Each manuscript shall contain a summary drawing attention to the nature and treatment of the problem studied, the character of the data and their utilization in the report, and the main conclusions reached.

4. For each manuscript so submitted, a special committee of the Directors (including Directors Emeriti) shall be appointed by majority agreement of the President and Vice Presidents (or by the Executive Committee in case of inability to decide on the part of the President and Vice Presidents), consisting of three Directors selected as nearly as may be one from each general division of the Board. The names of the special manuscript committee shall be stated to each Director when notice of the proposed publication is submitted to him. It shall be the duty of each member of the special manuscript committee to read the manuscript. If each member of the manuscript committee signifies his approval within thirty days of the transmittal of the manuscript, the report may be published. If at the end of that period any member of the manuscript committee withholds his approval, the President shall then notify each member of the Board, requesting approval or disapproval of publication, and thirty days additional shall be granted for this purpose. The manuscript shall then not be published unless at least a majority of the entire Board who shall have voted on the proposal within the time fixed for the receipt of votes shall have approved.

5. No manuscript may be published, though approved by each member of the special manuscript committee, until forty-five days have elapsed from the transmittal of the report in manuscript form. The interval is allowed for the receipt of any memorandum of dissent or reservation, together with a brief statement of his reasons, that any member may wish to express; and such memorandum of dissent or reservation shall be published with the manuscript if he so desires. Publication does not, however, imply that each member of the Board has read the manuscript, or that either members of the Board in general or the special committee have passed on its validity in every detail.

6. Publications of the National Bureau issued for informational purposes concerning the work of the Bureau and its staff, or issued to inform the public of activities of Bureau staff, and volumes issued as a result of various conferences involving the National Bureau shall contain a specific disclaimer noting that such publication has not passed through the normal review procedures required in this resolution. The Executive Committee of the Board is charged with review of all such publications from time to time to ensure that they do not take on the character of formal research reports of the National Bureau, requiring formal Board approval.

7. Unless otherwise determined by the Board or exempted by the terms of paragraph 6, a copy of this resolution shall be printed in each National Bureau publication.

(Resolution adopted October 25, 1926, as revised through September 30, 1974)

Contents

Acknowledgments

The papers in this volume were presented at a National Bureau of Economic Research conference held in Richmond, Virginia, on 6–7 October 1995. Financial support from the Ford Foundation is gratefully acknowledged. I would also like to thank Kirsten Foss Davis, Rob Shannon, and Deborah Kiernan for their dedicated assistance with the conference and the volume.

Introduction

Robert C. Feenstra

A magazine devoted to international economics recently asked a panel of experts to grade the performance of the Japan/trade policies undertaken by the Clinton administration ("Grading the Clinton Japan/Trade Policy" 1994). The results ranged from B+ to Z, with the latter being lower than an F. Less surprising than the range of scores (who would expect economists to agree?) was the attention given by nearly every person to the market-opening policies being pursued by the United States. Gone are the days in which the United States was evaluated by its ability to negotiate multilateral policies of mutual benefit to a broad group of countries; instead, the focus is on results-oriented policies in specific markets and with particular trading partners. There is little agreement, however, on whether the policies pursued have been helpful or harmful: the two lowest grades given to the Clinton administration came from individuals who felt that the actions taken toward Japan were either too harsh and a form of "affirmation action" promoting U.S. industries or too weak and "likely to prove ephemeral." Such is the state of affairs in the evaluation of recent U.S. trade policies!

The papers in this volume take a more dispassionate look at these policies and evaluate their effect with the benefit of hindsight and statistical inference. Of foremost concern are the policies affecting U.S.-Japan trade and investment, and nearly half the papers focus on these issues. A second section of the volume deals with the U.S. response to so-called unfair trading practices, while the final section contains an analysis of various industry- and country-specific trade policies. Three general themes arise from the papers. The first is that some policies can act as both import protection and export promotion. An ex-

Robert C. Feenstra is professor of economics at the University of California, Davis, and director of the International Trade and Investment Program at the National Bureau of Economic Research. He is also the editor of the *Journal of International Economics*.

ample is provided by the recent policies directed at the U.S. automobile industry, as examined by James Levinsohn. In that case, the goal of increasing Japanese purchases of U.S. auto parts (export promotion) was implemented through the threat of high tariffs on U.S. imports of Japanese luxury autos (import protection), with the result that the two cannot really be separated. A more complex example comes from the negotiations on antidumping in the Uruguay Round, discussed by Robert E. Cumby and Theodore H. Moran, where U.S. exporting and multinational firms—pursuing their own agendas— did not act as an effective counterweight to domestic firms seeking greater protection from imports.

The second general theme is that the threat of protection can often have effects that are as pronounced as when policies are actually implemented. This is illustrated by the response of the Japanese to the threatened tariffs on luxury automobiles but also by their response to threatened protection in other industries, which involved making direct investments in the United States, as analyzed by Bruce A. Blonigen and Robert C. Feenstra. Threats also lead to measurable reactions from firms faced with possible antidumping duties, discussed by Thomas J. Prusa, and from countries faced with Section 301 actions, discussed by Kimberly Ann Elliott and J. David Richardson in the section on "unfair" trade. The third theme is that domestic regulatory policy has as much effect on trade and investment patterns as trade policy itself. This is illustrated by the paper by Andrew R. Dick, dealing with the telecommunications industry; by the paper by David E. Weinstein, dealing with foreign investment in Japan; and by the papers in the final section, which deal with the effect of macroeconomic policy on U.S. wheat exports and on unemployment in Canada following the free trade agreement with the United States.

Arguably, the automobile industry—defined to include both finished cars and the manufacture of automobile parts—received the most trade policy attention throughout the 1980s and 1990s. The import competition faced by U.S. producers during the 1980s was offset by the application of a "voluntary" export restraint (VER) with Japan. This restraint had the further effect of encouraging foreign investment in the United States, as a result of which, with Japanese nameplates being produced in the United States, the VER became redundant by the end of the decade. Attention then shifted to the automobile parts industry, which had a very low foreign market share in Japan. In an effort to expand this share, the Clinton administration proposed a 100 percent tariff on thirteen Japanese luxury cars and threatened to implement this tariff unless the Japanese agreed to expand their purchases of automobile parts. The choice of instrument was strategic: a uniform tariff against all Japanese automobile imports would not have been effective since the majority of Japanese cars were produced in the United States. In this case, the threat apparently paid off, in that the Japanese agreed to various quantitative goals for the purchase of automobile parts. Levinsohn considers what would have happened had the tariff on luxury cars been implemented. He finds that the reduction in profits of the

Japanese manufacturers would have been very large, which may explain their decision to agree to various goals for the purchase of automobile parts. Surprisingly, he also finds that U.S. prices would have risen by nearly the full amount of the tariffs: there would have been little incentive for the Japanese producers to absorb some part of the tariff and pass though only a portion to U.S. consumers.

Among the quantitative goals gained in this "carwars" episode, the Japanese agreed that their firms in the United States, and elsewhere would purchase more automobile parts; that they would increase the foreign market share in Japan; and that they would expand their transplant production in the United States. It can be questioned whether some of these targets could have been met even without the U.S. threat. In particular, the number of Japanese manufacturers in the United States has been rising steadily, and these firms all do some business with U.S. parts suppliers. The changing magnitude of these parts purchases is studied by Deborah L. Swenson. She makes use of a unique data set collected from the foreign trade zones (FTZs) in the United States within which the Japanese automobile producers (and many other firms) operate. Since these data provide trade flows to and from FTZs, the separate purchases of U.S. and Japanese parts can be quantified, and the effect of exchange rates and other factors on the sourcing decision can be estimated. Swenson finds that exchange rate fluctuations are important, and that there is a tendency for Japanese purchases of U.S. parts to grow over time, but this growth is not enough for the differences between these firms and their U.S. counterparts to be eliminated.

It was suggested above that the VER with Japan in automobiles resulted in the inflow of foreign direct investment. It is surprising, however, that the number of transplant firms grew so large that the VER became redundant. This suggests that the foreign firms were responding, not only to the actual protection, but also to the threat of protection. This hypothesis is tested by Blonigen and Feenstra, who measure the threat of protection by the initiation of antidumping or "escape clause" cases filed against a particular foreign industry. They test whether the use of these cases results in additional inflows of foreign direct investment and, conversely, whether the foreign investment lowers the probability of future protection. Using data on inflows of Japanese firms to the United States, support for both these hypotheses is obtained. These results confirm the idea of quid pro quo foreign investment that has been advanced by Jagdish Bhagwati, among others (see the references to chapter 3 of this volume).

Looking at the opposite side of this issue, Weinstein investigates the level and determinants of foreign direct investment in Japan. The conventional wisdom has been that, measured by the share of employment or sales accounted for by foreign affiliates, the foreign presence in Japan is at most 1 percent. This is extremely low in comparison with other industrial countries. Weinstein argues that this estimate is in fact incorrect and that the actual foreign presence is at least 5 percent of sales or employment: still at the low end compared to other countries, but five times higher than the conventional wisdom! To explain why foreign investment has not been higher, many authors have pointed to the *keiretsu* system of cross-shareholding and corporate control. Weinstein questions whether this system developed in order to limit foreign takeovers. He suggests instead that various Japanese financial regulations have had the effect of encouraging cross-shareholding between manufacturing and financial firms and among related firms in the manufacturing sector.

Regulatory policies are also the focus of the paper by Dick, dealing with the telecommunications industry in the United States and Japan. In the early 1990s, the attempts of Motorola to enter the cellular telephone market in the Tokyo area led to extended discussions between government officials from the United States and Japan, which mirrored similar attempts to enter the market for radio pagers in the 1980s. Dick puts these actions into their historical context, arguing that deregulation in both countries since the 1970s, has had a profound effect on bilateral trade. Deregulation in the United States, including the divestiture of AT&T, had the effect of increasing imports from Japan (especially of terminal equipment) and other countries such as Canada (of network equipment). But deregulation in Japan had the effect of increasing imports from Hong Kong and Asia (of terminal equipment), with more limited increases of imports from Canada (of network equipment), with the result that the United States did not gain in terms of exports. The conclusion is that the vigorous enforcement of antitrust law in the United States (leading to the AT&T divestiture) had the effect of increasing the trade deficit with Japan, where comparable deregulation policies were not followed.

The second section of the volume is devoted to policies that are a response to "unfair trade," that is, situations in which the United States perceives that foreign industries or countries are engaged in practices particularly detrimental to domestic interests. An example is dumping: when foreign industries export their products at below their home prices or average costs. This practice has long justified the use of antidumping duties under U.S. and multilateral trade laws, but these provisions were renegotiated under the Uruguay Round of negotiations. The paper by Cumby and Moran argues that the new provisions are surprisingly lenient in terms of the criteria used to determine whether dumping has occurred and that they therefore protect domestic producers. The question that the authors pose is why the executive branch of the government did not act as an effective counterweight to industry demands in this instance. The answer leads to a fascinating insiders' account of negotiations during the Uruguay Round, in which, as one discussant observed, the "names were omitted to protect the guilty."

One reason that these authors focus on the antidumping laws is because these trade policies have been found to have very substantial effects, over and above those that occur when duties are actually applied. The paper by Prusa investigates some of these effects. Using highly disaggregated data for the same line-item tariff codes at which investigations occur, he finds that the investigation itself has the effect of restricting imports and raising the price from the countries named in the investigation; of course, these effects persist and are amplified if duties are applied. However, the net protection offered to U.S. firms is less than these results suggest because of significant trade diversion toward countries that are not named in the investigation. These countries are able to increase their import volumes to the United States and raise their prices following the application of duties on the named countries, with the result that the overall volume of imports continues to grow. In addition to quantifying the effect of antidumping investigations on import prices, Prusa provides the first estimates of the extent of trade diversion to nonnamed countries.

The use of antidumping duties is only one means by which the United States responds to perceived unfair trade, and, by necessity, this practice is restricted to particular commodities and countries. A more general response is contained in Section 301 of the Trade Act of 1974, which authorized the president to take action against "unreasonable, unjustifiable, or discriminatory" practices of foreign trade partners. These provisions were extended in the so-called Super 301 provisions of the Omnibus Trade and Competitiveness Act of 1988, which authorized the annual compilation of a list of countries engaged in egregiously unfair practices and subsequent negotiations to eliminate these practices. If the practices are indeed eliminated, then the action can be judged as "successful" from the U.S. point of view. Elliott and Richardson investigate the factors contributing to the perceived success or failure of the Section 301 actions. This study extends the work presented in Bayard and Elliot (1994) and adds to it a statistical analysis of the factors determining success (the earlier study used case methods). Among other conclusions, the authors find that the vulnerability of the foreign country influences the success of a 301 action, as does the simplicity of the foreign policies being targeted and the linkage of the action of some measure of reciprocity. In contrast, there is no evidence that cases involving the highest U.S. stakes are necessarily the most successful.

The final section of the volume turns to U.S. policies that have targeted specific industries or countries. Of chief concern to advocates of industrial policy has been the high-technology industries, which are sometimes argued to benefit other industries in a spillover process and to be of strategic interest for national security. Both these arguments have been used to justify U.S. support for the development of flat panel displays, as described by Kala Krishna and Marie Thursby. Much of the information on this industry is proprietary, and these authors provide details that are not readily available, including the very high magnitude of subsidies provided by the Clinton administration. Rather than evaluating the overall social cost or benefit of these subsidies, Krishna and Thursby focus on one particular aspect that is also of relevance to other industries: whether subsidies are provided to capacity acquisition or to R&D expenditures. Both these policies were considered under the National Flat Panel Display Initiative. These authors find that subsidies to capacity acquisition can have the perverse effect of reducing the steady-state level of R&D, which implies that the R&D subsidy is the preferred instrument for achieving long-term cost reductions.

The second industry considered—agriculture—is at the opposite end of the spectrum in that the subsidies provided cannot be justified by any technological spillover or national security argument but rather are the result of political economy considerations. One program that has been in effect since 1985 is the Export Enhancement Program (EEP), which provides export subsidies to a range of commodities, especially wheat. In 1985, exports of wheat were very low by historical standards, leading to a large accumulation of U.S. stocks. Pinelopi K. Goldberg and Michael M. Knetter argue that these events should be attributed to the appreciation of the U.S. dollar during 1980–85. With the subsequent depreciation, export volumes should have returned to their historical levels, but this was not the case: exports were lower than expected. One explanation for this finding is the increased productivity and export subsidies provided to wheat by the European Community. These findings suggest that the EEP was ineffective in stimulating wheat exports and that, to the extent that it led to the increased use of subsidies within Europe, it may even have been counterproductive.

Attention is turned from policies favoring specific industries to those favoring specific geographic locations in the paper by Gordon H. Hanson. Under the offshore assembly provisions of U.S. tariff laws, components that are exported, assembled abroad, and reimported into the United States receive preferential tariff treatment. Predictably, this provision has had the effect of encouraging the location of plants in Mexico near the U.S. border. Surprisingly, however, it has also encouraged the location of "twin plants" in the United States, at border cities near to their Mexican counterparts. Hanson estimates that fully half the growth in durable-goods activities in these U.S. cities is due to the expansion of assembly plants in Mexico. He also discusses how the choice of location is likely to be affected by the North American Free Trade Agreement (NAFTA).

The final paper, by Keith Head and John Ries, considers the other American border—that with Canada—and the effect of the Canada-U.S. Free Trade Agreement of 1988. While this agreement attracted less attention in the United States than the subsequent agreement with Mexico under NAFTA, it was widely debated and criticized in Canada. The fear was that Canadian industries would not be able to compete head-on with U.S. industries and would therefore be forced to downsize and lay off workers. In fact, in the years following the agreement, there was unusually high unemployment in Canada, but this was due at least in part to the restrictive monetary policy. Head and Ries attempt to disentangle from industry-level data the changes in Canadian output and employment that were consistent with trade liberalization and the remaining changes that appear to be due to other factors. Using a model of monopolistic competition, they find that a significant part of the reduction in Canadian output cannot be explained by this framework. They explore the extent to which macroeconomic policy, or other factors, is consistent with the additional unemployment that occurred.

References

Bayard, Thomas O., and Kimberly Ann Elliott. 1994. *Reciprocity and retaliation in U.S. trade policy.* Washington, D.C.: Institute for International Economics.
"Grading the Clinton Japan/trade policy." 1994. *International Economy* 8, no. 6 (November/December): 18–23.

I U.S.-Japan Trade and Investment

1   Carwars: Trying to Make Sense of U.S.-Japan Trade Frictions in the Automobile and Automobile Parts Markets

James Levinsohn

Sometimes, the line between trade promotion and trade protection is a fuzzy one. This is especially true in the automobile industry. For example, in an apparent effort to induce Japan to buy more U.S. cars and car parts, the United States recently threatened 100 percent tariffs on a handful of Japanese luxury cars. Trade promotion or trade protection?

The debate on U.S.-Japan trade promotion and trade protection in the automobile industry is frequently heated and pitched. The goal of this paper is to make sense of the sequence of recent events in which the United States developed a large bilateral trade deficit in automobile parts with Japan, which then led to the threatened tariffs on Japanese luxury cars, which in turn led to Japanese promises to buy more U.S. parts. Along the way, some of the questions addressed are the following: What are the root causes of the U.S. trade deficit in automobile parts? Why did the United States target thirteen luxury cars produced by Japan instead of a more broadly based tariff or a tariff on automobile parts? How would the profits of domestic, Japanese, and European firms have been affected by the proposed 100 percent tariff? How much of the tax burden would have been borne by U.S. consumers and how much by the Japanese firms? Readers should note, however, that this paper does not attempt to resolve the "big-picture" issue of how closed the Japanese automobile market may be.

The paper is organized as follows. Section 1.1 addresses the question of how the United States and Japan came to the brink of a trade war in the summer of

James Levinsohn is professor of economics and of public policy at the University of Michigan and a research associate of the National Bureau of Economic Research.

The author is grateful to Steven Berry, Edward Leamer, Ariel Pakes, and Amil Petrin for many helpful conversations, to Amil Petrin for research assistance, and to Mike Hewitt for background research assistance.

1995. This section discusses how structural differences in the U.S. and Japanese automobile parts industries may have contributed to trade frictions. Section 1.2 analyzes the logic (such as it was) that led from the parts dispute to the threatened tariff. Section 1.3 analyzes the likely consequences of the threatened tariff using a detailed econometric model of industry equilibrium. Conclusions are gathered in section 1.4.

1.1   Trade Promotion and Trade Protection in the 1990s: How Did We Get to Where We Are?

Trying to understand the sequence of events that led to the threatened 100 percent tariffs on thirteen Japanese luxury cars is tricky business, for logic, analysis, and common sense will get one only so far. On the surface, what began as a dispute about how many parts the Japanese should buy from U.S. parts manufacturers led to a threatened tariff on Japanese luxury cars and resulted, in the end, in Japanese promises to buy more U.S. parts. How was it that these events came to pass?

The very notion that trade in automobile parts could lead to a major trade dispute is indicative of the large changes the automobile industry has undergone in the last ten years. Not that long ago, Japanese cars were made in Japan, and American cars were made in the United States. Suppliers to the assemblers were located close to the assembly factories as transport costs mattered. U.S. assemblers dealt mostly with U.S. parts manufacturers, and the same was true in Japan. There simply was not a lot of international trade in automobile parts.

By the mid-1980s, the volume of trade began to increase. Table 1.1 gives the U.S.-Japan trade balance in automobile parts for 1985–94. In that period, the U.S.-Japan bilateral trade deficit in automobile parts went from about $3 billion to almost $13 billion. This section discusses the role that industry structure might have played in explaining the figures in table 1.1.

Table 1.1   **U.S.-Japan Trade in Automobile Parts, 1985–94 (in $million)**

Year	Imports of Parts	Exports of Parts	Balance
1985	3,280	200	−3,080
1986	6,220	224	−5,996
1987	7,586	259	−7,327
1988	9,293	451	−8,842
1989	10,595	619	−9,976
1990	10,410	871	−9,539
1991	9,960	826	−9,134
1992	10,816	1,035	−9,781
1993	12,339	1,130	−11,209
1994	14,334	1,485	−12,849

Source: U.S. Census Bureau.

1.1.1   Industry Structure in the United States and Japan

The relations between assemblers and their parts suppliers differed in the United States and Japan, and this is largely a product of history. The ways in which they differed have important implications for the deficit observed in the later years in table 1.1.

First, consider the structure of the U.S. automobile parts industry. In the United States, there was a long history of vertical integration in the automobile industry. At one extreme was Henry Ford's River Rouge plant, where it was loosely claimed that iron ore went in one end and cars came out the other. While the three U.S. automobile manufacturers have moved from this extreme, the industry is still quite vertically integrated. Consequently, many parts are still supplied by in-house suppliers.

At least until recently, the U.S. assemblers' relations with their suppliers were, at best, complicated. As explained in more detail in Womack, Jones, and Roos (1990), U.S. assemblers frequently supplied their potential parts manufacturers with detailed specifications of a particular part and then took bids based on price for a specified quantity. This emphasis on price did little to encourage capital investment and, especially, research and development by the suppliers. The emphasis on price is also sometimes claimed to have negatively affected the quality of contracted parts. Future price adjustments and negotiations were standard, and the ensuing relation was seldom one of cooperation. U.S. firms also purchased imported parts, and this practice was facilitated by stockpiling parts inventories. That is, in order to insure against parts becoming unavailable, U.S. firms would keep hefty inventories of parts. Hence, while transport costs would add to the cost of an imported part, the delays inherent in international shipping were not likely to be terribly costly, for inventories were available to buffer these delays. All these practices are changing, but understanding them helps explain some of the current issues in the automobile parts dispute.

The relation between Japanese automobile assemblers and their parts suppliers differs from the traditional relation in the U.S. industry. Japanese automobile assemblers are reputed to have developed a more long-term relation with their suppliers. The reasons for this are many, but they are due in part to historical as well as economic influences. Following World War II, Japanese automakers had a series of sequential decisions to make. They needed to decide whether to source parts domestically or through imports. Owing to stringent exchange controls and rules on imports following the war, they chose the former option. They then needed to decide whether to make their parts themselves or buy from outside sources. They chose not to adopt the U.S. pattern of vertical integration, this was probably due in part to the scarcity of capital following the war, in part to the lower wage structure that was prevalent among the parts suppliers, and in part to a strategy to lower investment risks (by limiting vertical integration, less capital was at risk).

Japanese OEMs (original equipment manufacturers) next needed to decide whether to seek either stable or floating relations with their suppliers and whether to make these relationships exclusive. When the Japanese OEMs realized their great dependence on outside suppliers, they anticipated several potential difficulties. First, some of their suppliers had a low level of technological competence. Second, with too many suppliers, any one supplier would have difficulty achieving economies of scale. Third, the cost of policing the OEM-supplier relation might be formidable. Certain criteria were established for suppliers. For example, potential suppliers were closely examined with regard to their reliability, financial soundness, and capacity to learn the necessary technology quickly. Also, the relations with suppliers had to last long enough to justify the large expenses encountered while screening different suppliers. Finally, the technological assistance and actual technology given to the supplier had to be kept out of the hands of rivals. These criteria led to the development of long-term exclusive relations with parts suppliers. For purposes of comparison, it is estimated that in 1987 a Japanese OEM would, on average, deal directly with two to three hundred parts makers (not including materials and equipment makers), while a comparable number for General Motors was in the range of up to thirty-five hundred (Mitsubishi Research Institute 1987).

The resulting structure of the parts industry in Japan resembled a pyramid in which the OEM was on the top, followed by first-tier suppliers. These first-tier suppliers were often controlled by the OEM through equity holdings, and, in any case, the OEM and the first-tier supplies typically developed a very close and long-standing working relation.

1.1.2 Implications for Trade Patterns

The different market structures in the automobile parts markets in Japan and the United States had implications for the pattern of international trade. In particular, the structure of the Japanese industry made it difficult for U.S. firms to sell there, while the Japanese were more successful selling in the United States. The reasons that U.S. firms had such small sales in Japan are often categorized under the catch-all term *structural impediments*. Four such examples are discussed below.

First, U.S. parts suppliers have traditionally relied on fully spelled-out blueprints, while Japanese OEMs often work closely with their suppliers on the design of the parts. This poses problems for U.S. parts makers who may not be accustomed to investing in the necessary engineering and design procedures. In particular, without technical centers in Japan, U.S. firms are often at a competitive disadvantage. Even U.S. firms that are accustomed to doing their own design often did not welcome the fact that many Japanese OEMs have contracts that stipulate that they have the right to provide supplier-prepared drawings to other suppliers if the OEM sees fit. Japanese suppliers are more willing to accept such arrangements when their long-term relations with the OEMs are more or less guaranteed.

Second, the Japanese system of long-term contracts may act as a structural impediment to trade. As the Japanese OEMs invested heavily in their major suppliers in terms of technical knowledge and screening processes for reliability, it became more expensive for the OEMs to switch to another (possibly U.S.) supplier. Another aspect of the contracts that has trade implications concerns the degree of information sharing often required of parts suppliers. While U.S. parts firms are generally accustomed to disclosing only prices and quality standards to the U.S. OEMs, Japanese OEMs expect more complete and open disclosure of costs and profit margins by their suppliers.

Third, the stringent quality guideline that the Japanese OEMs demand may act as a structural impediment to trade. U.S. parts suppliers faced competing influences when supplying domestic OEMs. While they had quality standards to meet, their chances of winning or renewing a contract with the Big Three improved if they could keep their costs very low. This trade-off, combined with often preannounced inspections by the OEM, led some parts makers (quite rationally) to compromise quality. Japanese OEMs treated the quality issue quite seriously. Like costs, the automaker set the objective quality level during the design process. The parts maker then pursued cost targets while maintaining the target quality levels. Rejection rates for Japanese parts suppliers are roughly one in one thousand and are closer to one in ten thousand for parts actually delivered. This heightened level of quality is due to extensive testing and a high degree of factory automation. It is also expensive, and the willingness of the suppliers to undertake this expense is surely related to the long-term nature of contracts.

The fourth and possibly greatest structural impediment to trade is the difference in inventory strategies between the U.S. firms and their Japanese counterparts. While the Big Three have often used inventory stockpiling in an effort to achieve long production runs and to insure against equipment breakdowns, defective parts, and interruptions in parts supplies, Japanese automakers instead rely heavily on a just-in-time (JIT) system. In turn, Japanese OEMs require their suppliers to work within the JIT system. This often means daily deliveries to assembly plants. The deliveries operate within a synchronized system in which parts are recognized by bar codes indicating the model and reference number of the targeted vehicle, the point of delivery, and the hour the vehicle will pass a specified assembly point. While some parts may be delivered only once a day, others such as headlights or batteries may be delivered every two to four hours. This system places great reliance on high parts quality as there are neither inventories nor time to test or inspect shipments. The system works well, but it not conducive to international trade in automobile parts since it requires parts suppliers to be in close geographic proximity to the factory.

These structural impediments are not inconsistent with complaints often heard on behalf of U.S. parts suppliers. Common complaints include an alleged unfair advantage given to Japanese suppliers (see the discussion involv-

ing the importance of long-term relations above), unreasonable delays in negotiations, difficulty in obtaining information needed for bids, design standards
that would require a massive production overhaul by U.S. parts suppliers, and
frequent product modification requests.

A final reason why the U.S. did not sell that many parts to Japan while
Japan sold more to the U.S. throughout the 1970s and early 1980s lay with the
exchange rate. During the 1970s, the exchange rate ranged from ¥200 to ¥350
per U.S. dollar. This made Japanese components look relatively inexpensive to
U.S. OEMs and, combined with the U.S. firms' emphasis on price, made imported parts relatively attractive.

All these reasons help explain the trade imbalance in automobile parts. Regulations in Japan may also have played a role, but much of the evidence here
is anecdotal and hard to quantify. For example, U.S. firms that attempted to
service the Japanese after market for parts (replacement parts for existing cars)
claimed that Japan's strict inspection of used cars limited their ability to compete. Some of these complaints had little to do with the different structures of
the U.S. and Japanese industries and instead seem more outrightly protectionist.[1] It is, however, difficult to judge how important to the parts trade these
regulations might be.

Prior to about 1981, the debate on the automobile parts trade was relatively
simple even if answers were not obvious. That is, it was well understood that
the Japanese did not buy many parts from U.S. suppliers and that this had a lot
to do with differing industry structures. Likewise, the U.S. industry structure
was more conducive to importing parts.

1.1.3   New Issues in the Automobile Parts Trade Debate: The VER Years

In May 1981, Japan agreed to a voluntary export restraint (VER) on exports
of automobiles to the United States. This led to an influx of direct foreign
investment (DFI) by Japanese automobile manufacturers. By 1985, Honda was
producing over 150,000 cars in Marysville, Ohio, and Nissan had started operations in Tennessee. In the years that immediately followed, Toyota, Mazda,
and Mitsubishi followed suit. During this same period, the weak yen began to
strengthen relative to the dollar. In 1985, exchange rate was about ¥236 per
dollar. By 1994, it was at about ¥100. Finally, by the early 1980s, the surge in
imported automobiles from Japan that occurred in the mid- and late 1970s had
aged such that the demand for after market parts for Japanese cars was now
increasing. All these phenomena had important implications for the automobile parts trade between the United States and Japan.

As noted above, Japanese OEMs frequently relied on parts suppliers with
whom they had long-established working relations. When the OEMs then

---

1. One (possibly outdated) example was a regulation that required the bulbs in both headlights
to be the same brand.

opened operations in the United States, they hesitated simply to drop their Japanese suppliers and instead buy solely from U.S. parts manufacturers. Hence, with the influx of DFI, some of the parts used in production in the United States were imported from Japan, and this led to an increase in the imports of parts. By definition, it takes a while for new working relations to become established ones. Over time, Japanese firms have indeed established relations with U.S. firms. (A popular advertising campaign for the Toyota Camry points out the many U.S. sources of key components of the Camry). Political pressure and domestic content legislation (real and threatened) surely played a role in getting Japanese OEMs to purchase parts made in the United States, but the dramatic strengthening of the yen was also important. With the exchange rate at ¥130 to the dollar, buying parts in dollars looked much more attractive than doing so when it was at ¥230. Hence, while Japanese OEMs operating in the United States have established relations with U.S. parts suppliers, this took time, and, in the interim, there was increased demand for parts from Japan.

The actual accounting of the automobile parts trade also became both more complicated and less informative in the presence of DFI. Many observers of the automobile parts trade focus on the bilateral trade balance in automobile parts between the United States and Japan. While perhaps a natural figure to focus on, this trade balance hides a great deal in an era with substantial DFI. To see this, consider the following hypothetical example. Suppose that Subaru's new plant in Indiana bought absolutely all its parts from U.S. firms—admittedly an extreme example. These purchases would not directly show up on the bilateral trade balance since they are domestic transactions. (While Suburu-Japan may end up buying fewer parts in Japan from its Japanese suppliers, this too is not an international transaction.) Hence, while much debate focuses on the bilateral trade balance, substantial changes in industry structure accompanying DFI may not even appear in this balance.

Another new phenomenon in the DFI era is the confusion regarding the very notion of nationality. When Japanese firms used parts made in Japan in OEM plants located in Japan and U.S. firms did analogously, accounting was pretty simple. That simplicity is long gone, and it has been replaced by complex relations that make the very idea of nationality tricky. When the notion of nationality is complex, if not outright confused, discussion of trade policy is similarly complex. As noted above, Japanese OEMs now produce in the United States. Many Japanese parts suppliers have also set up shop in the United States. By 1993, Japanese firms had invested in about 280 U.S. firms in the automobile parts sector. Of these, about half were joint ventures, while the other half were wholly owned subsidiaries. U.S. OEMs now have production facilities in Canada and Mexico, although most production remains in the United States. American parts manufacturers, however, have invested—heavily in some cases—in Mexico. Other parts producers have entered into the joint ventures with Japanese parts firms mentioned above. The result is a case in which one American consumer might buy a Toyota assembled in Kentucky with parts from a Japanese-owned firm in Indiana, a U.S.-owned firm in Mexico, a joint U.S.-Japan venture located in Ohio, and a Japanese parts firm in Japan. Using dated nomenclature, this consumer bought a *Japanese* car. Another consumer might buy a Ford Escort assembled in Hermosillo, Mexico, with parts manufactured by a joint U.S.-Japanese venture in Mexico. Using the same dated nomenclature, this consumer bought an *American* car. In this environment, discussions of traditional trade policy, which by their very nature are oriented around a well-defined notion of nationality, become both confusing and confused.

While much has changed in this era of DFI, it remains the case that U.S. parts manufacturers sell very little to Japanese OEMs located in Japan. A rough estimate is that U.S. firms have only about 1 percent of the OEM market in Japan. There have been indications, however, that some U.S. firms are making inroads in the Japanese parts market. For example, between 1986 and 1993, TRW saw its annual worldwide sales to Japanese automobile companies increase sevenfold to $500 million, accounting for about 10 percent of its total automobile parts sales. TRW initially invested heavily in joint ventures with Japanese companies supplying the U.S. plants of Toyota and Nissan. Once TRW found this niche, it began supplying these firms back in Japan. Except for air bag components and some electronics, TRW makes the products for its Japanese OEMs in Japan, allowing them to participate effectively in the JIT system. Other firms are following suit. Since 1991, GM has operated a technical center in Japan to develop automobile parts, and its components sales in Japan have increased 50 percent since the center opened. In 1993, Ford ACG began operating a technical center for electronic components in Hiroshima, hoping to expand sales to Mazda, Nissan, and Toyota. Ford is also investing $50 million in a new technical center near Tokyo expected to open in late 1995. These changes may lead to a larger U.S. presence in the Japanese parts market, but history suggests that such changes take time.

In 1992, President Bush and the U.S. automakers attempted to hurry matters along with Bush's well-publicized trip to Tokyo. Although the president was criticized for so blatantly pursuing U.S. commercial interests, he did secure a promise from the Japanese to purchase more automobile parts from American companies. Japan pledged to purchase $19 billion worth of U.S. automobile parts in fiscal year 1994. Whether owing to this pledge or to the natural course of events, Japanese automakers purchased $19.9 billion worth of parts in fiscal year 1994 (*Automotive News,* 17 July 1995). Most of these purchases ($15.4 billion) were parts used in the Japanese firms' transplant operations in the United States. As discussed above, many of these transactions were, from an accounting perspective, domestic transactions between the transplant and the U.S. parts firm. Japan also pledged to purchase $3.6 billion worth of parts for export to Japan in fiscal year 1994, and it fell about $0.6 billion short of this pledge, again suggesting that, in the Japanese automobile parts industry, location matters.

1.2   Why a Threatened Tariff on Thirteen Japanese Luxury Cars?

In 1995, President Clinton threatened a 100 percent tariff on thirteen Japanese luxury cars. It is not obvious that any single and narrowly defined issue triggered this threat. Clearly, the United States was concerned about its large bilateral trade deficit with Japan, and automobiles and automobile parts were a large portion of this. But, while the Big Three publicly complained about the difficulty of selling cars in Japan, most industry observers concluded that the Japanese market was not where the Big Three would make their mark in Asia. To be sure, there were significant barriers to selling cars in Japan (as claimed by the Big Three), but, at the same time, it was also the case that the cars that U.S. firms sold were not terribly well suited to the Japanese market. As noted above, the relative merits of these arguments are not addressed in this paper. In either case, the United States was not likely significantly to redress its bilateral trade deficit by exporting large quantities of cars to Japan.

If it were to redress the bilateral trade deficit via the automobile industry trade, the United States was left with three options. It could discourage the import of Japanese cars, encourage the export of U.S. automobile parts, and discourage the import of Japanese automobile parts. The first and third options clearly involve trade protection, while the second involves trade promotion. Pursuing the trade promotion option in this case, absent any sort of threat, would prove difficult. As discussed in the previous section, the structural reasons behind the bilateral trade deficit in automobile parts were deep-rooted. The first and third option provided such a threat, but each of these also posed problems.

Consider first the possibility of tariffs on Japanese automobile parts. The end users of these parts were in some cases American producers and in others transplant firms in the United States. To the extent that U.S. OEMs were using Japanese parts, a tariff would raise their costs—an option not greeted with enthusiasm.[2] The other end user of imported parts was the transplant factories. But these firms employed U.S. workers, and raising the cost of cars produced by these factories would negatively affect employment. This, too, was not an especially attractive option.

This left the possibility of placing tariffs on Japanese cars. Leaving aside issues involving violation of the GATT and possible actions the World Trade Organization (WTO) might take, tariffs on Japanese cars still posed problems.

---

2. From an economic viewpoint, higher costs might still impart an advantage to the U.S. firms if their competition faced yet higher costs from the tariff.

At the heart of these problems was the fact that many of the high-volume Japanese cars were in fact made in the United States. In the data set used in the econometric analysis in the next section, cars sold by Japanese firms in the 1994 calender year totaled 2.65 million (out of total U.S. sales of 8.782 million). Of these, 1.793 million are cars whose nameplate was produced in the United States. Hence, if the United States wanted to tax Japanese cars on a broad basis, this would involve taxing transplant production as well as imports. Placing a tax on transplant production, however, is at best complicated and at worst probably infeasible. In principle, the United States could renegotiate its tax treaty with Japan to effectively alter the taxes paid by the transplants. These taxes, however, are not directly based on sales; rather, they are based on accounting profits (i.e., they are not a per-unit production tax). Furthermore, the tax treaty is not industry specific, so any changes to the treaty in order to try to tax transplant auto production would also possibly affect all Japanese direct investment. Tax treaties seem too blunt a tool.

Suppose, then, that the United States restricts potential tariffs to nameplates not made in the United States. Imports of these Japanese nameplates totaled about 855,000 in the 1994 calendar year.[3] Of these, about one-quarter were models with retail prices in excess of $30,000. (There were thirteen Japanese models in 1994 with base prices above about $30,000.) In terms of revenue (as opposed to number of cars), these Japanese luxury models accounted for almost 40 percent of the value of imports. There were no Japanese cars with base prices in excess of $30,000 produced in the United States. Japanese luxury cars, then, were an easily targeted and at least potentially effective group of products on which to place a tariff.

Seen from a different angle, Japanese automobile producers had, by 1994, done a very effective job of insuring themselves against tariffs by the United States. While the more expensive models were still produced in Japan, the models with the largest sales were also produced in the United States.

Faced with a bilateral trade deficit that was viewed as troubling by politicians,[4] the United States opted for threatened tariffs on a limited set of cars in order to promote, among other things, an agenda of trade promotion in the automobile parts sector. Whether the threatened tariffs would actually benefit American OEMs depended on the substitution patterns of consumers. They would, however, almost certainly hurt Japanese OEMs, and therein lay the threat. The next step in analyzing the policy is to estimate the likely consequences of a tariff on Japanese luxury cars, and this is the topic of the next section.

3. Actual imports were higher since this figure does not include imports of nameplates made in both the United States and Japan. That is, imports of the Honda Accord and Toyota Camry, among many others, are not included here.

4. In this paper, I take it as given that the bilateral trade deficit was a topic of concern. From an economic viewpoint, this is not obviously sensible, but it seemed to constitute the political reality at the time.

1.3   The Threatened Tariffs, Their Estimated Consequences, and the Resulting Trade Promotion

1.3.1   Policy Details

On 16 May 1995, President Clinton announced 100 percent tariffs on thirteen Japanese luxury cars to go into place four days later, with the sanctions becoming final on 28 June. This schedule gave Clinton and his trade representative, Mickey Kantor, a few weeks to see if brinksmanship might prove a successful strategy for trade promotion.

The details of the announced tax involved a 100 percent tariff on the landed cost of the following thirteen models: the Lexus (Toyota) LS400, SC400, GS300, SC300, and ES300; the Infiniti (Nissan) Q45, J30, and I30; the Acura (Honda) Legend and 3.2TL; the Mazda 929 and Millenia; and the Mitsubishi Diamante. Of these models, the Millenia had the lowest base price ($26,435), while the LS400 was the most expensive ($51,680). None of these cars sold in especially large quantities, although the Legend and the ES300 were the most popular by a factor of almost two. Slightly under 40,000 of each sold in 1994. This compares with sales of about 365,000 for the Honda Accord alone.

Although the news media treated the tariff as if it would simply double the price consumers paid, this was simplistic and incorrect. The tariff would apply to the price that obtained in equilibrium after the tariff was imposed, and there is no reason to believe that the equilibrium price would be invariant to a tariff. Also, the 100 percent figure referred to the landed price, not the list price. What this figure translates to as a percentage of list price varies by model, but the leading trade publication, *Automotive News,* reported the tariff, as a percentage of list price, to be about 65 percent in the case of the Lexus LS400. For example, the landed value of this particular model was estimated to be $33,280, while the dealer invoice was about $42,000, and the list price was $51,680.[5] In the analysis in this paper, an ad valorem tariff of 65 percent is used, although this figure is admittedly approximate and in reality would vary by model.

1.3.2   Modeling the Policy

In order to model the equilibrium that would obtain in the presence of the proposed tariff, one must model both consumer behavior and firm behavior. The basic setup is taken from Berry, Levinsohn, and Pakes (1995a). For purposes of brevity, an intuitive discussion of these methods is given here, and the interested reader is referred to Berry, Levinsohn, and Pakes (1995a) for a (much!) more in-depth discussion.

The model estimated has two parts—a utility-based consumer framework

---

5. Consumers also pay a 10 percent luxury tax on the portion of the price above $32,000.

on the demand side and a cost-function-based model of a multiproduct oligopolistic firm on the supply side. Each is discussed in turn.

Following a strategy developed by Pakes (1986), demand in this model is computed by aggregating over simulated heterogeneous consumers. Consumers' utility functions are assumed to have the same functional form, but the parameters of the function vary across the population. This is because consumer tastes vary throughout the population. The distribution of tastes is one of the primitives that is estimated. I assume that tastes for product attributes such as horsepower, weight, and size are normally distributed in the population. The estimation procedure estimates the mean and variance of these normal distributions. Price is treated a bit differently than other product attributes. I assume that sensitivity to price is inversely proportional to income and that it is income that varies throughout the population. Rather than estimating the distribution of income as, say, the distribution of taste for horsepower is estimated, the empirical distribution of income is used. There is also a random idiosyncratic component to utility. A simulated consumer, then, consists of a draw from each of the distributions of tastes and income as well as a draw from the distribution of idiosyncratic terms. This simulated consumer then chooses either to buy a car or to spend nothing and instead buy the "outside good." The utility of the outside good is normalized to zero, and its presence allows substitution out of the automobile market. Conditional on this set of draws, one can then compute which product gives this simulated consumer the greatest utility. One can imagine simulating about 90 million consumers (the number of households in the United States), hence effectively simulating the demand for automobiles. One would keep track of the most preferred product of each of these consumers and aggregate up to compute market shares. Loosely speaking, the objective of the estimation procedure is to find the means and variances of the underlying distribution of tastes that come as close as possible to fitting the observed market shares.

The description given above ignores many important aspects of the demand side of the model. These include econometric issues such as allowing for product characteristics that are unobserved by the econometrician but observed by the consumer, the probable correlation of these unobserved characteristics with price and the econometric endogeneity thus induced, and sampling techniques (in particular, importance sampling). The role of the distribution of idiosyncratic tastes and how this interacts with ensuing policy analysis are also mostly omitted. These issues are discussed in BLP.

On the supply side of the model, each product is assumed to be produced with constant returns to scale, and a (log) marginal cost function is estimated for each product. Marginal cost is assumed to depend on attributes of the product as well as cost shifters such as wages and exchange rates (when applicable). The firms are modeled as multiproduct oligopolists who set prices in a Nash fashion (i.e., Bertrand competition). That is, firms set prices to maximize firm-level profits, taking as given the prices of their competitors. To compute the prices that maximize profits, firms make use of information on demand elasticities. In a no-tax equilibrium, price is composed of marginal cost plus the markup. Since the demand system is not a constant elasticity system, markups will depend on quantities demanded (i.e., demand elasticities vary along the demand schedule). The demand and pricing sides of the model are simultaneous because demand depends on prices and the prices set by the firms depend on quantity demanded. Put another way, a firm's first-order conditions for optimal prices depend on demand elasticities, and the underlying (indirect) utility function itself depends on the prices that firms charge. The pricing and utility sides of the model are estimated simultaneously.

Modeling the 100 percent tax involves changing the firm's first-order condition and recomputing an equilibrium under the assumption that firms still maximize profits, that consumers still maximize utility, but that there is now a wedge between the price consumers pay and the price firms receive for a subset of products.[6] In this case, that wedge is assumed to be an ad valorem tax of 65 percent of the producer price that obtains in the new equilibrium.

1.3.3   Data and Results

The model is estimated using twenty years of annual data from 1975 to 1994.[7] Product attributes entering the utility function of consumers are a constant, the ratio of horsepower to weight, size (defined as length times width of the car, a dummy variable for whether the base model of the car had air conditioning as standard, and a dummy variable if it was made by a non-U.S. based company (i.e. foreign). Recall that for each of these attributes, the mean of the distribution of tastes for the attribute as well as the variance of this distribution is estimated. A parameter on the price term is also estimated. Prices are given in constant terms and the list price is used. For a discussion of the issues surrounding the use of list versus transaction price, see Berry, Levinsohn, and Pakes (1995b).

On the cost side, marginal cost shifters are a constant, the logs of horsepower divided by weight, size, the lagged exchange rate, wages, a dummy variable for air conditioning as standard, a trend term, dummy variables for Japan and Europe, and these dummy variables interacted with the trend term.

Table 1.2 gives the estimated parameters of the primitives of the model. The top panel gives the means of the distribution of tastes for the product attributes entering the demand side. The second panel gives the estimated standard deviations of these distributions. A large and precisely estimated standard deviation (σ) may be interpreted as capturing heterogeneity in the population concerning how the attribute contributes to utility. A demand side attribute in this model

6. An additional assumption is that the set of products that firms produce does not change. Just how reasonable this assumption may be is discussed below.
7. The data set is available on request as a MIME attachment to email. Send requests to JamesL @umich.edu.

Table 1.2   **Estimated Parameters of the Demand and Pricing Equations: 2,470 Observations**

Variable	Parameter Estimate	Standard Error
Demand-side parameters:		
Mean (β's):		
Constant	−6.697	1.046
HP/weight	1.414	1.095
Size	4.689	.463
Air	.934	.194
Foreign	−4.317	.611
Standard deviations (σ_β's):		
Constant	2.191	1.445
HP/weight	3.320	1.688
Size	1.295	.907
Air	.739	.791
Foreign	5.774	.579
Term on price (α):		
(y/p)	46.728	5.336
Cost-side parameters:		
Constant	−2.172	.686
ln(HP/weight)	.564	.072
ln(size)	1.190	.122
Air	.482	.040
Trend	−.008	.006
Japan	−1.299	1.133
Japan×trend	.016	.012
Euro	3.363	.493
Euro×trend	−.034	.006
lag ln(e-rate)	−.028	.017
ln(wage)	.895	.159

Note: HP = horsepower; e-rate = exchange rate.

is considered to be important if either its mean or its standard deviation is precisely different from zero. That is the case with all automobile attributes in this specification. Finally, although the mean of the distribution of taste for foreign cars is negative, it turns out that the elasticity of demand with respect to this dummy variable is indeed positive. This is because most of the consumers who place a negative value on foreign cars do not in fact buy a car.

The term on price is precisely estimated. Its implications for elasticities and hence markups are discussed below. All 2,470 products, however, face elastic demand at the estimated parameters.

Most marginal cost shifters are precisely estimated. The only estimated coefficients not significantly different from zero are those on the general trend, those on the lagged exchange rate, and those on the Japan dummy and interaction variables. All product attributes enter marginal cost positively and precisely.

Perhaps the easiest way to interpret the reasonableness of the estimated coef-

Table 1.3	A Sample from 1994 of Estimated Price–Marginal Cost Markups of (Potentially) Taxed Models, Based on Table 1.1 Estimates		
	Price ($)	Markup ($) over MC $(p - MC)$	Fraction of Markup
Acura Legend	33,800	8.048	.351
Acura Vigor	26,350	5.965	.334
Infiniti Q45	50,450	12.988	.380
Infiniti J30	36,950	9.655	.386
Lexus ES00	31,200	7.925	.375
Lexus GS300	41,100	10.806	.388
Lexus LS400	51,200	13.164	.380
Lexus SC300	40,000	10.501	.388
Lexus SC400	47,500	12.285	.382
Mazda Millenia	25,995	5.518	.313
Mazda 929	32,200	7.278	.334
Mitsubishi Diamante	25,750	5.373	.308

Note: MC = marginal cost.

ficients is to examine the markups that they imply since markups imply information about both marginal costs and underlying demand elasticities. The list price (in 1994 dollars) as well as the markup of twelve of the thirteen cars subject to the proposed tariff are given in table 1.3. One of the cars that would have been subject to the tax, the Infiniti I30, was not sold in 1994. Another of the cars, the Acura 3.2TL, was also not sold, but this car is basically a rebadged Acura Vigor, so the Vigor is used as a proxy for the 3.2TL. In table 1.3, one sees that the markups vary from about 30 percent of list price to about 38 percent. The more expensive models tend to have the higher percentage markups, suggesting that these models have relatively less elastic demand.

The estimates in table 1.2 above completely specify the underlying distribution of tastes in the population on the demand side of the model and the firm's first-order condition on the cost side. The model is an equilibrium model of the automobile market. Households are maximizing utility, while firms are simultaneously maximizing profits. Modeling the threatened tariff involves perturbing this equilibrium by altering the first-order conditions for the firms that produce the models subject to the tariff. One then recomputes the prices and quantities for which the new first-order conditions hold.

The main difference between the tariff and the no-tariff equilibria is that the tariff introduces a wedge between the price consumers pay and the price the firms receive. This wedge is taken to be 65 percent of the new equilibrium (post-tariff) producer price. Table 1.4 lists the twelve models targeted with tariffs that were sold in 1994. The first column lists the 1994 base model list price, while the second column lists the producer price that would obtain in the presence of the 65 percent tariff. These figures are surprising to those used

Table 1.4   **Prices with Implementation of the Threatened Tariff, Based on Table 1.1 Estimates**

	Price ($) without Tariff	Producer Price ($) with Tariff	Consumer Price ($) with Tariff
Acura Legend	33,800	33,264	54,886
Acura Vigor	26,350	27,108	44,728
Infiniti Q45	50,450	45,805	75,578
Infiniti J30	36,950	35,053	57,837
Lexus ES300	31,200	30,665	50,598
Lexus GS300	41,100	38,311	63,213
Lexus LS400	51,200	46,475	76,684
Lexus SC300	40,000	37,391	61,695
Lexus SC400	47,500	43,435	71,668
Mazda Millenia	25,995	27,195	44,872
Mazda 929	32,200	32,313	53,317
Mitsubishi Diamante	25,750	27,111	44,733

to thinking about taxes in models of perfect competition with a representative consumer. In those models, the tax burden is shared between the consumers and the firm, with burdens distributed according to relative elasticities. Those models, however, do not characterize the U.S. automobile market very well. The estimates of the producer price that would obtain with a 65 percent tariff show remarkably little price change as a result of the imposition of the tariff. The price received by producers falls in the cases of nine of the twelve models, although these declines are not large. The largest decline (relative to the no-tax price) is only about 9 percent. In three cases, the price received by producers actually rises. What is going on here?

There are three intertwined explanations. First, in models in which goods are strategic complements, a tax will tend to exert an upward influence on the price received by the producer. In a Bertrand model with linear demands, all goods are strategic complements. While the equilibrium concept assumed here is Bertrand, demand is not linear. It turns out that about half the product pairs are strategic complements. Hence, in these cases, a tariff shifts reaction functions out and tends to increase equilibrium prices. Whether the producer price will increase so much as to result in a producer price higher than the no-tariff price is an empirical issue. Second, in this model, consumers are heterogeneous. When the tariff is applied to some products, the consumers who substitute away from those products are the price-sensitive consumers. The consumers who continue to buy the car at the post-tariff price are those who have relatively inelastic demand for the taxed product. After the tariff, then, the firm faces a more inelastic demand for its product, and this will tend to move prices higher. Again, the magnitude of this influence is an empirical matter. Third, and this is closely related to the second factor, the idiosyncratic term in the utility function is assumed to have an extreme value ("logit") distribution. An empirical implication of this is that, at *any* price, there will be some consumers whose idiosyncratic tastes are such that a particular product is still bought. This phenomenon is not unique to the logit assumption. If the idiosyncratic term were normally distributed ("probit"), there would still be the occasional draw from the tail of the distribution. These draws from the tails of the unbounded distributions will give rise to at least some demand for every product at any price. This phenomenon will also tend to exert an upward influence on price. The relative importance of this (as well as ways around the problem) is the topic of continuing research. In summary, producer prices tend to fall a small amount, but this is not uniform across products.

With relatively unchanged producer prices, consumer prices with the tariff rise substantially. These prices are given in the last column of table 1.4. Most prices rise by about 60 percent. Hence, the price of the top-of-the-line Lexus sedan rises from $51,200 to over $76,000. The price of the top-of-the-line Infiniti Q45 also exceeds $75,000. An important cautionary note is due here. The figures in table 1.4 assume that the firms continue to play a static Bertrand game and maximize prices accordingly. If news reports following the announcement of the threatened tariffs are to be believed, this is not a realistic assumption. Soon after the tariffs were announced, for example, Toyota stated that it would not change the price of the cars subject to the tariff. This implies that Toyota was prepared to absorb the $20,000–$30,000 tariff. As a long-run strategy, this probably could not be sustained. As a short-run strategy, it is somewhat puzzling, although presumably it helped placate their dealer network.

Although the producer prices of the taxed models did not increase substantially with the tax, the ensuing high consumer prices would have exacted a heavy toll on sales and profits. Table 1.5 addresses these issues. The first column gives the sales that actually occurred in the 1994 calendar year. Note that none of the models threatened with tariffs have very large sales. For purposes of comparison, almost 370,000 Honda Accords were sold during this period, and the corresponding number of the Ford Taurus was almost 400,000. Of the models listed in table 1.5, the least expensive Lexus (the ES300) had the highest sales, and these totaled just over 39,000. The second column in table 1.5 lists the variable profits associated with each model. This is just the producer price minus marginal cost (the markup) times sales. These numbers should be treated with some caution as it is not completely clear what constitutes variable profits in an industry with such huge fixed costs. Still, they provide a baseline for comparison. These figures suggest that, while sales are not huge, profits of some of these models are indeed quite substantial. The estimates imply that the Acura legend, the Lexus ES300, and the Lexus LS400 each earned a bit more than $400 million for their respective parent firms. These large numbers are due to the significant markups on these models.

When the tariff was threatened, car dealers that sold the affected models claimed that sales would fall drastically should the tariff go into effect. My

Table 1.5   **Sales and Profits with Implementation of the Threatened Tariff, Based on Table 1.1 Estimates (sales are in 1,000s; profits are in $1,000,000)**

	Sales without Tariff	Profit without Tariff	Sales with Tariff	Profit with Tariff
Acura Legend	35.709	424.277	9.836	111.598
Acura Vigor	8.469	74.582	1.952	18.665
Infiniti Q45	11.949	229.092	3.896	56.597
Infiniti J30	22.718	323.769	6.935	85.683
Lexus ES300	39.108	457.476	10.671	119.119
Lexus GS300	13.939	222.340	4.447	58.530
Lexus LS400	22.443	436.140	7.299	107.354
Lexus SC300	4.537	70.330	1.436	18.516
Lexus SC400	7.392	134.052	2.391	33.643
Mazda Millenia	24.423	198.962	5.296	49.505
Mazda 929	9.206	98.929	2.376	25.799
Mitsubishi Diamante	18.096	143.544	3.822	35.514

estimates suggest that the dealers were right on target. With the imposition of the tariff, sales plummet. Sales of the taxed models fall, in aggregate, from about 218,000 to just over 60,000. Although the decline in sales varies by model, most models see their sales fall around 75 percent. For example, Legend sales fall from 35,706 to 9,836, while those of the newly launched Mazda Millenia fall from 24,423 to 5,296. Hence, while producer prices remain mostly unchanged, the correspondingly high consumer prices drive demand way down. Profits accordingly fall. Again defined as the markup times sales, profits fall drastically. Declines are typically on the order of 75 percent. For example, profits from the Lexus LS400 fall from $436 million to $107 million. Profits from half the models subject to the tariff fall below $50 million, and this raises the issue of whether these models will survive.

The new car industry is marked by tremendous fixed costs. If variable profits are too low, a model will not prove profitable to develop. With this sort of calculus in mind, it seems probable that, while the taxed models will not disappear immediately, the firms producing them may decide to discontinue some models when model change time comes. Making firm predictions would require detailed information on fixed costs, and such information is not readily available. Nonetheless, the issue of whether, say, Nissan will continue with its Infiniti line when the time comes for remodeling or whether they will develop new models when profits are so low is real.

Table 1.5 is useful for doomsayers who claimed that the proposed tariffs would really hurt the Japanese firms. That table, however, does not put the figures into any sort of firm-level perspective. The broader issue is whether the parent firms would be substantively hurt by the proposed tariffs. One might imagine that consumers who did not buy a Lexus might instead buy a top-of-

Table 1.6   **Firm Profits by Country of Origin (in $million), Based on Table 1.1 Estimates**

	Profits without Tariff	Profits with Tariff
Total Japanese profits	12,165.861	10,638.131
Total U.S. profits	34,572.571	34,921.828
Total European profits	3,852.204	44,443.364

the-line Camry or Avalon (both Toyotas), hence diminishing the tariff's effect on Toyota. Another issue not addressed in the previous tables is who, if anyone, gains from these tariffs. It was widely speculated that the real beneficiaries of the proposed tariffs would be, not American firms, but rather European firms. This would be true if the consumers who substituted away from the taxed products instead bought the typically upscale European products.

Table 1.6 begins to address these issues. Rather than looking at one product at a time, the table looks at profits at a much more aggregate level. This table puts the likely effect of the threatened tariff in a broader context. Japanese profits fall by about $1.5 billion, which represents a decline of approximately 12.5 percent. Whether this is a large decline depends on one's perspective. For a 100 percent tariff, one might argue that a 12.5 percent decline in profits is not that big. On the other hand, for a tariff as narrowly targeted as the one under consideration, a 12.5 percent overall decline might seem large. In any case, the proposed tariff would clearly hurt the Japanese firms. Who gains? The figures in table 1.6 suggest that the real winner would be the European firms. European profits increase by about 15 percent. U.S. profits are basically unaffected. Consumers who switch away from the targeted high-end Japanese cars tend to switch to other Japanese cars and European cars. According to my estimates, U.S. firms just do not win many new customers with the proposed tariffs. Furthermore, some of those customers who do switch to domestic cars are among the more price sensitive, and this works toward lowering markups.

1.3.4   Actual Outcomes

The previous section estimated what would have happened had the tariffs been put permanently into place. In fact, on 28 June 1995, about six weeks after the tariffs were first announced, they were withdrawn. This is consistent with the decline in Japanese profits in table 1.6, although political concerns were surely important.

The trade pact announced on 28 June affected many players in the U.S.-Japan automobile market—U.S. parts producers, Japanese OEMs, U.S. OEMs, as well as retail dealerships. The effect of the agreement on each is discussed in turn.

The biggest winners of the trade pact were U.S. parts manufacturers. The net effect of the pact for parts makers is estimated to be a $9 billion increase in Japanese purchases of parts from North American suppliers by 1998.[8] While some increase surely would have occurred naturally, the $9 billion figure represents almost a 50 percent increase in parts purchases. The pledge to purchase more American parts bears much resemblance to a similar pledge obtained by President Bush in 1992. Recall that that agreement entailed a pledge to increase parts purchases by about $8.5 billion. That pledge was met. There are, however, reasons to suspect that it will be harder to meet the pledged increase this time. When the previous pledge was announced, several Japanese OEMs had plans to build new transplant factories, the Japanese market share was increasing annually, and the yen was falling rather dramatically. All these factors facilitated meeting the earlier pledge. Now, only Toyota remains in an expansion mode in the United Sates, as other firms do not have major expansion projects in the works.[9] Japanese market share seems to be leveling off, and few observers expect the yen to continue to decline at the rate seen from 1991 to 1995. All this suggests that meeting the pledge may be more difficult this time around. On the other hand, as discussed in section 1.1 above, U.S. parts manufacturers seem to be adapting to working with Japanese OEMs, and this process will continue.

The specific parts of the trade pact dealing with increased parts purchases include commitments from Japan's Big Five (Toyota, Honda, Mazda, Mitsubishi, and Nissan) to buy $6.75 billion more in parts from U.S. suppliers, meet NAFTA local content standards by 1998, increase transplant production from 2.1 million in 1994 to 2.65 million in 1998, and import $6 billion worth of foreign parts by 1997, $2 billion of which will come from the United States. Japan also agreed to a series of administrative changes that are expected to contribute to opening up Japan's market for replacement parts. These changes include an end to inspections not requiring welds or rivets (expect some regulation-induced technological progress in car repair!); eased standards for garages, which is expected to increase competition and hence increase demand for U.S.-made parts; a promise to further review the restrictive list of parts that can be replaced only by certified garages; removing shock absorbers, struts, power steering, and trailer hitches from the list; a promise to respond within thirty days to U.S. requests to remove a part from the list; and permitting a new class of garages that will specialize in brakes, transmissions, and mufflers.

Japanese OEMs were mostly affected by the parts pledges discussed above. As noted, these pledges may be difficult to fulfill. Japanese OEMs' production and sales were also mildly affected by the threat of sanctions. Lexus decreased June production by about five thousand units, although U.S.-bound production increased soon afterward. Infiniti also saw June production fall, only for that fall to be made up in July. Acura delayed the launch of its 3.2TL model by

---

8. Much of this section is drawn from reporting in *Automotive News* (3 July 1995).

9. Honda is also expanding, but these plans had been in progress long before the announced trade pact.

two months owing to the sanctions. Mazda production had been cut before the sanctions were put into place and was not really affected by the sanctions, while Mitsubishi delayed its 1996 Diamante by six to eight weeks. In no case did the sanctions and resulting decrease in production result in unexpected shortages.

U.S. OEMs benefited mostly from potentially increased access to the Japanese market. The details suggest that, relative to the parts deal, this is pretty minor. For example, Ministry of International Trade and Industry (MITI) agrees to write all Japanese automobile dealers to tell them that they are free to sell foreign vehicles and to announce that pressure (from Japanese OEMs) not to sell such vehicles could violate Japan's competition laws. Japan also agrees to survey dealers for interest in selling foreign cars and pass the survey results on to U.S. OEMs.[10]

Car dealers in the United States that carried the models threatened with the tariffs were also big winners from the trade pact in the sense that they avoided a potential disaster. They are not big winners in the sense that they are left clearly better off than they were prior to the entire trade dispute. Had the tariffs been put into place, however, the estimates reported in the previous section suggest that sales would have plummeted and new models might not have been forthcoming.

What about enforcement and monitoring of the trade pact? The pact does not contain specific quotas, other numerical targets, or timetables for gauging progress. Nor are specific sanctions mentioned should pledges go unfilled. Rather, the United States and Japan agree to work to speed progress should matters move too slowly. In sum, monitoring and enforcement are minimal. It remains to be seen how important this might be.

1.4   Conclusions

The story of recent trade frictions between the United States and Japan in the automobile parts market goes as follows. Initially, there was not much trade as Japanese cars were made in Japan with mostly Japanese parts and the same was mostly true of North American cars. Most of what trade did exist consisted of U.S. imports of Japanese parts. U.S. OEMs had a very different relation with their parts suppliers than did Japanese OEMs. These differences contributed to a growing bilateral trade deficit in auto parts. In an effort to address this deficit, the U.S. threatened tariffs on thirteen Japanese cars. This might seem like a very indirect way to address the parts trade, but more direct avenues were either ineffective or too costly. The threatened tariffs would have resulted in drastically reduced sales of the thirteen models, and Japanese profits in total would have fallen around 12.5 percent, while the European firms would have captured

---

10. Estimates suggest that these changes will result in about two hundred more outlets for U.S. cars in Japan by 1997. It is not clear, however, on what this estimate is based.

many of the lost Japanese sales. U.S. firms would have been pretty much unaffected by the tariffs. An unenforced trade pact resulted in which Japan agreed to buy substantially more U.S. parts and the United States agreed to drop the threatened tariffs. The pact is one of trade promotion, although it resulted from a threat of trade protection. As noted at the outset, the line between trade promotion and trade protection is thin indeed.

References

Automotive News. Various 1995 issues. Detroit: Crain Communications.

Berry, Steven, James Levinsohn, and Ariel Pakes. 1995a. Automobile prices in market equilibrium. *Econometrica* 63:841–90.

———. 1995b. Voluntary export restraints on automobiles: Evaluating a strategic trade policy. Working Paper no. 5235. Cambridge, Mass.: National Bureau of Economic Research.

Mitsubishi Research Institute. 1987. The relationship between Japanese auto and auto parts makers. Tokyo. Mimeo.

Pakes, Ariel. 1986. Patents as options: Some estimates of the value of holding European patent stocks. *Econometrica* 54:755–84.

Womack, James P., Daniel T. Jones, and Daniel Roos. 1990. *The machine that changed the world.* New York: Harper Collins.

2 Explaining Domestic Content: Evidence from Japanese and U.S. Automobile Production in the United States

Deborah L. Swenson

The ongoing U.S. trade deficit in automobiles and automobile parts remains a central focus of trade disputes between the United States and Japan. There are many margins on which this deficit could change. These include export volumes, production location, and domestic product content. However, this deficit has continued, despite large changes in the assembly pattern of U.S.—purchased automobiles. For example, in 1994, the United States purchased 2.69 million Japanese nameplate automobiles. This was roughly the same number as the 2.78 million purchased in 1990. However, 1.45 million, or 54 percent, of the vehicles sold in 1994 were assembled in U.S. transplant operations, as compared with only 38 percent four years earlier. In light of the shift in production, the apparent immobility of the automotive deficit raises the question as to whether multinational production arrangements, such as automobile transplant production in the United States, ultimately have any effect on the trade balance between nations. In particular, these facts raise the question of whether the national identity of the firms, as opposed to production location alone, determines international sourcing decisions. This paper begins to address this question by studying the production of U.S. and foreign automobile firms in U.S. foreign trade zones.

Although roughly 30 percent of imports in general arrive through the intrafirm trade of multinationals, and the percentage is much higher in the auto industry, there has been little examination of the factors shaping these flows and firm decisions. Among theoretical treatments of this issue, considerations of factor costs, increasing returns to scale in production, contracting difficulties, and the circumvention of protection have figured prominently in the de-

Deborah L. Swenson is professor of economics at the University of California, Davis, and a faculty research fellow of the National Bureau of Economic Research.

scription of motivations for multinational activity.[1] Indeed, these rationales are not necessarily exclusive. Unfortunately, a dearth of firm-level data on multinational firms' activity in trade has impeded widespread empirical observation and characterization of these effects.

This papers considers one aspect of multinational activity, the domestic content decision of U.S. and foreign automobile firms in the United States.[2] Observation of this activity is facilitated by the U.S. operation of the foreign trade zone (FTZ) program. The evidence shows that, although the domestic content of U.S. automakers is higher overall than that of Japanese automobile firms, the difference is shrinking as the operations age. It should also be noted that, although Japanese manufacturers may initially have located in the United States for political reasons, Japanese automobile assembly operations appear to be affected by relative prices, just as U.S. production facilities are. These conclusions are supported by observation of domestic input content.

The paper proceeds as follows. Section 2.1 discusses factors that may influence the foreign and domestic content of automobile production in the United States, including the institutional details of the U.S. foreign trade zone program. Section 2.2 provides a simple model of the demand for inputs, which links the relative demand for domestic and foreign inputs to movements in factor costs. The model is then tested in section 2.3. Concluding comments and discussion are presented in section 2.4.

2.1 Foreign Trade Zones: Design and Usage

2.1.1 Trade Flows and Multinational Activity

The predicted effect of multinational activity on trade depends largely on the international conditions that are used to construct the model for prediction. For example, Helpman and Krugman (1985) describe the effects of multinational production in the context of a conventional factor model. They demonstrate that the presence of multinational production can enhance or diminish the volume of trade. The degree of intraindustry trade that occurs in this setting depends largely on the distribution of factors. Since headquarter services are assumed to be capital intense in production, intrafirm headquarter services, however, flow in a single direction and originate from the capital abundant country. In contrast, Markusen and Venables (1995) consider an alternative

---

1. For examples of these arguments, see Helpman (1984), Markusen (1984), Ethier (1986), and Bhagwati et al. (1987).

2. In addition to trade talks regarding Japanese sales and purchases in the automotive sector, policy concern regarding domestic content is exhibited by the American Automobile Labeling Act. This act requires that, as of the 1995 model year, vehicle stickers include information on the location of automobile assembly as well as the percentage of U.S./Canadian content. These stickers must also include the production location of the engine and transmission as well as the country of origin for all major sources of content.

framework in which multinational activities can originate from multiple locations. Firms have many potential modes of operation, including existence as a national firm that exports to, or as a multinational firm that produces in, many locations. When firms decide how to serve foreign markets, they must weigh the opposing forces of transport and tariff costs, which impede export sales, against the importance of scale economies in production, which raise the cost of multinational activity relative to production in a single location. In the Markusen and Venables model, multinationals initially enhance the volume of trade but may ultimately diminish the volume of trade if the multinational form of operation becomes increasingly prevalent over time.

Since we observe elements of both models in the international environment, it is not possible to form a single prediction regarding the effect of multinationals on trade. It is likely that the ultimate effect of multinationals on trade volumes will depend on the characteristics of the industry as well as on the underlying sources of comparative advantage across countries. In this case, the overall effects have to be observed industry by industry.

To date, few studies have examined the importance of multinational firms in trade. One exception is Zeile (1995), who considers a number of measures that demonstrate the relative importance of U.S. value added, or parts, in multinational production. Zeile's results are based on a panel of multinational firms operating in the United Sates. This work documents that there are significant differences across industries and countries in the measures of U.S. economic activity associated with multinational firms. Zeile observes that Japanese multinationals incorporate a smaller percentage U.S. content in their U.S. production, relative to other multinationals operating in the United States. Zeile suggests that this observed difference may reflect Japanese methods of subcontracting as well as the relatively high portion of Japanese firm investment that was greenfield as opposed to acquisition.

An ongoing question in this literature is whether multinational activity enhances or substitutes for market service by export. In one recent analysis, Blomstrom, Lipsey, and Kulchycky (1988) study the case of U.S.- and Swedish-headquartered multinationals and conclude that the activities are complementary. In another study, Brainard (1993) performs a cross-industry analysis, describing the relative sales of multinationals generated by affiliate activity as compared with export. This work discovers that affiliate activities rise in importance with transportation costs, tariffs, and other trade barriers but that the relative importance of affiliate activities falls when it is confronted by higher barriers to foreign investment. In addition, Brainard finds that plant scale and proprietary firm assets also affect the modes of serving foreign markets, providing evidence that the relative importance of multinational activity conducted by affiliates responds to industry characteristics. In light of this characterization, this paper seeks to describe and measure the responsiveness of domestic content in the automobile industry.

2.1.2   The Foreign Trade Zone Program

Data from the U.S. foreign trade zones program form the basis of this study. The foreign trade zones program was created in 1934 in an effort to encourage international trade in general and the reexport of products in particular. However, the program was of little use to producers until modifications were rendered in later years. In its initial form, the foreign trade zones program could not be used for production or assembly purposes. The 1950 Boggs amendment expanded the activities that could be performed within foreign trade zones to include manufacture. A second major change was a 1980 Treasury Department ruling that limited the dutiable value of products leaving foreign trade zones to the cost of the components contained in those products.

The foreign trade zones program operates along two tiers. General purpose zones are available for use by most industries. Both foreign and domestic firms are allowed to operate within these zones. However, sensitive industries, such as automobiles and steel, must operate within the more regulated foreign trade subzone program. By the end of the 1980s, the automobile industry accounted for more than 80 percent of all foreign trade subzone shipments.

It is no coincidence that all U.S. automobile assembly plants currently in the United States have sought and obtained foreign trade subzone status. Automobile assemblers benefit from three tariff reductions that are provided by operation within a foreign trade zone. The most important provision is one that enables producers to reduce the tariffs they owe in the case of inverted tariffs. *Inverted tariffs* refers to the situation in which the tariff levied on intermediate inputs is higher than the tariff applied to the import of the final product. Normally, firms utilizing imported components pay the tariffs associated with each individual component. However, if a firm produces within the boundaries of a foreign trade zone, the firm may elect to pay either the tariff rate assessed on the final good or the tariff rate that applies to the imported components. The obvious benefit is the firm's ability to select the lowest of the two rates.

Currently, the ability to reduce tariffs when an inversion exists is lauded as a provision that helps U.S. assemblers remain competitive with foreign assemblers. A rationale for the program is elimination of the cost disadvantages that might face U.S. assemblers who use imported components. Suppose, for example, that the foreign firm produces a product with foreign parts and completes the assembly abroad. When the product is shipped to the United States, it pays the tariff rate that applies to the assembled good. In cases of tariff inversion, a U.S. firm, performing assembly in the United States, could pay a higher tariff on the same foreign components. This ability to circumvent "inverted tariffs" is particularly important for producers in the automobile industry, where the tariff rate on finished cars is 2.5 percent and the rate on many automobile parts ranges from 4 to 11 percent.[3] A further tariff benefit accruing to

---

3. "Inverted tariffs" in the automobile industry originated from U.S. Tariff Act of 1930.

zone users is the ability to delay tariff payments. In general, firms must pay customs duties within ten days of a product's entry into the United States. However, firms located in foreign trade zones are entitled to delay payment of customs duties until ten days after their products have left the foreign trade zone for their destination markets. The magnitude of this second benefit is proportional to inventory held within the subzone. Further, for finished products that are exported out of the United States, no tariff is due on the imported components that were used in production. Finally, the presence of foreign trade zones provides one last benefit for automobile producers who practice just-in-time production techniques. The time required for customs is reduced by as much as five days, enabling firms to produce more efficiently.[4]

Foreign trade subzone benefits are not automatic. Automakers who wish to gain foreign trade zone status for their assembly operations are required to apply for firm-level subzone status, and they are further required to renew these subzone privileges periodically. Foreign trade subzones are granted to firms and are attached to general purpose foreign trade zones. Hence, a firm cannot apply for subzone status unless there is a general purpose zone to which it can attach itself. As long as this qualification is met, however, there are essentially no moving costs entailed in the creation of a foreign trade subzone. Automakers typically request that their current manufacturing facilities be given subzone status, and the boundaries of the subzone are defined accordingly.

In the larger context, it should be mentioned that the foreign trade zone program cannot be used to circumvent other trade policies. To begin, although producers have the choice of paying the lower of the intermediate inputs tariff and the final product tariff on imported components, operations within a foreign trade zone or subzone cannot be used to avoid the payment of antidumping duties. Further, although products that are reexported from trade zones pay no U.S. tariffs on their use of imported components, the North American Free Trade Agreement (NAFTA) is explicit that foreign trade zones cannot be used to avoid the payment of any North American tariffs on products that are subsequently exported to Mexico or Canada.

2.1.3 Trends in Foreign Trade Zone Usage by Automobile Producers

A growing portion of trade in automobiles and automobile parts enters the United States through the foreign trade zones program. By 1993, the volume of automobile trade entering foreign trade zones was over $12 billion. Over half this amount entered special purpose foreign trade subzones, where domestic assembly or activity was conducted before the products were shipped for final sale.[5] Table 2.1 displays some of the trends in automakers' usage of foreign trade zones. First, it is notable that more than 90 percent of the zone

---

4. Products that are sourced through foreign trade zones may move more quickly since they avoid some customs clearance formalities.

5. Automobile activity represented 51.4 percent of all subzone foreign receipts in 1993. In turn, automobile parts constituted 92.8 percent of these auto subzone foreign receipts.

Table 2.1   U.S. Content and U.S. Shipments of FTZ Subzone Auto Assemblers

	U.S. Firms			Foreign Firms		
Year	No. of Sites	% Domestic Shipments	% Domestic Inputs	No. of Sites	% Domestic Shipments	% Domestic Inputs
1984	9	90.3	90.6	3	96.0	35.1
1985	15	90.8	91.5	5	96.9	32.0
1986	20	92.1	90.5	5	97.3	29.2
1987	22	92.1	91.3	4	98.5	41.3
1988	25	91.8	88.6	5	95.2	49.3
1989	29	90.1	87.6	6	94.4	52.8
1990	29	91.6	91.0	6	93.8	59.6
1991	28	93.4	95.0	6	92.6	64.1
1992	28	93.2	95.9	6	89.8	68.8
1993	28	91.8	95.4	6	88.5	66.7

Source: Foreign Trade Zones Board, annual reports; and author's calculations.
Note: "% domestic shipments" is the percentage of shipments from the foreign trade subzone that is shipped to U.S. destinations. "% domestic inputs" is the percentage of inputs entering the foreign trade subzone from U.S. locations. The percentages have been weighted by zone shipments.

shipments are destined for the domestic market whether the assembly is completed by a U.S. or by a foreign firm. However, the usage of domestic inputs by U.S. and foreign automakers differs markedly. In 1993, foreign automobile firms sourced two-thirds of their inputs from the United States, while U.S. firms sourced more than 95 percent of their inputs from the United States. Nonetheless, U.S. sourcing by foreign firms has grown dramatically. In 1984, foreign firms purchased only 35 percent of their inputs in the United States.

Tables 2.2 and 2.3 track individual firm usage of automobile foreign trade subzones. Foreign and U.S. firms exhibit a few distinct trends in their foreign trade zone operations. To begin, most domestic manufacturers had their trade zones in place by 1988, while foreign firms were continuing to open new zones. The one exception was Volkswagen. Volkswagen opened its U.S. facility before the other foreign producers and closed its U.S. production facility in 1988. It should also be noted that three subzones contain international joint venture activity; NUMMI, Autoalliance, and Diamond-Star.[6] While there is some heterogeneity in the sourcing and shipping activity between firms that are headquartered in the United States, or abroad, U.S. plants have uniformly higher domestic input content and shipping. Although the entry of new zone operators obscures the overall aging process of zone activity, it also appears that foreign firms use an increasing percentage of inputs sourced from the United States.

Table 2.4 compares automobile industry activity represented by the foreign

6. For the purposes of this paper, zones are classified as an international joint venture if the output from the zone results in automobiles sold under both U.S. and foreign nameplates.

Table 2.2   Volume of Automobile Foreign Trade Subzone Activity, 1984, 1988, and 1992

	1984			1988			1992		
	Zones (No.)	Inputs ($million)	Shipments ($million)	Zones (No.)	Inputs ($million)	Shipments ($million)	Zones (No.)	Inputs ($million)	Shipments ($million)
GM	0			10	13,118	14,324	16	16,560	17,232
Ford	7	5,222	6,916	10	15,993	24,462	10	11,020	8,928
Chrysler	3	4,470	7,344	6	4,866	4,830	6	4,320	4,344
Toyota	0			1	38	17	1	1,958	1,957
Nissan	1	356	367	1	924	932	1	1,368	1,352
Honda	1	816	755	1	2,635	2,715	2	4,844	4,908
Volkswagen	1	327	332	1	277	307	0		
Subaru-Isuzu	0			0			1	869	887
JV[a]	0			2	876	894	3	3,156	3,102
Total	13	11,191	15,714	32	38,727	48,481	40	44,095	42,710

Source: Foreign Trade Zones Board, annual reports; and author's calculations.

Note: Zones represented include assemblers and parts makers. All input and shipment values are deflated to 1982 dollars.

[a]Joint ventures between U.S. and Japanese partners.

Table 2.3   Sourcing and Shipping Activities of Automobile Foreign Trade Subzones, 1984, 1988, and 1992

	1984			1988			1992		
	Zones (No.)	% Domestic Inputs	% Domestic Shipments	Zones (No.)	% Domestic Inputs	% Domestic Shipments	Zones (No.)	% Domestic Inputs	% Domestic Shipments
GM	0			10	94.4	92.1	16	97.3	93.3
Ford	7	85.9	92.8	10	84.7	91.6	10	90.9	93.1
Chrysler	3	92.1	86.3	6	87.3	87.4	6	95.1	91.8
Toyota	0			1	48.5	86.1	1	66.1	88.8
Nissan	1	20.0	99.8	1	32.8	99.9	1	52.0	94.8
Honda	1	29.6	97.7	1	60.7	96.9	2	83.7	89.1
Volkswagen	1	63.8	87.7	1	35.4	91.0	0		
Subaru-Isuzu	0			0			1	59.9	98.7
JV[a]	0			2	31.7	93.6	3	57.9	87.9
Total	13	84.1	90.1	32	82.9	91.3	40	87.5	92.0

Source: Foreign Trade Zones Board, annual reports; and author's calculations.

Note: Zones represented include assemblers and parts makers. Firm averages weight plant observations by plant shipments.

[a]Joint ventures between U.S. and Japanese partners.

Table 2.4   U.S. Imports Shipped to Affiliates, 1992

	Shipped by Foreigners				Shipped by Foreign Parent Group			
	Total ($million)	% Capital Equipment	% Goods for Resale without Further Manufacture	% Goods for Further Manufacture	Total ($million)	% Capital Equipment	% Goods for Resale without Further Manufacture	% Goods for Further Manufacture
All industries	182,152	.945	69.995	29.059	134,292	.685	74.258	25.057
Manufacturing	50,919	1.601	28.592	69.805	34,401	1.576	30.563	67.861
Transportation equipment	5,665	3.513	16.452	80.035	4,882	4.035	16.459	79.496
Wholesale trade	109,833	.144	93.320	6.536	88,761	.169	92.414	7.417
Motor vehicles and equipment	34,524	.113	90.974	8.913	28,644	.136	89.806	10.054

Source: U.S. Department of Commerce (1994, table G-35).

trade zones data set of this paper with aggregate trade statistics and with other industries. It is not possible to provide an exact match since the Department of Commerce classification system places foreign automakers under one of two different categories rather than under a single category that encompasses these firms' automotive production activity. In particular, the Department of Commerce classifies each foreign firm according to its primary line of business. In this taxonomy, some automotive firms are designated as manufacturing, while others are designated as wholesale trade. As with manufacturing in general, the bulk of imports brought to affiliates in the transportation equipment sector is used for further manufacture. However, in contrast with the manufacturing aggregate, the transportation sector imports capital equipment in twice the proportion. Nonetheless, the transportation equipment sector imports capital equipment at the low amount of 3.5 percent of affiliate imports. The transportation sector sources a much higher percentage of its imports shipped to affiliates directly from the foreign parent, relative to the manufacturing sector as a whole.

To date, no work has been done on the foreign trade zones program. However, work has examined the Overseas Assembly Provision (OAP). This program is similar in that it is meant to mitigate tariff-induced disadvantages faced by U.S. component makers. When the United States imports products that are assembled abroad, the OAP exempts from duty that portion of the U.S.-imported final product that can be attributed to U.S. components. The general finding in this area, as demonstrated by Finger (1976) and Mendez (1993), is that the OAP has increased the activity of U.S. parts industries at the same time that it has reduced the activities of U.S. assemblers.[7]

2.2 A Model of Zone Usage

To motivate the empirical work that follows, we construct a stylized model to describe the demand for auto components of domestic and foreign origin. For expositional ease, the notation and explanations that follow consider representative U.S. and Japanese firms that are both producing in and selling to the U.S. market. In fact, it is assumed that multinational firms exist in equilibrium at all times, although the volume of their activities may change.

Multinational firms are assumed to use both domestic and foreign inputs in their production processes according to a constant elasticity of substitution production function. The output of a typical U.S. firm, Y_{US}, is a function of U.S. inputs, X_{US}, and Japanese inputs, X_J. Each of the N_{US} varieties of U.S. inputs and N_J varieties of Japanese inputs enters the production function symmetrically, and the elasticity of substitution between any two inputs is σ

$$Y_{US} = [N_{US}X_{US}^{(1-1/\sigma)} + N_J X_J^{(1-1/\sigma)}]^{1/(1-1/\sigma)}$$

7. Grossman (1982) shows that the OAP may actually cause intraindustry trade in homogeneous products, as domestic and foreign producers may perceive differential input costs.

Japanese firms producing in the United States are also expected to have a constant elasticity of substitution production function, which reflects the output generated by the U.S. and Japanese inputs entered into the production process. However, since Japanese firms are headquartered in Japan, we introduce the possibility that Japanese firms use U.S. inputs less efficiently than they do Japanese inputs.[8] The differential efficiency related to the use of non-Japanese inputs is captured by the term δ_{US}. It is assumed that $0 < \delta_{US} < 1$.[9] Hence, the overall Japanese production function is as follows:

$$Y_J = [\delta_{US} N_{US} X_{US}^{(1-1/\sigma)} + N_J X_J^{(1-1/\sigma)}]^{1/(1-1/\sigma)}$$

Firms maximize profits, taking input prices into consideration. The price of a typical U.S. part is P_{US}, while the price of a representative Japanese part is P_J. In light of the production technology, the respective demands for U.S. inputs by Japanese and U.S. producers in the United States are

$$X_{US,J} = \delta_{US}^{\sigma}(P_{AGG}^J/P_{US})^{\sigma}Y_J; \quad X_{US,US} = (P_{AGG}^{US}/P_{US})^{\sigma}Y_{US}.$$

At the same time, the respective demands for Japanese inputs by Japanese and U.S. producers in the United States are determined by

$$X_{J,J} = (P_{AGG}^J/P_J)^{\sigma}Y_J; \quad X_{J,US} = (P_{AGG}^{US}/P_J)^{\sigma}Y_{US}.$$

It is important to note that the composite price of inputs, P_{AGG}, differs for Japanese and U.S. firms in a fashion that reflects any differential efficiency in the utilization of parts sourced from different locations. In particular, the aggregate price that applies to Japanese parts demand places a weight on U.S. parts prices that is less than or equal to the weight placed on U.S. parts prices by U.S. producers:

$$P_{AGG}^J = [\delta_{US}^{\sigma}P_{US}^{(1-\sigma)} + P_J^{(1-\sigma)}]^{1/(1-\sigma)}; \quad P_{AGG}^{US} = [P_{US}^{(1-\sigma)} + P_J^{(1-\sigma)}]^{1/(1-\sigma)}.$$

The value of U.S. content in Japanese production depends on the price and variety of U.S. inputs used as well as the quantities of each variety demanded by Japanese producers. We can now compare the value of U.S. input content to the total value of inputs used by Japanese firms through the following calculation:

$$\frac{P_{US}N_{US}X_{US}}{P_{US}N_{US}X_{US} + P_J N_J X_J} = \frac{\delta_{US}^{\sigma}}{\delta_{US}^{\sigma} + (N_J/N_{US})(P_{US}/P_J)^{\sigma-1}}.$$

As one would expect, the relative value of U.S. content is rising in the Japanese price of inputs and declining with increases in the U.S. price of inputs. It is

---

8. Bergsten and Noland (1993) describe how the method of supplier contracting in Japan may increase the proclivity of Japanese assemblers for Japanese parts produced by suppliers with whom they have ongoing arrangements.

9. It is possible that U.S. firms also have a differential efficiency in their use of U.S. and foreign inputs. Incorporation of this idea would only strengthen the conclusions that follow. Further explanation of the δ_{US} term will be provided in the following section.

important to note as well that the Japanese price expressed in dollars is generated by the price in yen multiplied by the exchange rate, $P_J = e \times P_J^*$.

Since a high portion of components purchases are intrafirm in nature, whether the parts are produced in the United States or abroad, it is assumed that the parts are priced at marginal cost. It is possible that there are scale economies that are present in the production of intermediate inputs. However, this possibility is excluded here in order to prevent cost feedback that affects total demand. More discussion of product demand is included in the following section.

The U.S. content embodied in U.S. production takes a similar form, and prices exert influence in a comparable fashion, as is shown in the final equation:

$$\frac{P_{US}N_{US}X_{US}}{P_{US}N_{US}X_{US} + P_J N_J X_J} = \frac{1}{1 + (N_J/N_{US})(P_{US}/P_J)^{\sigma - 1}}.$$

In light of this set of equations, the following conclusions emerge. First, for a given set of Japanese and U.S. prices, the U.S. content of U.S. firm production will be higher than that of Japanese firms. In fact, this situation will be exacerbated if U.S. firms use Japanese inputs less efficiently than Japanese firms do since the preference for own-country inputs will be strengthened. Second, if the dollar depreciates, the domestic content embodied in either U.S. or Japanese production should rise since dollar depreciation causes the relative price of U.S. inputs to fall.

However, it is possible that Japanese production might not respond to exchange rate movements. Japanese motivation for producing in the United States could arise from the desire to gain North American content or the desire to circumvent protectionist moves in the United States.[10] Additionally, the need to fulfill content requirements for other tariff privileges might also modify the sourcing plans of firms. If so, these motives related to the degree of protection and form of regulation could cause the domestic content of Japanese production to be much higher than the preceding set of equations indicates.[11] If Japan were maintaining a certain level of domestic content in the United States to achieve these alternative objectives, then one would expect that the level of U.S. content would not change with exchange rate movements since content would be held to the minimum threshold needed to satisfy the requirement.

2.3 Data and Estimation

In this section, I test the model of parts purchases that was developed in the previous section. It is important to emphasize that the test is one that examines

10. This is the situation described by Bhagwati et al. (1987).

11. For discussions of content regulations, see Lopez-de-Silanes, Markusen, and Rutherford (1993) or Krishna and Krueger (1995).

the location from which components are sourced as opposed to the nationality of the party from whom the components are purchased.[12] In particular, I am seeking to discover the responsiveness of firms in their decision to buy U.S. or foreign parts. In all cases, I am seeking to explain the percentage of total inputs, μ, that are of domestic origin. The first set of tests follows the functional form that is proposed by the model and is estimated by nonlinear least squares. However, the results are subsequently estimated by tobit, in order to examine the sensitivity of the results to functional form and to augment the regressors.

The preceding section suggests that domestic input content is determined by relative prices of inputs, the variety of inputs, and firm preferences. Hence, the estimating equation that is used in this section assumes the form

$$\mu = \frac{\delta_{US}^{\sigma}}{\delta_{US}^{\sigma} + \left(\dfrac{N_J}{N_{US}}\right)\left(\dfrac{P_{US}}{P_J}\right)^{\sigma-1}}.$$

The relative efficiency of using U.S. parts is measured by δ_{US}. In the case of U.S.-headquartered firms, δ_{US} is set equal to one. In the case of foreign firms, the value of δ_{US} is estimated. The relative number of Japanese parts and U.S. parts, N_J/N_{US} is also set equal to one rather than estimated.[13] Hence, the estimation that proceeds from this point is the determination of the elasticity of substitution and the degree of discount, if any, that foreign producers associate with the use of U.S. parts. The purchase of domestic and foreign inputs is collected from the annual reports of the Foreign Trade Zones Board and is used to construct the measure of domestic content. The price of U.S. parts relative to Japanese parts is proxied alternatively by the relative automotive wage rates in the two countries and by the exchange rate.

2.3.1   Joint Venture Production

Before continuing, there is one last data issue to be resolved. In particular, there were three international joint ventures by the conclusion of the estimation period. For the purposes of this paper, joint ventures are deemed to be facilities that produce models that are sold under both U.S. and foreign nameplates.[14] Table 2.5 experiments with the classification of these U.S./foreign joint ventures to see whether they can be classified as a unique hybrid or whether these operations are more similar to either U.S. or foreign automobile production. Columns 1 and 2 analyze two subsets of the data and assume that the estimated elasticity of substitution is the same for all types of automaker. In column 1, joint ventures are compared with pure foreign automakers operating in the

---

12. However, Zeile (1995) shows that 94.6 percent of automobile firm imports are intrafirm.

13. Attempts were made to estimate the ratio of Japanese to U.S. parts, but the results were too large to be sensible. Also, since there are fully integrated automobile assemblers in both the United States and Japan, it seems likely that the relative number of parts types should differ drastically.

14. This restrictive definition of *joint venture* excludes Subaru-Isuzu, which involves two Japanese firms. However, none of its output is sold under a U.S. nameplate.

Table 2.5   Domestic Input Content and Firm Type, 1984–93

	(1)	(2)	(3)	(4)	(5)	(6)
σ, group	1.838	2.670				
	(.487)	(.422)				
σ, United States				2.700	2.701	2.700
				(.435)	(.417)	(.414)
σ, foreign			2.191		1.872	
			(.547)		(.781)	
σ, joint venture (JV)			1.665	2.251	1.665	
			(.863)	(1.758)	(1.408)	
σ, foreign/JV[a]						2.203
						(.784)
δ, foreign	.925		.823			.826
	(.063)		(.054)			(.009)
δ, joint venture		.865		.861		.860
		(.113)		(.136)		(.129)
Adjusted R^2	.763	.797	.768	.796	.789	.792
N	79	284	79	284	341	341

Note: Estimates are by nonlinear least squares. Standard errors are in parentheses. Joint ventures represent twenty-two year-firm observations.

[a]The elasticity of the foreign and joint venture observations estimated jointly.

United States. The results indicate a slight difference; the pure foreign ventures exhibit an apparent discount on their use of domestic parts relative to the joint venture manufacturers. In column 2, the joint venture producers are compared with U.S. producers. The results suggest that joint venture producers discount the use of U.S. parts relative to U.S. makers.

Columns 3 and 4 repeat the subset groupings that were tested in the first two columns of table 2.5. However, the estimation now relaxes the assumption that all automakers have the same elasticity of substitution. Instead, each type of automaker is allowed to have a unique elasticity of substitution. Column 4 reveals that the joint venture producers appear to be less flexible than the U.S. makers, as is shown by their estimated elasticity of substitution of 2.25. It is shown as well that the joint venture makers appear to place a discount on U.S.-sourced parts relative to the U.S. firms.

Finally, the entire sample is tested in columns 5 and 6 of table 2.5. Here, each type of firm is allowed to have its own elasticity of substitution in its purchasing of parts. In column 5, it is assumed that no discount applies to the foreign purchase of U.S. parts. This column shows that U.S. firms have an estimated elasticity of substitution that is more than 50 percent larger than the estimated elasticity of foreign or joint venture firms. In column 6, it is assumed that foreign firms and joint ventures have a common elasticity of substitution but that they may have different discount rates in their use of U.S. parts. Again, the estimated elasticity for U.S. firms is much higher than that for the foreign or joint venture firms in the sample. On the other hand, the estimated discount

Table 2.6   **Domestic Input Content and Firm Characteristics, 1984–93**

	Production Type		Production Volume		Number of Models	
	Assembler (1)	Parts (2)	High (3)	Low (4)	More than 2	2 or Fewer
σ, United States	2.692	2.749	2.058	4.615	2.670	2.719
	(.451)	(1.021)	(.544)	(.917)	(.632)	(.639)
σ, foreign/JV	2.388	−1.951	2.353	2.306	4.763	2.335
	(.867)	(4.469)	(1.042)	(1.644)	(4.307)	(.965)
δ, foreign/JV	.853	.813	.834	.884	.762	.966
	(.081)	(.128)	(.110)	(.128)	(.081)	(.103)
Adjusted R^2	.792	.784	.781	.812	.787	.799
N	295	46	189	106	146	149

Note: Estimates are by nonlinear least squares. Standard errors are in parentheses. Production volume is deemed high if the number of cars produced in the calendar year was 207,000 or higher. Low volume represents output below that threshold. Number of models counts the number of automobile nameplate vehicles produced within the individual zones. JV = joint venture.

factors of foreign and joint venture operators are very close in magnitude. Since the joint venture firms have elasticities that are similar in magnitude to the pure foreign firm elasticities, the following estimation assumes that the foreign firm and joint venture observations can be classified together as foreign. The specification further assumes that foreign and joint venture producers have the same discount factor in their use of U.S. parts.

Table 2.6 investigates a number of subsets in the data in order to gauge whether any of the factors provide meaningful insight into the estimated elasticities of substitution or the input discount factor, δ. Columns 1 and 2 separate the assembly zones from zones that specialize in the production of parts. Although the elasticity of substitution for U.S. firms is virtually identical to the previous estimates, the results show that foreign or joint venture assemblers have a higher elasticity of substitution than was estimated in the previous table. However, a differential still remains.

Columns 3 and 4 distinguish the automobile assemblers by production volume. Automobile zones producing 207,000 or more vehicles per calender year were deemed high volume, and zones producing fewer vehicles were classified as low volume. Automobile firms are broken out according to production volume since the automobile industry is known for its high fixed costs of production. We might assume that a firm with high production volume would be more sensitive to cost changes than a low-volume firm since the low-volume firm could not justify producing parts in multiple locations even if relative prices changed. This reluctance would be most pronounced in the case of engine or transmission production, where fixed costs are especially high, causing reliance on scale production.

Data on automobile zone volume was collected by matching each foreign trade zone with the automobile plant data published in the *Automotive News Market Data Book*. During the sample period, the median U.S. assembly site plant (both foreign trade zone and non–foreign trade zone) produced 207,000 vehicles. Of those plants producing within a zone, the median number of vehicles produced was 227,000.[15] These results suggest that foreign and domestic assemblers have similar elasticities of substitution but that the notable differences emerge from the low-volume sample. In the low-volume sample, U.S. firms are much more responsive to exchange rate–induced price changes than are foreign producers in the United States.

Finally, the data are separated according to the number of nameplate vehicle types produced in each zone. The rationale for this separation is to see whether the difference in foreign and domestic elasticities relates to the fact that foreign zones typically produce fewer car models in each zone than do U.S. producers. Column 5 includes all assemblers who produce three or more vehicle types in a zone, and column 6 includes all those with two or fewer vehicle nameplates. Vehicle diversity cannot be excluded as a determinant of U.S.-foreign differences. However, the imprecision of the estimated foreign elasticity makes it difficult to draw conclusions as to whether production diversity plays a role.

2.3.2 Tobit Estimates

Although the previous estimates have the advantage of following directly from the model of parts demand and result in direct estimates of the elasticity of substitution, they suffer from a few drawbacks. The main reason for using tobit analysis here is to see how estimated domestic content responds to price changes when a larger set of firm characteristics is considered. It is true that the elasticity of demand could be estimated as a function of plant age or other characteristics. However, results were not stable or precisely estimated when this was performed with this paper's data set. The estimating equation now takes the form

$$\mu = \alpha + \alpha_{US} - \beta e + \gamma X + \xi.$$

As before, content varies over time as relative prices change. These price changes are captured alternatively by exchange rate movements, measured by *e,* and later by the direct measurement of factor input prices. Now, however, the level of U.S. content in production also depends on a U.S. shift term, α_{US}, and firm characteristics, X. The error term is measured by ξ.

Table 2.7 provides a baseline estimate in column 1. As expected, the results show that the average U.S. firm utilizes 31.5 percent more domestic value added than does the average foreign firm. This baseline estimate assumes further that all firms react similarly to exchange rate movements, and the estimated effect again confirms that dollar depreciation causes the share of U.S. inputs to rise. Column 2 adds another indicator variable to capture differences

15. The numbers are different because some firms were slower to open zones than others.

Table 2.7   **Auto Production in U.S. Foreign Trade Zones, 1984–93**
                     (dependent variable: domestic inputs/total inputs)

	(1)	(2)	(3)	(4)	(5)
United States	.315	.294	.204	.588)	
	(.028)	(.027)	(.850)	(.831)	
Parts		−.161	−.146	−.099	−.200
		(.035)	(.033)	(.034)	(.030)
Log(exchange rate)	−.162	−.218			
	(.094)	(.092)			
Log(exchange rate)			−.233	−.254	−.135
×United States			(.090)	(.088)	(.068)
Log(exchange rate)			−.318	−.245	−.135
×foreign			(.171)	(.167)	(.070)
Age			.088	.081	.012
×foreign			(.010)	(.010)	(.010)
Age²			−.005	−.005	.0001
×foreign			(.007)	(.001)	(.0007)
Total shipments				.005	.002
				(.001)	(.001)
Constant	1.257	1.544	1.724	1.365	1.204
	(.428)	(.421)	(.791)	(.773)	(.313)
Firm effects	No	No	No	No	Yes
N	341	341	341	341	341
Log likelihood	16.55	26.47	60.28	69.80	156.51

Note: Standard errors are given in parentheses.

between parts makers and assemblers. While the results are qualitatively similar to the baseline estimates, the estimation finds that parts makers have domestic content that is roughly 16 percent lower than that of assemblers.

Column 3 introduces the possibility that foreign and domestic firms may have different responses to the movement of the exchange rate and actually suggests that the response is higher for the foreign firms in the sample. The specification also includes measures of the zone's age, where age is the number of years of zone operation. The age variable used applies only to the case of foreign firms. When age was included more generally, the estimated effects varied substantially and were not precisely estimated. It is likely that the age of the subzone activity is more meaningful in the case of foreign operations since they are more recently opened. Here we find that foreign firms source an increasing portion of their parts from the United States as their zones age but that the level of growth diminishes over time.

Column 4 adds another control for the total shipment size of the zones. It is learned that zones with higher shipments use a greater percentage of U.S. parts. The inclusion of this regressor brings the value of the foreign response to the exchange rate back down to a magnitude that is slightly smaller than that of U.S. firms. Finally, column 5 estimates firm fixed effects. The results are qualitatively similar to the previous specification. Overall, the results suggest

Table 2.8   Auto Production in U.S. Foreign Trade Zones, 1984–93
                   (dependent variable: domestic inputs/total inputs)

	(1)	(2)	(3)	(4)
United States	.316	.316	.323	.304
	(.028)	(.028)	(.028)	(.027)
Relative wage	−.079	−.088	−.061	−.083
	(.051)	(.056)	(.059)	(.058)
Relative energy cost		.003	.0002	−.073
		(.171)	(.170)	(.165)
Relative iron cost		.049	.050	.053
		(.079)	(.079)	(.076)
Relative wage			−.141	−.213
×foreign			(.111)	(.108)
Parts				−.176
				(.036)
Constant	.514	.500	.494	.530
	(.026)	(.034)	(.035)	(.034)
N	341	341	341	341
Log-L likelihood	16.24	16.46	17.27	28.66

Note: Standard errors are given in parentheses.

that many of the observed differences between foreign and U.S. firms are caused by age and production volume differences.

Rather than relying solely on the exchange rate to proxy for relative price effects, I now work with specifications that include a number of prices that should directly affect the costs of production in the auto industry. Table 2.8 sequentially adds measures of ore costs and energy costs to the estimating equations. Each of the results implies that a rise in the relative cost of labor in the United States will reduce the domestic content of U.S.-produced automobiles. In contrast, relative energy and iron prices enter with a perverse positive coefficient. This suggests that the use of domestic inputs relative to total inputs increases when the U.S. prices of these inputs rise. However, none of these estimates are significant. And, importantly, the continued U.S. indicator variable shows that U.S. firms utilize 30 percent greater levels of domestic inputs, even after controls have been added for input prices. It is the relative price of labor that plays the most decisive role in parts sourcing decisions.

2.3.3   Specification Checks

Table 2.9 examines the tobit estimating assumption that the regression errors are homoskedastic. Since the errors could be related to firm size, the first two columns divide the dependent variable, percentage domestic content, first by the square root of shipment size and next by the square root of zone production volume. While the first normalization provides results that are qualitatively similar to earlier tobit analysis, the second, based on production volume, does

Table 2.9   **Specification Tests (dependent variable: domestic inputs/total inputs)**

	(1)	(2)	High Volume (3)	High Volume (4)	Low Volume (5)	Low Volume (6)
United States	.09	−.01	.63	.60	.61	.32
	(.22)	(.02)	(.22)	(.23)	(.24)	(.18)
Real×	−.23	.01	−.29	−.31	−.20	−.47
United States	(.12)	(.01)	(.16)	(.18)	(.20)	(.14)
Real×	−.16	−.01	−.13	−.12	−.18	−.20
foreign	(.17)	(.02)	(.12)	(.13)	(.09)	(.08)
Age	−.01	.001	−.02	−.02	−.004	−.005
	(.01)	(.0004)	(.01)	(.01)	(.005)	(.005)
Foreign×	−.05	−.003	.06	.07	.07	.04
Age	(.03)	(.002)	(.03)	(.03)	(.03)	(.02)
Foreign×	.003	.0001	.001	.0001	−.005	−.002
Age^2	(.002)	(.0002)	(.002)	(.002)	(.002)	(.002)
Constant	.50	.03	.44	.45	.51	.81
	(.18)	(.02)	(.17)	(.18)	(.22)	(.16)
Log likelihood	10.88	1,262.25	56.41	47.99	110.94	123.41
N	340	242	232	219	109	122

Note: Tobit estimation. Standard errors are given in parentheses. The dependent variable is divided by the square root of total shipments in col. 1. It is divided by the square root of production volume and multiplied by ten in col. 2. Columns 3 and 5 are relative to the all production median of 207,000 units. Columns 4 and 6 are relative to the all FTZ production median of 227,529 units.

not. A further difference between columns 1 and 2 is that production volume applies only to automobile assemblers who produce completed vehicles. Since total shipments represents the dollar value of shipments, it includes parts makers and assemblers.

Under the assumption that there will be less heteroskedasticity of errors if data are analyzed according to production volume subsets, the tobit analysis is redone on subsamples of the data that are classified as high or low volume. As was learned previously, in the nonlinear least squares estimates, the biggest apparent differences appear when low-volume producers are compared. However, this result is sensitive to the volume classification selected: median of all automobile production or median of all foreign trade subzone production. Nonetheless, in three of the four estimates of price responsiveness in columns 3–6, U.S. firms exhibit greater sensitivity in all but column 5. And this result is robust to the inclusion of firm age effects, which were found to affect the price responsiveness.

2.4 Conclusions

This paper studies the domestic content decisions of domestic and foreign automobile makers in the United States between 1984 and 1993. The results show that, although the domestic content of Japanese firms has risen over time, differences are not being eliminated completely. Also, the apparent elasticity of substitution is lower for Japanese than for U.S. firms. If one assumes that the demand for Japanese nameplate automobiles will remain roughly constant, regardless of assembly location, these results suggest that, although transplant production may reduce the U.S. automotive deficit with Japan, it will not eliminate it.

The fact that the relative domestic input content of automakers responds to relative production costs provides two implications for multinational activity. To begin, this sensitivity to relative costs suggests that foreign automakers are not purely motivated by the goal of circumventing U.S. trade restrictions. If this were the single reason for transplant activity in the United States, we would expect the degree of U.S. content to be kept to a minimum that would not change with external conditions. Next, some studies, such as Klein and Rosengren (1994), claim that foreign investment outlays are not measurably altered by movements in relative wages. It may be true that foreign investment outlays do not respond to relative wage movements, but it would be incorrect to infer that no other real activities were affected. These results suggest that real wage movements may nonetheless have important consequences since multinationals can adjust their activities along other margins such as domestic versus foreign content. Further work is needed to provide an integrated understanding of the various margins along which multinational activity is conducted.

References

Automotive News Market Data Book. 1984–1994 (annual). Detroit: Crain Automotive Group.

Bergsten, C. Fred, and Marcus Noland. 1993. *Reconcilable differences? United States–Japan Economic Conflict.* Washington, D.C.: Institute for International Economics.

Bhagwati, Jagdish N., Richard A. Brecher, Elias Dinopoulos, and T. N. Srinivasan. 1987. Quid pro quo foreign investment and welfare: A political-economy-theoretic model. *Journal of Development Economics* 27 (1–2): 127–38.

Blomstrom, Magnus, Robert E. Lipsey, and Ksenia Kulchycky. 1988. U.S. and Swedish direct investment and exports. In *Trade policy issues and empirical analysis,* ed. Robert E. Baldwin. Chicago: University of Chicago Press.

Brainard, Lael S. 1993. An empirical assessment of the proximity-concentration trade-off between multinational sales and trade. Working Paper no. 4580. Cambridge, Mass.: National Bureau of Economic Research, December.

Ethier, Wilfred J. 1986. The multinational firm. *Quarterly Journal of Economics* 101:805–33.

Finger, J. M. 1976. Trade and domestic effects of the offshore assembly provision in the U.S. tariff. *American Economic Review* 66:598–611.

Foreign Trade Zones Board. 1984–92. Annual report to the Congress of the United States. Washington, D.C.

Grossman, Gene M. 1982. Offshore assembly provisions and the structure of protection. *Journal of International Economics* 12:301–12.

Helpman, Elhanan. 1984. A simple theory of international trade with multinational corporations. *Journal of Political Economy* 92:451–71.

Helpman, Elhanan, and Paul R. Krugman. 1985. *Market structure and foreign trade: Increasing returns, imperfect competition, and the international economy.* Cambridge, Mass.: MIT Press.

Klein, Michael W., and Eric Rosengren. 1994. The real exchange rate and foreign direct investment in the United States: Relative wealth vs. relative wage effects. *Journal of International Economics* 36:373–89.

Krishna, Kala, and Anne Krueger. 1995. Implementing free trade areas: Rules of origin and hidden protection. Working Paper no. 4983. Cambridge, Mass.: National Bureau of Economic Research, January.

Lopez-de-Silanes, Florencio, James R. Markusen, and Thomas F. Rutherford. 1993. Anti-competitive and rent-shifting aspects of domestic-content provisions in regional trade blocks. Working Paper no. 4512. Cambridge, Mass.: National Bureau of Economic Research.

Markusen, James R. 1984. Multinationals, multi-plant economies, and the gains from trade. *Journal of International Economics* 16, nos. 3–4: 205–26.

Markusen, James R., and Anthony J. Venables. 1995. Multinational firms and the new trade theory. Working Paper no. 5036. Cambridge, Mass.: National Bureau of Economic Research, February.

Mendez, Jose A. 1993. The welfare effects of repealing the offshore assembly provision. *Journal of International Economics* 34:1–22.

U.S. Department of Commerce. Bureau of Economic Analysis. 1994. *Foreign direct investment in the United States: 1992 benchmark survey.* Washington, D.C.: U.S. Government Printing Office.

Zeile, William J. 1995. Imported inputs and the domestic content of production by foreign-owned manufacturing affiliates in the United States. Washington, D.C.: Department of Commerce. Typescript.

3   Protectionist Threats and Foreign Direct Investment

Bruce A. Blonigen and Robert C. Feenstra

Avoiding protectionist measures by establishing production facilities in the protectionist country is one of the oldest explanations for foreign direct investment (FDI). Recent papers have added a new extension to this traditional "tariff-jumping" explanation to analyze the possibility that the threat of protection may induce FDI. One explanation is that, as the probability of protection rises, foreign firms may engage in more FDI, ceteris paribus, to establish a presence in the host country as an insurance policy in case protectionist barriers arise. This anticipatory tariff jumping may be especially important since there may be a substantial lag in establishing a plant in the host country and a firm may lose substantial market share if it does not have a plant in the host country when protectionism is put into place. The majority of papers on protection-induced FDI, however, have hypothesized that foreign firms (and/or governments) use FDI as a quid pro quo for a lower future threat of protection.

The concept of quid pro quo FDI was formally introduced by Bhagwati (1985) and refined in subsequent papers, including Bhagwati et al. (1987), Dinopoulos (1989), Wong (1989), Dinopoulos and Wong (1991), Dinopoulos (1992), and Bhagwati, Dinopoulos, and Wong (1992). Grossman and Helpman (1994) is the most recent and fully specified analysis of this idea. In short, the quid pro quo hypothesis is that a firm may decide to invest in a foreign country (even at a loss potentially) to reduce the "threat" of protection in future periods to keep its export markets open. There have been a number of instances in which it is quite clear that the Japanese have offered FDI as a quid pro quo to avert U.S. protectionism. One of the most recent and obvious examples is the U.S.-Japan deal that averted a trade war in automobiles and automobile parts

Bruce A. Blonigen is assistant professor of economics at the University of Oregon. Robert C. Feenstra is professor of economics at the University of California, Davis, and director of the International Trade and Investment Program at the National Bureau of Economic Research. He is also the editor of the *Journal of International Economics*.

in June 1995. When faced with prohibitive tariffs on luxury automobiles, Japanese automakers promised substantial expansions of their automobile plants in the United States—an interesting concession since the main issue was supposedly access of U.S. firms to the Japanese market. However, there may be reasons to believe that induced FDI is not a general phenomenon. In particular, Dinopoulos (1989) shows that one primary reason quid pro quo FDI may not occur is the existence of a free-rider problem. Specifically, if one foreign firm invests in an export market to reduce protectionist pressure, all firms in the industry that export to the same market may benefit. The larger the free-rider problem, the less likely quid pro quo FDI, and the problem may preclude the phenomenon from arising. For this reason, testing whether the threat of protection affects FDI flows is important and relevant.

Despite the solid theoretical work in this area, only one other known paper has empirically explored the relation between FDI and the threat of protection. Azrak and Wynne (1995) test whether the predicted probability that a U.S. antidumping case will reach a final affirmative decision against a Japanese product affects quarterly Japanese manufacturing FDI in the United States. Azrak and Wynne run into a common problem with empirical analysis of FDI: extremely aggregated data. Using fifty-eight observations over fourteen years of manufacturing FDI, they find modest support that the probability of protection affects FDI flows.

This paper extends Azrak and Wynne in numerous ways. First, observations of Japanese FDI into the United States across four-digit Standard Industrial Classification (SIC) manufacturing industries from 1981 to 1988 are used to test a number of hypotheses that arise from the theory of protection-induced FDI. Since antidumping (AD) and escape clause (EC) investigations are often targeted at very specific products, it makes sense to analyze the threat of protection from these sources at a much more disaggregated industrial level.[1]

Unlike previous analysis, this paper is careful to estimate separately the effect of tariff jumping of actual protection as distinguished from FDI that is induced by the threat of protection. Separate estimation of these two different types of FDI is important for two reasons. First, induced FDI has potentially different welfare implications than tariff jumping of actual protection. Second, there is quite likely a correlation between industries with actual protection in place and those with high predicted probabilities of protection. Estimation using only one of these as an explanatory variable may lead to biased conclusions since it does not allow separate identification of the two different effects.[2]

---

1. For example, it may be more difficult to discern the effect of an affirmative case on Japanese cyanuric acid imports on manufacturing FDI than it is to discern the case's effect on cyanuric acid's associated four-digit SIC industry, Cyclic Organic Crudes and Intermediates.

2. Azrak and Wynne (1995) looked at the effect of the threat of protection in isolation, without modeling the effects of protection in place. By not controlling for actual protection, which is most likely highly correlated with greater probability of protection, it is not clear whether their significant results lend support for induced FDI or tariff jumping.

Finally, we address whether induced FDI is due to anticipatory tariff jumping or quid pro quo considerations. Whereas Azrak and Wynne model FDI as a function of the threat of protection, quid pro quo theory maintains that the threat of protection is a function of lagged FDI as well. Thus, we model and test this second connection between FDI and the threat of protection. To further identify when quid pro quo FDI occurs, we note that political motivations behind FDI behavior can be gleaned by the *type of FDI* a foreign firm engages in and the *type of protection* foreign firms may be able to defuse with FDI. The type of FDI matters because acquisition FDI may be more likely to create ill will than to defuse protectionist pressure in the host country industry. The type of protection matters because political factors have been shown to influence EC investigations more than AD investigations. Thus, quid pro quo influences should be especially strong in nonacquisition FDI flows with respect to EC investigations.

Our empirical analysis confirms at the four-digit SIC level that the threat of protection strongly influences Japanese FDI into the United States. In fact, our estimates find that the threat of protection effect on Japanese FDI flows rivals the effect of actual protection on these flows. In addition, our results suggest that quid pro quo intentions play a major role in this response of FDI to the threat of protection. First, the threat of protection substantially increases nonacquisition FDI, the type of FDI that would be appropriate to defuse a protectionist threat, but has little effect on acquisition FDI. Second, nonacquisition FDI has a stronger response to the threat of EC protection than it does to the threat of AD protection. Again, this suggests that threat-responding FDI is politically motivated since EC investigations are more likely to be responsive to political appeasement. Finally, our estimates are able to determine when FDI is successful in defusing the threat of protection in future periods. Not surprisingly, the strongest evidence for successful quid pro quo FDI is when firms use nonacquisition FDI to defuse the threat of EC protection.

The paper is organized in four sections. Section 3.1 briefly reviews the literature on quid pro quo FDI and presents testable hypotheses of the relation between the threat of protection and FDI. Section 3.2 presents the econometric model and data used to test the hypotheses presented in section 3.1. Section 3.3 gives results, and section 3.4 concludes.

3.1   The Effect of a Protectionist Threat on FDI: Testable Implications

The quid pro quo FDI hypothesis rests on the assumption that foreign firms and/or governments believe that they can use FDI to defuse the threat of protection in future periods by appeasing special interest groups in the potentially protectionist country. Bhagwati, Dinopoulos, and Wong (1992) indicate a number of different ways in which FDI may reduce the probability of protection. On the one hand, it may be directed at gaining the goodwill of the host country's government, which represents the "supply of protection." Presumably, the products manufactured by foreign firms will be more palatable to the host government if they are produced using host country labor. On the other hand, quid pro quo FDI may be intended to placate the groups who are potential "demanders" of protection. These potential demanders include firms, labor unions, and towns/communities in the host country that may be affected by increased import penetration and organized enough to lobby the government for protection. In this respect, Wong (1989) presents a model that specifically models labor union behavior and its lobbying efforts for protection, where employment levels of its members are endogenously determined by import protection and FDI.

Sometimes it may be difficult to identify which groups quid pro quo FDI is intended to appease. For example, Japanese automotive firms geographically located U.S. production in areas that did not have unionized automotive workers. Thus, in this instance, appeasement of labor must not have been a goal of these Japanese firms. There is the additional question of whether FDI is quid pro quo to the specific industry or a more broad appeal to the host government, regardless of the specific industry's view of the FDI. This depends on how large a role a specific industry can play in host government protection. Given U.S. protectionist laws, under which industries petition for relief in a formal process, one would guess that appeasement of the industry (if not its industry groups) would be a primary goal of the quid pro quo FDI. In summary, quid pro quo FDI implies the following general relation between FDI flows and the threat of protection:

$$(1) \qquad \text{threat}_{t-1} \to \text{FDI}_t \to \text{threat}_{t+1}.$$

This leads to the following testable hypotheses:

Hypothesis 1: FDI flows from a foreign country are positively affected by the perceived threat of protection to its export markets in the host country: $\text{threat}_{t-1} \to \text{FDI}_t$.

Hypothesis 2: FDI defuses the future probability of protection: $\text{FDI}_t \to \text{threat}_{t+1}$.

We decompose the quid pro quo theory in these two hypotheses for the following reason. First, it highlights that there is an inherent lag to the process. This represented lag structure is not an artificial construct, but empirically important. The threat of protection variable is lagged one period from FDI in hypothesis 1 since it is assumed that it takes a period for a foreign firm to change its level of FDI in response to changes in the threat of protection. Given the significant lag in establishing new or additional FDI, this is appropriate even if the length of one period is a year. Furthermore, it will take time for FDI to appease special interest groups lobbying for protection in an industry and defuse the threat (hypothesis 2). In other words, it may take time for the foreign firms to become involved in the host country industry and be able to influence its political machinery.[3]

A second reason for two separate hypotheses is that, whereas hypothesis 1 is compatible with either quid pro quo FDI or anticipatory tariff jumping, hypothesis 2 allows a separate test for quid pro quo intentions only. When increased FDI is observed in response to a rising protectionist threat in the host country (hypothesis 1), is it because the foreign firms believe that they can defuse the protectionist threat and continue exporting in future periods, or is it because they anticipate future protection and want to get established in the host country by the time the protection is in place? The former is quid pro quo FDI, the latter anticipatory tariff jumping. Anticipatory tariff jumping may be important since there may be a substantial lag in establishing a plant in the host country and a firm may lose substantial market share if it does not have a plant in the host country before protectionism is in place. Disentangling which intention motivates the foreign firm to engage in FDI in the face of rising protectionism is difficult, and the firm may be motivated by both.[4]

One drawback of testing hypothesis 2 is that it can determine whether quid pro quo FDI is occurring only if quid pro quo FDI is successful. Specifically, FDI may be offered with quid pro quo intentions, but it may not be successful in attaining a lower threat of protection. Thus, failure to find a negative correlation between the threat of protection and lagged FDI does not necessarily mean that FDI is not motivated by the desire to reduce the threat of protection; it means simply that it may have failed. To better explore if there are political motivations behind FDI flows, we can look at what types of protectionism Japanese FDI responds to. Azrak and Wynne (1995) use AD decisions as an indicator variable to estimate the probability of protection. This paper includes both AD and EC affirmative decisions as indicators. However, AD and EC investigations often lead to different forms of actual protection and thus have potentially varying consequences. In particular, Finger, Hall, and Nelson (1982) describe AD investigations as following a "technical track," whereas EC investigations follow a "political track." They find that whether an EC investigation will reach an affirmative decision and lead to actual protection depends on political factors, such as industry structure and an industry's ability

---

3. In addition, we found little correlation between current FDI and the threat of protection in our data, but we obtained significant results with lagged FDI.

4. Dinopoulos and Wong (1991) make a different distinction between forms of FDI that occur previous to protectionism than the one made here. They distinguish between "protectionist-threat-responding" FDI and quid pro quo FDI. They model a Cournot-type game between foreign firms and domestic labor unions, in which the labor unions choose lobbying efforts to raise the probability of protection and foreign firms choose FDI to lower the probability. They define *protectionist-threat-responding protection* as FDI by foreign firms when they are "reacting to protectionist threat in a Nash fashion" and *quid pro quo FDI* as FDI meant to "defuse the protectionist threat as a Stackelberg leader." We find this distinction unintuitive since, in both cases, the foreign firm is investing to lower the threat of protection. Other papers on quid pro quo FDI implicitly refer to both these types of FDI as quid pro quo.

to lobby for protection. In contrast, the final decision in an AD case depends on technical facts that are used to determine whether there exists a difference between the foreign firm's home price and its export price (i.e., dumping) and whether the domestic industry has been injured. It is important to note that the president of the United States has the final decision on whether to enact protectionism in the case of an affirmative EC investigation, whereas affirmative AD cases lead automatically to duties.[5] As described above, quid pro quo FDI is specifically intended to affect the political process of protectionism. This suggests a third hypothesis:

Hypothesis 3: Quid pro quo FDI is more likely in the case of EC investigations than in AD ones.

Testing hypothesis 3 will allow a distinction between anticipatory tariff jumping and quid pro quo. Specifically, with anticipatory tariff jumping, it is expected that the response of FDI flows with respect to higher probabilities of EC and AD protectionism are similar, whereas a relatively larger response toward the threat of EC protectionism is expected if FDI is affected by quid pro quo considerations.

Analysis of the type of FDI in which foreign firms choose to engage may also provide information on the firms' political motivations. Bhagwati, Dinopoulos, and Wong (1992) note that political perceptions involved with quid pro quo FDI can be very sensitive. For example, they admit that increased Japanese FDI into the United States may eventually create "ill will rather than goodwill" if it comes to be perceived as a threat, like import penetration. Despite this, no one has commented on whether certain forms of FDI may be more likely to appease special interest groups and are therefore more appropriate for quid pro quo FDI. These considerations will help distinguish between quid pro quo and anticipatory tariff jumping.

Politically, it is reasonable to expect that quid pro quo FDI would occur through new plants (or "greenfield" FDI), plant expansions, or joint ventures[6] rather than acquisitions, for the following reasons. First, not all acquisitions are "friendly," which may increase the threat of protectionism rather than reduce it. But even those acquisitions that are "friendly" may cause hostility with the target firm's labor and/or community, although they may be acceptable to the target firm's management. These former groups are typically not a significant part of the acquisition agreement. Thus, they may be hostile to the change in ownership and the adjustment process it implies, a process that may be even

5. Duties from an affirmative AD decision may not be imposed if the petitioning industry withdraws or suspends its petition. This may occur in the case where the petitioning industry and foreign firms have made an alternative bargain. For example, AD cases in computer chips from Japan in 1985 were suspended in lieu of the semiconductor agreement between the two countries.
6. The discussion that follows focuses only on the political difference between acquisitions and new plants or plant expansion. Joint ventures seem to be an obvious way to try to appease host country firms in the same industry, as pointed out by Bhagwati, Dinopoulos, and Wong (1992).

more difficult because of cultural differences with new foreign owners. There-fore, of the three lobby groups that are among the potential demanders for protectionism, acquisition FDI may appease only one group (the firm's deci-sion makers) and aggravate the other two (labor and the community). However, these considerations may be mitigated if the target company was on the brink of closing and all groups connected with the target firm are aware of that re-ality.

In addition, the acquisition may increase protectionist sentiments from other firms in the industry, who may appeal to government to prevent foreign firms from "buying up" their industry. This clearly was the case with the proposed merger of Fujitsu's semiconductor business and Fairchild Semiconductor Cor-poration in 1986. At the time, one industry analyst was quoted in the *Wall Street Journal* (27 October 1986) as saying, "Right now protectionist senti-ments are mixed, and I don't think this merger in itself will result in sanctions or opposition by the U.S. government. But when you have one of the best high tech semiconductor companies in the business sell to the Japanese, it's got to raise some eyebrows. And if it's the beginning of a trend of Japanese snapping up weakened U.S. companies, the government might have to respond."

A second contrast between acquisition and greenfield investment is related to the timing of job creation in the host country. The immediate effect of a new plant or plant expansion is the creation of new jobs and all the publicity that goes with the initial hiring process. The long-run effect of greenfield invest-ment may mean no new jobs or even lost jobs in the overall economy if the new foreign plant leads to job displacement elsewhere in the industry. But uncertain future losses, potentially dispersed in small amounts across many firms and communities, may have little political weight in the face of the initial large job creation. Acquisitions have no such immediate positive effect. In fact, acquisi-tions can often bring reorganizations and accompanying immediate job losses. Again, the exception is a target company that is known to be on the brink of closure. In this instance, there may be an opportunity for the foreign company to play the role of the white knight and "save jobs."

In contrast to quid pro quo FDI, an argument can be made that anticipatory tariff jumping is more likely to take the form of acquisition FDI. Anticipatory tariff jumping implies that it is important for the firm to establish a presence in the market before protection is in place. However, some forms of FDI, espe-cially construction of a new plant (or greenfield), may take a year or longer to complete. Others have noted that the quickest form of FDI is most likely an acquisition. Thus, with anticipatory tariff jumping, where time is apparently crucial, one would expect to see acquisition FDI. This discussion leads to a fourth testable hypothesis:

Hypothesis 4: Quid pro quo FDI is more likely to take the form of greenfield FDI, while anticipatory tariff jumping is more likely to involve acquisition FDI.

3.2   Empirical Model and Data

To test hypotheses 1–4 formally, we focus on Japanese FDI into the United States and the role of protectionist pressure in explaining those patterns across manufacturing industries over time. Proponents of quid pro quo FDI have pinpointed Japanese investment patterns in the United States as a likely area for observing the phenomenon. Bhagwati, Dinopoulos, and Wong (1992) explicitly state, "There is certainly some plausible, more-than-anecdotal evidence that the acceleration in Japanese DFI [direct foreign investment] in the United States in the early 1980's was due to a mix of 'political' reasons: some partly in anticipation of the imposition of protection, and others partly to defuse its threat" (p. 189). As they report, a survey by the Japanese Ministry of International Trade and Industry (MITI) of Japanese firms undertaking foreign investment between 1980 and 1986 found that many were motivated by "avoiding trade friction." This is not surprising since trade groups in Japan publicly encouraged Japanese firms to invest to lower the threat of protection in the United States during this time. For example, the *New York Times* (2 May 1984) reported that, "fearful of trade friction, the Communications Industry Association of Japan, a trade group, has cautioned its members to avoid explosive increases in exports and to build factories in the United States, according to Haruo Ozawa, its president."

Japanese industrial structure may make observation of quid pro quo FDI more likely as well. MITI and *keiretsu* industrial linkages have been cited often as elements in the Japanese economy that may allow a greater degree of industrial collusion there than in other developed countries. We will test for the importance of *keiretsu* relations in the FDI decision below. By facilitating coordination of FDI and export flows, the unique Japanese institutional and industrial structures may lessen any potential free-rider problem inherent in an industry faced with protectionist threats in its export markets.

3.2.1   Econometric Model

Testing the relation between FDI and the threat of protection is difficult precisely because it is impossible to measure or observe the threat of protection directly. However, the formal institutional process in the United States that accompanies EC and AD protection provides perhaps the best indication of when protectionist pressures in a U.S. industry are high. As successive GATT rounds have reduced most-favored-nation tariff rates and long-standing quota arrangements, EC and AD laws are the main ways that new protectionism has occurred in the United States in the past decades. AD and EC investigations also focus on very specific products and industries, which makes the threat of protection industry specific and thus more easily identified. Thus, an indication of the threat of protection is whether imports in an industry become subject to an affirmative EC or AD decision.[7] We can use this indicator variable to model the relation between the underlying latent variable and explanatory variables by assuming that

$$(2) \qquad\qquad Z^*_{i,t-1} = W_{i,t-1}\gamma + \eta_{i,t-1},$$

where

$$Z_{i,t-1} = 1 \text{ if } Z^*_{i,t-1} > 0,$$
$$Z_{i,t-1} = 0 \text{ if } Z^*_{i,t-1} < 0,$$

and where $Z^*_{i,t-1}$ is the threat of protection in industry i and year $t - 1$, $Z_{i,t-1}$ is the associated indicator variable of whether an affirmative AD or EC decision is made, $W_{i,t-1}$ are explanatory variables that represent industrial, political, and overall U.S. economic factors that influence the threat of protection, γ is the parameter vector, and $\eta_{i,t-1}$ is the error term, assumed to be $N(0,1)$.[8] Appropriate estimation of this model can be done with a standard probit model. A number of studies have analyzed a similar model to help predict which industries will have successful AD or EC investigations brought against U.S. imports, including Takacs (1981), Salvatore (1987), and Coughlin, Terza, and Khalifah (1989). Unlike past studies, we use the model to determine whether previous FDI lowers the threat of protection (hypothesis 2) by including lagged FDI as an explanatory variable in $W_{i,t-1}$.

The unobservable nature of the threat of protection also affects estimation of whether the threat of protection affects FDI (hypothesis 1). To test hypothesis 1, assume that Japanese FDI in industry i in year t is specified as

$$(3) \qquad\qquad Y_{it} = X_{it}\beta + Z^*_{i,t-1}\delta + \varepsilon_{it},$$

where Y_{it} is an $(n \times 1)$ vector of Japanese FDI, X_{it} is an $(n \times k)$ vector of k explanatory variables besides the threat of protection variable, β is a $(k \times 1)$ vector of coefficients, $Z^*_{i,t-1}$ represents the threat of protection last period, δ is its associated coefficient, ε_{it} is an $(n \times 1)$ error term, and $n = i \times t$. Once again, the variable $Z^*_{i,t-1}$ has an asterisk associated with it because we cannot observe this variable; rather, we observe $Z_{i,t-1}$. Whereas the latent variable is the dependent variable in equation (2), the latent variable is in the explanatory

7. Section 301 trade actions, which are neatly analyzed in Bayard and Elliott (1994), were also considered as possible indications of a protectionist threat. However, the majority of 301 activity with respect to Japan has targeted market access of U.S. firms in Japan with respect to products that Japan does not import to the United States (specifically, tobacco and citrus fruit products). Other 301 actions with respect to Japan occurred simultaneously with an AD or EC investigation of the same subject product. Thus, it would be impossible to separate out the effect of the 301 action from the AD or EC action we model.

8. The variables in eq. (2) are written as lagged variables with subscript $t - 1$ since this equation will generate predicted probabilities of protection to explain next-period FDI, as predicted by theory and modeled in eq. (4) below.

variables of equation (3), and estimates using the observable indicator variable as a proxy need not be consistent (see Goldberger 1972; and Pagan 1984). However, whether the latent variable is observable to the agents being modeled is important for testing. In this case, the unobservable variable (the threat of protection) is not only unknown to the researcher but also most likely unknown to the agents being modeled, the foreign firms making FDI decisions. Thus, assuming that foreign firms use the same information set as is available to us (W_{it} in eq. [2]), the predicted (i.e., expected) probability of protection from equation (2), $\hat{Z}_{i,t-1}$, not the unobservable threat of protection, $Z_{i,t-1}^*$, is the appropriate regressor. Thus, hypothesis 1 is tested with

(4) $$Y_{it} = X_{it}\beta + \hat{Z}_{i,t-1}\delta + \varepsilon_{it}.$$

In summary, from estimating equation (2), we obtain estimated predicted probabilities of filings for all industries i across all years $t - 1$, $\hat{Z}_{i,t-1}$. Assuming that the error terms of the two equations are independent, this predicted probability, $\hat{Z}_{i,t-1}$, can be substituted in (4) to obtain consistent maximum likelihood estimates (see Maddala 1983, 117–23).[9]

Assuming that the error terms are independent is consistent with the relation between the threat of protection and FDI shown in equation (1), whereby FDI levels and the threat of protection are not contemporaneously (i.e., simultaneously) determined. Current values of each variable are affected by lagged, predetermined values of the other. Provided that the threat of protection and FDI are not correlated with their own past values two periods before, the two equations' error terms are independent. Because it is more likely that noncontemporaneous correlation exists with FDI, we correct for this in equation (4), as described below. As mentioned, equation (2) by itself has been the subject of empirical investigation, as a number of papers have modeled the probability that a U.S. industry will file an AD and/or an EC petition, including Takacs (1981), Herander and Schwartz (1984), Salvatore (1987), Coughlin, Terza, and Khalifah (1989), Moore (1992), Baldwin and Steagall (1994), Azrak and Wynne (1995), and Hansen and Prusa (in press). Relying primarily on these studies and hypothesis 2, we include the following as explanatory variables in estimating equation (2): (1) previous-period real Japanese import growth in industry; (2) previous-period real domestic shipment growth of U.S. industry; (3) share of Japanese imports in industry i of total Japanese imports in United States; (4) share of Japanese imports in industry i to total imports in industry i; (5) union presence in U.S. industry i; (6) industry wage to value added; (7)

---

9. This situation can be contrasted with the case in which a variable is unobservable to the researcher but known to the agents in the process being modeled. This is the classic case of latent variable estimation, where simply inserting the predictions from eq. (3) for $Z_{i,t-1}^*$ in eq. (2) will lead to inconsistent standard errors in the linear setting and has unknown properties in the nonlinear setting used in this paper (see Goldberger 1972; and Pagan 1984). Because it is likely that foreign firms are removed from actual observation of the U.S. protectionist threat, the assumption used here does not seem restrictive and makes estimation more tractable.

previous period AD/CVD (countervailing duty) investigations of other countries' imports in industry; (8) real U.S. GNP growth; and (9) lagged FDI.

Variables 1, 3, and 4 capture how prominent Japanese import penetration has been in the industry in absolute terms, relative to total Japanese imports in the United States, and relative to other countries' imports in the industry. The more prominent the Japanese import penetration, the more likely a petition is filed by the U.S. domestic industry for relief. Variable 2 is intended to capture how well the U.S. industry is performing since an injury test in AD investigations is a statutory requirement for affirmative determinations. Lower real shipment growth should raise the probability of an affirmative decision. Variables 5 and 6 are intended to assess how prominent and powerful U.S. labor interests are in an industry since, as Bhagwati, Dinopoulous, and Wong (1992) point out, labor groups can be a strong and important lobby group for protectionist pressure. Thus, a larger labor presence should increase the likelihood of an affirmative AD or EC petition.

Justification for including variable 7 and expecting a positive correlation is that, once an industry has employed substantial fixed costs for filing an initial case and acquiring institutional knowledge of U.S. protectionist law, the marginal cost in future periods of filing for relief is much lower. Trade diversion from previous cases may also play an important role. When a number of foreign countries' imports of a certain product suffer AD or CVD duties, this competition barrier can benefit not only the U.S. industry but also the foreign importers that did not come under investigation. Thus, these nonsubject imports can often increase substantially, raising the probability that they come under future investigations. Finally, variable 8 relates to economy wide factors that may influence the likelihood of filings across years, and variable 9 tests hypothesis 2.

The theory of FDI suggests a number of explanatory variables for equation (4)—in addition to the threat variable—that have performed well in previous empirical analyses. As discussed in the data section below, we use a panel data set of Japanese FDI in the United States across four-digit SIC manufacturing industries and the years 1981–88. Thus, the specified explanatory variables address both the cross-sectional and the time-series dimensions of the dependent variable, Japanese FDI into the United States.[10]

One of the more prominent theories of FDI is internalization. Internalization, which arose out of the transactions cost literature, postulates that firms with more firm-specific assets are more likely to engage in FDI. For these firms, external market transactions with another party, such as exporting or licensing, may not adequately take advantage of firm-specific assets, as would be the case if the transactions were internalized (i.e., setting up one's own oper-

---

10. Many empirical studies of FDI explore either theories that explain cross-sectional variation of FDI patterns (e.g., Kogut and Chang 1991) or theories that explain variations in aggregate FDI across years (e.g., Froot and Stein 1991; and Martin 1991). For studies that use panel data, see Ray (1989) and Blonigen (1995).

ations in the foreign country).[11] To proxy Japanese industries that enjoy larger stocks of these firm-specific assets, we use R&D expenditures by industry and expect a positive coefficient. R&D expenditures have been used by a number of other empirical studies similarly (e.g., Martin 1991; and Grubaugh 1987) and show significant explanatory power.

Exchange rate changes have shown explanatory power in a number of empirical studies (see Swenson 1994; Ray 1989; Froot and Stein 1991; Azrak and Wynne 1995; and Blonigen 1995). Both Froot and Stein (1991) and Blonigen (1995) present theoretical models that predict that dollar depreciations relative to the yen increase Japanese FDI into the United States. Thus, the yen-dollar exchange rate is included with an expected negative sign.

Other studies examining foreign countries' investment patterns in the United States over time have included real GNP growth in the foreign country as an explanatory variable (see Ray 1989; and Martin 1991). One would expect higher growth rates of overall economic activity to be positively correlated with a country's investment both within the foreign country and abroad. Thus, we include Japanese real GNP growth and expect a positive sign.[12]

We also include a variable specific to Japanese economic behavior: *keiretsu* relations. Lawrence (1991, 1993) details important ways in which *keiretsu* relations may influence Japanese economic activity and shows empirically that it has a substantial effect on the level of imports and inward FDI in Japan. The large horizontal *keiretsus* of Japan are centered around the Japanese economy's largest banks. One way in which firms affiliated with a *keiretsu* may be different with respect to their outward FDI behavior is perhaps through their easier access to and the lower cost of external financing because of these *keiretsu* linkages to a major bank. In addition, Dinopoulos (1989) showed that market structure considerations may affect the phenomenon of quid pro quo FDI, as discussed above. Thus, we include the degree of *keiretsu* linkages across a Japanese industry and expect a positive sign.

One of the oldest explanations for FDI is the avoidance of protection that is in place; that is, tariff-jumping. Once protectionist barriers are erected to foreign imports, foreign firms invest in the protectionist country to get behind the tariff wall. Thus, we include a protection variable to indicate the presence of EC or negotiated trade agreements with Japan or AD duties in place in an industry on Japanese products. We assume that relative levels of protection from other sources in the U.S. economy (i.e., most-favored-nation tariff rates and long-standing quotas) remain unchanged over our sample and thus have no effect on changes in FDI flows over our sample.

---

11. For example, licensing another firm in a foreign country involves "transactions" costs if your firm has superior marketing abilities.

12. Martin (1991) found this variable to be statistically significant in explaining Japanese investment in the United States.

3.2.2   Data

To test the model, we must necessarily rely on numerous data sources, each with potential limitations in coverage and otherwise. The most difficult variable with respect to data is information on Japanese FDI flows into the United States. Credible testing of our model requires both cross-sectional detail and a time-series dimension, as explained above. Thus, we rely on a yearly publication by the International Trade Administration (ITA) at the Department of Commerce (DOC), *Foreign Direct Investment in the United States.* The appendix of this publication contains a compiled list of FDI transactions reported in public sources during the year, including the type of investment,[13] the foreign investor and country, the four-digit SIC of the U.S. investment,[14] the state in which it is located, and the dollar value of the transaction. The disaggregate nature of the ITA data (specifying individual observations of FDI by type, country, and four-digit SIC industry) distinguishes them from the data published annually by the Bureau of Economic Analysis (BEA) in the *Survey of Current Business,* which reports more aggregate statistics. However, the BEA relies on private survey data, whereas the ITA records FDI from publicly available sources. Figure 3.1 graphs two comparable aggregate measures of Japanese FDI activity from 1979 to 1989, with one line representing the number of Japanese manufacturing FDI occurrences in the United States reported by the ITA and the other representing a BEA measure of Japanese outlays for acquisitions and new establishments in the United States. It is easy to see that the two series follow each other closely (the correlation is 0.91), suggesting that the ITA consistently matches the private survey data of the BEA. In addition, the ITA count data patterns for broad manufacturing groups were matched to BEA data with strong, positive correlation coefficients as well.[15]

Dollar values of FDI are not necessarily a matter of public record; thus, dollar values for observations are reported by the ITA database only about half to two-thirds of the time. Thus, we specify our dependent variable in equation (4) as the discrete number of FDI occurrences in a four-digit industry i in year t. To model this dependent variable correctly, we employ a discrete probability model, negative binomial, to obtain maximum likelihood estimates.[16] The panel nature of the data is a concern as well, however, particularly serial correlation problems. If lagged FDI is correlated with current FDI in the sample, estimates need not be consistent. Thus, we assume that each industry i has its

---

13. The different types of FDI that it separately identifies are acquisitions and mergers, new plants, joint ventures, plant expansions, reinvested earnings, equity increases, and other.

14. With acquisitions, this means the four-digit SIC classification of the target firm.

15. Correlation coefficients between the two series were 0.79 for machinery, 0.73 for chemicals and their allied products, 0.66 for primary and fabricated metals, and 0.70 for other manufacturing.

16. Kogut and Chang (1991) use the same database and use a negative binomial specification as well.

— Dollar value of investment outlays in   – – – Counts of FDI occurrences (ITA)
hundreds of thousands (BEA)

Fig. 3.1   Measures of Japanese manufacturing FDI activity in the United States, 1979–89
Source: Bureau of Economic Analysis (BEA) data are taken from various issues of the *Survey of Current Business,* and the International Trade Administration (ITA) data are from the appendix of the annual *Foreign Direct Investment in the United States.*

own unobservable propensity to engage in FDI, θ_i, which is independently and identically distributed across industries. Conditional on θ_i, FDI for a given industry in one period is independent of its FDI in other periods.[17] Following Hausman, Hall, and Griliches (1984), assume that the ratio $\theta_i/(1 + \theta_i)$ is distributed as a beta random variable with shape parameters (a, b). Using this beta density, the joint probability of an industry's acquisitions over the panel of years

(5) $pr(Y_{i1}, \ldots, Y_{iT} \mid X_{i1}, \ldots, X_{iT})$

$$= \frac{\Gamma(a + b)\Gamma(a + \Sigma\gamma_{it})\Gamma(b + \Sigma\ Y_{it})}{\Gamma(a)\Gamma(b)\Gamma(a + b + \Sigma\ \gamma_{it} + \Sigma Y_{it})}\left[\Pi_t \frac{\Gamma(\gamma_{it} + Y_{it})}{\Gamma(\gamma_{it})\Gamma(Y_{it} + 1)}\right],$$

where $\gamma_{it} = \exp(Q_{it}\pi)$, and Q_{it} and π are the combined regressor matrix and associated coefficients, $[X_{it}, \hat{Z}_{i,t-1}]$ and $[\beta|\delta]$ in equation (4). Maximum likelihood techniques estimate a and b in addition to our coefficient vector, $[\beta|\delta]$.

17. This assumption is similar to that used by Staiger and Wolak (1994).

Significant changes in the AD law came into place in 1980. In addition, tariff schedules and the SIC system underwent substantial changes in the late 1980s, creating consistency problems with a number of important variables across this time period. As a result, we limit our sample to the years 1981–88. Missing observations in some explanatory variables leave a sample of 299 four-digit manufacturing industries over eight years.[18] The history of AD and EC investigations against Japanese products during 1980–87 is listed in table 3.1, of which the affirmative decisions are used as an indicator of the threat of protection.[19] A data appendix discusses sources for the other variables used in the analysis.

3.3 Results

Our analysis begins with testing equation (2) and the hypothesis that lagged FDI affects the threat of protection. The predicted probabilities are then used in estimating equation (4) and testing the hypothesis that FDI is affected by previous-period threat of protection. After initial estimates, we test the effect of different forms of possible new protection (hypothesis 3) and different forms of FDI (hypothesis 4) on the estimated relations. As discussed above, testing of equation (2) provides evidence of whether FDI is successful in defusing the threat of protection, while equation (4) tests whether and to what extent the threat of protection motivates firms to engage in FDI.

Column 1 of table 3.2 presents initial maximum likelihood probit estimates of the probability of an AD or EC filing in industry i in year $t - 1$. Overall, the equation shows a good fit, as the likelihood ratio test easily rejects the null hypothesis that the coefficients of the equation are jointly zero. In addition, most of the explanatory variables have their expected sign. In particular, Japanese import growth and penetration variables are all positively related to a higher probability of protectionism in an industry. Previous-period investigations of other countries' imports in the industry are highly significant as well, suggesting that, once the U.S. industry has incurred the fixed costs of familiarizing itself with U.S. protection laws, it is more likely to file future petitions for relief and obtain protection. However, contrary to hypothesis 2, there is no significant relation between lagged FDI and the threat of protection in these initial estimates.

To test whether the type of protection matters in finding a quid pro quo relation in equation (2), we separately estimate the threat of EC protection and AD protection in columns 2 and 3 of table 3.2. As expected, the results are more encouraging. In particular, with respect to the threat of EC protection,

18. Import data for some of the four-digit industries were missing, and, in a few cases, import levels jumped from zero to positive levels and back again, making import growth figures noncalculable. In addition, shipment data were missing for a couple of industries.
19. Data used for these cases are from 1980–87, not 1981–88, because the threat of protection equation is lagged one period.

Table 3.1 **AD, CVD, and EC Investigations Affecting Japanese Products, 1980–87**

Investigation Type	Year	Product	SIC	Decision
AD	1980	Pipes and Tubes of Iron and Steel	3312	Negative
AD	1980	Menthol	2865	Negative
EC	1980	Motor Vehicles	3711	Negative[a]
AD	1981	Steel Wire Nails	3315	Terminated
AD	1981	Amplifiers	3662	Affirmative
AD	1981	Stainless Steel Clad Plate	3312	Affirmative
EC	1981	Fishing Rods and Parts	3949	Negative
AD	1982	Seamless Steel Pipes	3312	Affirmative
AD	1982	High Capacity Pagers	3662	Affirmative
AD	1982	Portland Cement	3241	Negative
EC	1982	Tubeless Tire Valves	3714	Negative
EC	1982	Heavyweight Motorcycles	3751	Affirmative
EC	1982	Stainless Steel & Alloy Tool Steel	3312	Affirmative
AD	1983	Polyester Fabric	2221	Terminated
			2241	Terminated
AD	1983	Tapered Roller Bearings	3562	Negative
AD	1983	Cyanuric Acid	2865	Affirmative
AD	1983	Spindle Belting	2399	Negative
AD	1983	Steel Valves	3492	Negative
AD	1983	Titanium Sponge	3339	Affirmative
EC	1983	Stainless Steel Table Flatware	3914	Negative
AD	1984	Cellsite Transceivers	3662	Affirmative
AD	1984	Eyeglass Lenses	3851	Withdrawn
AD	1984	Calcium Hypochlorite	2819	Affirmative
AD	1984	Stainless Steel Wire Cloth	3496	Terminated
AD	1984	Neoprene Laminate	2822	Affirmative
AD	1984	Cellular Mobile Phones	3661	Affirmative
EC	1984	Nonrubber Footwear	3143	Negative
			3144	Negative
			3149	Negative
EC	1984	Carbon & Specialty Steel Products	3312	Affirmative
			3315	Affirmative
			3317	Affirmative
EC	1984	Unwrought Copper	3331	Affirmative
EC	1984	Certain Canned Tuna	2091	Negative
EC	1984	Potassium Permanganate	2819	Negative
EC	1984	Nonrubber Footwear	3143	Affirmative
			3144	Affirmative
			3149	Affirmative
AD	1985	Offshore Platform Jackets	3441	Affirmative
AD	1985	Nylon Impression Fabric	2221	Terminated
			2241	Terminated
AD	1985	64K DRAMs	3674	Affirmative
AD	1985	EPROMs	3674	Affirmative
AD	1985	256K DRAMs	3674	Suspended
EC	1985	Electric Shavers	3634	Negative

Table 3.1   (continued)

Investigation Type	Year	Product	SIC	Decision
EC	1985	Certain Metal Castings	3321	Negative
			3322	Negative
			3492	Negative
			3494	Negative
			3499	Negative
			3523	Negative
			3524	Negative
			3531	Negative
			3585	Negative
			3714	Negative
			3732	Negative
EC	1985	Apple Juice	2037	Negative
AD	1986	Butt-weld Pipe Fittings	3494	Terminated
			3498	Terminated
AD	1986	Butt-weld Pipe Fittings	3494	Affirmative
			3498	Affirmative
AD	1986	Clear Glass Mirrors	3211	Negative
AD	1986	Tapered Roller Bearings	3562	Affirmative
AD	1986	Malleable Pipe Fittings	3494	Affirmative
			3498	Affirmative
AD	1986	Forged Steel Crankshafts	3566	Negative
AD	1986	Silica Filament Fabric	2221	Affirmative
AD	1986	Portland Cement	3241	Negative
AD	1986	Color Picture Tubes	3671	Affirmative
EC	1986	Wood Shingles and Shakes	2499	Affirmative
EC	1986	Steel Fork Arms	3537	Negative
AD	1987	Copier Toner	2865	Negative
AD	1987	Butt-weld Pipe Fittings	3494	Affirmative
			3498	Affirmative
AD	1987	Forklift Trucks	3537	Affirmative
AD	1987	Brass Sheet and Strip	3351	Affirmative
AD	1987	Bimetallic Cylinders	3559	Negative
AD	1987	Nitrile Rubber	2822	Affirmative
AD	1987	Granular PTFE Resin	2821	Affirmative

Source: U.S. International Trade Commission (USITC) annual reports and concordances maintained at the USITC.

[a]Despite the negative decision by the U.S. International Trade Commission, the president imposed protection on this product, and thus this observation is treated as an affirmative decision in the statistical analysis.

FDI lagged one period and FDI lagged two periods have the expected negative sign, although they are statistically insignificant at the 90 percent confidence level. In contrast, lagged FDI is positively correlated with the threat of AD protection, and FDI lagged one period is statistically significant at the 90 percent confidence level. This suggests either that quid pro quo FDI was unsuccessful in defusing an AD protectionist threat or that there is anticipatory tariff

Table 3.2   **Probit Estimates for Predicting Affirmative Decisions on Japanese Products across Four-Digit SIC Manufacturing Industries, 1980–87**

	Threat of Protection	Threat of EC Protection	Threat of AD Protection
Constant	−3.170***	−4.899***	−2.969***
	(.339)	(.787)	(.373)
Lagged real Japanese import growth	.005**	.004*	−.012
	(.002)	(.003)	(.072)
Lagged real domestic shipments growth	−.578	−.636	−.287
	(.679)	(1.067)	(.797)
Share of Japanese imports to total Japanese imports	3.485*	10.912**	1.159
	(1.782)	(5.015)	(2.462)
Share of Japanese imports to total all imports	.798*	−.469	1.201**
	(.429)	(.842)	(.496)
Union presence	.006	.017*	.004
	(.006)	(.010)	(.006)
Industry wage to value added ratio	.178	3.370**	−1.105
	(.938)	(1.690)	(1.114)
Past investigations of other countries' imports	.911***	.529	1.137***
	(.200)	(.400)	(.212)
U.S. real GNP growth	.091**	.126*	.670
	(.038)	(.066)	(.435)
FDI lagged 1	.110	−.961	.133*
	(.078)	(.639)	(.080)
FDI lagged 2	.008	−1.722	.036
	(.103)	(1.497)	(.104)
FDI lagged 3	.049	.643**	.057
	(.106)	(.278)	(.107)
Log likelihood	−129.48	−42.69	−97.44
Restricted log likelihood	−156.79	−64.75	−120.35
Likelihood ratio test	54.62	44.12	45.82
Observations (N)	2,392	2,392	2,392

***Asymptotic *t*-test significant at the 99 percent confidence level.
** Asymptotic *t*-test significant at the 95 percent confidence level.
* Asymptotic *t*-test significant at the 90 percent confidence level.

jumping in the face of an AD protectionist threat. This accords with hypothesis 3, that political appeasement is difficult with "technical track" AD investigations. Differences in the other regressors also show that the threat of EC protection is influenced by political factors more than the threat of AD protection is. In particular, the degree of union presence and the industry wage to value added, both signs of labor's political strength in an industry, are significantly correlated with the threat of EC protection but not with the threat of AD protection.

Table 3.3 explores how different forms of lagged FDI may affect the threat of EC protection.[20] Specifically, column 1 specifies lagged Japanese nonacquisition FDI, whereas column 2 lags Japanese acquisition FDI. Hypothesis 4 suggests that previous nonacquisition FDI should be more likely to defuse the threat of EC protection than acquisition FDI, and the results show some support for this. The coefficients on nonacquisition FDI lagged one and two periods are larger, and the one-period lag is significant at the 95 percent confidence level, suggesting stronger support for successful quid pro quo FDI with nonacquisition FDI than with all forms of FDI in general. In further support of hypothesis 4, the coefficients on lagged acquisition FDI are statistically insignificant with respect to the threat of EC protection. The one inexplicable result is the strong positive correlation between nonacquisition FDI three periods before and the threat of EC protection.

Before discussing estimation results for equation (4), it should be noted that a variety of specifications were tried for the dependent variable in equation (2). As noted earlier, our dependent variable takes the value of one when an investigation occurred that led to an affirmative ruling (i.e., led to protection). Specifying the binary variable as taking on the value of one when any investigation occurred (both those that ended in an affirmative ruling and those that did not) leads to similar, but slightly weaker, results. This is logical in the sense that foreign firms may have information that negative cases are less likely to lead to protection, and thus economic behavior will change less than in a case that will lead to an affirmative decision. We also tried specifying three options (no investigation, investigation/negative decision, and investigation/affirmative decision) with multinomial logit and ordered logit and probit specifications. These specifications led to similar, but slightly weaker, results. In addition, the various predicted probabilities generated by these models performed quite similarly to regressors in testing of equation (4).

We next turn to estimation of equation (4), using predicted probabilities from equation (2) as estimated in column 1 of table 3.2. Column 1 of table 3.4 presents initial estimates of the Japanese FDI equation using a random effects negative binomial model. The equation shows excellent fit, as the likelihood ratio test easily rejects the null hypothesis that the slopes are equal to zero at a 99 percent confidence level. In addition, most of the traditional explanatory variables are of expected sign and consistent with other empirical studies of FDI. In particular, the effect of movements in the exchange rate and the theory of internalization (as proxied by R&D expenditures) show strong support.

With respect to this paper's main focus, the predicted probability of protection is positively correlated with greater FDI activity in an industry at the 99 percent confidence level. Actual protection in place has the expected positive sign but is statistically insignificant. At first glance, this seems surprising.

---

20. For the sake of brevity, we do not show how different forms of lagged FDI affect AD protection. However, results show that lagged acquisition FDI has a particularly strong positive correlation with the threat of AD protection, whereas this is less the case with nonacquisition FDI.

Table 3.3   **Probit Estimates for Predicting EC Affirmative Decisions on Japanese Products across Four-Digit SIC Manufacturing Industries, 1980–87**

	EC Threat of Protection	EC Threat of Protection
Constant	−5.014***	−4.452***
	(.808)	(.659)
Lagged real Japanese import growth	.004*	.004*
	(.003)	(.002)
Lagged real domestic shipments growth	−.630	−.628
	(1.082)	(1.001)
Share of Japanese imports to total Japanese imports	11.402**	5.346***
	(4.977)	(1.984)
Share of Japanese imports to total all imports	−.588	−.185
	(.862)	(.735)
Union presence	.018*	.015*
	(.010)	(.009)
Industry wage to value added ratio	3.440**	2.747*
	(1.691)	(1.560)
Past investigations of other countries' imports	.517	.559
	(.398)	(.368)
U.S. real GNP growth	.139**	.097*
	(.068)	(.059)
Nonacquisition FDI lagged 1	−1.123**	
	(.567)	
Nonacquisition FDI lagged 2	−2.000	
	(1.568)	
Nonacquisition FDI lagged 3	.816***	
	(.307)	
Acquisition FDI lagged 1		−2.448
		(48.01)
Acquisition FDI lagged 2		−2.601
		(59.12)
Acquisition FDI lagged 3		−2.437
		(65.08)
Log likelihood	−42.24	−47.11
Restricted log likelihood	−64.75	−64.75
Likelihood ratio test	45.02	35.29
Observations (N)	2,392	2,392

***Asymptotic t-test significant at the 99 percent confidence level.
** Asymptotic t-test significant at the 95 percent confidence level.
* Asymptotic t-test significant at the 90 percent confidence level.

However, the majority of tariff jumping may occur in only the first few years of new protection. If the effect of protection on FDI behavior diminishes substantially over time, the presence of protection may not be significant in a data set with a time-series dimension, as used here. A second reason for insignificance may stem once again from pooling different forms of FDI. Firms may

Table 3.4 **Random Effects Negative Binomial Estimates of Japanese FDI across Four-Digit SIC Manufacturing Industries, 1981–88**

	All FDI	Acquisition FDI	Nonacquisition FDI
Constant	2.395***	2.459*	1.783***
	(.480)	(1.435)	(.536)
Exchange rate	−.014***	−.014***	−.014***
	(.001)	(.002)	(.001)
R&D expenditures	.282***	.255***	.301***
	(.063)	(.056)	(.063)
Keiretsu linkages	.004	.008	.003
	(.004)	(.005)	(.004)
Japanese real GNP growth	−.017	.013	−.027
	(.045)	(.075)	(.050)
Actual protection	.274	.380	.425**
	(.186)	(.390)	(.212)
Probability of protection	5.384***		
	(.711)		
Probability of EC protection		.189	5.541***
		(4.064)	(1.742)
Probability of AD protection		7.584*	5.182**
		(4.251)	(2.147)
a	6.288***	27.14	5.560***
	(1.500)	(35.99)	(1.427)
b	.666***	.631*	.682***
	(.092)	(.164)	(.106)
Log likelihood	−1,287.28	−551.91	−1,066.61
Restricted log likelihood[a]	−1,617.43	−659.82	−1,412.66
Likelihood ratio test	660.30	215.82	692.10
Observations (*N*)	2,392	2,392	2,392

[a]The coefficients are restricted to slopes equal to zero, intercept equal to the mean of the dependent variable, and *a* and *b* equal to one.

***Asymptotic *t*-test significant at the 99 percent confidence level.
** Asymptotic *t*-test significant at the 95 percent confidence level.
* Asymptotic *t*-test significant at the 90 percent confidence level.

engage in certain types of FDI in response to actual protection, just as we have hypothesized differences in FDI with respect to the threat of protection. Blonigen (1995) found little relation between protection and acquisition FDI and suggests that, if protection tends to occur in industries where foreign firms have a competitive or technological advantage, they may be less inclined to acquire a firm in the host country than to set up their own operations. This suggests that foreign firms will use nonacquisition FDI to tariff jump, not acquisition FDI.

Columns 2 and 3 of table 3.4 test the effect of different forms of FDI and different forms of protectionist threat on equation (4) results. The dependent variable is split into acquisition FDI and nonacquisition FDI, and the threat of protection variable is split into the threat of AD protection and the threat of EC protection. The results are generally consistent with the predictions of hypotheses 3 and 4.

In column 3, there is a significant direct correlation between nonacquisition FDI and the threat of AD and EC protection. Acquisition FDI does not show a similar strong relation with the threat of protection, particularly the threat of EC protection. This supports the notion that foreign firms do not use acquisition FDI to respond to protection that can be politically influenced. Interestingly, both forms of FDI respond strongly to the probability of AD protection. However, nonacqusition FDI responds in a stronger fashion to EC protection than AD protection, which is what hypothesis 3 predicts. Interestingly, the two sets of estimates show differential effects of actual protection on different forms of FDI. In support of Blonigen (1995), the two sets of estimates show that actual protection has a statistically strong direct relation with nonacquisition FDI but not with acquisition FDI. In essence, there is little support that acquisition FDI is influenced by protection or the threat of protection.

3.4   Conclusion

This paper has confirmed that the threat of protection has a substantial effect on nonacquisition Japanese FDI in the United States in the 1980s. In addition, there is evidence that threat-responding FDI by the Japanese had political intentions of defusing the threat of protection as suggested by quid pro quo theory. This is seen in the type of FDI used to respond to protectionist threat and the type of protectionist threat that elicited a greater FDI response by the Japanese. The success of FDI in defusing the threat of protection is apparently determined by the type of FDI used and the type of protection targeted: nonacquisition FDI defuses EC protection.

But what is the relative effect of actual protection and the threat of protection on nonacquisition FDI? In this nonlinear context, coefficient estimates are difficult to interpret. In addition, the protection variable is a dummy variable taking on the values of only zero or one. One way to generate an estimate of these variables' effect is to simulate the effect of changes in the variables on the expected value of the dependent variable. In the case of the dummy variable, compare the mean at the two different values it may take. Fixing the other regressors at their means, and using our estimated coefficients from column 3 of table 3.4, in-place protection means a 53 percent increase in the expected number of FDI occurrences in an industry for a given year. A similar simulation shows that, if the threat of an EC affirmative decision rises from 5 to 10 percent, the expected number of FDI occurrences rises by approximately 32 percent. An identical simulation with respect to the threat of AD protection increases expected FDI by approximately 30 percent. These simulations are sensitive to the value of the other regressors and starting points for the variable in question but give some indication that the threat of protection rivals the effect of actual protection on FDI flows.

Data Appendix

Probability of Protection: Equation (2)

1. *Lagged real Japanese import growth.* Data on Japanese imports at the four-digit SIC level were obtained from a database maintained at the U.S. International Trade Commission (USITC) and based on official statistics of the U.S. Customs Service and concordances between Tariff Schedules of the United States Annotated (TSUSA) product codes and SIC categories. These figures were deflated using industry-specific price indexes taken from statistical tables in the *Economic Report of the President* (1994) to get real levels. Finally, last-period growth rate over the previous period was calculated.

2. *Lagged domestic industry real shipments growth.* Data on U.S. domestic shipments by four-digit SIC were taken from various issues of the *Census of Manufactures*. These figures were deflated using industry-specific price indexes taken from statistical tables in the *Economic Report of the President* (1994) to get real levels. Finally, last-period growth rate over the previous period was calculated.

3. *Share of Japanese industry's imports to total Japanese imports to the United States.* Data on both Japanese imports and total annual Japanese imports to the United States at the four-digit SIC level were obtained from a database maintained at the USITC, as indicated above. Then, for each industry i, this variable is defined as the ratio of Japanese imports in industry i in year t to total Japanese imports to the United States in year t.

4. *Share of Japanese industry's imports to industry imports from all countries.* Data on both Japanese imports and total imports by industry to the United States at the four-digit SIC level were obtained from a database maintained at the USITC, as indicated above. Then, for each industry i, this variable is defined as the ratio of Japanese imports in industry i in year t to all imports to the United States in industry i in year t.

5. *Union presence.* This variable is taken from Freeman and Medoff (1979). Estimates were for three-digit SIC level and thus repeated at the four-digit level for this study. The variable is defined as percentage of union membership of all workers in column 3 of Freeman and Medoff's table 2, beginning on page 155.

6. *Industry wage to value added ratio.* This variable is taken from various issues of the *Census of Manufactures*.

7. *Investigations in industry of other countries in previous two years.* This variable is taken from various issues of *The Year in Trade* and *Annual Report of*

the USITC. The variable is defined as one if an AD or a CVD petition has been filed on other countries' products in industry *i* in the previous two years.

8. *U.S. real GNP growth.* This variable is taken from statistical tables in the *Economic Report of the President* (1994).

9. *Lagged FDI.* The same source is used for this variable as is used for the dependent variable in equation (4) discussed in text.

Foreign Direct Investment: Equation (4)

1. *R&D expenditures.* This variable is defined as company and other (except federal) R&D funds as a percentage of net sales in R&D-performing manufacturing companies, by industry, taken from National Science Foundation (1993, 18). The majority of these figures were reported at the two-digit SIC level and then applied to our four-digit-SIC-level data. Some of the more important industries, including chemical (SIC 28), primary metals (SIC 33), industrial machinery (SIC 35), electrical machinery (SIC 36), transportation (SIC 37), and instruments (SIC 38), were detailed at the three-digit SIC level by the National Science Foundation figures.

2. *Yen-dollar exchange rate.* This variable is taken from statistical tables in the *Economic Report of the President* (1994).

3. *Japanese real GNP growth.* This variable is taken from the *Japan Statistical Yearbook.*

4. Keiretsu *linkages.* This variable is calculated in similar manner to that used by Lawrence (1993). *Industrial Groupings in Japan, 1988/89* (1988) lists major firms, their revenues, and their *keiretsu* linkages by industry. The *keiretsu* linkage variable was constructed by calculating the percentage of revenues in each industry that could be attributed to a firm with *keiretsu* affiliation.

5. *Actual protection.* This variable is taken from various issues of *The Year in Trade* and *Annual Report of the USITC.* The variable is defined as one if AD duties or VERs are in place for industry *i* in year *t* and zero otherwise.

References

Annual report of the USITC. Various issues. Washington, D.C.: U.S. International Trade Commission.

Azrak, Paul, and Kevin Wynne. 1995. Protectionism and Japanese direct investment in the United States. *Journal of Policy Modeling* 17, no. 3: 293–305.

Baldwin, Robert E., and Jeffrey W. Steagall. 1994. An analysis of ITC decisions in antidumping, countervailing duty and safeguard cases. *Weltwirtschaftliches Archive* 130, no. 2: 290–308.

Bayard, Thomas O., and Kimberly Ann Elliott. 1994. *Reciprocity and retaliation in U.S. trade policy.* Washington, D.C.: Institute for International Economics.

Bhagwati, Jagdish N. 1987. VERs, quid pro quo FDI and VIEs: Political-economy-theoretic analysis. *International Economic Journal* 1: 1–14.

Bhagwati, Jagdish N., Richard A. Brecher, Elias Dinopoulos, and T. N. Srinivasan. 1987. Quid pro quo foreign investment and welfare: A political-economy-theoretic model. *Journal of Development Economics* 27:127–38.

Bhagwati, Jagdish N., Elias Dinopoulos, and Kar-Yui Wong. 1992. Quid pro quo foreign investment. *American Economic Review* 82, no. 2:186–190.

Blonigen, Bruce A. 1995. Explaining Japanese foreign direct investment in the United States. Ph.D. diss., University of California, Davis.

Census of Manufactures. Various issues. Washington, D.C.: U.S. Government Printing Office.

Coughlin, Cletus C., Joseph V. Terza, and Noor Aini Khalifah. 1989. The determinants of escape clause petitions. *Review of Economics and Statistics* 71, no. 2:341–47.

Dinopoulos, Elias. 1989. Quid pro quo foreign investment. *Economics and Politics* 1:145–60.

———. 1992. Quid pro quo foreign investment and VERs: A Nash bargaining approach. *Economics and politics* 4:43–60.

Dinopoulos, Elias, and Kar-Yiu Wong. 1991. Quid pro quo foreign investment and policy intervention. In *International trade and global development: Essays in honor of Jagdish Bhagwati,* ed. K. A. Koekkoek and C. B. M. Mennes. London: Routledge.

Economic Report of the President. 1994. Washington, D.C.: U.S. Government Printing Office, February.

Finger, J. M., H. Keith Hall, and Douglas R. Nelson. 1982. The political economy of administered protection. *American Economic Review* 72, no.3:452–66.

Foreign direct investment in the United States. Various years. Washington, D.C.: U.S. Department of Commerce, International Trade Administration.

Freeman, Richard B., and James L. Medoff. 1979. New estimates of private sector unionism in the United States. *Industrial and Labor Relations Review* 32, no. 2:143–74.

Froot, Kenneth A., and Jeremy C. Stein. 1991. Exchange rates and foreign direct investment: An imperfect capital markets approach. *Quarterly Journal of Economics* 106, no. 4:1191–1217.

Goldberger, Arthur S. 1972. Maximum-likelihood estimation of regressions containing unobservable independent variables. *International Economic Review* 13, no. 1:1–15.

Grossman, Gene, and Elhanan Helpman. 1994. Foreign investment with endogenous protection. Working Paper no. 4876. Cambridge, Mass.: National Bureau of Economic Research.

Grubaugh, Stephen G. 1987. Determinants of direct foreign investment. *Review of Economics and Statistics* 69, no. 1:149–52.

Hansen, Wendy L., and Thomas J. Prusa. In press. Cumulation and ITC decision-making: The sum of the parts is greater than the whole. *Economic Inquiry.*

Hausman, Jerry, Bronwyn H. Hall, and Zvi Griliches. 1984. Econometric models for count data with an application to the patents-R&D relationship. *Econometrica* 52, no. 4:909–38.

Herander, M. G., and J. B. Schwartz. 1984. An empirical test of the impact of the threat of U.S. trade policy: The case of antidumping duties. *Southern Economic Journal* 51, no. 1:59–79.

Industrial groups in Japan, 1988/89. 1988. Tokyo: Dodwell Marketing Consultants.

Japan statistical yearbook. Various years. Tokyo: Japan Statistical Association.

Kogut, Bruce, and Sea Jin Chang. 1991. Technological capabilities and Japanese foreign direct investment. *Review of Economics and Statistics* 73, no. 3:401–13.

Lawrence, Robert Z. 1991. Efficient or exclusionist? The import behavior of Japanese corporate groups. *Brookings Papers on Economic Activity,* no. 1:311–41.

———. 1993. Japan's low levels of inward investment: The role of inhibitions on acquisitions. In *Foreign direct investment,* ed. Kenneth Froot. Chicago: University of Chicago Press.

Maddala, G. S. 1983. *Limited-dependent and qualitative variables in econometrics.* Cambridge: Cambridge University Press.

Martin, Stephen. 1991. Direct foreign investment in the United States. *Journal of Economic Behavior and Organization* 16:283–93.

Moore, Michael. 1992. Rules or politics? An empirical analysis of ITC antidumping decisions. *Economic Inquiry* 30:449–66.

National Science Foundation. 1993. *Selected data on research and development in industry: 1991.* Arlington, Va.

Pagan, Adrian. 1984. Econometric issues in the analysis of regressors with generated regressors. *International Economic Review* 25, no. 1:221–47.

Ray, Edward John. 1989. The determinants of foreign direct investment in the United States, 1979–85. In *trade policies for international competitiveness,* ed. Robert C. Feenstra. Chicago: University of Chicago Press.

Salvatore, Dominick. 1987. Import penetration, exchange rates, and protectionism in the United States. *Journal of Policy Modeling* 9, no. 1:125–41.

Staiger, Robert, and Frank Wolak. 1994. Measuring industry specific protection: Antidumping in the United States. Working Paper no. 4696. Cambridge, Mass.: National Bureau of Economic Research.

Survey of Current Business. Various issues. Washington, D.C.: Bureau of Economic Analysis, U.S. Department of Commerce.

Swenson, Deborah L. 1994. Impact of U.S. tax reform on foreign direct investment in the United States. *Journal of Public Economics* 54, no. 2:243–66.

Takacs, Wendy E. 1981. Pressures for protectionism: An empirical analysis. *Economics Inquiry* 19:687–93.

Wong, Kar-yui. 1989. Optimal threat of trade restriction and quid pro quo foreign investment. *Economics and Politics* 1:277–300.

The year in trade. Various issues. Washington, D.C.: U.S. International Trade Commission.

4   Foreign Direct Investment and *Keiretsu:* Rethinking U.S. and Japanese Policy

David E. Weinstein

For twenty-five years, the U.S. and Japanese governments have seen the rise of corporate groups in Japan, *keiretsu,* as due in part to foreign pressure to liberalize the Japanese market. In fact, virtually all works that discuss barriers in a historical context argue that Japanese corporations acted to insulate themselves from foreign takeovers by privately placing shares with each other (See, e.g., Encarnation 1992, 76; Mason 1992; and Lawrence 1993). The story has proved to be a major boon for the opponents of a neoclassical approach to trade and investment policy. Proponents of the notion of "Japanese-style capitalism" in the Japanese government can argue that they did their part for liberalization and cannot be held responsible for private-sector outcomes. Meanwhile, proponents of results-oriented policies (ROPs) can point to yet another example of how the removal of one barrier led to the formation of a second barrier.

While agreeing with the basic conjecture that high levels of corporate ownership may work to deter takeovers in Japan, the argument presented here suggests that it is not cultural or institutional factors that produce corporate groups and high levels of stable shareholding but rather conventional government pol-

David E. Weinstein is research associate professor in the School of Business Administration at the University of Michigan and associate professor of economics at Harvard University.

The author is grateful to the Ministry of Finance for allowing him to be a visiting scholar at the Institute for Fiscal and Monetary Studies during the summer of 1995 when this draft was prepared. While too many people helped him there to thank each of them individually, he especially thanks Satoshi Ohuchi for arranging interviews. In addition to the Ministry of Finance, the author thanks the Nomura Fund and the Japan Securities Research Promotion Foundation for financial support. Special thanks also go to Theresa Carney, Dennis Encarnation, Takuo Imagawa, Robert Lawrence, Ed Lincoln, Mark Mason, Paul Sheard, and Akihisa Tamaki for greatly improving the author's understanding of this topic. Jeff Bernstein, Takatoshi Ito, Hugh Patrick, Mark Ramseyer, and Klaus Wallner made extensive and invaluable comments on an earlier draft of this paper that were enormously helpful in preparing the final draft. Finally, the author thanks Robert Feenstra for suggesting that he look at the "1 percent" number in the first place.

icy. The focus on "conventional" policies is important. One does not need to rely on government encouragement and other nonbinding mechanisms of Japanese industrial policy in order to understand the rise of Japanese corporate groups. The incentives to form these groups can, to a large degree, be traced to tax, regulatory, and other policies that are conventional in the sense that their effects can readily be understood within a standard neoclassical economic paradigm.

The failure to recognize the role played by conventional policies in the formation of Japanese corporate groups has led to tremendous frustration on both sides of U.S.-Japan negotiations. The United States claims that, despite Japanese concessions, very little has changed. The Japanese, for their part, have grown tired of continual U.S. complaints over sector after sector. To some extent, this is the result of a failure on both sides to face the facts. On the Japanese side, this involves recognizing that they have created a financial system through tremendous government interventions based on dubious economic rationales. But the problem is not only a Japanese one. As this paper will try to demonstrate, the U.S. position has been influenced by poor data and insufficient attention to the underlying government incentives to form distinctive Japanese corporate structures. This has led to a belief that standard principles of economics do not apply in the case of Japan and that U.S. policy is continually hindered by hidden informal regulations.

Considering the willingness of policy makers to believe that trillions of yen worth of securities changed hands because of government *encouragement* or a fear of *potential* foreign takeovers, it is not surprising that many in the United States have decided that process-oriented policies are not tenable and have favored ROPs. Unfortunately for the proponents of these policies, it is not just academic economists who think that ROPs are bad economics; most Japanese do too. The current political climate in Japan strongly favors deregulation. The implementation of ROPs, however, requires greater government intervention, which is likely to further entrench bureaucrats and generate future problems. As the most recent automobile parts negotiations revealed, the unpopularity of ROPs makes them very difficult to implement in practice.

All this suggests that we reexamine the evidence in favor of ROPs and the notion that conventional policies are not important. The remainder of the paper therefore focuses on two issues. First, a reexamination of the data suggests that levels of foreign direct investment (FDI) into Japan are not nearly as out of line with international levels as is widely believed. This conclusion is based on the fact that much of the data underlying the analysis of FDI into Japan is highly problematic. Second, after finding that even after adjusting for various factors the level of FDI in Japan is still low, the paper explores government interventions that may continue to inhibit foreign takeovers through the promotion of stable shareholding.

4.1 Data Issues

One of the biggest problems in studying the level of FDI in Japan is that most of the Japanese data are highly flawed and that the U.S. data give only a very imperfect picture of the structure of foreign firms in Japan. Consider the case of one of the most widely cited pieces of evidence showing that Japan has inordinately low levels of FDI. In 1988, Julius and Thomsen presented international evidence on the level of FDI in various countries that showed, among other things, that, while foreign firms in Japan accounted for only 1 percent of Japanese sales, foreign firms' sales in the United States accounted for 10 percent of all sales in 1986. The number was so striking that it soon became widely cited in academic articles (see, e.g., Graham and Krugman 1989, 25; Graham and Krugman 1993, 16; Lawrence 1993, 85; and Krugman and Obstfeld 1994, 162). With many prominent economists citing this number, it was only a matter of time before it was influencing policy makers. Indeed, the first Clinton/Tyson *Economic Report of the President* (1994, 216) justified the U.S.-Japan Framework Talks coverage of direct investment issues by citing the 1 percent figure.

The source of the 1 percent figure is a publication by the Japanese Ministry of International Trade and Industry (MITI) entitled *Gaishikei kigyo no doko* (Foreign-owned-firm trends). Usually, MITI data are of the highest quality, but unfortunately, this is a rare exception. The problem is that only about half of all firms surveyed actually responded. This 50 percent response rate probably overstates the coverage because the survey covers only affiliates that have more than 33 percent foreign ownership: far higher than the 10 percent number reported in the U.S. *Survey of Current Business.* Companies like Mazda are not counted as foreign affiliates in the Japanese data, although they would be counted in the U.S. data. Since foreign direct investments are often quite lumpy in the sense that a single acquisition can move the aggregate numbers substantially, omissions like Mazda, which is one-quarter owned by Ford, can create a very different picture of the level of foreign presence in a market. For example, owing to the Mazda omission, even if the MITI response rate for other firms in transportation equipment had been 100 percent, they would have reported only around one-third of the sales of companies that are more than 10 percent foreign owned.

Furthermore, the response rate varies year to year and sector by sector, making it difficult to interpret longitudinal and cross-sectional comparisons of the importance of foreign firms in Japan. The differences in reporting rates are likely to be quite large across sectors. While MITI does not report response rates by sectors, a similar survey conducted by Toyo Keizai found that response rates differed by as much as 100 percent across sectors, with nonmanufacturing reporting significantly less than manufacturing. All this suggests that great caution should be used in inferring much about the distribution of FDI from the MITI numbers.

Many studies have focused on the inflows or levels of foreign capital stocks in Japan as an alternative to the MITI survey results. Unfortunately, it is not just the MITI numbers that vastly understate the level of FDI in Japan: the numbers published by the Bank of Japan (BOJ) and the Ministry of Finance (MOF) are also inaccurate measures of FDI flows and stocks relative to the FDI numbers published for the United States in the *Survey of Current Business*.[1] It is worth first noting, however, that one factor in the MOF numbers tends to make them appear larger than the BOJ numbers. The MOF statistics are based on foreign firm notifications about future investments, not actual investments. This means that the numbers will overstate actual investments somewhat because firms that notify the MOF that they will invest but then cancel their plans will not be counted. Hence, in 1992, the MOF reported that inward FDI was $4.1 billion, but the Bank of Japan numbers used in the balance-of-payments statistics reported only $2.7 billion of investments. The MOF numbers are not necessarily larger than the BOJ numbers on a year-to-year basis, however. If a firm notifies in one year but conducts all or part of the investment in the subsequent year, then the MOF will record the investment in the year of notification, but the BOJ will record the investment when it actually occurred.

The rest of the biases in the MOF and BOJ numbers make estimating the capital stock of foreign firms almost impossible. First, the MOF numbers do not count investments of less than ¥30 million, and the BOJ leaves out investments of less than ¥5 million. On the basis of the size breakdown of foreign firms in Japan given by *Gaishikei kigyo soran* (General survey of foreign-owned firms), a source I will examine later, this means that approximately one-third of all firms are left out of the MOF numbers and that 10 percent are left out of the BOJ figures. A bigger problem stems from the fact that FDI arising from retained earnings, the opening and expanding of branches, and the purchase of land do not appear in the MOF statistics.[2] Since the vast majority of the increase in the FDI stock by U.S. accounting methods occurs because existing foreign firms expand operations, the difference in accountng in the Japanese numbers serves to lower the Japanese numbers by a factor of three or four relative to the U.S. numbers. In addition, loans were not counted until 1985, and acquisition of unlisted stocks is not included, which further pushes down the numbers.

On top of these distortions, the MOF reports of aggregate FDI stocks are calculated by summing up nominal *dollar* investments over time. In other words, if a foreign firm made a $1 million investment in Japan when the exchange rate was ¥360/$1.00, then that investment would still count as $1 million today in the aggregate stock numbers despite the fact that exchange rate movements alone should have increased it by a factor of four. In fact, simply adjusting the reported MOF numbers by a price index, the exchange rate, and the assumption that foreign firms' capital stock grew at the same rate as the

---

1. The analysis of this BOJ and MOF data is drawn from Matsuoka and Rose (1994).
2. Land does appear in the BOJ numbers.

domestic Japanese capital stock would increase the reported level of Japan's FDI stock from $26 billion in 1992 to over $100 billion. Indeed, this number probably significantly understates the level of assets under the control of foreign corporations because it does not include assets purchased by borrowing or by funds supplied by Japanese partners. Given these considerations and the others mentioned, the stock of FDI in Japan could be as much as ten to twelve times higher than the reported levels. This is not to say that it is likely that the numbers are that high, only that the data are so bad that it is not unreasonable to think that the official numbers are off by an order of magnitude.

Given these data problems, various authors have tried to use U.S. numbers as an indicator of the level of FDI in Japan. The numbers from the Bureau of Economic Analysis are clearly superior to the Japanese numbers, but the problem with using U.S. numbers as a proxy for total FDI is that the level of FDI in Japan is very imperfectly correlated with the level of U.S. FDI in Japan. U.S. firms account for 46.5 percent of all foreign firms operating in Japan, but the distribution of U.S. firms differs significantly from the distribution of non-U.S. affiliates. Relative to other foregn affiliates, U.S. firms are more heavily concentrated in manufacturing than in services, but there is enormous variation across sectors. For example, U.S. firms are underrepresented in banking and in petrochemicals, where only 14 and 6 percent of all foreign affiliates are from the United States. On the other hand, they are vastly overrepresented in sectors like precision instruments and information services, where over 75 percent of all foreign affiliates are U.S. firms. This makes it extremely difficult to draw inferences about the overall level of FDI in a sector from the U.S. distribution.

All this raises the question of whether it would be possible to obtain a more accurate estimate of the stock of FDI in Japan. As the previous analysis has suggested, the government data are so poor that all one can conclude is that the actual level of sales by foreign affiliates or FDI is probably somewhere between four and twelve times larger than the reported levels. Fortunately, there are two private sources of FDI data in Japan that are significantly better than the government sources: one published by Nihon Keizai Chosakai and the other by Toyo Keizai (*Gaishikei kigyo soran*). The coverage is similar, and I will focus on the latter.

In 1992, Toyo Keizai conducted a survey of 3,402 foreign companies in Japan (about 30 percent more than the MITI source) and had a response rate of 83 percent. The data contain a fairly large number of missing observations, especially for smaller companies, so I built a sample containing foreign firms in Japan that employed more than ninety-nine employees. This yielded 533 firms, but even in this sample there were 157 firms that did not report sales numbers for 1992.[3] Using only the firms for whch we had data, the total sales of foreign affiliates stood at ¥40.3 trillion, or 5.3 percent of all gross output in

---

3. Most firms in Japan do not have fiscal years that correspond to calendar years, so, in general, the fiscal year that most overlapped with the calendar year was chosen.

Japan: over five times higher than previously published numbers![4] To obtain an estimate of the sales of the 105 firms for whch we had employment but not sales data, I regressed log sales on log employment and used the estimated coefficients to estimate the sales for the firms that only had employment data.[5] Adding in these firms raised the total of foreign sales to ¥43.0 trillion, or 5.6 percent of all sales. If we assume that the 1,243 firms employing ninety-nine or fewer workers have sales linearly distributed between zero and the sales of the smallest firm in my sample, then this implies that foreign firms sell 5.7 percent of all sales in Japan. These numbers still underestimate the true level of sales because of the 82 percent response rate to the questionnaire. For example, some large firms like Nippon ABS or Suzuka Fuji Xerox, with close to twelve hundred workers apiece, were left out of the sample. Adding these firms in would raise the number still further.

It is worth remembering that, even if foreign firms' share of the Japanese market stands at 6 percent, it is still lower than that in most other OECD countries by a factor of two or three. Furthermore, because of historic restrictions on majority-owned affiliates, the stock of majority-owned foreign firms is even more out of line with international averages. However, given that the stock of FDI is highly correlated with new inflows, which, in turn, are largely a measure of the expansion of existing firms, it is not surprising that recent Japanese liberalizations have not brought stocks in line with international averages. Furthermore, considering Japan's high corporate tax rate and the high cost of land, labor, utilities, and other nontradables, it is easy to come up with a large list of other reasons why multinationals often choose other countries in which to locate foreign affiliates.

Probably the most controversial reason why foreigners do not invest in Japan has to do with the difficulty of conducting takeovers in Japan. Mergers and acquisitions constitute one of the major mechanisms through which U.S. firms enter foreign markets, and the difficulty of conducting takeovers in Japan has often been argued to be an important factor in understanding why foreign penetration of Japan still remains lower than in most OECD countries. More specifically, it is often argued that the large amounts of shares held by Japanese corporate groups act as a major impediment to FDI. Indeed, there have been an enormous number of anecdotes that have piled up over the years suggesting that the large number of shares held by Japanese corporate groups, or *keiretsu,* work to make takeovers exceedingly difficult in Japan. One approach to testing this hypothesis is to use econometric evidence that controls for various factors and to see whether sectors with high *keiretsu* shares have lower levels of FDI. Unfortunately, given the crudeness of the data and the complexity of the theories, the results are often very difficult to interpret. Furthermore, this approach leaves open the question of why these shareholding patterns have emerged in

---

4. Figures do not include construction because no firms reported numbers to Toyo Keizai.
5. Manufacturing and nonmanufacturing firms were treated separately throughout.

particular sectors. Economists have made great contributions to the Japanese industrial organization literature arguing that many of these seemingly irrational arrangements may in fact be efficient, but these discussions are somewhat unsatisfying because the theories have difficulty explaining why there is so much variation in corporate ownership of securities over time.

The remainder of this paper will ignore most of what has been written on *keiretsu* in order to highlight the role played by conventional government interventions. Two caveats are in order. First, the government regulations presented here are by no means the only ones present or relevant: to catalog all such regulations would result in a book (or books) instead of a paper.[6] Instead, I have tried to highlight the policies that I feel are most important to the debate. My focus on the market for corporate control stems from the fact that corporate takeovers are a major mechanism by which U.S. firms conduct FDI. Second, I ignore most of the economic and sociological contributions to the understanding of Japanese corporate groups not because I think that they are unimportant but rather because I want to focus on the regulatory issues.[7]

4.2   The Ownership Puzzle

During the late 1960s and early 1970s, Japan substantially liberalized its controls on FDI. At roughly the same time, there was a substantial rise in corporate ownership. It is therefore not surprising that these two phenomena were linked by both Japanese and foreign researchers. Just as with the 1 percent number, a consensus was achieved that the rise of cross-shareholding in Japan was a product of FDI. Consider the following passage from Viner (1988, 88), which is representative of a much wider literature:

> In 1971, an amendment to the Securities Exchange Law introduced a system of notification for takeover bids and, in 1972, Bendix Corporation made a tender offer for part of the equity in a small firm (Jidosha Kiki). These events prompted Japanese corporations to consider measures that would prevent foreign firms from initiating hostile takeovers of domestic companies. Thus, it was decided that mutual shareholding, if established on a more widespread basis, could render foreign takeovers virtually impossible in many cases. With this in mind, hundreds of corporations (with unofficial Ministry of Finance encouragement) that were not members of a *keiretsu* systematically expanded their mutual shareholdings. Companies within *keiretsu* increased their mutual shareholding to the legal limit. As a direct result . . .

6. For example, Ito (1992) is one of many books in Japanese on deregulation. The chapter on financial market deregulation focuses on the regulation of interest rates, bank deposits, consumer credit, banking hours, and electronic transfer fees. These are all likely to have very important effects on consumers, but I do not discuss them here because their effect on corporate ownership is less clear.

7. Readers interested in learning more about sociological and economic approaches should see Gerlach (1992) and Aoki and Patrick (1994).

the percentage of shares held by corporations rose 12.7% [in just one year, 1971–72].

In terms of the history of thought on Japanese *keiretsu,* this quote is fascinating because virtually every verifiable fact mentioned is wrong! First, MOF data reveal that the percentage of shares held by corporations rose 9.7 percent, not 12.7 percent: an overestimate of 31 percent.[8] Second, the statement "companies within *keiretsu* increased their mutual shareholding to the legal limit" is correct only in the sense that more than one company was at the legal limit in 1972. In a sample of presidents' club members constructed using 1972 data from *Kigyo keiretsu soran,* city banks could have hit their legal limit of 10 percent ownership 124 times. This actually occurred in only three cases. Although it is difficult to test the same hypothesis for nonfinancials, considering that most of them held less than 1 percent of the shares of the other companies in the group, it is highly unlikely that the legal cross-shareholding limit was binding for many of them either.[9]

What about the role of government? It is true that Japan passed its first takeover law in 1971, but, as Ramseyer (1987) has argued, takeovers were not illegal before the law—there just were no rules governing them. The 1971 law simply created rules governing takeovers. Indeed, one of the reasons for the passage of the law was to make takeovers, especially by foreigners, more difficult (Adams and Hoshii 1972, 190). In this sense, Viner's argument is the equivalent of arguing that monopolies could not have existed in the United States until the Sherman Antitrust Act. Furthermore, neither the legal change nor the Bendix bid could possibly have driven most of the cross-shareholding because they occurred too late. Figure 4.1 shows the evolution of equity ownership in Japan. It is clear that much of the increase in financial and nonfinancial corporate ownership occurred in the period between 1965 and 1971, long before either the legal change or the takeover bid.[10] In fact, ownership by financials, the companies at the core of financial groups, seems to follow a generally smooth upward trend between 1968 and 1988. Finally, the statement that the MOF "encouraged" cross-shareholding suggests that major realignments in the structure of Japanese capital markets can be achieved through unconventional means. However, as we will soon see, the main problem with focusing on MOF encouragement is that it obfuscates the fact that a very real intervention occurred.

One explanation for the rise in cross-shareholding in the late 1960s, often suggested by other authors, is that the fear of foreign takeovers arising from

8. Tokyo Stock Exchange (TSE) data indicate that the increase was even smaller: only 7.6 percent. For an explanation of the two data sources, see n. 11 below.

9. The important legal factor limiting ownership for nonfinancials is that a subsidiary cannot own shares in a parent.

10. Total corporate shareholding is relatively flat over the earlier period because of the disappearance of investment trusts and securities companies as large holders. The reasons for their demise will be discussed later.

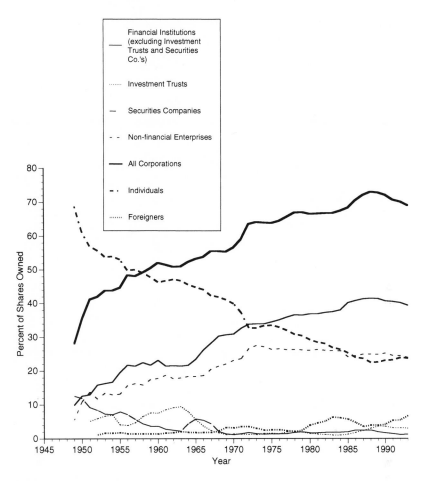

Fig. 4.1   Movements in Japanese equity ownership
Source: Takahashi (1994).
Note: See n. 11.

future liberalization generated the increase. As Mason (1992) documents, Japanese government and industry leaders placed the blame for the increase in shareholding squarely on fears of foreign entry following market liberalization. Unfortunately, for those trying to understand the phenomena, the hypothesis is difficult to test because it is predicated on the fear of an event that never happened. But, here again, the numbers raise serious questions. First, in 1966, corporations already owned over half of all outstanding shares, which raises the question of why it was that Japanese firms felt vulnerable to takeovers when corporations owned 55 percent of their shares but safe at 66 percent. Certainly, it is possible that the increase in shareholding was due to the increase in holdings by companies who had less than fifty percent of their shares in the hands of stable shareholders. However, this raises another puzzle concerning why it was that, before the threat of liberalization, corporate ownership was so high. Second, it is hard to see how something as trivially small as FDI could drive enormous shifts in ownership. For most of this time period, and even after liberalization, the level of FDI was so low that, had the entire inflow gone toward the purchase of equity, foreign ownership of Japanese securities would have increased by only a few tenths of a percentage point. As one can see from table 4.1, foreign ownership of Japanese securities increased by only 0.9 percentage points over this time period.[11] It seems unlikely that, in response to this modest increase in foreign ownership, Japanese corporations bought up 11 percent of the market. Indeed, this enormous response is even more puzzling considering that corporate ownership today is only 5 percentage points higher than it was in 1975 even though the share of foreign ownership has doubled.[12]

It is not just the data that make it difficult to believe that the rise in corporate shareholding in Japan was in response to foreign takeovers. In order to believe that Japanese firms were good takeover targets, one must either believe that Japanese managers were inferior to foreign managers or that Japanese firms were undervalued. However, considering the fact that between 1965 and 1975 the return on the Tokyo Stock Exchange (TSE) index was around 100 percentage points higher than the return on the S&P 500 *before* factoring in currency adjustments, it is hard to argue that Japanese firms were systematically badly managed from a shareholder standpoint. Similarly, it also seems doubtful that the only people who could have appreciated the fact that Japanese stocks were undervalued were foreigners.

All this suggests that we dig a little deeper into the data. The following sections explore the policies that explain why the largest corporate holders of equity in Japan—insurance companies, banks, and nonfinancial enterprises—decided to invest so heavily in securities.

4.3   Insurance Companies

It turns out that the reason for the rise of the Japanese insurance industry is easy to locate: the Japanese tax code. The major tax advantage offered to life insurance companies is that they have had a monopoly in tax-free individual investment plans. Premiums paid into life insurance policies or for pension plans administered by life insurance companies are tax deductible up to

---

11. The data in fig. 4.1 above are not directly comparable with that in table 4.1 because the TSE (the source for fig. 4.1) does not include shares listed on the over-the-counter market while the MOF numbers do until 1966. Prior to the creation of the second section of the TSE in 1961, this creates some big differences in the numbers, especially for nonfinancial holding. This is why there is a (spurious) slight upward trend in nonfinancial holdings in fig. 4.1 prior to 1961 that does not appear in the numbers shown in table 4.1. Figure 4.1 was based on TSE numbers because the TSE series start earlier and, after 1985, are more comprehensive than the MOF numbers.

12. In fact, foreign portfolio investment in Japan exceeds that in the United States.

Table 4.1   **Percentage Ownership of Equity by Investor**

	1955	1960	1965	1966a[a]	1966b[a]	1970	1975	1980	1985	1990	1993
Government	.6	.5	.3	.3	.2	.2	.2	.2	.2	.6	.6
Corporate	44.3	51.5	53.2	53.7	53.9	56.6	63.7	66.5	68.5	72.1	69.0
Financial institutions	27.7	30.2	32.0	32.5	35.3	33.5	37.4	40.5	42.9	46.9	45.1
City & trust banks					11.8	14.0	16.4	17.7	19.7	21.6	21.7
Insurance companies					12.6	15.1	16.1	17.4	17.4	17.3	16.5
Life insurance					9.3	11.1	11.4	12.5	12.7	13.2	12.7
Property and casualty insurance					3.3	4.0	4.7	4.9	4.7	4.1	3.8
Other financials					1.8	1.8	1.9	2.2	2.3	2.7	2.6
Investment trusts	3.3	6.3	5.0	3.3	3.7	1.4	1.6	1.5	1.4	3.6	3.0
Securities companies	7.2	3.5	5.3	5.0	5.4	1.2	1.4	1.7	2.1	1.7	1.3
Other corporations	16.7	21.3	21.3	21.2	18.6	23.1	26.3	26.0	25.6	25.2	23.9
Individuals	53.4	46.7	44.9	43.8	44.3	40.1	33.5	29.3	25.4	23.1	23.7
Foreigners	1.7	1.3	2.1	2.2	1.6	3.1	2.5	4.0	6.0	4.2	6.7

Source: Zaisei kinyu tokei geppo.

[a]In 1966, the MOF changed its method of measuring ownership. This makes the numbers in this table not directly comparable with those in fig. 4.1 (for details, see n. 11). The numbers prior to 1966 are comparable with 1966a and those afterward are comparable with 1966b.

¥25,000, 50 percent deductible for the next ¥25,000, 25 percent deductible for the next ¥50,000, and then fully taxable afterward. Thus, a typical taxpayer has a strong tax incentive to purchase life insurance or pension policies up to ¥100,000 per year to a life insurance pension fund. Similarly, there is an additional tax incentive that provides a tax deduction of ¥15,000 on contributions of ¥20,000 for property and casualty insurance (*An Outline of Japanese Taxes* 1994, 53). These numbers, however, underestimate the historical importance of the tax incentives. Inflation has largely eroded the value of this subsidy over the years. For example, in 1961, a taxpayer who contributed ¥60,000 to an insurance-type pension plan could deduct half his total payments from his taxable income. Considering that 83 percent of taxpayers in that year had incomes of less than ¥500,000, these subsidies made insurance an obvious channel for investment funds (*An Outline of Japanese Taxes* 1961, 205).

Given the absence of IRAs and most other forms of tax-free investments in Japan, the Japanese tax code made insurance plans the preferred individual investment vehicle for many Japanese, and the renowned savers of Japan poured money into them.[13] In 1993, approximately one-quarter of all Japanese financial wealth was tied up in insurance policies. Indeed the value of life insurance contracts in 1990 was 4.75 times larger than national income. Relative to the rest of the world, this is an enormous number. For example, in the same year, the next highest country was Korea, at 2.7 times national income, with

---

13. The big exception was tax-free postal savings accounts, or *maruyu,* which were abolished in the late 1980s. I will turn to the role of postal savings later in the paper.

most of the West far further behind (*Zaisei kinyu tokei geppo* 1994).[14] The reason for the high levels of insurance is that virtually all Japanese policies contain maturity benefits. In fact, death benefits constituted less than a third of all life insurance payments in 1993. In contrast, maturity payments and lump-sum annuities accounted for 62 percent of all payments, with payments for hospitalizations and operations accounting for most of the remainder.

Japanese households have therefore chosen to save primarily through two types of investment vehicles. Either they have invested through insurance companies, or they put their money in bank or postal accounts. While this may help explain why Japanese buy so much insurance, it does not explain why Japanese insurance companies buy so much equity. For example, stockholding constituted 11.5 percent of U.S. insurance firms' assets, in comparison with 20.3 percent in Japan. U.S. firms invest very heavily in public and private bonds, but these constituted only about 10 percent of Japanese holdings. Much of the remainder of insurance companies' assets is composed of loans and foreign securities. This makes Japanese insurers look quite similar to banks. In fact, the terms on endowment policies (i.e., policies with a maturity value) offered by insurers and bank time deposits are quite close in Japan. This contrasts sharply with the West, where the return on deposits is generally substantially higher (Bronte 1982, 102).

In order to understand equity holding by insurance companies, we need to examine the pattern of ownership at the firm level. Table 4.2 is a matrix showing the pattern of ownership among presidents' club members of the Mitsui group in 1993. The presidents of all these firms attend regular meetings that do not involve the planning of collective strategy so much as the sharing of information. The elements in the table indicate the percentage of shares of the row company owned by the column company. One of the striking features of this table is that, for fifteen of the twenty-five stock companies, total group ownership stands at less than 20 percent, and in no case is more than 40 percent of the equity of a company held by the entire group. With typically around 80 percent of group member equity held by nongroup holders, it is hard to argue that financial *keiretsu* have "unassailable control over all outstanding equity" (Encarnation 1992, 75).[15] The issue seems to be not why *keiretsu* hold so many shares but rather why it is that banks, insurance companies, and firms, *in general,* tend to buy and hold on to so much equity.

A second interesting feature of this table is that, despite the common tendency to call Mitsui a "bank-centered group," the largest single shareholder is not a bank but a life insurance company. The Mitsui group is not alone in this respect. In four of the six largest groups, the largest single shareholder is an insurance company. Not only are insurance companies very large holders of

14. For reference, the numbers for other countries were as follows: the United States, 2.15; Canada, 2.4; France, 2.2; the United Kingdom, 1.3; and West Germany, 1.0.

15. Encarnation is actually referring to the Mitsubishi *keiretsu,* whose ownership structure was quite similar to Mitsui's.

Table 4.2 Percentage of Shares Held by Members of the Mitsui Group in 1993

Owned\Owners	1	2	3	4	5	6	7	8	9	10	11	12	13	14	15	16	17	18	19	20	21	22	23	24	25	26	Sum.
1 Sakura Bank, Ltd.	x	1.66	3.49	1.06	.88	?	.11	?	.93	.13	.21	.14	.45	.92	.33	?	.06	.20	.29	.24	.20	?	1.48	.49	.25	2.56	16.1
2 M. Trust	2.51	x	4.24	1.73	1.34	?	.20	?	2.91	.08	.73	.22	1.24	1.55	.97	?	.17	.40	.64	.49	.23	?	1.27	.54	.62	1.79	23.9
3 M. Life Ins.	x	x	x	x	x	x	x	x	x	x	x	x	x	x	x	x	x	x	x	x	x	x	x	x	x	x	x
4 M. Mar & Fire	4.82	4.33	5.11	x	3.55	?	.20	?	1.52	.13	.49	.36	1.35	.87	.20	?	.07	.58	.26	.64	.09	?	.42	1.32		2.12	28.4
5 M. & Co.	4.93	3.91	4.69	2.71	x	?	.11	?	.12	.91	.06	.09	.15	.79	.11	?	.12	.21	.10			?	.42	.28	.22	.38	20.3
6 M. Mining	4.97	6.37	9.29	2.08	5.53	x	2.96	?	2.03	.33		.31	.11	.75		?	1.97		.49	2.91		?					37.0
7 M. Construction	4.66	5.13	6.78	1.17	2.10	?	x	?	15.7		.18					?				.19	.24	?					39.3
8 Mitsukoshi, Ltd.	4.59	3.89	4.27	.81	.22	?	x	x	.21					x		?				x		?					14.0
9 M. Fudosan	4.64	5.42	2.86	1.72	.34	?	.97	?	x	.17	.07	.24		.19		?	.02			.02	.13	?	.25	.16			17.2
10 M. O.S.K. Lines	3.71	4.22	4.11	2.98	.69	?		?	.51	x						?						?		3.78	1.05		21.2
11 M.-Soko	4.99	7.14	8.85	5.87		?	.90	?	.87		x		.43			?			.45			?					29.9
12 Sanki Engineering	4.16	3.37	9.46	1.70		?	.35	?			.22	x				?					.14	?		1.18			20.6
13 Nippon Flour Mill	4.99	6.61	6.25	5.21	2.65	?	.36	?	.17	.05	.36		x			?		.03				?		.15			26.4
14 Toray Industries	4.49	4.61	4.89	1.43	.56	?	.14	?	.02		.05		.02	x		?				.07		?		.15	.17		16.5
15 New Oji Paper	3.49	3.08	3.48		.23	?		?							x	?						?		.20	.17		10.7
16 Nippon Paper Inds.	2.69	2.78	4.05	1.85		?		?	.15							x						?					10.8
17 M. Toatsu Chem.	4.99	4.50	3.75	2.30	1.78	?	.33	?		.05	.16				1.04	?	x	.05	.14			?		.09			18.1
18 Denki Kagaku Kog.	3.11	3.23	6.82	2.67	1.45	?		?								?	x	x				?					17.3
19 M. Pet. Industries	4.99	5.19	4.32	2.21	4.14	?	.17	?		.19	.19			11.5		?	2.62		x			?		3.26			38.6
20 Onoda Cement	4.99	5.75	4.87	2.15	.86	?	.12	?	.28						.44	?			x	x		?		.21			19.7
21 Japan Steel Works	4.86	4.65	6.50	1.85		?	.50	?	1.02			.08				?					x	?					19.5
22 M. Min & Smelting	2.48	4.42	4.09	.87	.50	?	.26	?	.45	.09						?	.14	.00		.00	.04	x					13.2
23 Toshiba	3.73	2.27	2.90	1.32	.41	?	.01	?	.06					.04	.04	?	.02			.04	.04	?	x	.03	.58		11.5
24 M. Eng. & Ship.	2.44	3.14	3.99	2.07	2.36	?		?	.41	1.87		.30		.29	.26	?				.12	.14	?		x		.61	18.0
25 Ishikawajima-HHI	1.54	2.26	1.56		.72	?		?	.07							?						?	4.26		x		10.4
26 Toyota Motor	4.95	2.39	2.23	2.45	.25	?	.06	?	.04			.06				?					.05	?	.15	.06		x	12.7
Average	3.44	3.06	3.72	1.61	.81	?	.14	?	.56	.17	.1	.07	.17	.44	.16	?	.08	.07	.09	.1	.05	?	.54	.4	.2	.53	

Source: Kigyo keiretsu soran (1995).

Note: M. = Mitsui. A "?" indicates that shareholding data were not available in *Kigyo keiretsu soran.* Underlined numbers indicate a cross-shareholding. *x*'s indicate that shareholding is not legally permitted because the firms cannot hold shares in themselves or because the firm is not a stock company. Entries in the double boxed area highlight nonfinancial cross-shareholding, and those in the single-lined area are manufacturing cross-shareholders.

equity within Japanese financial groups, but their holdings are also relatively stable. In 1980, for example, Mitsui Life and Mitsui Fire and Marine (formerly, Taisho Fire and Marine) held 3.85 and 1.99 percent of the presidents' club member stocks, in comparison to 3.72 percent and 1.61 percent today. This pattern of "stable shareholding" can be seen in aggregate data as well. Although insurance companies held 17 percent of all equity in Japan, these firms accounted for only 1 percent of all sales and purchases (Takahashi 1994). By contrast, foreigners, with less than half the level of equity ownership, executed thirteen times more sales and purchases. The shareholding patterns of Japanese insurers is closely connected to the patterns of purchases of insurance in Japan. Table 4.3 presents the results of a 1993 American Chamber of Commerce survey of presidents' club members. The data clearly show that the vast majority of property and casualty insurance for each of the presidents' club members was purchased from the insurance company that had the largest shareholding in the company. Unfortunately, similar data are not available for the life insurance sector, but discussions with both Japanese and U.S. members of the industry suggest that it is likely that a similar picture would emerge were the data available.

McKenzie (1992) and others have argued that one of the primary functions of this stable shareholding is to make it more difficult for another company to take over the insurance purchaser. In other words, Japanese insurance companies do not simply sell insurance; they also sell their willingness to remove a certain percentage of shares from active trading. The reason why they offer both products stems from their inability to compete effectively in the insurance market. Property and casualty insurance, in Japan, is not sold through brokers but rather through case agents who typically handle only one or two insurance companies' products. These case agents are often owned by the companies that purchase the insurance. This means that, if management decides to use a particular insurance company, they can influence the case agent to carry only that insurer's policies. For automobile insurance, these agency commissions typically account for 17.9 percent of the total premium cost even for policies sold to repeat customers.[16] In the United States, 60 percent of automobile insurance is sold through nonagency channels like direct marketing or telemarketing, which largely eliminates these middlemen. This largely accounts for the fact that the expense ratio (the share of the insurance premium that does not cover the actuarial risk cost) is 14 percentage points higher in Japan than in the United States.

However, it is doubtful that it is simply the absence of sufficiently diligent antitrust enforcement that makes this system tenable. Stable shareholding is costly for insurance companies, and, in a free market, there would be an incentive for these insurers to offer cheaper insurance to companies that did not

---

16. The description of the automobile insurance market is drawn from my interview with Theresa Carney at Cygna Insurance.

Table 4.3   **Mitsui Group Insurance Business (1991)**

Core Company	Case Agents	Insurance Companies	Estimated Share of Insurance	% of Insurance Company Shareholding in Core Company
Sakura Bank	Yowa	Mitsui M&F	25	1.1
		Nippon F&M	75	
		Others		
	Horai	Mitsui M&F	Unknown	
		Other 18 companies		
	Keihanshin Hoken Daiko	Dowa F&M (main)	Over 50	
		Mitsui M&F	Unknown	
		Others		
Mitsui Trust Banking	Sanshin Shinko	Mitsui M&F	90	1.7
		Others	10	
Mitsui Life Ins.	Onyu	Mitsui M&F	100	
Mitsui Co.	Mitsui Co. (Ins. Div.)	Nonmarine:		2.7
		Mitsui M&F	80	
		Other	20	
		Marine:		
		Mitsui M&F	100	
Mitsui Mining Co.	Sanko Shoji	Mitsui M&F	100	2.1
Mitsui Construction Co.	Sanken Shoji	Mitsui M&F	100	1.2
Sanki Engineering Co.	Sanshin Sangyo	Mitsui M&F	100	1.7
Nippon Flour Mills Co.	Suehiro Kogyo	Mitsui M&F	100	5.2
Toray Industries, Inc.	Toray Agency	Mitsui M&F	Nearly 100	1.4
		Tokio M&F		
		Sumitomo M&F		
Oji Paper Co.	Oji Fudosan	Mitsui M&F	Unknown	
		Others		
	Kyoei Shokai (general agt)	Mitsui M&F	45	
		Other 21 companies	55	
Mitsui Toatsu Chemicals	Santo Sangyo	Mitsui M&F	100	2.3
Mitsui Petrochemical Inds., Ltd.	Sun Business	Mitsui M&F	Top share	2.2
		Others		
Onoda Cement Co.	Onoda Fudosan	Mitsui M&F	90	2.2
		Others	10	
	Azuma Kogyo	Mitsui M&F	90	
		Others	10	
The Japan Steel Works, Ltd.	Fuji Shokai (general agt)	Mitsui M&F	80	1.9
		Sumitomo F&M	20	
		Others		

(continued)

Table 4.3   (continued)

Core Company	Case Agents	Insurance Companies	Estimated Share of Insurance	% of Insurance Company Shareholding in Core Company
Mitsui Mining & Smelting Co.	Mitsui M&S staff service	Mitsui M&F	100	.9
Toshiba Corp.	Toshiba Ins. Service	Mitsui M&F	30	1.3
		Nippon F&M (main)	40	1.9
		Others	30	
Mitsui Engineering & Shipbuilding	Sanko Zitsugyo	Mitsui M&F	80	2.2
		Others	20	
Toyota Motor Corp.	Toyota Tsusho	Mitsui M&F	Top share	2.5
		Others		
Mitsukoshi, Ltd.	Sanbi	Mitsui M&F	50	.8
		Other 10 companies	50	
Mitsui Real Estate Development Co.	Mitsui R.E.D. Sales	Mitsui M&F	Top share	1.7
		Others		
Mitsui O.S.K. Lines, Ltd.	Shosenmitsui Kosan	Mitsui M&F	50	3.0
		Sumitomo M&F	50	3.1
Mitsui Warehouse Co.	Tokyo Sanshin Service	Mitsui M&F	95	5.9
		Others	5	
Average		Mitsui M&F	88.3	
		All related insurers	94.4	

Source: American Chamber of Commerce (1993).

Note: Dowa F&M once belonged to Taiyo-Kobe Bank Group, now merged into Sakura Bank, which holds 4.99 percent of the shares of Dowa F&M. Sakura's three case agents handle their premerged bank's business, Yowa for Taiyo Bank, Horai for Mitsui Bank, and Keihanshin Hoken Daiko for Kobe Bank.

require the insurer to take out big equity positions. Here, government regulation plays an important role. In the nonlife sector, this regulation has largely arisen from the government's exemption of the Premium Rating Agency (PRA) from the Antimonopoly Law. The PRA sets uniform rates for motor vehicle, compulsory motor liability, fire, earthquake, and accident insurance (Carroll 1994, 15). Ostensibly, this agency exists to make sure that price competition does not drive insurers into bankruptcy, but the net effect is to enforce high prices in the market.

Furthermore, the Ministry of Finance historically has not been very receptive to the development of new insurance products. Typically, the approval process for new insurance products requires that the developer make public virtually all the relevant data on the product. Since this means that companies that do not innovate can enter the market without paying for much of the research and development, the returns to innovation are largely eliminated. This helps explain why, in the automobile insurance sector, there are no differences in policy rates based on age or driving history.

In life insurance markets, the situation is somewhat different. Here, again, there have been efforts to set fees above market rates, but firms have been able to offer investors guaranteed investment contracts (GICS). These contracts offer investors a guaranteed minimum return on their insurance policies and are one of the major reasons why many Japanese insurers are currently in deep financial trouble following the recent decline in stock prices. Theoretically, these investment contracts should be the dimension along which competition should wipe out the rents and therefore the stable shareholding. McKenzie (1992) has argued that competition in insurance is stifled by extensive sharing of information as well as the tacit cooperation of the MOF in an insurance cartel. The problem with this argument is that many industries are characterized by extensive information sharing and are quite competitive. For example, one can easily find out the prices of all computers sold through catalog stores, but one would hardly consider that sector uncompetitive. Indeed, considering the homogeneity of life insurance, one should expect it to be very competitive. As for the ability of the MOF to enforce a cartel in insurance, while the MOF did restrict entry, it is hard to see how it could prevent life insurance firms that had agreed to keep returns low ex ante from obtaining high returns ex post. In general, cheating seems to have plagued other Japanese attempts to form cartels. For example, Weinstein (1995) examined cartels formed by the Ministry of International Trade and Industry and found that virtually all of them were failures. Why should insurance be any different?

Basic cartel theory tells us that, in order for a cartel to be sustainable, there must be a credible enforcement mechanism to ensure that those firms that violate cartel prices will not reap a gain. In all likelihood, none of the MOF's regulations are sufficiently rigid or enforceable to maintain a cartel in insurance. A more reasonable place to look for an enforcer is the Ministry of Posts and Telecommunications (MPT), which administers the vast postal insurance fund and postal savings system. In 1993, the value of funds in the postal insurance plan equaled just over ¥74 trillion: equal to roughly half the assets held by Japan's twenty-seven private-sector life insurance firms. This makes the Japanese post office the world's largest provider of life insurance, with the biggest Japanese company, Nippon Life, being less than half as large. In addition, when measured in deposits, the Japanese post office is also the world's largest bank. At the end of 1993, the value of deposits in the Japanese postal savings system stood at ¥184 trillion, which accounts for about a quarter of all deposits in Japan.

One is tempted to think of the postal savings, insurance, and pension plans as vestiges of Japan's past development strategy. The system was founded around one hundred years ago during a time when few banks existed and the government wanted to channel savings into productive purposes. However, far from dying a graceful death, the numbers demonstrate that funds under the administration of the Japanese post office have been growing at a tremendous rate. Most striking is postal pensions, which have increased from a forty-year low of ¥1.3 billion in 1980 to over ¥1 trillion today. Funds in the Japanese postal insurance fund have increased as well, more than doubling between 1987 and the end of 1993. Finally, the postal savings system has succeeded in increasing its deposits by ¥100 trillion over the last ten years (Ministry of Posts and Telecommunications 1994). No one can really justify the postal savings system on efficiency grounds, yet it continues to grow.

What is important to recognize about this system is that the rates set by the post office on its pension and insurance plans are not determined by the returns on the investments of government financial institutions. According to Japanese law, the rates set on postal accounts must reflect current market rates. In effect, the MPT (often in conjunction with the MOF) sets rates by surveying private-sector rates and then choosing a rate that maintains its "competitiveness" in the market. If private rates are high, then postal rates are high, and, if private rates are low, then postal rates will be low as well. The MPT is intent on maintaining a certain share of the market, and quite often the returns to postal accounts are higher than those in the private sector. This eliminates much of the gain that could be realized by private-sector firms in the market. They can compete again each other, but, if one firm's market share starts to encroach on that of the postal system, the postal rates will move to eliminate the firm's competitive advantage. By always setting a "competitive price," the post office can eliminate the gains from competition, thereby providing a credible enforcement mechanism to support collusion in Japanese financial markets.

Indeed, the Japanese debate on the privatization of the postal savings system demonstrates the fact that the postal savings system exerts an anticompetitive influence on banks. There have been a number of suggestions to break the postal savings system up and create around ten banks. Regional banks, in particular, have strongly opposed this on the grounds that these new banks would create fierce competition. But, of course, this fear is warranted only if current rates on deposits are below competitive levels.

By keeping rates on deposits low either through stifling competition or by direct regulation of deposit rates (which remained in force throughout much of the postwar period), the government increased incentives for funds to be invested through insurance companies. These regulations may have increased the incentives for stable shareholding by Japanese insurers. In other words, it may be government policies, not Japanese business practices, that are the problem.

4.4 Bank-Firm Links

It is not just insurance companies that face heavy government interference; Japanese banks must also compete with the government. The economics of a system in which banks are both large lenders and shareholders in firms while firms also hold large shares in banks has been analyzed extensively elsewhere (see, e.g., Sheard 1994; and Aoki and Patrick 1994); hence, it makes little sense to go through all the arguments about the costs and benefits of this type of corporate governance structure here. This section will therefore focus on some of the regulations and laws that help support this structure.

A striking feature of table 4.2 above is that, while there is very little cross-ownership of shares among manufacturing firms, these firms own substantial amounts of shares of the financial firms. Of eighty-eight possible cross-shareholds among manufacturers, cross-shareholding occurred only eight times, and most of these shareholds involved less than 1 percent of the firm's equity. Adding in nonfinancial, nonmanufacturing firms raises the ratio of actual cross-shareholds relative to total possible cross-shareholds to 16 percent: slightly higher but still quite low. In fact, it is quite clear from the table that virtually all cross-ownership of corporations takes the form of financial firms taking large positions in nonfinancials and these nonfinancials taking large positions in the financials. While a manufacturing firm was one of the top twenty shareholders of another manufacturer only 4 percent of the time, all manufacturers held shares in all the financials, and manufacturers were the top twenty shareholders of their group banks in 28 percent of the cases. These data suggest that cross-shareholding is largely a phenomenon among financials or between financials and nonfinancials. While nonfinancials often hold share in other nonfinancials, the amount of reciprocation is actually quite small.

Once again, the tax code plays an important role in these relationships. While the only form of tax-deductible investing open to Japanese households has traditionally been through insurance policies, a major source of investment funds arises from private corporate pension funds. Private pension funds are one of the largest single holders of shares in the United States, but they account for less than 10 percent of all shareholding in Japan. The primary reason for this difference is a 1962 amendment to the tax law that created tax advantages for the formation of pension plans (Adams and Hoshii 1972, 110). Under this amendment, firms were able to create tax-free pension plans, funded either by the employer or by the employees, if the money were invested either through insurance companies or through trust banks. This tax law is one of the principle reasons why trust banks were able to become not only major lenders to firms but also major shareholders.

However, regulation has exerted a fairly important restraint on the ability of these trust banks to compete. In order to obtain the tax benefits, trust banks and insurance companies that manage pension funds must invest in very specific types of assets that are determined by the MOF. Ostensibly, the objective of these restrictions is to prevent pension money from being invested in risky assets, but a subsidiary effect is to impose a fair degree of homogeneity on the portfolio composition and therefore the return. Investments must follow the 5-3-2 rule: 50 percent of the money must be invested in secured bonds or loans, 30 percent may be invested in stocks, and 20 percent in real estate or real estate trusts (Adams and Hoshii 1972, 110). These restrictions make it difficult for banks and insurance companies to offer differing returns, and, as we have seen before, the lack of competition in financial product markets often leads to stable shareholding. Indeed, in 1980, for example, the return on large pension funds managed by trust banks varied (after commissions) by less than 1 percentage point (Bronte 1982, 238).

The effect of these regulations was probably compounded by taxes on securities transactions, mandatory minimum fees for brokerage services, a bond underwriting cartel, restriction of international capital movements, and restrictions on the opening of bank branches. These regulations tended to favor debt as a source of outside financing and tended to reinforce relational banking in Japan.[17] Japan's prohibition of holding companies following the dissolution of the prewar *zaibatsu* probably also enhanced the position of banks within Japanese corporate groups. Thus, with both the capital and the absence of restrictions on corporate shareholding below a certain level, Japanese banks were in a relatively good position to monitor Japanese corporations. It is not surprising that, as monitors, certain Japanese banks took large equity positions in firms that they sought to monitor and tended to hold on to these positions.

However, it is also important to remember that the same argument explaining stable shareholding in insurance markets also works in lending markets. A tremendous amount of the money collected in the postal savings system is pumped back into the economy through loans from various government institutions. Government banks like the Japan Development Bank and the Export-Import Bank are well known, but these are only the tip of the iceberg. There are over a hundred semigovernment financial institutions operating in Japan (Bronte 1982, 149). In 1991, these public financial institutions accounted for 31 percent of all lending in Japan. (*Economic Statistics Annual* 1994, 250). Considering that these financial institutions set rates in order to maintain a certain share of the market, it is not inconceivable that these institutions diminish the incentives of banks to compete through lower interest rates. While this effect is probably most pronounced in small business lending and agriculture, industrial lending by public institutions is by no means limited to these sectors.

Explaining why it is that nonfinancials are such large holders in financials is more difficult. Sheard (1994) finds that, while nonfinancials own less than a quarter of all outstanding equity, about 58 percent of all the equity in his sample of twenty-one banks is held by nonfinancials. Nonfinancials have a particularly large equity stake in the firms that supply them with capital. Considering that banks make up about one-sixth of all the equity on Japanese exchanges, this implies that nonfinancial ownership of nonfinancial firm equity is probably around 17 percent, which is not very different from average total

---

17. The bond cartel and the restrictions on international capital flows disappeared by the early 1980s. The tax on securities transactions was reduced in 1989.

nonfinancial ownership in the United States. In other words, most of the relatively higher level of nonfinancial ownership of equity is due to the main bank system. Sheard argues that nonfinancials buy and hold on to bank shares in order to provide a collective enforcement mechanism that ensures that banks perform their role as monitors. This implies that the same regulations that created the main bank system may also have increased shareholding by nonfinancials as well.

It is also possible that interest rate regulation may play a role here as well. Interest rate regulations on bank loans created the "compensating-balance" system in Japan. In order to circumvent interest rate restrictions, banks required that firms that received loans deposit a sizable portion of that loan with the bank. These compensating balances raise the effective interest rates on loans. It is not inconceivable that, in order to get loans in a capital rationed market, some firms also agreed to become stable shareholders in the banks as well.

4.5   Vertical Groups

Just as Japanese financial groups have recently attracted a tremendous amount of attention, vertical groups, too, have often been the center of trade and investment friction. Ownership by these nonfinancials accounts for fully one-third of all corporate ownership in Japan. While the rise of this ownership is often blamed on foreign investment, the development of these groups is also quite closely linked to conventional policies. Vertical groups are composed of an assembler who is surrounded by a large number of smaller suppliers that are technically independent. There is a fairly large body of literature examining these relationships in terms of their efficiency and social origins. Once again, I will focus on the government regulations that have helped produce this system.

In order to understand the government regulations, we need to be clear about what we are explaining. The most common source used for analyzing these manufacturing groups is the Dodwell Marketing Consultant's *Industrial Groupings in Japan*. With only around forty groups listed, that source underestimates the importance of these groups in Japan. Table 4.4 is drawn from Toyo Keizai's *Nihon no kigyo guruupu*, which contains data on over one thousand manufacturing groups.[18] About half of all related firms in Japan typically appear to be located either in the same industry as the manufacturer or in distribution. As various authors have noted, these relationships are fairly stable. Three-quarters of the eighty-two hundred related firms for which we have detailed data were in the same manufacturing group ten years earlier.

Many researchers have questioned how it is that Japanese firms have been

---

18. It is ironic that Americans refer to these groups by the Japanese word *keiretsu* but that Japanese refer to these groups with the English word *group* (*guruupu* in Japanese pronunciation).

Table 4.4   Distribution of Subsidiaries and Related Companies by Industry

Company's Industry	No. of Parent Cos.	No. of Subs. & Rel. Cos.	% in Same Ind.	Food	Textiles	Glass, Cement, Etc.	Iron & Steel	Nonfer. Metals	Ferro-alloys	Gen. Mach.	Electric Mach.	Trans. Eq.	Other Manufac.	Nonmanu.	W-sale & Retail	Other Services
All industries	2,057	25,293	30.9	628	571	403	266	296	479	716	1,110	499	1,295	14,809	5,553	8,065
Manufacturing	1,157	13,778	31.5	458	375	327	193	274	379	628	1,043	457	1,017	6,143	3,203	2,559
Food	95	1,167	32.9	384	1	1	0	1	2	4	1	1	29	604	392	207
Textiles	71	1,012	33.8	22	342	6	1	1	6	23	20	4	60	392	208	171
Glass, cement, concrete, ceramics	49	488	41.8	2	0	204	1	2	14	11	8	0	32	174	83	70
Iron & steel	53	697	22.6	1	0	18	157	16	69	28	13	9	64	253	72	153
Nonferrous metals	41	699	28.8	3	0	8	6	201	38	11	31	5	75	217	94	86
Ferroalloys & other steel products	53	385	29.6	0	1	2	5	10	114	12	1	4	26	178	125	39
General machinery	152	1,312	25.5	1	1	2	2	7	38	334	27	35	86	685	358	287
Electric machinery	158	1,888	42.2	1	0	15	2	10	16	41	797	20	64	790	402	367
Transportation equipment	99	1,408	26.2	4	1	3	15	5	43	85	11	369	90	698	344	329
Other manufacturing	386	4,727	30.3	40	29	68	4	21	39	79	134	10	491	2,152	1,125	850
Nonmanufacturing	900	11,515	30.2	170	196	76	73	22	100	88	67	42	278	8,666	2,350	5,506
Wholesale & retail	275	4,091	35.7	122	192	28	67	15	85	44	33	10	147	2,843	1,843	949

Source: Nihon no kigyo guruupu (1995).

Table 4.5   **Capital Finance of Vertical Group Members in 1984**

	Number of Subsidiaries and Related Companies	Core Company's Ave. Lending Share (%)	Ave. % of Shares Held by Core Company	% Capitalized at under ¥100 Million[a]
Kanebo	132	31.37	87.46	53.19
Asahi Kasei	145	11.89	56.44	44.94
Nippon Steel	150	3.51	30.34	52.79
Nittetsu Steel Pipe	108	5.90	66.98	60.00
Sumitomo Metals	104	7.89	44.74	55.39
Kobe Steel	83	3.78	34.94	55.13
Hitachi	211	7.64	70.07	59.23
Toshiba	199	9.90	74.29	55.35
Mitsubishi Electric	179	2.57	30.08	58.33
Nippon Electric	143	7.88	59.78	57.56
Fujitsu	123	12.44	76.89	46.02
Matsushita Electric	455	15.70	78.67	37.72
Sony	87	21.70	92.77	21.67
Mitsubishi Heavy Industries	132	5.22	42.55	55.41
Nissan	21	24.54	74.57	61.48
Toyota	164	6.76	59.79	62.67
Honda	249	19.66	89.76	21.21
Average	158	11.67	62.95	50.48

Sources: Kigyo keiretsu soran (1984); *Nihon no kigyo guruupu* (1994).
[a]Data are for 1992.

able to form these very stable relationships in which buyers and suppliers continue to deal with each other for decades. The data suggest that assemblers very often ensure that their suppliers do not take advantage of long-term relationships the old-fashioned way: they own them. One of the striking features of these groups is the high degree of corporate ownership by the assemblers in the parts suppliers. Table 4.5 presents evidence on seventeen such groups of large assemblers. What is most striking in the table is the degree of ownership held by the lead group firms in the affiliated companies. It is important to remember that this table simply is expressing average ownership positions: there are cases where assemblers do not own a large share of their affiliates. For example, of the 127 first-tier Hitachi affiliates, there are three suppliers that have no shares owned by Hitachi.[19] These sorts of firms become more frequent when you add in the smaller firms that supply the affiliates and form the full Hitachi group, but often that is because they are owned by firms that are largely owned by Hitachi.

The high degree of ownership within these groups raises the question of why

19. First-tier suppliers are only those suppliers that have relationships with Hitachi directly. Table 4.5 also includes firms that are affiliated with Hitachi's suppliers.

Japanese firms do not simply vertically integrate. There are many efficiency arguments for why a firm might not want to do this, but let us ignore them in order to focus on the role of government policy. In table 4.5, we see that slightly over half of all firms in the selected vertical groups were capitalized at under ¥100 million in 1992. Because the selected groups contain some of the largest firms in Japan and large firms tend to have large suppliers, it is likely that, for the economy as a whole, an even greater share of vertical group members is composed of small firms. Table 4.6 presents evidence on the size breakdown of the members of manufacturing groups for a much broader sample of firms. Unfortunately, capitalization data are difficult to come by for this sample, but data on the number of employees are readily available.[20] These data suggest that, even if we exclude firms with no employees or those for which data are unavailable, three-quarters of the members of Japanese vertical groups have fewer than two hundred employees. This number is probably closer to 84 percent if one considers that the firms that do not report data are most likely small.

The size of these firms is relevant when one considers the vast array of policies in place in Japan to a assist small and medium-sized enterprises (SMEs). While the definition of what constitutes a SME varies somewhat by industry and by government program, according to the Corporate Tax Law, firms that are capitalized at less than ¥100 million and report earnings of less than ¥8 million are SMEs. In practice, this last requirement is generally not binding. For example, according to the Japanese tax agency, the average firm capitalized between ¥50 and ¥100 million had average earnings of ¥5.6 million in 1993, well within the upper bound. These firms typically report very low average earnings because they are allowed to file "blue returns." Filing a blue return enables them to carry losses forward for up to five years, carry them back one year, and take special depreciation allowances, and, most important, the ability of the government to audit their books is severely circumscribed.[21] In other words, it is probably not too outrageous to say that, in Japan, only very poorly managed small firms report profits![22]

It is important to remember, however, that firms that can legally be classified as small are not necessarily small by conventional standards. Because capitalization is a poor measure of firm size, especially for firms that grow through debt or retained earnings, often quite large suppliers can qualify as small

20. Actually, capitalization numbers are available, but data analysis would require the entry by hand of over twenty-five thousand capitalization numbers to obtain the sample statistics.

21. In principle, the books of a firm filing a blue return can be audited only if the authorities catch a calculation error (see Income Tax Act, sec. 155A and B, and Corporate Tax Law sec. 130). These and other advantages are discussed in *An Outline of Japanese Taxes* (1994, 127).

22. While 53.1 percent of all firms capitalized under ¥100 million reported a loss in 1992, only 30.5 percent of larger firms did. In the category of firms capitalized under ¥1 million, a whopping 67 percent reported a loss (*Kokuzeicho tokei nenposho* 1992). All the difference is not due to tax evasion, however. Part of the reason why larger firms report losses less frequently reflects the fact that the profits of large firms are an average of profitable and unprofitable sections.

Table 4.6 Size Breakdown of Japanese Subsidiaries

Industry	Number of Workers in Parent Co.	Number of Workers in Subs.	Total Number of Subs.	% of Employees by Firm Size								
				0 or Unknown	<30	30–39	40–49	50–99	100–199	200–499	500–999	1,000+
All industries	6,279,200	3,976,700	25,293	13	33	6	5	15	12	10	4	3
Manufacturing	3,129,000	1,914,500	8,224	11	21	6	5	17	16	14	5	4
Nonmanufacturing	3,150,200	2,062,200	17,069	14	39	6	5	13	10	8	3	2

Source: Nihon no kigyo guruupu (1995).

firms.[23] For example, virtually all the firms capitalized in the ¥50–¥100 million range in the Hitachi group had over two hundred employees, and one had over a thousand. Because the government has been slow to adjust the criteria for classifying firms as small, in the 1970s it was even easier for larger firms to qualify as small firms. For example, in 1970, the capital criterion for being an SME was the same as it is today, but at that time a firm capitalized between ¥50 and ¥100 million on average and employed 222 workers, as opposed to an average of just over 100 today.[24] This implies that older suppliers are more likely to be classified as small firms than newer ones. Indeed, because of this historical legacy, probably about 70–80 percent of all group members are capitalized at under ¥100 million.

If a firm can be classified as an SME, it is eligible for far more tax breaks and subsidies than in most other industrialized countries. For example, while the Japanese corporate tax rate for earnings of over ¥8 million is 37.5 percent (which is the marginal rate for most large companies), the tax rate for earnings of ¥8 million and under is only 28 percent.[25] According to the MOF, this makes the Japanese corporate tax schedule more progressive than that in the United Kingdom, France, and Germany (*Zaisei kinyu tokei geppo* 1995). The United States, however, has significant tax reductions for firms with earnings of less than $75,000, but consolidated reporting makes it more difficult for a firm to organize itself as a collection of smaller enterprises.[26] Japanese consolidated reporting of financial statements did not begin until 1977, but major loopholes allow firms to create dummy corporations in order to evade Japanese taxes.

One of the most important loopholes is the fact that the Japanese Corporate Tax Law does not distinguish between small enterprises that are wholly owned subsidiaries and those that are not.[27] This provides firms with a tremendous tax

23. Since capitalization is the number of shares times the par value of the shares, it has almost no relation to firm size for older companies.

24. While the capitalization criterion has been the same since at least as far back as 1967, the earnings criterion has been steadily raised from ¥3 million in 1967 to ¥8 million in 1981 (*Zaisei kinyu tokei geppo* 1995, 75).

25. Neither number includes prefectural, city, or enterprise taxes, which tend to increase the differential.

26. U.S. law requires consolidated tax reporting when firms are over 80 percent owned by a parent or other members in a corporate group or if the parent has 80 percent of the voting power (Code, sec. 1504[a]). While this provides a tax incentive for U.S. firms to spin off 80 percent–owned subsidiaries, the tax incentives are probably smaller in the U.S. than in Japan. First, U.S. taxes are considerably less progressive than Japanese taxes when one includes state and prefectural taxes for firms with earnings over $50,000. This tends to decrease the incentive to spin off subsidiaries. Second, U.S. law requires that outside investors would have to be part of any subsidiary that was spun off for tax purposes. The requirements that outside investors hold some shares may result in unacceptable releases of information or control that offset the gains from forming a vertical group.

27. This is not true of all other laws. Some laws require small firms to have fewer than a certain number of workers (usually three hundred), not more than half their capital from a large firm, and/or not more than half their directors from a large firm. These laws are summarized in Small and Medium Enterprise Agency (1994).

incentive to spin off subsidiaries that are taxed at much lower rates. In addition, this may also help explain why foreign companies often complain that Japanese firms buy from their affiliated companies even if the price is not competitive. If the affiliate is taxed at a lower rate than the parent, it makes sense to try to record as much profit as possible in the affiliate. Unless the affiliate is so inefficient that the cost of production exceeds the outside price by more than the tax subsidy, assemblers should rely on their affiliates even if the outside price is lower.

In addition to these tax measures, there are at least twenty other laws that create a variety of other benefits for SMEs. For example, SMEs borrowed approximately ¥30 trillion in low-interest loans in 1994 from the Small Business Finance Corporation, the People's Finance Corporation, and the Central Bank for Commercial and Industrial Cooperatives (Small and Medium Enterprise Agency 1994). In fact, lending by these government institutions accounted for approximately 10 percent of all lending to SMEs. This, of course, does not include loans from other public financial institutions, worker-training subsidies, subsidies for technological development, and various measures for "structural adjustment assistance."

The second major loophole is that subsidiaries are allowed to have different taxable years than their parents.[28] This is true even for firms that do not qualify as SMEs. For example, while none of Toyota's first-tier suppliers would qualify as SMEs, only one of these suppliers closed it books on the same date as Toyota did in 1994. Even subsidiaries that were 100 percent owned by Toyota closed their books on different dates. Allowing subsidiaries to close their books on different days from their parents permits firms to manipulate tax payment schedules in order to reduce their tax burden. For example, an assembler might pay off its suppliers prior to closing the books in order to reduce its profits and therefore its tax liability. If the supplier then incurred the costs of producing and delivering the parts before its books closed, the group can succeed in delaying its tax payment.

Tax incentives not to vertically integrate are an even stronger incentive in distribution. In addition to the disincentives to open large stores in Japan generated by the Large Scale Retail Law, Japanese tax law grants large advantages to small retailers and wholesalers.[29] Consider the direct tax benefits: first, all their tax burden is reduced from 37.5 to 28 percent, and, second, small stores do not need to charge the 3 percent consumption tax. If firms' income stands at around 10 percent of sales, then these two measures mean that small retailers in Japan have a 4 percentage point price advantage over their larger counterparts before one even begins to count all the other subsidies and policies avail-

28. I am grateful to Gary Saxonhouse for suggesting that I explore this possibility.

29. The Large Scale Retail Law is essentially a zoning restriction that has made it more difficult for large stores to open up new branches. Recent reforms to the law following the Structural Impediments Initiative have reduced these restrictions to some degree.

able to them as SMEs. The existence of these tax incentives suggests that small stores may remain a feature of Japanese retail regardless of the future of the Large Scale Retail Law.

It is important not to conclude from these examples that the tax code is the only reason for vertical groups in Japan. Japan's ban on holding companies probably plays an important role in favoring vertical groups relative to conglomerates. Obviously, there are many other reasons why firms choose not to vertically integrate in both Japan and the United States, and there are a lot of members of corporate groups for whom these benefits do not apply. For example, virtually all members of the Nissan and Isuzu groups are large firms with the same closing date as their parents. However, in both groups, the affiliate with the largest number of employees closes its books on a different date than its parent. Defenders of the tax code would argue that these large affiliates, Unisia Jecs (in the case of Nissan) and Zexel (in the case of Isuzu), are independent companies, but the fact they are 30 and 20 percent owned by their respective buyer firms makes this independence less clear.

Furthermore, newly created affiliates are required to have the same closing date as their parents. In order words, while these policies for SMEs historically may have greatly contributed to the formation of vertical groups, their importance for the future is beginning to wane. In fact, the rate of creation of new affiliates has fallen sharply over the last decade, but it is difficult to tell how much of this is due to the recent economic downturn and how much is due to the reduction in incentives to form these organizations.

4.6   Reexamining the Link between FDI and Cross-Shareholding

The discussion, so far, helps to identify how conventional government policies helped shape the structure of corporate ownership in Japan. Tax policies favored certain financial institutions and industrial structures. When this was combined with regulations that limited or eliminated certain types of price competition, Japanese economic agents circumvented these regulations through distinctive forms of shareholding. While these arguments work well to explain levels and trends, they do not explain the shifts in trends that occur roughly between 1965 and 1973. Since it was these movements that motivated the initial argument in favor of a link between FDI and cross-shareholding, it is important that we examine this period in greater detail.

The story begins in 1963, when, following a rapid rise in stock prices, there was a crash in the Japanese market.[30] Between April and December 1963, the average share price on the first section of the Tokyo Stock Exchange fell by 27 percent. Many firms and individuals lost money, which prompted the MOF and the Bank of Japan to decide that it was necessary to prop up the market. Early

---

30. I am indebted in part to Paul Sheard for suggesting that I explore this direction. Much of the material for the discussion of the stock market bailout was drawn from Sheard (1986).

in 1964, the Japanese government formed a public/private venture called the Japan Joint Securities Corporation (Nihon Kyodo Shoken Kabushiki Gaisha), which had the mission to put a floor on the Japanese market by buying up securities whose prices were "too low." Initially, this firm was financed by private-sector banks and low-interest loans from the Bank of Japan, although, as time went on and the firm needed more capital, insurance companies were asked to participate as well.

The Joint Securities Corporation began purchasing securities at a tremendous rate. In its first year of operation, it purchased 1.6 billion shares at a cost of ¥190 billion (Nihon Kyodo Shoken Zaidan 1978). This accounted for 2 percent of all shares and 3 percent of the entire value of the market. Very quickly, however, it became apparent that this was not sufficient to put a floor on the market. In 1965, Yamaichi securities as well as the smaller Oi (now Wako) securities failed. A large number of other securities companies were also in trouble because, like Yamaichi and Oi, they had used the equity in their trust accounts as collateral to borrow heavily from banks in order to finance the purchase of more stocks. With the slump in stock prices, these firms were no longer solvent (Adams and Hoshii 1972, 171). In order to stave off a new rash of bankruptcies, the BOJ extended ¥28 billion in low-interest loans to Yamaichi and another ¥5.3 billion to Oi via city banks. In addition, a second semigovernment institution, the Japan Securities Holding Association (Nihon Shoken Hoyu Kumiai), was formed to prop up share prices further. By July of that year, this association had purchased an additional ¥230 billion in equities from investment trusts and securities companies.

In the end, these two institutions purchased 5.2 percent of all shares listed on the TSE, and the BOJ estimates that the overall cost of the intervention was close to ¥500 billion. However, since the Joint Securities Corporation was restricted to purchasing equity only from the first section of the exchange, where most core corporate group firms are listed, ownership of the first section was probably closer to 6 percent (Adams and Hoshii 1972, 199). The government also created various less visible incentives for firms to buy up securities through the extension of loans from the BOJ to banks. For example, between 1964 and 1970, the value of new shares purchased by Japanese banks increased by approximately the same amount as the increase in money lent them by the BOJ.

Purchasing 6 percent of the market had the desired effect on stock prices, but now the semigovernment institutions faced the problem of what they were going to do with the shares they had purchased. The express objective of the government was to transfer the shares into "stable" holders (Adams and Hoshii 1972, 199), which meant that these shares would be transferred directly to corporations that would not sell them in the short term. Indeed, 90 percent of the shares held by the Japan Joint Securities Corporation and 75 percent of the shares held by the Japan Securities Holding Association were sold to corporations during the next five years (Moriki and Isozaki 1988, 395). The sales of these securities probably account for a large portion of the faster increase in nonfinancial corporate ownership over the late 1960s. In other words, Japanese banks and firms bought more shares because the government subsidized their purchase through low-interest lending.

This intervention is probably more important than other legal changes over the period. For example, Mason (1992) argues that one reason for the continued rise in nonfinancial corporate ownership between 1966 and 1973 was changes in the laws covering private placement of securities. Private placements are private sales of equity, often at very low prices, to selected persons or firms such as directors, employees, suppliers, or distributors (Japan Securities Research Institute 1994). These transfers are often made to corporate shareholders who are unlikely to sell in response to a takeover bid. Alternatively, they can also be seen as a payment mechanism. In 1966, Mason (1992, 205) argues, the Japanese commercial code was changed in order to make these transactions easier. In order to block a third-party allocation that was proposed by management, two-thirds of the existing shareholders would have to vote against it (Adams and Hoshii 1972, 193). Ostensibly the reason given by the firms was to reduce the chance of foreign takeovers, but in practice these sales may have enriched the recipients of the stock and enabled management to become further entrenched. Following a rapid increase in these private placements in the early 1970s, the securities industry finally clamped down on private placement transactions in 1973 (Japan Securities Research Institute 1994).

While this story initially sounds compelling, it probably explains only a small part of the increase in cross-shareholding for several reasons. First, many of the private placements that occurred in the 1950s and 1960s were made by companies whose stock was not trading publicly. In many of these cases, existing shareholders had preemptive rights, which meant that they had the option to stock issued to third parties at the same price.[31] In addition, since a below-market-value issuance of stock to a third party would violate the board's duty of loyalty to the shareholders, whether the board approved the sale or not, existing shareholders could block an issuance that harmed them. This makes it unlikely that many issuances were made at prices that were below the true value of the stocks. It is not just legal issues that would have made it difficult for Japanese managers to use private placements to sidestep existing shareholders. The data also do not seem to support this hypothesis. Figure 4.2 shows the value of private placements relative to equity outstanding as well as the value of the placement over the par value of the stock relative to the amount of money raised by the placement. Since par values are typically substantially below market values, this last measure gives some indication of the discount of the shares. A few things are apparent from the graph. First, while private

31. I am grateful to Mark Ramseyer for clarifying the legal issues related to this first point for me. Technically, existing shareholders were limited to purchasing up to their percentage interest in the new company.

Fig. 4.2   Private placement of securities

Source: Takahashi (1994).

Note: The discount equals $[1 - (\text{par value of private placements})/(\text{value of private placements})]$. High discounts imply that the shares were sold at close to par.

placements were made at significant discounts prior to 1972, in later years they were conducted at prices that were substantially above the par value of the stocks. Second, despite the legal change, private placements did not increase much between 1966 and 1973 relative to the total market. Third, although there was a surge in private placements in 1971 and 1972, the magnitude of these placements was minute relative to the size of the market. Even if we assume that these shares were released at half their market value and that all private placements went to corporations (both of which are generous assumptions), then these issues still could only account for no more than 5–10 percent of the increased corporate shareholding in the first two years of the decade and even less overall.

The most plausible explanation for the rise in 1972 probably has nothing to do with government policy at all. In 1972, the TSE posted its single largest percentage gain over the last thirty years. With stock prices at a record high, 498 firms, close to one-third of all listed firms, issued equity at a total value of over ¥1 trillion. This constituted a 4 percent increase in the value of the TSE: another thirty-year record. Of the approximately five hundred share issuances in that year, however, only forty-three were private placements. The vast majority of issuances in both value and number were public offerings or offers to existing shareholders. Since the majority of the shares issued in 1972 were offered to the public, in most cases foreigners or any existing shareholders could just as easily have purchased the shares as particular Japanese firms. The notion that cross-shareholding grew in these years through quiet side deals does not seem to be borne out by the data. On the contrary, the Japanese government played an important and active role in the formation of corporate groups through conventional policies that subsidized their formation.

4.7   Conclusion: Toward a Process-Oriented Policy

In this type of analysis, one is tempted to draw comparisons with the United States and argue that the difference between the two systems is due to Japanese regulation. It is often taken for granted that the U.S. system of diversified ownership of corporations is the "deregulated" benchmark against which other countries should be judged. Indeed, many a proponent of the Japanese *keiretsu* system has run up against the economists' retort, "If Japanese corporate groups are so good, why don't we see them develop in the United States?" The answer, it turns out, has to do largely with U.S. securities market regulations that have the opposite effect of Japanese regulations: U.S. laws tend to force high levels of diversification by large U.S. financial institutions.

Table 4.7 (drawn from Roe 1990) presents the major restrictions on portfolio choices by U.S. financial enterprises. Very little comment is needed. The reason why financial firms do not take out large positions in individual firms and actively try to manage them is that in most cases it would be illegal or tax disadvantaged. Furthermore, joint actions by financials that would involve pooling their shareholdings are also difficult to accomplish owing to other regulations.[32] In the light of these restrictions, it is entirely possible that high levels of equity holdings by a single financial entity, as often happens in Japan, may be more the result of free market factors than the automistic holdings more common in the United States. In other words, maybe the problem is not that Japanese regulations make takeovers too difficult but that U.S. regulations make them too easy!

There is little doubt that Japan is not going to privatize the post office or eliminate tax perks for various financial institutions and small businesses overnight. However, it is also important to recognize that there is increasing pressure within Japan to make these changes. Often foreign pressure (*gaiatsu*) can be helpful for the proponents of economic liberalization, especially when these liberalizations play one political group or ministry off against another. It is along these fault lines—areas where politically powerful constituencies hold opposing views—that U.S. policy is likely to be most effective.

---

32. These are discussed in greater detail in Roe (1990). The problematic regulations covering group action include filing papers ahead of time regarding the intentions of the joint action, restrictions on communications within the group, and restrictions on short-term sales by group members.

Table 4.7   **Important Ownership Restrictions for U.S. Financial Institutions**

Institution	Assets in $Trillions (1989)	Restriction	Source
Banks	3.2	Stock ownership prohibited.	Glass-Steagall Bank Act
Bank holding companies	.3	No more than 5 percent of the voting stock of any nonbank.	Bank Holding Act of 1956
Bank trust funds	.7[a]	No more than 10 percent of assets in any one company.	Comptroller regulations
		Active bank control could trigger bank liability to controlled company.	Bankruptcy case law
Life insurers	1.3	No more than 2 percent of assets can be placed in a single company.	New York Insurance Law (for insurers doing business in New York)
		No more than 20 percent of assets can be held in stock.	New York Insurance Law
Property and casualty	.5	None.	Same
Open-end mutual funds	.5	For half of portfolio: No more than 5 percent of fund assets can be invested into stock of any issuer, and fund may not purchase more than 10 percent of the stock of any company. For other half: No more than 25 percent of fund assets can be placed in a single stock. Otherwise tax penalties apply.	Investment Company Act of 1940: Subchapter M of the Internal Revenue Code
		Must get SEC approval prior to joint action with affiliate, i.e., a fund needs SEC approval before acting jointly to control a company of which it and its partner own more than 5 percent.	Same
Pensions	1.2	Must diversify unless clearly sensible not to.	Employment Retirement Income Security Act of 1974

Source: Roe (1990).
[a]1988.

Consider the potential for pressure on Japanese corporate tax rates. Currently, in Japan not only foreign firms would prefer lower corporate tax rates; the leading enterprise organization, Keidanren, has also been engaged in an ongoing battle to lower Japanese corporate tax rates. Japanese firms feel that high corporate taxes hurt them relative to foreign competitors. These forces have successfully reduced the maximum corporate tax from 42 percent in 1981 to 37.5 percent today. The lowest tax bracket has only fallen from 30 to 28 percent over the same time period. If Japan were to lower the tax rate for large corporations further, that would tend to increase FDI, reduce Japan's trade surplus, stimulate investment, and diminish the incentives for vertical groups. Not bad for a simple process-oriented policy.

Pressuring for deregulation in insurance is another potentially high-effect area. Considering the vast array of regulations in the U.S. market, this would have to be a bilateral negotiation at the very least, but there certainly is strong support within Japan for deregulation here, too. In the framework talks, progress was made on easing the acceptance of new insurance products, reducing insurance rate regulations, and introducing insurance brokers, but clearly this is an area where more could be done. For example, the innovative Japanese insurance companies, banks, and the MOF are not happy with the "competition" offered by the MPT and other government institutions. Once again, this provides a potential area for mutual gain.

Deregulation of investment vehicles is a further area that might work to improve Japanese efficiency and diminish the importance of corporate groups. The MOF restrictions on the types of funds that can manage tax-free investments and the portfolios of these firms seem unnecessary. The argument that, without MOF guidance, firms will invest in risky assets seem hollow in the light of MOF regulations that required that firms invest in the now depressed real estate sector. Deregulation in this area is likely to have wide ranging effects on the structure of corporate ownership in Japan.

This list of potential process-oriented policies is only a small sample of those that are likely to have profound effects on the structure of Japanese industrial organization. The United States has a clear interest in Japanese efforts to deregulate their financial markets. It is a shame that the United States ends up talking about numerical targets instead.

References

Adams, T. F. M., and I. Hoshii. 1972. *A financial history of the new Japan*. Tokyo: Kodansha International.

American Chamber of Commerce in Japan. Financial Services Committee. 1993. *Insurance sector report, 1993: A study of Japanese insurance procurement practices within keiretsu groups*. Tokyo.

Aoki, M., and H. Patrick, eds. 1994. *The Japanese main bank system*. New York: Oxford University Press.

Booz, Allen and Hamilton, Inc. 1987. *Direct foreign investment in Japan: The challenge for foreign firms*. Tokyo.

Bronte, Stephen. 1982. *Japanese finance: Markets and institutions*. London: Euromoney.

Budget Bureau. Ministry of Finance. 1995. *The Japanese budget in brief.* Tokyo.

Carroll, J. 1994. The not-so-brave new world of Japanese insurance: To liberalize or not to liberalize. *The Journal* (September).

Dodwell Marketing Consultants. Various years. *Industrial groupings in Japan.* Tokyo.

Economic report of the president. 1994. Washington, D.C.: U.S. Government Printing Office.

Economic statistics annual. Various issues. Tokyo: Bank of Japan.

Encarnation, D. 1992. *Rivals beyond trade: America versus Japan in global competition.* Ithaca, N.Y.: Cornell University Press.

Gaishikei kigyo no doko (Foreign-owned-firm trends). Various issues. Tokyo: Okurasho Insatsu Kyoku (Ministry of Finance Printing Bureau).

Gaishikei kigyo soran (General survey of foreign-owned firms). Various issues. Tokyo: Toyo Keizai.

Gerlach, M. 1992. *Alliance capitalism.* Berkeley and Los Angeles: University of California Press.

Graham, Edward M., and P. Krugman. 1989. *Foreign direct investment.* Washington, D.C.: Institute for International Economics.

————. 1993. The surge in foreign direct investment in the 1980s. In *Foreign direct investment,* ed. Kenneth A. Froot. Chicago: University of Chicago Press.

Ishi, H. 1993. *The Japanese tax system.* 2d ed. New York: Oxford University Press.

Ito, T. 1992. *Shohisha jushi no keizaigaku* (Consumer-centered economics). Tokyo: Nihon Keizai Shimbunsha.

Ito, T., and M. Maruyama. 1991. Is the Japanese distribution system really inefficient? In *Trade with Japan: Has the door opened wider?* ed. P. Krugman. Chicago: University of Chicago Press.

Japan Securities Research Institute. 1994. *Securities market in Japan, 1994.* Tokyo.

Julius, D., and S. Thomsen. 1988. Foreign-owned firms, trade, and economic integration. In *Tokyo Club Papers* 2. Royal Institute of Economic Affairs.

Kigyo keiretsu soran (Compendium of enterprise groups). Various issues. Tokyo: Toyo Keizai.

Kokuzeicho tokei nenposho (National Tax Agency's yearly statistical data book). Various issues. Tokyo: National Tax Agency.

Krugman, Paul, and Maurice Obstfeld. 1994. *International economics: Theory and Policy.* 3d ed. New York: Harper Collins.

Lawrence, R. 1993. Japan's low levels of inward acquisitions: The role of inhibitions on acquisitions. In *Foreign direct investment,* ed. Kenneth A. Froot. Chicago: University of Chicago Press.

Mason, M. 1992. *American multinationals and Japan: The political economy of capital controls, 1899–1980.* Cambridge, Mass.: Harvard University Press.

Matsuoka, M., and B. Rose. 1994. *The DIR guide to Japanese economic statistics.* New York: Oxford University Press.

McKenzie, C. 1992. Stable shareholdings and the role of Japanese life insurance companies. In *International adjustment and the Japanese firm,* ed. Paul Sheard. St. Leonards: Allen & Unwin.

Ministry of Posts and Telecommunications. 1994. *Yusei tokei: Heisei 6 nendohan* (Postal statistics for 1994). Tokyo: Okurasho Insatsu Kyoku (Ministry of Finance Printing Bureau).

Moriki, A., and S. Isozaki, eds. 1988. *Okurasho hyaku-nijunenshi* (The 120-year history of the Ministry of Finance). Tokyo: Keizai Konwakai.

Nihon Keizai Chosakai (Japanese Economy Research Group). Various years. *Keiretsu no kenyu* (Research on groups). Tokyo.

Nihon Kyodo Shoken Zaidan. 1978. *Nihon kyodo shoken kabushiki gaisha shi* (History of the Japan Joint Securities Company). Tokyo: Kyodo Insatsu Kabushiki Gaisha.

Nihon no kigyo guruupu (Japanese enterprise groups). Various issues. Tokyo: Toyo Keizai.

Nishimura, K. 1991. Entry barriers, monopoly profits and production efficiency: The case of the Japanese retail trade sector. University of Tokyo, Department of Economics. Mimeo.

An outline of Japanese taxes. Various issues. Tokyo: Okurasho Insatsu Kyoku (Ministry of Finance Printing Bureau).

Patrick, H., and T. Rohlen. 1987. Small-scale family enterprises. In *The political economy of Japan,* vol. 1, *The domestic transformation,* ed. K. Yamamura and Y. Yasuba. Stanford, Calif.: Stanford University Press.

Ramseyer, J. M. 1987. Takeovers in Japan: Opportunism, ideology and corporate control. *UCLA Law Review* 35:1–64.

Roe, M. J. 1990. Political and legal restraints on ownership and control of public companies. *Journal of Financial Economics* 27:7–41.

Ryutsu tokei shiryoshu (Book of distribution statistics). Various issues. Tokyo: Ryutsu Keizai Kenkyujo (Economics of Distribution Research Institute).

Sheard, P. 1986. Intercorporate shareholdings and structural adjustment in Japan. Research Paper no. 140. Canberra: Australia-Japan Research Centre.

———. 1994. Interlocking shareholdings and corporate governance in Japan. In *The Japanese firm: Sources of competitive strength,* ed. M. Aoki and R. Dore. New York: Oxford University Press.

Small and Medium Enterprise Agency. 1987. *Chusho kigyo shisaku no aramashi: Showa 62 nendohatsu* (Outline of the measures for small and medium enterprises for 1987). Tokyo.

———. 1994. *Chusho kigyo shisaku soran* (General survey of measures for small and medium enterprises). Tokyo.

Takahashi, Koji, ed. 1994. *Shoken tokei nenpo* (Annual securities statistics). Tokyo: Tokyo Shoken Torihikijo Tyosabu (Tokyo Stock Exchange, Research Department).

Viner, A. 1988. *Inside Japanese financial markets.* Homewood, Ill.: Dow Jones–Irwin.

Weinstein, D. 1995. Evaluating administrative guidance and cartels in Japan, 1957–1988. *Journal of the Japanese and International Economies* 9:200–223.

Weinstein, D. 1996. Structural impediments to foreign direct investment in Japan: What have we learned over the last 450 years? In *Foreign direct investment in Japan,* ed. E. Graham and M. Yoshitomi. Brookfield, Vt.: Edward Elgar.

Zaisei kinyu tokei geppo (Public finance and monetary monthly statistics). Various issues. Tokyo: Okurasho Insatsu Kyoku (Ministry of Finance Printing Bureau).

5   U.S.-Japan Telecommunications Trade Conflicts: The Role of Regulation

Andrew R. Dick

For more than fifteen years, the telecommunications equipment sector has played a prominent role in straining trade relations between the United States and Japan. The industry's most recent trade dispute was precipitated by Motorola's charge that technical standards effectively barred its entry into Japan's cellular telephone market. Cellular systems face the technical challenge of transferring calls as customers roam from one company's cells to another. In both the United States and Japan, this challenge was solved by establishing regulatory standards to ensure compatibility among local service providers. However, compatibility did not extend internationally between the United States operating standard (developed jointly by Motorola and AT&T) and the Japanese standard (developed by Nippon Telephone and Telegraph [NTT]). While Japanese cellular companies surmounted the U.S. standards barrier by modifying their equipment for export, Motorola's entry strategy into Japan relied instead on lobbying for market access guarantees under U.S. trade law.

After contentious and prolonged negotiations between the office of the U.S. trade representative (USTR) and the Ministry of International Trade and Industry (MITI), a compromise was reached in 1987. Japan agreed to license Motorola with a local partner (Daini-Denden [DDI]) to supply cellular service outside the Tokyo-Nagoya corridor using Motorola's standard. The Tokyo-Nagoya corridor would be served by Nippon Idou Tsushin (IDO) operating on NTT's standard, and NTT itself would offer cellular service throughout Japan. Motorola originally accepted this compromise but by 1989 had reasserted its claim of market access barriers by arguing that its cellular system remained

Andrew R. Dick is an economist with the Antitrust Division of the U.S. Department of Justice.

The analysis and conclusions presented in this paper do not purport to reflect those of the U.S. Department of Justice. For their valuable comments, the author thanks Takatoshi Ito, Ed Leamer, Lionel Olmer, and NBER conference participants. UCLA's Center for American Politics and Public Policy kindly provided research support.

117

disadvantaged because it was not fully portable within Japan. Under renewed pressure from the USTR and Japan's Ministry of Posts and Telecommunications, IDO and NTT agreed to cede radio spectrum for Motorola service in the Tokyo-Nagoya corridor. In 1993, the United States extracted additional spectrum concessions that gave Motorola and NTT equal population coverage, effectively nullifying NTT's ten-year head start in its local market.

The market access charges raised during the cellular dispute were not unfamiliar to the industry. Once telecommunications equipment began trading internationally in volume beginning in the late 1970s, the industry attracted ongoing congressional scrutiny. In 1979, a congressional task force charged Japan with "using their protected home market to improve their telecommunications technology while exporting as much as they can into the open American market" (U.S. Congress 1979, 33). Responding to congressional pressure, the USTR began negotiations with Japan in 1981, seeking to stem the widening bilateral trade imbalance. These early negotiations yielded few tangible results, however, and exports to Japan remained almost level, while imports continued nearly to double annually. In 1985, the United States elevated the dispute by including telecommunications equipment in the Market-Oriented Sector-Selective (MOSS) talks. Despite this renewed negotiating pressure, however, the bilateral imbalance continued to widen. The apparent failure of negotiations finally culminated in the passage of the Telecommunications Trade Act of 1988, which authorized the USTR to impose unilateral sanctions against trading partners for "unfair trade practices" in the industry. Motorola was among the first to use the act as a credible threat for pressing its market access demands in the cellular telephone dispute.

Political rhetoric and policy demands notwithstanding, the American and Japanese telecommunications equipment industries historically have been highly similar in their structures and openness to trade. In 1978, despite congressional claims of unequal market access, *both* countries remained tightly closed. Imports represented less than 5 percent of domestic equipment purchases in both markets, and the United States actually held a larger share of the Japanese market (3.4 percent) than Japan did in the United States (1.2 percent) (*Japan Electronics Almanac* 1984; *U.S. Industrial Outlook* 1980). If, as U.S. trade negotiators asserted, Japan had been pursuing a policy of import protection as export promotion during this period, there is nothing in the market share data to suggest that this strategy had been successful.[1]

Not until the early 1980s, as telecommunications markets were deregulated globally, did persistent imbalances emerge in market penetration. By 1992, once deregulation was effectively concluded in the United States and Japan, import penetration in the United States had grown sixfold to 30.5 percent, and

---

1. Krugman (1984) demonstrates how import protection in a decreasing-cost industry can raise firms' export market share by guaranteeing them a secure domestic market. However, Dick (1994) finds no supporting evidence for a wide cross section of decreasing-cost industries in the United States.

Japan's share of U.S. telecommunications equipment purchases had risen eight-fold to 9.8 percent (*Japan Electronics Almanac* 1994; *U.S. Industrial Outlook* 1994). By comparison, import penetration in Japan had risen only modestly to 5.9 percent, with U.S. shipments continuing to account for less than 5 percent of Japanese imports. Trade policy—in the traditional sense—appears unlikely to have played a major role in generating these imbalances. Tariff rates on telecommunications equipment historically have been low and relatively uniform in the two countries, and U.S. firms have not regarded Japanese nontariff charges on imports as a serious impediment to market access.[2]

An alternative explanation for telecommunications equipment trade patterns is suggested by the "industrial organization approach to international trade." The central insight of that literature is to acknowledge that foreign trade flows are influenced by the domestic market's structure and the form of contractual relations among firms.[3] Historically, telecommunications markets in the United States and Japan (and in most other industrialized countries) were organized around domestic monopoly suppliers of telephone service. These firms either produced their own equipment directly through a wholly owned subsidiary, as in the case of AT&T and Western Electric, or purchased their equipment from a small family of preferred suppliers, as in the case of Japan's NTT and NEC.[4] In both countries, the historically small number of equipment suppliers, combined with their preferential procurement ties to service carriers, were the direct outgrowth of economic and regulatory "barriers to entry" that shaped the industry's structure and organization.

In this paper, I define a barrier to entry to exist in an industry if economic fundamentals or policy choices (i) allow only a small number of suppliers to coexist in the market or (ii) favor preferential, long-term contracts over competitive, arm's-length transactions. The United States and Japan erected regulatory barriers to entry in telecommunications by directly barring competition from independent equipment producers and by indirectly encouraging monopoly service carriers to tightly control equipment distribution within their network. For particular categories of equipment, these regulatory barriers were reinforced by economic barriers to entry. Economic barriers arose naturally from economies to scale (on the supply side) and network economies (on the demand side) and served both to limit the sustainable number of suppliers and to discourage arm's-length sourcing. Common economic and regulatory barriers generated highly similar market structures and contracting practices in the

---

2. Post–Tokyo Round tariff rates on U.S. imports of telecommunications products ranged from 0.4 to 6.0 percent. Tariff rates in Japan ranged from 4.5 to 9.2 percent (U.S. International Trade Commission 1984, tables 1 and 3). In a 1984 survey by the International Trade Commission of U.S. telecommunications equipment producers, only two respondents of fifty-three cited Japanese nontariff charges on imports as an important barrier to trade (U.S. International Trade Commission 1984, table F1).

3. Important summary references include Helpman and Krugman (1985, 1989).

4. The Nippon Electronic Corp. was the head of NTT's small equipment supply family.

United States and Japan and effectively curtailed trade in telecommunications equipment for both countries until the late 1970s.

During the next decade, deregulation in both countries gradually exposed telecommunications monopolies to competition, and what followed was a complete restructuring of the equipment market and contracting practices.[5] These changes coincided with three major transformations in telecommunications equipment trade patterns. First, with little correlation to trends in total merchandise, durable goods, or advanced technology trade balances, the United States abruptly began a persistent trade deficit in telecommunications equipment after 1982. Second, this trade deficit emerged in both "low-technology" and "high-technology" product segments, although the deficits' timing and persistence varied distinctly within the industry. Finally, these changes initially were unique to the United States and were driven primarily by trade with Japan. Only later were they repeated in U.S.-Asian and European-Japanese trade patterns.

The central question addressed by this paper is the role that deregulation played in first precipitating and then ultimately sustaining the U.S.-Japan trade imbalance in telecommunications equipment. Adopting the industrial organization approach to international trade, the paper assesses how foreign trade patterns were shaped by changes in domestic market structure and contracting practices induced by deregulation. The analysis concludes that deregulation played an essential role in each of the three major transformations in U.S. telecommunications equipment trade.

First, the time profile of the industry's bilateral trade imbalance closely tracks major changes in domestic market structure and contracting practices prompted by U.S. deregulation. Japanese deregulation occasionally reinforced these effects, while in other instances its effect on the bilateral trade imbalance was largely neutral. Second, the consequences of U.S. deregulation varied predictably within the industry according to the origin of entry barriers. Monopolies in "low-technology" terminal equipment, which had been sustained solely by regulatory barriers to entry, were quickly eroded by international factor cost differentials following early deregulation. By contrast, monopolies in "high-technology" network equipment, which were sustained additionally by economic barriers to entry, were eroded only by the combination of proactive deregulation and major technological advances. Finally, the initial uniqueness of the U.S.-Japan trade imbalance can be partially attributed to differences in the timing and scope of deregulation in the two countries. These differences impinged on both economic and regulatory barriers to entry.

The organization of the paper is as follows. Section 5.1 reviews the major transformations affecting U.S. telecommunications equipment trade during the

---

5. The political and economic forces leading to deregulation largely lie beyond the scope of this paper, which will concentrate on the effects of regulatory policy. Noll and Rosenbluth (1993) describe many of these forces as they relate to regulatory changes in the United States and Japan.

past decade and a half. Section 5.2 develops an empirical linkage between industry structure and foreign trade to explain patterns in "low-technology" terminal equipment trade. Section 5.3 undertakes a parallel analysis for "high-technology" network equipment. Finally, section 5.4 concludes by drawing implications for ongoing changes in the telecommunications equipment industry's structure.

5.1   Transformations in U.S. Telecommunications Equipment Trade

International trade in communications equipment has been a relatively recent phenomenon. Prior to the mid-1970s, equipment procurement historically had been confined within national borders in most industrialized countries, including the United States and Japan. Gradually, changes in technology and regulation opened national markets to foreign trade. This section documents three major transformations that shaped U.S. telecommunications equipment trade during the past fifteen years. First, the industry abruptly began a large and persistent trade deficit after 1982, distinguishing itself from trends in U.S. merchandise, durable goods, and advanced-technology trade. Second, the trade deficit's timing and persistence varied distinctly for low-technology terminal equipment versus high-technology network equipment. Third, these transformations initially were limited to U.S.-Japan trade, although subsequently they spread to U.S.-Asian and European-Japanese trade. These unique features of telecommunications trade led the United States to single out this industry for special bilateral negotiations, believing that Japanese trade practices and policies were primary contributors to the industry's difficulties.

5.1.1   Comparisons of Sectoral Trends

Having been a small net exporter of telecommunications equipment for almost a decade, after 1982, the United States abruptly began a persistent trade deficit. This reversal cannot be attributed simply to trends in U.S. overall merchandise trade or to trends for durable manufactures or advanced technology products in general. Figure 5.1 compares the trade balance for telecommunications equipment (scaled by industry shipments; series 1) with the total U.S. merchandise trade balance (scaled by GNP; series 2) for a twenty-five-year period.[6] Until 1982, the two series were strongly correlated. Industry and merchandise trade were approximately balanced until 1974, and even in later years, as telecommunications equipment moved into surplus while merchandise trade was in deficit, the two series rarely diverged by more than 3 percent. Since 1982, however, the two series have exhibited little correlation. After deregulation forced the breakup of AT&T, the U.S. trade balance in telecommunications equipment deteriorated at a rate nearly four times faster than the merchandise trade balance. In 1989, the telecommunications equipment deficit

---

6. Series numbers refer to data for figures appearing in app. A.

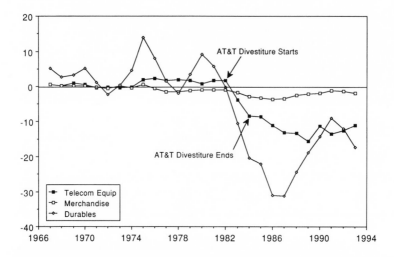

Fig. 5.1   Telecommunications equipment, merchandise, and durables trade balances (as a percentage of industry shipments or GNP)

Sources: U.S. Industrial Outlook (1970–74); *Statistical Abstract of the United States* (1971, 1981, 1994).

peaked at over 15 percent of industry shipments, while the merchandise trade deficit never reached 4 percent of GNP throughout the decade.

Narrowing the focus to durable manufactures confirms telecommunications equipment's unique recent history. The remaining series in figure 5.1 plots the U.S. trade balance for durable goods (scaled by sectoral shipments; series 3) over the same twenty-five-year period. Before 1982, the durable goods balance fluctuated widely in response to real exchange rate movements, while the telecommunications equipment balance remained essentially stable for fifteen years. This disparity was particularly evident between 1980 and 1982, when the (scaled) durable trade balance fell from 9.2 percent to −0.2 percent in response to a 32 percent real appreciation of the dollar, while the (scaled) telecommunications equipment trade balance actually rose modestly. After 1982, both trade balances deteriorated, but again their timing was not synchronized. As the dollar began its real depreciation in 1986, the durables trade deficit narrowed sharply, while the telecommunications equipment deficit merely stabilized.

Trade balance movements in telecommunications equipment also are distinguished from trends in other leading-edge industries. Figure 5.2 compares (unscaled) trade balances for telecommunications equipment and a basket of advanced-technology products between 1982 and 1993 (series 4 and 5).[7] Tele-

---

7. Since 1982, the Department of Commerce has tracked trade balances for a basket of products that employ leading-edge technologies. The basket covers the following sectors: advanced materials, aerospace, biotechnology, electronics, flexible manufacturing, information and communications, life sciences, nuclear technology, optoelectronics, and weapons.

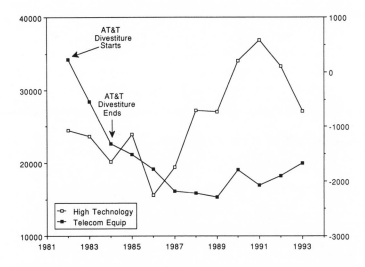

Fig. 5.2 Telecommunications equipment and high-technology trade balances (in millions of current dollars). Left axis: high-technology products; right axis: telecommunications equipment.
Sources: U.S. General Accounting Office (1992); *U.S. Industrial Outlook* (1982–94); *Statistical Abstract of the United States* (1994).

communications equipment is distinguished by both the level and the direction of change in its trade balance. While the United States maintained a surplus in advanced technology products throughout the decade, telecommunications equipment was consistently in deficit after 1982. The advanced-technology trade surplus also grew slightly over the decade (in nominal terms), while the telecommunications equipment trade deficit instead widened sharply.

5.1.2 Comparisons of Intraindustry Trends

While telecommunications equipment distinguished itself from aggregate and sectoral trade trends, it also exhibited substantial intraindustry variation in the timing and persistence of trade deficits. Telecommunications systems consist of three interconnected components: terminals, transmission lines, and switches. Terminals are used to send and receive voice and data communications. *Terminal equipment* includes handsets, modems, facsimile machines, and simple key telephone sets that allow access to multiple lines and services such as call forwarding and conferencing. *Network equipment* collectively refers to switches and transmission lines. Switches act like the central nervous system of the network by controlling call routing across telephone exchanges and service carriers.[8] Switches may be located either in a telephone company's premises (central office switches, or COSs) or in a customer's facilities (private branch exchanges, or PBXs). Transmission lines complete the network system

8. Switches also perform complementary functions such as tracking calls for billing purposes.

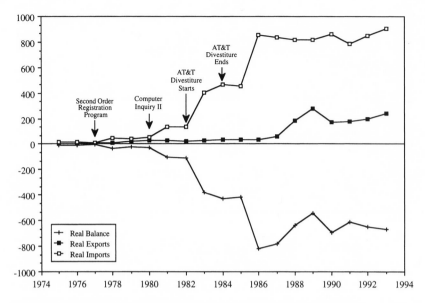

Fig. 5.3   U.S. trade in terminal equipment (in millions of 1982 dollars)
Source: Electronic Market Data Book (1975–94).

by connecting individual switches. Transmission can occur either along wires and optical fibers (wireline communication) or over the electromagnetic spectrum by microwave, radio, and satellites (wireless communication).

The United States has run a persistent trade deficit in terminal equipment since the effective inception of international telecommunications trade in 1975, as summarized in figure 5.3 (series 6–8). The sharpest deterioration in this trade balance occurred between 1980 and 1986, when the terminal equipment deficit ballooned in real terms from $30 to $820 million before narrowing slightly in later years. These movements were driven overwhelmingly by imports, which grew from less than $50 million during the late 1970s to exceed $850 million by 1986. As a share of domestic consumption, imports rose from less than 2 percent during the mid-1970s to 11.2 percent by 1981 and to 55.3 percent by 1986 (series 9). Through this period, Japan supplied between 37 and 43 percent of terminal equipment imports, making it the largest foreign supplier to the U.S. market (U.S. International Trade Commission 1984, table H-14). After 1985, Taiwan, Hong Kong, and South Korea displaced Japan to become major suppliers to the United States of generic telephone equipment. In contrast to import trends, U.S. terminal equipment exports remained stable and below $60 million until the late 1980s, when development of specialty, software-intensive equipment and deregulation of European telecommunications markets allowed U.S. exports to grow gradually to $200–$250 million.

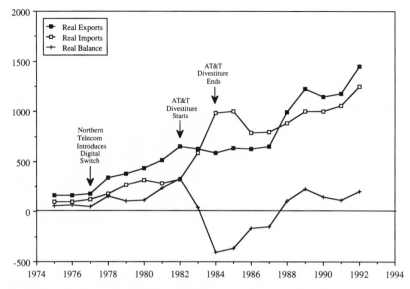

Fig. 5.4   U.S. trade in network equipment (in millions of 1982 dollars)
Source: Electronic Market Data Book (1975–94).

After 1990, U.S. imports of (generic) terminal equipment outstripped exports of (specialty) terminal equipment by a four-to-one ratio.

Network equipment, by contrast, maintained a relatively small trade surplus through 1982, as summarized in figure 5.4 (series 10–12). Between 1982 and 1984, however, the United States abruptly became a substantial net importer as real imports more than tripled from $319 to $983 million and imports doubled as a share of network equipment purchases to reach 16.3 percent (series 13). Since 1984, growth in imports and import penetration has been more modest, reflecting a solidification of network equipment supply relations. Canada's Northern Telecom has remained the largest supplier of U.S. network equipment imports (with a 57.9 percent share in 1989), reflecting the early foothold that the firm achieved after introducing digital technology switches in 1977. The remainder of the U.S. import market has been divided almost evenly between Japan's NEC, Fujitsu, Toshiba, and Hitachi (with a combined share of 18.8 percent) and Europe's Siemens and Ericsson (with a combined share of 15.5 percent).[9] Throughout this period, U.S. real exports of network equipment remained relatively stable and did not begin growing until after 1987, in response to European telecommunications deregulation. This delayed export growth, reinforced by dampened import growth after 1984, helped return the

---

9. My calculations, based on data in Vietor and Yoffie (1993, 162). Shares sum to less than 100 percent because the country of origin of some imports could not be determined.

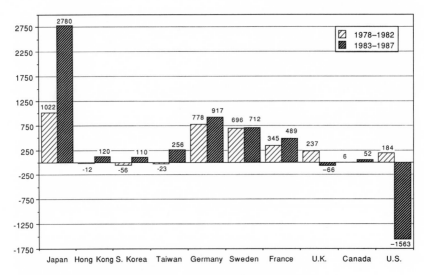

Fig. 5.5   Average trade balances for major telecommunications equipment producers (in millions of current dollars)
Source: Organization for Economic Cooperation and Development (1991).

United States to a small trade surplus in network equipment beginning in 1988, although it continued to be a large net importer from Japan.

5.1.3   Comparisons of Regional Trends

The perception of the telecommunications equipment trade imbalance as a "U.S.-Japan problem" can be attributed to the industry's third transformation. In the early 1980s, the United States was virtually the only major producer of telecommunications equipment to become an overall net importer—a shift that was precipitated largely by its trade relations with Japan. Only later did patterns in U.S.-Japan trade spread to U.S.-Asian and Japanese-European trade.

Figure 5.5 compares trade balances among ten major telecommunications equipment producers between 1978 and 1987. The countries divide themselves naturally into three groups. The first group consists of the United States and Japan, which experienced the largest changes in their industry trade balances. During this decade, the United States moved from a surplus of $184 million to a deficit exceeding $1.5 billion, while Japan's trade surplus grew from $1.0 to $2.8 billion. The second group includes smaller Asian producers (Hong Kong, South Korea, and Taiwan), which became net exporters by supplying generic terminal equipment to the United States in large volume after the mid-1980s. The final group consists of European producers and Canada, which maintained comparatively stable trade balances over the decade. An exception was the United Kingdom, which began telecommunications deregulation in 1984 and, like the United States, became a net importer of equipment.

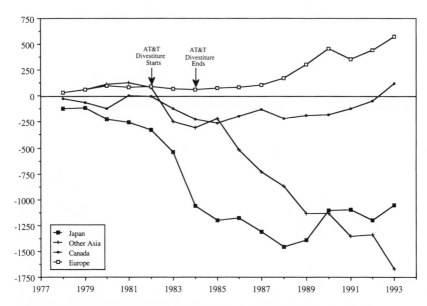

Fig. 5.6   U.S. telecommunications equipment regional trade balances (in millions of 1982 dollars)
Source: U.S. Industrial Outlook (1978–94).
Note: "Other Asia" consists of Hong Kong, South Korea, and Taiwan.

By disaggregating trade balances regionally, figure 5.6 (series 14–25) confirms the initial uniqueness of the U.S.-Japan imbalance. Through 1990, the largest U.S. regional trade deficit was with Japan. Between 1982 and 1989, Japanese imports grew from $356 to $1.62 billion, while U.S. exports to Japan rose from just $25.0 to $236.4 million. The eventual narrowing of the U.S.-Japan trade deficit stemmed not from subsequent growth in U.S. exports but instead from the substitution of terminal equipment imports from smaller Asian producers—principally Hong Kong, South Korea, and Taiwan. Import *growth rates* from these three sources had actually matched or exceeded Japanese import growth since 1984, but import *levels* remained constrained by the residential effects of industrialized countries' regulatory barriers that had confined equipment producers to their normal markets. U.S.-Japan trade also distinguished itself from the relative stability of the U.S. regional trade balance with Europe and Canada. Historically, the United States maintained a moderate trade surplus with Europe, which widened in the late 1980s, following the deregulation of major European telecommunications markets. The United States historically maintained a moderate deficit with Canada, which widened after 1982, following the deregulation of the United States market.[10]

10. Trade with both of these regions has been concentrated overwhelmingly in network equipment.

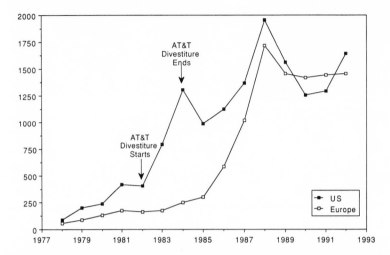

Fig. 5.7   Japanese telecommunications equipment regional trade balances (in millions of 1982 dollars)
Source: Japan Electronics Almanac (1981–84).

The initial uniqueness of the U.S.-Japan imbalance is reinforced by comparing it to Japan's trade with Europe in this industry, as summarized in figure 5.7 (series 26 and 27).[11] Prior to the mid-1980s, Japan's widening industry surplus was driven almost entirely by trade with the United States. The sharpest early growth in Japan's surplus also coincided with final deregulation of the U.S. telecommunications market between 1982 and 1984. Through 1985, by comparison, Japan maintained only a small trade surplus with Europe. Later, as Europe gradually began deregulating telecommunications, Japanese-European trade began to follow Japanese-U.S. patterns, with a four-year delay. By the early 1990s, the United States and Europe were experiencing comparably sized trade industry deficits with Japan.

5.1.4   Criteria for Explaining Trade Patterns

The distinct characteristics of telecommunications equipment trade patterns, summarized in figures 5.1–5.7, establish three criteria for a theory to explain the industry's trade dynamics. First, the fact that telecommunications equipment trade patterns diverged abruptly from general merchandise, durable goods, and advanced-technology trends after 1982 necessitates an explanation that is industry specific. Second, variation in the timing and persistence of the deficit across equipment categories implies that the explanation should take account of intraindustry differences in demand and technology features. Fi-

11. U.S. and Japanese industry classifications differ slightly, leading to discrepancies between the series depicted in figs. 5.6 and 5.7. Comparable data for Japan-Canada and Japan-Asia telecommunications equipment trade were unavailable.

nally, the fact that these trends initially were peculiar to U.S. trade with Japan implies that an explanation should emphasize interactions between these countries. At the same time, because these trends eventually spread to U.S.-Asian and Japanese-European trade, a complete explanation should also include reference to those countries' telecommunications markets and institutions. Sections 5.2 and 5.3 adopt these criteria to explain the origins and evolution of the U.S. telecommunications equipment industry's trade imbalance.

5.2   Trade Conflicts in Terminal Equipment

This section assesses how domestic market structure and procurement practices in the United States and Japan shaped bilateral trade in terminal equipment. Terminal equipment consists primarily of low-technology, labor-intensive products, including telephone handsets, answering machines, and modems. Economic barriers to entering terminal equipment production are minimal, as a result of rapid technology diffusion, minimal scale economies, and weak demand complementarities. However, through the late 1970s, regulatory barriers effectively excluded all but a few domestic suppliers in both U.S. and Japanese markets. The result was that terminal equipment imports remained below 2 percent of equipment purchases in both countries, despite the fact that U.S. labor costs were twelve times and Japanese labor costs six times higher than wages prevailing in Hong Kong, South Korea, and Taiwan.

U.S. deregulation lowered entry barriers in stages between 1977 and 1984 and was followed by a series of sharp jumps in terminal equipment import penetration, which eventually rose to exceed 85 percent. Japan initially accounted for the largest share of these imports, reflecting its head start in installed capacity that had been exclusively supplying the world's second largest captive telecommunications market. The conclusion of U.S. deregulation in 1984, coupled with a sharp rise in Japanese labor costs between 1985 and 1988, enabled Hong Kong, South Korea, and Taiwan to begin large-scale production of terminal equipment and eventually to displace Japan as leading exporters to the United States. Deregulation of the Japanese market after 1981, by comparison, had relatively little effect on the bilateral imbalance in terminal equipment. While Japanese imports from lower-cost Asian sources rose sharply, high U.S. labor costs continued to limit U.S. exports to a small range of specialty, software-intensive terminal equipment.

5.2.1   Economic Barriers to Entry

The economics of terminal equipment manufacturing traditionally did not erect perceptible barriers to entry. To begin, economies of scale were exhausted at very low rates of production. Huber (1987, 17-7) found that U.S. firms reached minimum efficient scale with as little as 3 percent market share, and Brock (1981, 235) confirmed that scale economies for terminal equipment were comparable to those for any other small electrical appliances. Production cost penalties therefore were unlikely to deter potential entrants from entering at a small scale.

Lack of access to manufacturing technologies also did not erect an economic barrier to entry in this industry. Technology for terminal equipment had grown increasingly standardized as a result of two forces. The first was the traditional routinization and labor intensification of manufacturing methods as the product cycle progressed, described by Vernon (1966).[12] The second was technology dissemination among firms that was hastened by AT&T's court-imposed obligation in 1956 to license its patents to all applicants at a "reasonable royalty." AT&T licenses proved to be particularly important to the development of Japan's telecommunications industry (Baughcum 1986, 83).

Finally, terminal equipment's inherent simplicity lessened possible barriers to entry from the demand side. Because terminal equipment required little customization or after-sale service, there was no economic necessity for the location of consumption to be tied geographically to the location of production. The position of terminal equipment as the final node in the telecommunications system would also facilitate entry. Each terminal instrument was linked to a network switch, rather than directly to other terminal equipment, thereby removing any technical necessity to assure complete uniformity among individual products.

The absence of economic barriers to entry has direct implications for industry structure, contracting practices, and foreign trade in terminal equipment. First, the U.S. market should have been able to support a large number of competitive suppliers. In practice, however, one firm—Western Electric—supplied over 85 percent of domestic terminal equipment demand. Second, non-discriminatory contracting should have been economically viable. In practice, however, terminal equipment was sold through exclusive contracts based on long-term supply relations. Finally, in an industry where economic barriers to entry were minimal, production locales should have been determined by relative factor costs. In 1975, average hourly compensation for manufacturing production employees was $6.36 in the United States, which compared with $3.05 in Japan and between $0.34 and $0.76 among smaller Asian producers (fig. 5.8, series 28–32).[13] Despite these substantial labor cost differentials, however, imported terminal equipment accounted for less than 2 percent of the U.S. (and Japanese) markets through the mid-1970s. In the absence of economic entry barriers, an explanation lies elsewhere for the U.S. terminal equipment indus-

12. As for many electronics products, the product life cycle for most telecommunications equipment involves a race to innovate leading-edge products followed by a race to routinize manufacturing processes to transform a proprietary device into a standardized commodity.

13. While time-series data on international labor costs are available only for a manufacturing composite, for at least one year these data are closely correlated in the cross section with compensation costs for electric and electronic equipment manufacturing. In 1983, average hourly compensation for this sector was $11.90 in the United States (compared with $12.10 for all manufacturing), $5.54 in Japan ($6.13), $1.29 in Korea ($1.20), and $1.31 in Taiwan ($1.27) (International Trade Administration 1986, 79).

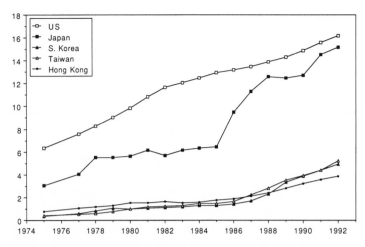

Fig. 5.8   Compensation costs for production workers in manufacturing industries (in current dollars per hour)
Source: International Comparisons of Hourly Compensation Costs for Production Workers in Manufacturing (1988, 1993).
Note: Compensation includes pay for time worked, other direct pay, social insurance, and private benefits.

try's extraordinarily high seller concentration, its reliance on exclusive supply contracts, and the apparent interdependence between supply and relative costs.

5.2.2   Regulatory Barriers to Entry in the United States

Until its divestiture on 1 January 1984, AT&T was both the largest manufacturer and the largest purchaser of telecommunications equipment in the United States. As the parent company for the Bell Telephone system, AT&T supplied all long-distance service through its Long Lines Department, while its twenty-four regional Bell operating companies (BOCs) supplied local service for 85 percent of the U.S. market.[14] AT&T's manufacturing subsidiary, Western Electric, supplied nearly all the entire Bell system's equipment requirements. Equipment was supplied under exclusive contracts, which established a multi-billion-dollar captive market for Western Electric. AT&T also owned the Bell Laboratories, which worked closely with the BOCs and Western Electric to develop and commercialize new equipment. This monopolistic market structure, which had evolved over decades of industry consolidation, was officially sanctioned by the Department of Justice in a 1956 consent decree that settled an antitrust complaint against AT&T.[15]

14. The remainder of the local market was served by a large number of independent telephone companies, of which GTE was the largest.
15. The antitrust complaint charged AT&T with a conspiracy to restrain trade in telephone service and charged AT&T's equipment subsidiary, Western Electric, with monopolizing the market for telephones and related equipment. The consent decree contained three central provisions:

Telecommunications was regulated at both the federal and state levels. The Federal Communications Commission (FCC) had jurisdiction for approving charges for interstate and international service, while states' public utility commissions (PUCs) set intrastate charges. Both agencies used traditional rate of return regulation, which set a maximum allowable profit rate for AT&T on telephone calls and equipment sales. Regulators also authorized the terms under which telephone service would be provided. Competitive entry was directly controlled by a regulatory mandate that "[n]o equipment, apparatus, circuit or device not furnished by the telephone company shall be attached to or connected with the facilities furnished by the telephone company" (Brock 1981, 239). The effect of this mandate was to prevent customers from legally purchasing a telephone from an independent company and then attaching it to AT&T's telecommunications network. While some unauthorized attachments did occur, AT&T aggressively monitored the number of telephones attached to each line, and the company penalized violators by seizing independent equipment or denying telephone service.

Entry was indirectly controlled further by regulations requiring subscribers to lease their terminal equipment from their local BOC, which in turn purchased the equipment exclusively from Western Electric. By tying telephone equipment to service, AT&T forced potential equipment suppliers to establish their own local telephone company to service their customers. State regulators generally declined to license new competitors in local telephone markets, and substantial economic barriers to entry existed in providing telephone service owing to large network economies. The result was that entry into telephone service was a roundabout and usually unprofitable route for entry into terminal equipment manufacturing. AT&T's tie-in strategy and exclusive supply arrangement with the BOCs therefore left little scope for competition in terminal equipment, from either domestic or foreign sources.

It is critical to underscore that telecommunications regulation provided AT&T with both the incentive to exclude competitors and the means to control equipment distribution. In the absence of a regulatory cap on its profit rate, AT&T could have charged (near) monopoly prices for telephone service. In an unregulated market, therefore, neither a tying arrangement nor exclusive contracting would have extended AT&T's market power from telephone service to the terminal equipment market because the monopoly profit could have been collected only once. Nor would an unregulated monopolist have chosen to manufacture terminal equipment unless it were the minimum-cost producer since a mandated purchase and leasing scheme would only have reduced the maximum profit that AT&T could extract from its (near) monopoly in tele-

---

First, as noted earlier, AT&T was required to license its patents on reasonable and nondiscriminatory terms. Second, AT&T was required to confine its activities to regulated common carrier service in the domestic market. Finally, Western Electric was permitted to manufacture equipment only for use within the Bell system.

phone service. In this situation, therefore, AT&T would have had no incentive to insist on leasing equipment to subscribers or to insist that its regional operating companies purchase their equipment under exclusive arrangements, unless these could be justified for purely cost-saving reasons.

But, under federal and state regulation, AT&T's allowable profit was constrained by the size of its rate base. Profits therefore depended on the firm's costs, and higher costs implied larger revenues and greater allowable profits, provided that demand was inelastic. A regulated AT&T therefore would profit by extending its (constrained) monopoly power from telephone service into the terminal equipment market by using sales under the tie-in and exclusive supply contract to expand its rate base. Regulation thus enabled a telephone company that controlled terminal equipment to earn profits on its sale *twice:* once at the manufacturing stage, by charging its subsidiaries inflated prices, and then again as profit on the rate base for the local telephone company, which leased the equipment to subscribers. If the BOCs had been allowed to purchase equipment from competitive sources, in lieu of the exclusive supply contracts, AT&T's downstream source of profit would have been eliminated by shrinkage of its rate base. And, if telephone subscribers had been permitted to purchase terminal equipment from competitive sources in lieu of the tie-in, both sources of AT&T profit would have been eliminated by shrinking the rate bases of both AT&T and the BOCs.[16]

Facing these regulatory incentives, AT&T vigorously protected its (near) monopoly by consistently opposing entrants' attempts to liberalize regulations governing independent equipment attachments. The first attempt to challenge AT&T's control over attachments to the network came in 1956 with the Hush-a-Phone case. The Hush-a-Phone was a simple cuplike device that snapped onto the end of a telephone to provide speaking privacy and shield out surrounding noises. The manufacturer of Hush-a-Phone petitioned the FCC to allow the attachment to be sold directly to telephone subscribers. AT&T vigorously opposed the petition, asserting that the device threatened network service quality. After protracted legal battles, the FCC eventually sided with Hush-a-Phone but tailored its ruling narrowly to carve out an exception solely for this device. The potential effect of the FCC ruling was dampened further when its implementation was left to local telephone companies, which engaged in delaying tactics for more than two decades before terminal equipment markets finally were opened to competition.

16. AT&T's tying of telephone equipment to service also facilitated nonlinear price discrimination that would not have been feasible in the absence of regulation. Subscribers that attach a higher valuation to service tend to demand more telephones per line. To charge a higher effective price per call to those subscribers, nonlinear price discrimination would combine a relatively low rate for telephone service with a relatively high leasing fee for terminal equipment. Because this metered pricing scheme placed the largest price-cost markup on the product for which entry was easiest (terminal equipment), however, a formal tying arrangement was necessary to support price discrimination. Regulatory barriers to entry in local telephone service markets provided the means for enforcing this tie-in and further raised AT&T's profits.

AT&T repelled a second entry challenge in 1986. The Carterphone was a relatively simple attachment that converted telephone signals into radio signals for broadcast to a mobile radio/telephone. AT&T opposed the Carter Electric Company's attempt to sell the attachment directly to final users. The FCC eventually ruled in Carter's favor but allowed AT&T to require purchasers of the Carterphone to lease a telephone-company-supplied coupling device for the asserted purpose of protecting the network from harm. In some cases, the charge for the protective device was as high as the monthly charge for basic telephone service (Brock 1981, 242). This discriminatory fee was structured to make it uneconomical for Carter to sell its attachment except to subscribers with very large telephone systems. The result was that FCC policy continued to maintain entry barriers in most of the U.S. terminal equipment market.

5.2.3   Deregulation of the U.S. Market

Under increasing domestic political pressure, the FCC began a gradual process of opening terminal equipment markets to competition, starting in the mid-1970s.[17] An initial opportunity to lower regulatory barriers to entry came in October 1975 with the FCC's first order registration program. The program sought to provide non-Bell equipment manufacturers with controlled access to AT&T's subscriber network. The FCC proposed to test independents' equipment, certify products that posed "no harm" to network quality, and permit those products to be attached legally to telephone lines by subscribers. In practice, however, the program did little to facilitate entry. Its narrow scope excluded the majority of terminal equipment (telephones, key sets, and PBXs), and AT&T and its subsidiary BOCs succeeded in delaying implementation of the modest deregulation order for two years.

The first meaningful deregulation of the U.S. terminal equipment market occurred in October 1977 with the adoption of the second order registration program. The program permitted telephone subscribers to attach directly most types of non–Western Electric terminal equipment (including telephones, key sets, and PBXs) to the AT&T network. Competitive entry quickly followed this partial lowering of regulatory entry barriers, confirming that, in the absence of economic barriers, supply would be determined by relative factor costs. Between 1977 and 1978, real imports of terminal equipment jumped 30 percent (from $11.2 to $44.1 million), and import penetration rose from 1.4 to 4.5 percent. During this period, Japan supplied approximately 45 percent of U.S. terminal equipment imports, amounting to just over 2 percent of total U.S. purchases (U.S. International Trade Commission 1984, table H-14). While imports grew rapidly, market access remained limited by an FCC requirement that subscribers notify their local telephone company when they attached non–Western Electric equipment. As with the earlier entry threat from Carterphone,

---

17. Appendix B provides a time line of major regulatory changes.

AT&T used this regulatory loophole to monitor attachments and to charge a discriminatory fee to subscribers using independent equipment. Surveillance proved to be very costly, however, and compliance rates with the FCC requirement were estimated at only 20 percent, indicating that the second order registration program did in fact begin to lower regulatory entry barriers (Brock 1981, 251).

Entry barriers were lowered again in 1980 when the FCC removed terminal equipment from rate-of-return regulation and required AT&T to sell terminal equipment to telephone subscribers directly rather than indirectly leasing equipment through the BOCs.[18] The immediate effect of the FCC order was to remove terminal equipment from AT&T's and the BOCs' rate bases. Because rate-of-return regulation had been the sole rationale for AT&T's exclusionary practice of tying telephone equipment and service, deregulation therefore eliminated AT&T's incentive to monopolize the local terminal equipment market. The result was a second surge in U.S. terminal equipment imports. Between 1980 and 1981, real imports of terminal equipment rose from $56.2 to $132.5 million, and imports increased as a share of domestic consumption from 5.9 to 11.2 percent in the same year (fig. 5.3 above, series 8 and 9). Japan's import share rose to 54 percent during this period, and its share of the U.S. market increased to just over 6 percent (U.S. International Trade Commission 1984, table H-14).

The final—and furthest-reaching—deregulation order was issued in August 1982, with the announcement of the Modification of Final Judgment (MFJ) as an out-of-court settlement to a 1974 antitrust suit against AT&T.[19] Under the terms of the MFJ, AT&T agreed to fully divest itself from the local BOCs by 1 January 1984. The centerpiece of the divestiture order was the severing of exclusive equipment supply contracts that had prevailed for five decades between AT&T and the BOCs. After 1982, the local telephone companies—which the MFJ now grouped into seven regional holding companies (RHCs)—were permitted to purchase terminal equipment directly from independent manufacturers. Henceforth, all equipment contracts involving AT&T were required to be negotiated on arm's-length, nonpreferential terms. The MFJ also prohibited the RHCs from vertically integrating upstream to supply their internal demand for telephone equipment. By divorcing the local carriers from their former parent company, requiring competitive contracting, and precluding self-supply, the MFJ removed the last remaining regulatory barriers to entry in the U.S. terminal equipment market.[20]

The conclusion of deregulation precipitated another surge in terminal equipment imports. Between 1982 and 1984, real imports jumped from $136.0 to

18. The order resulted from the FCC's Computer II Inquiry.

19. The agreement is known as the Modification of Final Judgment because it modified the terms of the original consent decree that the industry had operated under since 1956.

20. Under the MFJ's terms, AT&T was allowed to continue producing its own equipment for long-distance service. Western Electric was renamed AT&T Technologies after 1982.

$466.7 million, and import penetration tripled from 11.6 to 37.5 percent (fig. 5.3 above, series 8 and 9). During this period, Japan remained the largest foreign supplier of terminal equipment in the United States with a 14 percent share of all purchases, reflecting its 50 percent manufacturing labor cost advantage. However, Japan's share of U.S. imports also started to decline, falling from 54 percent in 1981 to 46 percent in 1982 and then 37 percent in 1983 as smaller, lower-cost Asian producers began large-scale manufacturing of terminal equipment (U.S. International Trade Commission 1984, table H-14).

Telecommunications regulation in the United States and most other industrialized countries had historically constrained terminal equipment manufacturers worldwide to supply only their local market. For Hong Kong, South Korea, and Taiwan, which had small domestic telecommunications markets, foreign regulatory barriers precluded expansion of capacity to exploit their considerable manufacturing labor cost advantage (fig. 5.8 above, series 28 and 30–31). Final deregulation of the U.S. terminal equipment market in 1982, however, opened a potential marketplace of 93 million telephone lines (Organization for Economic Cooperation and Development 1991, table 1). This market opportunity prompted large-scale investments in telecommunications equipment manufacturing in Hong Kong, South Korea and Taiwan, which permitted rapid growth in export sales to the U.S. market. In 1979, the three countries accounted for just 8.5 percent of U.S. imports of terminal equipment (and 0.3 percent of U.S. consumption). By 1982, their import share had risen to 28.4 percent (3.3 percent of U.S. consumption), and, by 1983, it had reached 45.3 percent (15.4 percent of U.S. consumption) (U.S. International Trade Commission 1984, table H-14).[21]

Between 1985 and 1988, Japanese manufacturing labor costs jumped 82 percent, bringing them to within 91 percent of U.S. rates (fig. 5.8 above, series 28 and 29). In response, terminal equipment production continued to shift toward Hong Kong, South Korea, and Taiwan, which maintained between a seven-to-one and ten-to-one labor cost advantage. After 1985, U.S. imports from the rest of Asia grew nine times as rapidly as imports from Japan (series 16 and 22). The import surge after 1985 was short-lived, however, as real U.S. terminal equipment demand peaked in 1986. Beginning in 1987, real consumption began falling in response to saturation of the U.S. market after five years of imports of generic terminal equipment from Asia. Thus, while real import growth slowed appreciably after 1986, when combined with an average 8.2 percent annual decline in real consumption between 1986 and 1992, import penetration rates continued rising and eventually exceeded 90 percent in this market (series 9).[22]

21. Individual country import shares in 1979 (and 1983) were as follows: Hong Kong, 1.8 percent (14.8 percent); South Korea, 3.4 percent (10.3 percent); and Taiwan, 3.2 percent (20.2 percent).

22. Real consumption of terminal equipment fell from $1.54 billion in 1986 to $961 million in 1992. Import penetration during this period grew from 55.3 to 88.1 percent (*Electronic Market Data Book* 1994).

5.2.4   Regulation and Deregulation in Japan

Japan's telecommunications equipment market closely resembled its American counterpart, the result of common economic fundamentals and very similar regulatory structures. In 1952, Nippon Telegraph and Telephone (NTT) was established as a publicly owned monopoly supplier of telephone service. Regulations by Japan's Ministry of Posts and Telecommunications (MPT) required telephone subscribers to lease their terminal equipment directly from NTT, which purchased equipment under a preferential agreement from a small family of suppliers headed by the Nippon Electronic Corporation (NEC).[23] NTT was given exclusive authority by the MPT to approve communications equipment for attachment to its network. NTT established technical specifications for equipment that were based on specific design criteria rather than general performance standards and wrote these specifications to favor NEC family members. NTT's certification procedures were complex and time consuming, and independent equipment manufacturers frequently faced difficulties in convincing NTT to divulge even what the technical criteria were. Further, for more sophisticated terminal equipment such as key telephones, separate approval was required for each individual installation.

These regulatory barriers and preferential contracting practices (supported by regulatory authority) effectively curtailed entry into terminal equipment manufacturing. Few Japanese manufacturers that were not associated with the NEC family supplied equipment to NTT. Japanese imports of terminal equipment from the United States totaled just $121,000 in 1978 (U.S. Congress 1980, 27). The strongest evidence of regulatory barriers, however, is found in the fact that Japan's overall import penetration ratio for terminal equipment was only 1.2 percent in 1978, despite Japan's six-to-one manufacturing labor cost disadvantage relative to small producers in Hong Kong, South Korea, and Taiwan (fig. 5.8 above, series 29–32) (*Japan Electronics Almanac* 1984, table 7).

Deregulation of Japanese telecommunications commenced four years after initial liberalization in the United States. In January 1981, the Japanese market was partially deregulated to permit telephone subscribers to purchase some terminal equipment directly from independent manufacturers. However, NTT retained its monopoly for supplying the first telephone in a subscriber's premises and retained its authority to inspect and certify independent equipment for compliance with technical standards before it could be connected to the network. Shortly thereafter, however, certification procedures were significantly liberalized by NTT's decision to accept test data from independent manufacturers to expedite certification of their products.[24] After 1981, NTT approved most

23. The NEC family included NEC, Fujitsu, Hitachi, and Oki. An exception to the mandatory equipment leases applied to large PBXs, where NTT allowed direct dealings between equipment suppliers and telephone subscribers.

24. NTT's revised procedures were pursuant to the Understanding on the Interconnect Market negotiated with the United States in 1981.

requests for attachments of independent terminal equipment (U.S. General Accounting Office 1983, 15). Despite deregulation, however, the U.S. share of the Japanese market rose just marginally to 1.1 percent (*Japan Electronics Almanac* 1984, table 7; U.S. International Trade Commission 1984, table H-14; *U.S. Industrial Outlook* 1984). While U.S. export continued to face some regulatory barriers to entering the Japanese market, the primary obstacle remained high U.S. manufacturing labor costs. For this reason, exports of terminal equipment to Japan were limited to software-intensive devices such as video conferencing and voice processing that required skilled assembly.

Deregulation of Japan's terminal equipment market was completed in April 1985, amid trade frictions with the United States and pressure from large Japanese telecommunications users seeking lower charges. The NTT Company Law and the Telecommunications Business Law were enacted to institute three regulatory reforms. First, NTT's monopoly over subscribers' first telephone was rescinded. Second, authority for equipment approval was removed from NTT and placed in an independent standards board, the Japan Approval Institute for Telecommunications, which instituted simplified and transparent certification procedures (Choy 1995). Finally, NTT was converted into a semiprivate corporation subject to competition from independent telephone service providers that were not tied to the NEC equipment family.

Despite apparent compliance by NTT with each reform, removal of these final regulatory barriers again had little effect on U.S. terminal equipment exports to Japan.[25] That the United States was at a 50 percent manufacturing labor cost disadvantage remained the central impediment limiting its exports to just 10 percent of Japan's total purchases of foreign terminal equipment. While U.S. exports rose by 30 percent after Japanese deregulation, they remained less than $5 million in total. By contrast, Japanese deregulation spurred rapid growth in terminal equipment production among smaller Asian countries, where manufacturing labor costs were one-quarter to one-seventh. After 1985, Japanese imports of terminal equipment from South Korea, Hong Kong, and Taiwan increased 160 percent annually. Asian imports accounted for 88 percent of total Japanese purchases of foreign terminal equipment and in absolute level were nine times greater than U.S. imports (*Japan Electronics Almanac* 1989, 165–67).

5.2.5 Summary

Regulatory policy played a dominant role in shaping terminal equipment markets in the United States and Japan. Despite minimal economic barriers to entry, regulatory barriers created and protected local monopolies that suppressed competitive entry. The result was that, through the mid-1970s, imports constituted less than 2 percent of U.S. and Japanese terminal equipment pur-

---

25. U.S. telecommunications companies generally attested to Japanese compliance with the 1985 reforms (U.S. General Accounting Office 1988, 22–23).

chases, despite substantial manufacturing labor cost disadvantages in both countries relative to low-age Asian sources. Deregulation occurred first in the United States, starting in 1977 and culminating in the 1982–84 dissolution of the Bell system. Deregulation followed in Japan between 1981 and 1985. In both countries, imports from comparatively lower-cost sources grew rapidly following deregulation. Japan benefited from U.S. deregulation and gained a substantial market share, only to be supplanted in the second half of the 1980s by still lower-cost Asian suppliers. In contrast, after Japanese deregulation, high factor costs continued to limit U.S. terminal equipment exports to a small range of complex, specialty products. The combined effect of deregulation in the U.S. and Japanese markets, therefore, was to create a substantial U.S. trade deficit immediately following the opening of those markets to competition.

5.3   Trade Conflicts in Network Equipment

This section assesses how domestic market structure and procurement practices in the United States and Japan shaped bilateral trade in network equipment. In both countries, trade historically had been limited by the presence of domestic monopoly suppliers with preferential ties to local service providers. This market structure was favored by the coexistence of substantial scale economies in production and network economies in demand. These economic entry barriers were reinforced by regulatory policies that favored exclusive supply relations and set design standards to exclude competitors. Economic and regulatory barriers together limited network equipment imports to less than 5 percent of the U.S. market and less than 1 percent of the Japanese market through the late 1970s (*Electronic Market Data Book* 1979; *Japan Electronics Almanac* 1984, table 7).

Entry barriers into the U.S. network equipment market were lowered by two complementary events. Together, they created a window of market contestability. The first event was the introduction of digital switches in 1977 by Canada's Northern Telecom, which offered substantial cost and quality advantages over AT&T's installed analog switching system. Digital technology threatened to erode economic barriers to entry by depreciating AT&T's sunk investments in its analog network. The second event was the Modification of Final Judgment in 1982, which split the Bell system. This regulatory reform directly undermined economic barriers to entry by proactively severing AT&T's exclusive equipment supply contracts with local telephone companies. Entry by Canadian and Japanese network equipment imports quickly followed the MFJ's adoption. In Japan, by contrast, economic barriers remained largely in place as a result of NTT's decision to delay adoption of digital switches in its local network, even as Japanese equipment producers were beginning to export digital technology. Japanese deregulation in 1985 also failed to encourage entry as it merely sanctioned competitive contracting without proactively severing existing supply relations. Asymmetries in market structure and contracting practices that persisted after deregulation explain why entry by Japanese (and Canadian) network equipment imports quickly followed U.S. deregulation while U.S. exports responded only weakly to Japanese deregulation.

5.3.1 Economic Barriers to Entry

Network equipment differs importantly from terminal equipment in its technology and demand characteristics. The practical effect of these differences is that, while terminal equipment markets and contracting could be structured competitively, network equipment's technology and demand characteristics encourage monopolistic market structures and preferential supply arrangements that discourage competitive entry. On the production side, substantial economies of scale naturally limit the viable number of suppliers for network equipment. Variable material costs are low, while the fixed investment associated with developing and fine-tuning a line of digital switches can require a five- to ten-year expenditure of $1–$1.5 billion (Hausman and Kohlberg 1989, 203). To recover this sunk expenditure, a firm requires between a 10 and a 15 percent share of the world market in switching equipment (Huber 1987, 14–18). Scale economies have permitted the survival of just seven switch manufacturers worldwide. Each firm historically enjoyed preferential procurement ties to its national telephone service carrier: AT&T (in the United States), NEC (Japan), Northern Telecom (Canada), Siemens (Germany), Ericsson (Sweden), Alcatel (France), and Plessey (the United Kingdom).[26]

On the demand side, network complementarities imply that the network's value rises proportionately with the number of interconnected subscribers. These connections are made through central office switches, which act as the central nervous system of the telephone network. Routing telephone signals within an exchange and between exchanges requires that switches be able to communicate with one another. For this reason, telephone companies consistently rate compatibility with existing equipment as among the most important criteria when selecting their current supplier of network switches (U.S. International Trade Commission 1984, table 9). Because switches are embedded with proprietary technologies, the simplest manner for a telephone company to ensure network compatibility is to limit procurement to a small number of suppliers. Accordingly, most telephone companies historically have contracted with no more than two suppliers for central office switches (Vietor and Yoffie 1993, 138). Opportunities for recontracting occur infrequently because of the very long replacement cycle for switches. For example, the mean time between failures for AT&T's 5ESS digital switch is approximately forty years, which implies that, once a contract is let, AT&T remains strongly favored for upgrades and add-on purchases for four decades. Together, the technology and

---

26. Economics of scale also extend to other network equipment. For example, AT&T produces all its transmission equipment and fiber cable at a single plant in the United States, as it does for switch production.

demand characteristics of network switches strongly encourage purchasers to develop long-term, exclusive relations with their suppliers, with the result that traditional sources retain an advantage over potential entrants into a market.

5.3.2   Regulatory Barriers to Entry in the United States

Complementing these economic barriers to entry were U.S. regulatory policies that directly limited both import and export trade in network equipment. Prior to AT&T's divestiture of the local BOCs in 1982, imports remained less than 8 percent of total purchases, and exports remained below 15 percent of industry shipments (series 11 and 13).

Western Electric retained its effective monopoly over network equipment supply through 1982.[27] During this time, AT&T accounted for more than 80 percent of U.S. purchases of central office equipment, and Western Electric manufactured most of the Bell system's requirements. The remaining equipment was purchased from independent suppliers and then resold by Western Electric, acting as the BOCs' exclusive procurement agent. The 1956 consent decree sanctioned these exclusive contracts and also required the BOCs to provide Western Electric with advance notice of proposed equipment purchases. In a 1974 antitrust suit against AT&T, the government contended that this arrangement gave Western Electric sufficient lead time to preempt entry by independent suppliers.

Regulatory policy further discouraged entry into the U.S. market by establishing unique network equipment design standards. The U.S. operated under the North American standard for most switching equipment, while the rest of the world generally followed standards developed by the International Telecommunications Union. The result was the balkanization of much of the world network equipment market for an extended period. Entering the U.S. market required that a foreign manufacturer adapt its equipment to conform with U.S. standards, at a cost ranging up to $500 million for central office switches. Often, the difficulties of customizing switches for the U.S. market proved to be insurmountable. After investing several hundreds of millions of dollars trying to adapt its switch for the United States, France's Alcatel abandoned its attempts at entry (Vietor and Yoffie 1993, 138–39).

U.S. exports of network equipment likewise were limited by the 1956 consent decree, which confined AT&T to domestic, regulated markets. The decree sought to prevent AT&T from exploiting its status as a regulated service provider to cross-subsidize export sales. While an unregulated firm could not benefit from subsidizing some customers at the expense of others, AT&T could have profited by lowering its export price in the (unregulated) foreign market, shifting capital costs from those sales into its rate base, and then raising its

---

27. The early deregulation orders in the late 1970s (discussed in sec. 5.2) pertained only to terminal equipment contracting and therefore did not disturb the preferential supply arrangements for network equipment.

regulated price to domestic customers in order to recoup forgone export revenues. To avoid this unintended consequence of domestic regulation, the consent decree simply precluded AT&T's expansion into export markets.

5.3.3   Deregulation of the U.S. Market

In contrast to terminal equipment markets, where the removal of regulatory barriers to entry was sufficient to allow international trade to occur, trade in network equipment required reductions in *both* regulatory and economic barriers. The coincidence of a major technological advance in network switching and the forced severing of existing supply relations by regulators was responsible for opening the U.S. network equipment market to international trade.

In 1977, Northern Telecom introduced digital central office switches and sparked the first major shift in the Bell system's procurement of network equipment.[28] Digital switching represented a technological breakthrough. Compared with the Bell system's installed network of analog equipment, digital technologies made possible unprecedented advances in the quality, speed, and capacity of call routing. According to Johnson (1993, 10), Northern Telecom's lead in digital switching was so commanding that it was able to overcome the BOCs' traditional reluctance to deal with new suppliers. Between 1977 and 1980, AT&T began integrating Northern Telecom switches into its network, and U.S. real imports rose by 150 percent (series 12). Northern Telecom also established a U.S. subsidiary, Northern Telecom International, to manufacture central office switches (COSs) locally. Despite Northern Telecom's early success, however, import penetration had reached just over 7 percent by 1980, reflecting the premium that remained on preserving compatibility within the existing analog network.

Not until the MFJ fully deregulated the U.S. market in 1982 were regulatory and economic entry barriers eroded sufficiently to allow substantial U.S. import trade in network equipment. Between 1982 and 1984, import penetration jumped from 7.8 to 16.3 percent as real imports more than tripled from $319.3 to $983.3 million (fig. 5.4 above, series 12 and 13). The effect of this import surge in network equipment is seen clearly in the U.S. overall trade balance for telecommunications equipment. Figures 5.1 and 5.2 above (series 1 and 5) date 1982 as the beginning of the secular decline in the industry's aggregate trade balance.

The 1982 MFJ has been described as "the greatest unilateral removal of a non-tariff barrier in international trade history" (Robinson 1991, 438). Prior to this order, open markets for telecommunications equipment were limited to less than 15 percent of total world demand, according to OECD estimates

28. Until 1956, Northern Telecom had been controlled by AT&T and had manufactured equipment designed by Western Electric and the Bell Telephone Laboratories. When the 1956 consent decree forced Western Electric to divest its foreign operations, AT&T complied by selling Northern Telecom to Bell Canada. Ironically, regulatory policy set the stage for the eventual entry of network equipment imports into the U.S. market.

(Noam 1989, 288). The breakup of AT&T more than doubled the potential market open to foreign equipment suppliers. Deregulation severed long-standing, exclusive supply relations at the time when digital switches were just beginning to be integrated into the U.S. telecommunications network. The combination of AT&T's breakup and growing demand for digital switching thus established a window of contestability in the mid-1980s. This window provided network equipment suppliers with their first real opportunity to penetrate the U.S. market.

The terms of AT&T's divestiture of the local exchanges steered the newly created regional holding companies (RHCs) toward purchasing a greater fraction of their network equipment from foreign suppliers. The deregulation order did this in three ways. First, and most directly, AT&T was forced to sever its preferential supply relations between Western Electric and the BOCs. While Western Electric (now renamed AT&T Technologies) was permitted to continue selling network equipment, all transactions had to be at arm's-length, and the RHCs could not show preference for AT&T equipment when "other procurement conditions were roughly equal." The divestiture also barred the RHCs from vertically integrating upstream to manufacture their own network equipment. Deregulation thus disrupted two obvious sources of supply for the RHCs. The result, not unexpectedly, was a sharp decline in AT&T sales of network equipment. However, because AT&T had controlled 85 percent of the domestic market prior to deregulation, few alternative *domestic* manufacturers were available to replace those sales.[29] Thus, it was inevitable that severing the industry's existing supply arrangements would lead to a surge in *imported* equipment.

Second, the MFJ provided an additional, one-time stimulus to the RHCs' demand for digital central office switches.that encouraged additional entry. To enable telephone subscribers to choose among competing long-distance carriers, the MFJ mandated that RHCs install switches that would provide "equal access" to their local network for all interexchange carriers. Existing analog switches in the Bell system could not be modified easily to provide equal access. This forced the RHCs to shift more quickly toward adopting digital switching technologies, whose flexibility allowed equal access. Again, under the terms of the MFJ, this new demand was satisfied primarily by unaffiliated suppliers, which, in the absence of significant independent domestic capacity, led to foreign entry. By the mid-1980s, however, almost all lines had been converted over to equal access, leading to a slowdown in new switch orders and, in turn, in imports.

Finally, the combination of deregulation and asset specificity in network equipment created a strategic incentive for the RHCs to diversify among suppliers. The fact that switches must be customized and carefully integrated into

---

29. The largest independent U.S. equipment supplier, GTE, had only a 3 percent share of the domestic digital switch market in 1982 (Crandall 1991, 84).

a telecommunications system creates the potential for postcontractual opportunistic behavior or holdups between contracting parties. The regulated Bell system solved this holdup problem through vertical integration between the dominant supplier of equipment (AT&T and its subsidiary Western Electric) and the major purchasers of equipment (the local BOCs). When deregulation split the Bell system, the potential for holdups between AT&T (as the supplier) and the RHCs (as independent purchasers) reemerged and created the strategic incentive for RHCs to diversify their equipment suppliers. The fear of holdups contributed to the RHCs' decision to purchase a greater fraction of their network equipment from foreign sources after deregulation.

Seven years after Northern Telecom's introduction of digital switches, and two years after the MFJ's implementation, import penetration in network equipment had risen to 16.3 percent (series 13). Both events played critical—and complementary—roles in opening the U.S. market to foreign trade. Their complementarity is evidenced by comparing Northern Telecom's sales before and after deregulation and by comparing sales by Northern Telecom and other foreign suppliers in the United States. While Northern Telecom's introduction of digital switches revolutionized network technology and gave the firm a potential early mover advantage, not until the MFJ severed AT&T's existing procurement contracts did Northern Telecom begin exporting switches in large volume to the United States. For example, U.S. imports from Canada (which consisted almost entirely of network equipment from Northern Telecom) rose in real terms only from $111.7 to $138.8 million between 1978 and 1981 but had grown to $342.8 million by the time the MFJ was fully implemented in 1984 (series 25). At the same time, while Northern Telecom's penetration was contingent on deregulation, its early entry into digital technology did confer an advantage over foreign competitors. For example, by 1989, Northern Telecom had grown to account for 58 percent of the import market for COSs and PBXs, while Japanese firms (NEC, Fujitsu, Toshiba, and Hitachi) held just a 19 percent share, and European firms (Siemens, Ericsson, and Mitel) held a 23 percent share.[30] In countries where telecommunications equipment systems were less extensive—and procurement relationships were less firmly entrenched—by comparison, other foreign suppliers gained dominant market shares. For example, NEC supplied 80% of Thailand's demand for COSs, 60% in Malaysia and 50% in Argentina (Vietor and Yoffie 1993, 172).

Deregulation created only a temporary window of contestability, however. This window was opened between 1982 and 1985, when U.S. demand for network equipment doubled from $3.06 to $5.99 billion (*Electronic Market Data Book* 1983, 1986). Responding to this opportunity, real imports more than tripled from $319.3 to $998.5 million during these three years (series 12). Because network switches have an average forty-year life span, however, contract opportunities again closed quickly after this date. Between 1985 and 1988,

---

30. My calculations, based on data in Vietor and Yoffie (1993, 162).

real demand for network equipment declined by 5 percent, real import growth slowed markedly, and the trade balance in this industry segment returned to its historical position of a small surplus.

Finally, deregulation also removed restrictions barring AT&T equipment exports that had been in place since the 1956 consent decree. AT&T was partially successful at exporting large PBXs and COSs, but export sales continued to be constrained by procurement regulations in importing markets. With the exception of the United Kingdom, which had privatized its telecommunications network in 1984, European equipment markets were not effectively deregulated until 1987, when technical standards were harmonized within the European Community and equal access requirements were mandated (Vietor and Yoffie 1993, 148–51). Thereafter, U.S. network equipment exports grew rapidly and were driven primarily by European liberalization (fig. 5.4 above, series 11).[31]

5.3.4   Regulation and Deregulation in Japan

The same regulatory policies governing Japan's terminal equipment market also covered sales of network equipment. Until 1985, NTT retained sole authority to lease and sell network equipment, which it purchased almost exclusively from a family of four suppliers headed by NEC. NTT's preferential supply relations were very similar to those negotiated between AT&T and the BOCs, although NTT itself was not vertically integrated into manufacturing. As with AT&T, these relations excluded both domestic and foreign sources of competition. Entry by independent Japanese equipment manufacturers into the approved family of suppliers were extremely rare. Likewise, as late as three years prior to deregulation, fewer than 1 percent of Japanese purchases of switching equipment were imports (Curran 1982, 194; *Japan Electronics Almanac* 1984, table 7).

In contrast to AT&T, equipment exports by the NEC family were not restricted by Japanese regulatory policy. However, exports remained limited by foreign regulatory and economic barriers. Prior to the MFJ's opening of the U.S. network equipment market in 1982, for example, only 10 percent of all Japanese switch exports were sold in the United States. (By comparison, significantly lower regulatory and economic barriers in the U.S. terminal equipment market by this date allowed Japan to sell 52 percent of these exports in the United States [*Japan Electronics Almanac* 1984, table 6].) Major destinations for Japanese switch exports were Asia and Central and South America, where telecommunications networks were less extensively developed and supply relations therefore were less firmly entrenched.

Japan's network equipment market was partially deregulated in 1985 with the passage of the NTT Company Law and the Telecommunications Business Law. Unlike deregulation three years earlier in the United States, which led to

---

31. Japanese exports to Europe also began rising sharply around this period, as indicated in fig. 5.7 above.

modest growth in import penetration, however, Japanese deregulation had very little effect on import trade and, in particular, on imports of U.S. network equipment. Three factors contributed to this asymmetry. First, Japanese deregulation simply withdrew government enforcement of exclusive procurement contracts without proactively severing existing supply relations. Deregulation converted NTT into a semiprivate corporation subject to competition from rivals who were not tied to the NEC equipment family. While this reform led to a gradual weakening of NEC-NTT procurement ties, it stopped well short of AT&T's divestiture of the BOCs, which both severed existing supply contracts and prompted a one-time demand surge to fulfill AT&T's equal access obligations. The NTT Company Law explicitly rejected a government commission's recommendation that NTT be forced to divest its local telephone operations in favor of new carriers (Harris 1988, 15). The result was that economic barriers to entry remained largely intact even after regulatory barriers were removed. Five years after Japanese deregulation, therefore, import penetration in switching equipment had risen to just 4.1 percent, and the U.S. share of the Japanese market had risen to just 2.9 percent (*Japan Electronics Almanac* 1993, 1994).[32]

The second factor explaining the asymmetric trade response following Japanese and U.S. deregulation stems from NTT's decision to maintain its analog switching network domestically, long after the introduction of Northern Telecom's digital switches. NEC, Fujitsu, and Hitachi each had developed digital COSs for the export market and had made preliminary sales to several regional exchanges in the United States (Hausman and Kohlberg 1989, 199). Despite the fact that these three firms also were members of the NEC family of preferred equipment suppliers in Japan, however, NTT chose to attempt to develop its own digital system for its local network. During the interim, existing analog switches remained in place. As late as 1980, only 26.7 percent of Japan's COSs had been converted over to digital, as compared to 44.6 percent of U.S. switches (McKinsey Global Institute 1992, exhibit 2E-14). the effect of this delayed introduction was to sharply limit Japanese demand for digital switches, including imported switches.

Finally, U.S. exports were hampered by Northern Telecom's earlier entry into digital technology. To the degree that Japanese deregulation opened its network equipment market to competition, entry was by Northern Telecom rather than AT&T. In the largest single procurement from a foreign supplier, AT&T lost a $250 million contract to supply central office switches to NTT for a six-year period beginning in 1987 (International Trade Administration 1986, 83). Northern Telecom's nearly ten years of production experience with digital switching provided the firm with a head start in penetrating the Japanese market.

32. For the comparable period centered around the AT&T divestiture, by comparison, U.S. import penetration for network equipment rose from 6.6 to 16.3 percent (*Electronic Market Data Book* 1982, 1990).

5.3.5   Summary

Regulatory policy played a complementary role with economic barriers to entry in shaping network equipment markets in the United States and Japan. In both countries, regulatory agencies supported business practices that sustained near monopoly control over the supply of network equipment. Deregulation led to trade only when it lowered both regulatory and economic barriers to entry. In the United States, the sequential introduction of digital switching and the proactive severing of existing supply relations met this condition. Imports rose, from both Canada and Japan, although the continuation of sunk investments in network equipment encouraged a substantially lower level of import penetration than arose in terminal equipment after deregulation. In Japan, delayed adoption of digital technologies and deregulation's failure to sever existing supply relations meant that economic barriers remained largely intact. This, combined with Northern Telecom's early mover advantage in digital switches, sharply limited U.S. exports of network equipment to Japan. The combined effect of regulatory changes in the United States and Japan, therefore, was to further expand the bilateral trade imbalance.

5.4   Lessons and Open Issues

A central conclusion of this paper is that domestic competition policy—and regulatory policy in particular—can have major repercussions for international trade. Telecommunications deregulation in the United States, and to a lesser extent in Japan, was driven primarily by domestic policy objectives and political realities (Noll and Rosenbluth 1993). Despite policy makers' inward focus, the deconcentration in market structure and opening of procurement networks that followed deregulation had profound implications for the industry's trade balance. These changes pushed telecommunications equipment to the top of the international trade policy agenda early in the Reagan administration, where it remained a source of friction between the United States and Japan for the remainder of the decade.

A second conclusion drawn from the analysis relates to the common intransigence of American and Japanese telecommunications service monopolies to accept competitive entry into equipment supply. U.S. trade negotiators have tended to overlook this commonality in order to enhance their current bargaining position. The USTR accused NTT of using discriminatory and needlessly stringent product standards to deter entry into its network and cellular equipment markets. Japan's historic reliance on stringent "voice quality" standards, in contrast to the U.S. practice of approving equipment provided that it did "no harm to the network," was a focal point of trade tensions during the MOSS negotiations. The arguments raised by U.S. trade negotiators against NTT, however, bear a striking resemblance to the complaints raised by AT&T's

would-be competitors during the 1950s. AT&T's success in excluding the innocuous Hush-a-Phone attachment for twenty years, arguing that it would harm network quality, attests to the common incentive of incumbent firms to use available regulatory barriers to maintain their monopoly position.

Finally, ongoing regulatory changes in telecommunications can be expected again to have important implications for international trade. Japan's Ministry of Posts and Telecommunications has proposed a divestiture of NTT modeled after the vertical disintegration of AT&T in 1982–84. NTT successfully resisted this reform when it was first proposed in 1985, but it now stands poised for a major reorganization in market structure and contracting ties to equipment suppliers. If these reforms are adopted, they would further erode economic barriers within Japan's telecommunications equipment market and could be expected to narrow the bilateral trade imbalance in network equipment. In the United States, passage of the proposed Telecommunications Act will expand deregulation by allowing regional telephone companies to provide long distance service and erode the regional BOCs' local service monopolies by allowing AT&T and cable television companies to enter these markets. To the extent that local service monopolies have mimicked AT&T's pre-1982 exclusionary equipment contracting practices, deregulation may further open the U.S. network equipment market to entry and international trade.

Appendix A

Table 5A.1   **Industry Data**

	Series 1, Telecom. Equip. Trade Balance ÷ Shipments (Fig. 5.1) (%)	Series 2, Merchandise Trade Balance ÷ GNP (Fig. 5.1) (%)	Series 3, Durables Trade Balance ÷ Shipments (Fig. 5.1) (%)	Series 4, Advanced-Technology Trade Balance (Fig. 5.2) ($millions)	Series 5, Telecom. Equip. Trade Balance (Fig. 5.2) ($millions)	Series 6, Terminal Equip. Trade Balance (Fig. 5.3) (1982 $millions)
1967	.551	.028	5.090	N.A.	17	N.A.
1968	.201	.010	2.630	N.A.	7	N.A.
1969	1.012	.051	3.310	N.A.	41	N.A.
1970	.478	.024	5.150	N.A.	24	N.A.
1971	−.472	−.024	1.090	N.A.	−24	N.A.
1972	−.247	−.013	−2.210	N.A.	−14	N.A.
1973	−.300	−.015	.460	N.A.	−18	N.A.
1974	−.111	−.006	4.640	N.A.	−7	N.A.
1975	1.989	.101	13.880	N.A.	124	−12.0
1976	2.228	.113	8.040	N.A.	150	−7.2
1977	1.750	.089	1.610	N.A.	150	−3.8
1978	1.861	.094	−1.850	N.A.	179	−32.2
1979	1.714	.087	3.380	N.A.	200	−19.7
1980	.806	.041	9.230	N.A.	100	−30.5
1981	1.745	.088	5.660	N.A.	256	−104.7
1982	1.644	.083	−.170	24,458	225	−111.8
1983	−3.881	−.196	−10.460	23,646	−542	−379.1
1984	−8.297	−.418	−20.430	20,220	−1,309	−431.1
1985	−8.483	−.427	−22.030	23,945	−1,503	−418.9
1986	−11.058	−.557	−31.040	15,640	−1,776	−820.3
1987	−13.205	−.665	−31.220	19,425	−2,183	−778.9
1988	−13.319	−.670	−24.310	27,241	−2,220	−634.7
1989	−15.587	−.784	−18.790	27,047	−2,288	−539.5
1990	−11.187	−.562	−14.370	34,081	−1,794	−689.9
1991	−13.511	−.679	−8.860	36,900	−2,065	−609.2
1992	−12.623	−.634	−11.930	33,300	−1,901	−648.8
1993	−11.049	−.554	−17.380	27,200	−1,664	−664.8

(continued)

Table 5A.1   (continued)

	Series 7, Terminal Equip. Exports (Fig. 5.3) (1982 $millions)	Series 8, Terminal Equip. Imports (Fig. 5.3) (1982 $millions)	Series 9, Terminal Equip. Import Penetration (%)	Series 10, Network Equip. Trade Balance (Fig. 5.4) (1982 $millions)	Series 11, Network Equip. Exports (Fig. 5.4) (1982 $millions)	Series 12, Network Equip. Imports (Fig. 5.4) (1982 $millions)
1967	N.A.	N.A.	N.A.	N.A.	N.A.	N.A.
1968	N.A.	N.A.	N.A.	N.A.	N.A.	N.A.
1969	N.A.	N.A.	N.A.	N.A.	N.A.	N.A.
1970	N.A.	N.A.	N.A.	N.A.	N.A.	N.A.
1971	N.A.	N.A.	N.A.	N.A.	N.A.	N.A.
1972	N.A.	N.A.	N.A.	N.A.	N.A.	N.A.
1973	N.A.	N.A.	N.A.	N.A.	N.A.	N.A.
1974	N.A.	N.A.	N.A.	N.A.	N.A.	N.A.
1975	2.9	14.9	N.A.	62.0	159.2	97.2
1976	5.6	12.8	1.8	68.6	163.7	95.1
1977	7.4	11.2	1.4	52.4	178.6	126.2
1978	12.0	44.1	4.5	157.1	334.7	177.6
1979	20.1	39.8	3.5	107.0	377.4	270.3
1980	25.7	56.2	5.9	117.0	435.3	318.3
1981	27.8	132.5	11.2	233.0	515.4	282.4
1982	24.2	136.0	11.6	334.2	653.5	319.3
1983	27.1	406.2	34.1	42.6	628.5	585.9
1984	35.5	466.7	37.5	−400.7	582.6	983.3
1985	35.0	453.9	29.1	−364.0	634.5	998.5
1986	34.4	854.7	55.3	−166.0	622.6	788.6
1987	58.1	836.9	80.2	−148.8	646.2	795.0
1988	183.1	817.8	86.2	109.9	992.6	882.7
1989	278.0	817.5	95.8	225.5	1,224.8	999.4
1990	174.0	863.9	96.5	143.8	1,143.5	999.7
1991	175.7	784.9	87.0	118.5	1,175.2	1,056.6
1992	197.8	846.6	88.1	202.9	1,450.0	1,247.1
1993	242.0	906.8	N.A.	N.A.	N.A.	N.A.

Table 5A.1   (continued)

	Series 13, Network Equip. Import Penetration (%)	Series 14, U.S. Trade Balance with Japan in Telecom. Equip. (Fig. 5.6) (1982 $millions)	Series 15, U.S. Exports to Japan of Telecom. Equip. (1982 $millions)	Series 16, U.S. Imports from Japan of Telecom. Equip. (1982 $millions)	Series 17, U.S. Trade Balance with Europe in Telecom. Equip. (Fig. 5.6) (1982 $millions)
1967	N.A.	N.A.	N.A.	N.A.	N.A.
1968	N.A.	N.A.	N.A.	N.A.	N.A.
1969	N.A.	N.A.	N.A.	N.A.	N.A.
1970	N.A.	N.A.	N.A.	N.A.	N.A.
1971	N.A.	N.A.	N.A.	N.A.	N.A.
1972	N.A.	N.A.	N.A.	N.A.	N.A.
1973	N.A.	N.A.	N.A.	N.A.	N.A.
1974	N.A.	N.A.	N.A.	N.A.	N.A.
1975	N.A.	N.A.	N.A.	N.A.	N.A.
1976	N.A.	N.A.	N.A.	N.A.	N.A.
1977	N.A.	N.A.	N.A.	N.A.	N.A.
1978	4.9	−124.3	8.1	133.6	27.9
1979	6.6	−112.0	17.3	129.3	63.5
1980	7.1	−221.5	20.4	241.9	95.7
1981	6.6	−257.3	22.8	281.1	85.1
1982	7.8	−331.0	25.0	356.0	90.0
1983	13.0	−539.1	29.4	568.5	71.4
1984	16.3	−1,058.6	30.7	1,088.4	60.5
1985	13.1	−1,203.6	42.2	1,245.8	78.8
1986	11.7	−1,181.5	82.5	1,264.0	82.5
1987	12.0	−1,311.0	79.3	1,390.3	104.0
1988	13.4	−1,457.8	126.2	1,584.0	171.7
1989	16.3	−1,389.1	236.4	1,625.5	300.0
1990	14.8	−1,107.1	263.7	1,370.9	456.0
1991	17.5	−1,100.6	311.9	1,412.5	351.8
1992	20.3	−1,202.7	277.3	1,480.0	444.4
1993	N.A.	−1,050.9	382.5	1,433.3	571.9

(*continued*)

Table 5A.1   (continued)

	Series 18, U.S. Exports to Europe of Telecom. Equip. (1982 $millions)	Series 19, U.S. Imports from Europe of Telecom. Equip. (1982 $millions)	Series 20, U.S. Trade Balance with Other Asia in Telecom. Equip. (Fig. 5.6) (1982 $millions)	Series 21, U.S. Exports to Other Asia of Telecom. Equip. (1982 $millions)	Series 22, U.S. Imports from Other Asia of Telecom. Equip. (1982 $millions)
1967	N.A.	N.A.	N.A.	N.A.	N.A.
1968	N.A.	N.A.	N.A.	N.A.	N.A.
1969	N.A.	N.A.	N.A.	N.A.	N.A.
1970	N.A.	N.A.	N.A.	N.A.	N.A.
1971	N.A.	N.A.	N.A.	N.A.	N.A.
1972	N.A.	N.A.	N.A.	N.A.	N.A.
1973	N.A.	N.A.	N.A.	N.A.	N.A.
1974	N.A.	N.A.	N.A.	N.A.	N.A.
1975	N.A.	N.A.	N.A.	N.A.	N.A.
1976	N.A.	N.A.	N.A.	N.A.	N.A.
1977	N.A.	N.A.	N.A.	N.A.	N.A.
1978	60.4	32.5	33.7	59.2	26.7
1979	92.4	28.9	61.2	88.9	27.7
1980	128.0	32.3	111.8	155.9	44.1
1981	113.1	28.0	127.6	197.1	69.5
1982	130.0	40.0	81.0	255.0	174.0
1983	118.4	47.0	−249.5	275.9	524.5
1984	138.3	77.8	−307.4	216.1	523.5
1985	200.8	122.0	−215.8	223.3	439.0
1986	206.2	124.7	−520.6	209.9	731.4
1987	221.1	117.2	−733.9	187.7	921.6
1988	329.7	158.9	−872.8	304.3	1,177.1
1989	448.2	148.2	−1,137.3	410.9	1,548.2
1990	642.9	186.8	−1,133.7	518.3	1,652.0
1991	616.5	263.8	−1,356.3	392.6	1,748.9
1992	729.8	285.3	−1,336.0	484.4	1,820.4
1993	878.9	307.9	−1,671.1	469.3	2,140.4

Table 5A.1   (continued)

	Series 23, U.S. Trade Balance with Canada in Telecom. Equip. (Fig. 5.6) (1982 $millions)	Series 24, U.S. Exports to Canada of Telecom. Equip. (1982 $millions)	Series 25, U.S. Imports from Canada of Telecom. Equip. (1982 $millions)	Series 26, Japan Trade Balance with U.S. in Telecom. Equip. (Fig. 5.7) (1982 $millions)	Series 27, Japan Trade Balance with Europe in Telecom. Equip. (Fig. 5.7) (1982 $millions)	Series 28, U.S. Labor Cost (Fig. 5.8) ($/hour)
1967	N.A.	N.A.	N.A.	N.A.	N.A.	N.A.
1968	N.A.	N.A.	N.A.	N.A.	N.A.	N.A.
1969	N.A.	N.A.	N.A.	N.A.	N.A.	N.A.
1970	N.A.	N.A.	N.A.	N.A.	N.A.	N.A.
1971	N.A.	N.A.	N.A.	N.A.	N.A.	N.A.
1972	N.A.	N.A.	N.A.	N.A.	N.A.	N.A.
1973	N.A.	N.A.	N.A.	N.A.	N.A.	N.A.
1974	N.A.	N.A.	N.A.	N.A.	N.A.	N.A.
1975	N.A.	N.A.	N.A.	N.A.	N.A.	6.36
1976	N.A.	N.A.	N.A.	N.A.	N.A.	N.A.
1977	N.A.	N.A.	N.A.	N.A.	N.A.	7.59
1978	−27.0	84.6	111.7	86.4	53.5	8.27
1979	−66.8˙	89.5	156.3	200.0	85.7	9.02
1980	−125.6	98.1	223.7	239.1	129.1	9.84
1981	.2	138.9	138.8	419.5	172.0	10.84
1982	−7.8	119.8	127.6	407.5	162.6	11.64
1983	−121.5	108.0	229.4	793.5	175.8	12.10
1984	−221.5	121.3	342.8	1,308.4	251.1	12.51
1985	−260.9	122.2	383.1	985.6	302.9	12.96
1986	−197.7	118.1	315.8	1,123.5	588.9	13.21
1987	−132.2	157.6	289.7	1,366.7	1,020.6	13.46
1988	−217.8	172.2	390.0	1,956.8	1,715.9	13.91
1989	−188.2	206.1	394.3	1,559.5	1,458.7	14.32
1990	−183.0	287.8	470.8	1,258.7	1,415.9	14.91
1991	−122.3	406.0	528.3	1,293.9	1,444.2	15.60
1992	−47.6	595.9	643.5	1,642.5	1,456.0	16.17
1993	120.6	770.8	650.2	N.A.	N.A.	N.A.

(*continued*)

Table 5A.1   (continued)

	Series 29, Japan Labor Cost (Fig. 5.8) ($/hour)	Series 30, S. Korea Labor Cost (Fig. 5.8) ($/hour)	Series 31, Taiwan Labor Cost (Fig. 5.8) ($/hour)	Series 32, Hong Kong Labor Cost (Fig. 5.8) ($/hour)
1967	N.A.	N.A.	N.A.	N.A.
1968	N.A.	N.A.	N.A.	N.A.
1969	N.A.	N.A.	N.A.	N.A.
1970	N.A.	N.A.	N.A.	N.A.
1971	N.A.	N.A.	N.A.	N.A.
1972	N.A.	N.A.	N.A.	N.A.
1973	N.A.	N.A.	N.A.	N.A.
1974	N.A.	N.A.	N.A.	N.A.
1975	3.05	.34	.39	.76
1976	N.A.	N.A.	N.A.	N.A.
1977	4.02	.59	.52	1.03
1978	5.54	.80	.61	1.18
1979	5.49	1.06	.78	1.31
1980	5.61	1.01	.98	1.51
1981	6.18	1.06	1.18	1.55
1982	5.70	1.13	1.22	1.67
1983	6.13	1.20	1.27	1.52
1984	6.34	1.28	1.48	1.60
1985	6.47	1.31	1.46	1.75
1986	9.47	1.39	1.67	1.89
1987	11.34	1.69	2.23	2.11
1988	12.63	2.30	2.82	2.40
1989	12.49	3.34	3.53	2.79
1990	12.74	3.88	3.95	3.20
1991	14.55	4.39	4.39	3.58
1992	15.16	4.93	5.19	3.89
1993	N.A.	N.A.	N.A.	N.A.

Sources: Series (1): *U.S. Industrial Outlook* (1970–94). Series (2): *Statistical Abstract of the United States* (1971, 1981, 1994). Series (3): Citibase (New York), main data tape, series GEXMD, GIMMD, and MDS. Series (4): U.S. General Accounting Office (1992); *Statistical Abstract of the United States* (1994). Series (5): *U.S. Industrial Outlook* (1982–94). Series (6)–(13): *Electronic Market Data Book* (1975–94). Series (14)–(25): *U.S. Industrial Outlook* (1978–94). Series (26)–(27): *Japan Electronics Almanac* (1981–94). Series (28)–(32): *International Comparisons of Hourly Compensation Costs for Production Workers in Manufacturing* (1988, 1993).

Appendix B

Table 5B.1   **Major U.S. and Japanese Regulatory Actions Affecting Telecommunications Equipment**

Date	Action	Significance
1956	AT&T consent decree	Agreement ending antitrust complaint allowed AT&T and Western Electric to remain vertically integrated, required AT&T to license all patents, and restricted AT&T to regulated activities in the domestic market
1956	Hush-a-Phone order	FCC permitted attachment of this independent device to telephones, but AT&T blocked implementation
1968	Carterphone order	FCC permitted customer-owned equipment to be connected to network but allowed AT&T to charge a discriminatory fee to those customers
1974	Antitrust case filed against AT&T	Department of Justice seeks to split AT&T from Western Electric (eventually settled by 1982 Modification of Final Judgment)
1975	First order registration program	FCC clarified standards for certifying independent attachments but excluded telephone sets, key sets, and PBXs; AT&T delays implementation for two years
1977	Second order registration program	Extends 1974 program to apply to telephones, key sets, and PBXs; independent equipment can be attached after certifying that it poses "no harm" to the network
1980	Computer II Inquiry	FCC removed terminal equipment from rate-of-return regulation and required AT&T to sell equipment through a separate subsidiary
1981	Understanding on the Interconnect Market (Japan)	Following partial deregulation of Japan's terminal equipment (interconnect) market, NTT liberalized certification procedures for independent equipment
1982	Modification of Final Judgment announced	Agreement ending 1974 antitrust complaint required AT&T to divest Bell operating companies (BOCs), severed AT&T's exclusive equipment supply contracts with BOCs, and organized BOCs into regional holding companies (RHCs) and barred them from manufacturing equipment
1984	Modification of Final Judgment's implementation completed	Implementation of Modification of Final Judgment completed on 1 January 1984
1985	Telecommunications Business and NTT Company Laws (Japan)	Deregulation of Japanese terminal and network equipment markets that rescinds NTT's monopoly over first telephone, establishes independent standards-setting board, and partially privatizes NTT subject to competition from rivals not tied to NEC's equipment family

References

Baughcum, Alan. 1986. Deregulation, divestiture, and competition in U.S. telecommunications: Lessons for other countries. In *Marketplace for telecommunications: Regulation and deregulation in industrialized democracies,* ed. Marcellus S. Snow. New York: Longman.
Brock, Gerald W. 1981. *The telecommunications industry: The dynamics of market structure.* Cambridge, Mass.: Harvard University Press.
Choy, Jon. 1995. A decade of deregulation and counting: Japan's telecommunications market. Report no. 28A. Washington, D.C.: Japan Economic Institute, 28 July.
Crandall, Robert W. 1991. *After the breakup: U.S. telecommunications in a more competitive era.* Washington, D.C.: Brookings.
Curran, Timothy J. 1982. Politics and high technology: The NTT case. In *Coping with U.S.-Japanese economic conflicts,* ed. I. M. Destler and Hideo Sato. Lexington, Mass.: D. C. Heath.
Dick, Andrew R. 1994. Does import protection act as export promotion? Evidence from the United States. *Oxford Economic Papers* 46, no. 1 (January): 83–101.
Electronic market data book. Various years. Washington, D.C.: Electronic Industries Association.
Harris, Robert G. 1988. Telecommunications policy in Japan: Lessons for the U.S. Business and Public Policy Working Paper no. BPP-35. University of California, Berkeley.
Hausman, Jerry A., and Elon Kohlberg. 1989. The future evolution of the central office switch industry. In *Future competition in telecommunications*, ed. Stephen P. Bradley and Jerry A. Hausman Boston: Harvard Business School Press.
Helpman, Elhanan, and Paul R. Krugman. 1985. *Market structure and foreign trade.* Cambridge, Mass.: MIT Press.
———. 1989. *Trade policy and market structure.* Cambridge, Mass. MIT Press.
Huber, Peter W. 1987. *The geodesic network: 1987 report on competition in the telephone industry.* Washington, D.C.: U.S. Department of Justice.
International comparisons of hourly compensation costs for production workers in manufacturing. Various years. Washington, D.C.: U.S. Department of Labor.
International Trade Administration. 1986. *A competitive assessment of the U.S. digital central office switch industry.* Washington, D.C.: U.S. Government Printing Office.
Japan electronics almanac. Various years. Tokyo: Dempa.
Johnson, Leland L. 1993. *U.S.-Japan trade relations in telecommunications equipment markets.* Santa Monica, Calif.: Rand.
Krugman, Paul R. 1984. Import protection as export promotion: International competition in the presence of oligopoly and economies of scale. In *Monopolistic competition and international trade,* ed. Henryk Kierzkowski. Oxford: Clarendon.
McKinsey Global Institute. 1992. *Service sector productivity.* Washington, D.C.
Noam, Eli M. 1989. International telecommunications in transition. In *Changing the rules: Technological change, international competition, and regulation in communications,* ed. Robert W. Crandall and Kenneth Flamm. Washington, D.C.: Brookings.
Noll, Roger G., and Frances M. Rosenbluth. 1993. Telecommunications policy in Japan and the U.S.: Structure, process, outcomes. Working Paper no. 349. Stanford University, Center for Economic Policy Research.
Organization for Economic Cooperation and Development. 1991. *Telecommunications equipment: Changing market structures and trade structures.* Paris.
Robinson, Kenneth G., Jr. 1991. Issues of international trade. In *After the breakup: Assessing the new post-AT&T divestiture era,* ed. Barry G. Cole. New York: Columbia University Press.

Statistical abstract of the United States. Various years. Washington, D.C.: U.S. Department of Commerce.

U.S. Congress. House Subcommittee on Trade. Committee on Ways and Means. 1979. *Task force report on United States–Japan trade.* Washington, D.C.: U.S. Government Printing Office.

———. 1980. *U.S.-Japan trade report.* Washington, D.C.: U.S. Government Printing Office.

U.S. General Accounting Office. 1983. *Assessment of bilateral telecommunications agreements with Japan.* GAO/NSIAD-84-2. Washington, D.C.: U.S. Government Printing Office.

———. 1988. *U.S.-Japan trade: Evolution of the market-oriented sector specific talks.* GAO/NSIAD-88-205. Washington, D.C.: U.S. Government Printing Office.

———. 1992. *High-technology competitiveness: Trends in U.S. and foreign performance.* GAO/NSIAD-92-236. Washington, D.C.: U.S. Government Printing Office.

U.S. industrial outlook. Various years. Washington, D.C.: U.S. Department of Commerce.

U.S. International Trade Commission. 1984. *Changes in the U.S. telecommunications industry and the impact on U.S. telecommunications trade.* Publication no. 1542. Washington, D.C.

Vernon, Raymond. 1966. International investment and international trade in the product cycle. *Quarterly Journal of Economics* 80 (May): 190–207.

Vietor, Richard H., and David B. Yoffie. 1993. Telecommunications: Deregulation and globalization. In *Beyond free trade: Firms, governments, and global competition,* ed. David B. Yoffie. Boston: Harvard Business School Press.

II   Response to "Unfair" Trade

6 Testing Models of the Trade Policy Process: Antidumping and the "New Issues"

Robert E. Cumby and Theodore H. Moran

6.1 Introduction: The Expansion of Trade Protection in the Midst of Trade Expansion

The trade policy process in the United States is producing dramatically opposite outcomes simultaneously. On the one hand, the United States has ratified both the North American Free Trade Agreement (NAFTA) and the Uruguay Round, which together include sweeping trade liberalization measures. On the other hand, from the perspective of many of those involved in the struggles over NAFTA and the Uruguay Round, those opposing trade liberalization or seeking new trade protection have battled with extraordinary intensity and, in significant areas, with some success. How is the trade policy process likely to evolve in the post-Uruguay Round era? Will models of policy formation that have been useful in the past continue to be relevant in the future?

This paper examines one of the most vigorously contested areas in the Uruguay Round, the case of establishing a framework for antidumping actions in the World Trade Organization (WTO). Here, efforts at trade liberalization were not successful. In fact, there was an extension and codification of a new protectionist regulatory regime worldwide, leavened only by some modest reforms

Robert E. Cumby is the Marcus Wallenberg Professor of International Financial Diplomacy at the School of Foreign Service, Georgetown University, and a research associate of the National Bureau of Economic Research. Theodore H. Moran is the Karl F. Landegger Professor of International Business Diplomacy at the School of Foreign Service, Georgetown University. In 1993-94 Cumby served as senior economist, Council of Economic Advisers, and Moran served as senior adviser for economics, policy planning staff, Department of State.

Gary Horlick and Ellie Shea provided extensive comments on an earlier draft of this paper. Those, along with the helpful comments of Robert Lawrence and other conference participants, are acknowledged with thanks.

of existing procedures. How did this campaign on behalf of antidumping protectionism succeed in the midst of a major tide flowing in the direction of liberalization, what does it say about how the process works, and what does it portend for the trade battles to come?

6.2   Models of the U.S. Trade Policy Process

The basic model of trade policy formation predicts protectionist outcomes. Policy making toward trade is an archetypical example of the collective-goods problem (Olson 1965; Schattschneider 1935; Cohen 1988; Baldwin 1985). Intense damage to concentrated groups will prevail over small individual benefits to diffuse populations in generating a policy response. Trade policy will be dominated by interests seeking relief through protection in general or possibly specifically through antidumping. There are three alternative models of the policy-formation process, however, that contradict the collective-goods logic to predict more liberal policies.

1. *Defying protectionism I: An institutional structure for the executive to save Congress from itself.* Popularly elected representatives find themselves faced by protectionist pressures of the collective-goods kind but want to do their duty in the larger national interest. Congress therefore delegates authority to undertake trade-liberalizing negotiations to the executive, with a fast-track institutional structure that allows the executive to save Congress from itself on behalf of the greater good. This explains liberal outcomes and would predict a split between the executive and Congress on antidumping, with the former winning out on behalf of a more liberal approach. (See Pastor 1980; Destler 1995.)

2. *Defying protectionism II: MNC and big exporter clout to expand market access abroad.* Helping explain liberal outcomes, special interest protectionism is offset by "special interest" market expansionism on the part of the big U.S. exporter and MNC (multinational corporation) trade-and-investment community. U.S. exporters and MNCs add their pressure from lobbying and PAC contributions to the weaker pressures from consumers. This would predict strong inside-the-beltway as well as corporate grassroots forces rising to confront those pressing an agenda of more restrictive antidumping laws. (See Destler, Odell, and Elliott 1987; Hufbauer 1989; McKeown 1984; Milner 1988.)

A "strategic-trade" qualification to this argument, advanced by Milner and Yoffie (1989), suggests that U.S. exporters and MNCs may support liberalization, not unconditionally, but only conditionally since they need the economies of scale that come from access to foreign markets to compete globally and fear the competitive boost that access to the U.S. market might give non-U.S. firms. Hence, U.S. MNCs withhold their support for liberalism at home unless it is strictly matched by reciprocity and balance in market-opening measures elsewhere. In the case of antidumping regulations, this "qualification" would predict particularly strong U.S. MNC effort to expand market access abroad without interference by antidumping forces in other nations, in return for which American multinationals help stifle domestic U.S. antidumping pressure groups.

3. *Defying protectionism III: The broader political and economic interests of the American hegemon (even a declining hegemon).* Charles Kindleberger and others postulate that an open international trading system requires a hegemonic power willing to bear a disproportionate share of the costs, risks, and burdens to keep the tendency toward shortsighted national self-interest under control.[1] The preponderant power, formerly the United Kingdom and now the United States, has a unique time frame and discount rate ("the long shadow of the future") as well as set of national political interests that predispose it to assume system maintenance duties for the benefit of all. This would predict strong efforts on the part of the foreign policy/national defense community to circumscribe antidumping protectionism at home and push for strong multilateral disciplines on its spread abroad.[2]

A qualification may be needed as American preeminence wanes, according to Walz (1979) and Mastanduno (1991). With the decline of American hegemony, national policy makers may place the search for relative gains above the search for mutual gains. They will support the latter only if the outcome is weighted to improve the relative position of the United States. In the case of antidumping, this qualification suggests that uppermost in the minds of U.S. policy makers will be the question of whether the outcome will leave the United States in a stronger or weaker position vis-à-vis America's major industrial rivals.

6.3 Background on Antidumping

U.S. antidumping law was originally intended to supplement domestic antitrust law and address international predatory pricing by foreign firms in the U.S. market. Predatory intent to injure was central in the determination of dumping. The first significant change to this original treatment of dumping came as early as 1921, when a new law omitted any reference to predation and provided for a remedy in the form of antidumping duties whenever foreign firms were found to be selling in the United States at less than fair value (below the price in the foreign markets or, in the absence of such a price, below the cost of production). Importantly, the 1921 law transformed dumping cases into

---

1. Kindleberger (1973, 1986) and Goldstein (1986, 1988); Coates and Ludema (1994) provide a formal, game-theoretic model of liberalization led by a dominant power.

2. Prestowitz (1988) presents a more "bureaucratic politics" version of this argument, that the foreign policy/national defense community weighs in to give away access to the U.S. market to foreigners so as to maintain cordial political relations with them.

administrative determinations rather than judicial proceedings, thereby soften-ing the rules of evidence and standards of proof.

Over time, a number of changes have been made in U.S. antidumping laws that have made them increasingly more restrictive. Two changes stand out in importance: the increasing reliance on a comparison of the U.S. price of im-ports to "constructed value" (an estimate of average cost plus profit and selling expenses) and the change in the administering authority from the Treasury De-partment to the Commerce Department in order to provide for more sympa-thetic treatment of petitioners.[3] Moreover, the details of the laws and of Com-merce's implementation of the laws have become biased toward finding larger margins and therefore more frequent positive dumping determinations.[4] Three examples illustrate these biases in the law and its implementation prior to the Uruguay Round. First, as the law permitted, Commerce compared a six-month average of foreign prices to individual U.S. (import) prices and ignored any U.S. prices that take place above the average foreign price when computing dumping margins. Thus, an exporter would be found to be dumping unless its price on every transaction in the United States is above the average price in the exporter's home market. Second, when Commerce used estimates of con-structed value instead of foreign prices, the law mandated that overhead of 10 percent and a profit margin of 8 percent be added to fully allocated production costs. In contrast, recognizing that competitive firms may set price below aver-age total cost for a number of reasons, U.S. courts require that price be below marginal cost or average variable cost and that it be possible to recoup short-term losses through subsequently higher monopoly prices before a firm's pric-ing practices run afoul of the antitrust laws. Because the antidumping laws compare U.S. prices to average total cost, and because U.S. firms' margins are often smaller than 18.8 percent, a double standard evolved under which a for-eign firm would be found to be dumping in the U.S. market even if it had the same costs and charged the same price as a U.S. competitor who faced no legal problems. Third, when the exporter failed to provide the information requested by Commerce in the format desired, Commerce would use the "best informa-tion available" (generally obtained from the petitioner) to compute dumping margins.

In addition to the faulty microeconomics that underlies the U.S. approach, the biases in Commerce's procedures have become so severe that it reached negative determinations in only 3 percent of its final determinations between

---

3. The Trade Act of 1974 requires that sales in the exporter's home market that take place below (an estimate of) cost should be excluded from calculations. Not only does this raise the average and therefore the resulting dumping margin when price comparisons are used, but it also often reduces the number of foreign prices available for comparison by enough to justify ignoring the exporter's home market prices and comparing prices in the U.S. market to constructed value. The change in administering authority took place as part of congressional approval of the Trade Agreements Act of 1979.

4. The biases in Commerce's methods are described and thoroughly analyzed in several contri-butions in Boltuck and Litan (1991).

1988 and 1992 (Arnold 1994). The view that Commerce's procedures are biased in favor of petitioners is shared by a number of U.S. trading partners and led them to push for greater discipline on antidumping actions as part of the Uruguay Round negotiations.

The central issue for antidumping in the Uruguay Round was therefore a choice between attempting to circumscribe antidumping protectionism at home and abroad and legitimizing the U.S. approach in the new Uruguay Round agreements as the standard that would then become commonplace in foreign markets. From the beginning of the Uruguay Round negotiations, the Reagan and Bush administrations' negotiators consistently pressed for the latter. During the Bush administration, the U.S. negotiators, along with those from the European Community (EC), resisted including antidumping in the negotiations at all. U.S. negotiators finally acquiesced but consistently defended U.S. antidumping practices and, at the end of 1989, formed what Horlick and Shea call a "non-aggressive pact" to resist changes to either of their antidumping practices (Horlick and Shea 1995, 12). The U.S. negotiators never attempted to use the multilateral negotiations as an "antiprotectionist counterweight" (Destler 1995).

The negotiations dragged on well past the initial deadline of December 1990 owing to disputes on a number of matters. In December 1991, GATT director general Dunkel produced a draft agreement to serve as the basis for further negotiations. Given the history of U.S. pressure, the Dunkel text did not embrace a sweeping reform of antidumping practices but did include a number of restrictions that were aimed at reducing the extent of bias against imports that had developed in the United States and elsewhere. For example, the draft required that, when conducting antidumping investigations, the authorities compare average prices in the home and foreign markets or compare individual transaction prices in the two markets (rather than average prices in one market to transactions prices in the other market); required that actual data on profitability (but only on above-cost sales) be used when calculating constructed cost; and placed restrictions on the use of the best information available.

6.4   Determining the Outcome on Antidumping Policy

6.4.1   Internal Debate in the New Administration

In principle, the new administration could have reopened the entire spectrum of debate on antidumping, including the constructed-cost/price discrimination standard, as might be expected from an administration devoted to expanding the export potential of the country's industries. Such an effort did take place informally in the summer of 1993, via circulation of discussion papers across agencies on a personal basis (a U.S. government equivalent of the *samizdat* process). But the authors of such documents were quickly tracked down by those who had responsibility for enunciating "official" policy positions, reminded of the requirement for agency clearance of all such papers, threatened with exclusion from the deliberative process if they did not play by the rules, and warned about the loss of credibility in interagency debate if they ventured too far out in front.[5]

In practice, then, there was no "bottom-up review" of antidumping in the new administration. The initial policy battle began from where the previous administration had left off, with the more circumscribed but nonetheless significant question of whether to try to shape the new international regime at the margin in ways that would favor consumers and exporters (and economic efficiency) or to reinforce the protection afforded domestic producers not only in the United States but around the world.

Beginning in late September, the terms of debate (as defined by the office of the U.S. trade representative [USTR] with the backing of the National Economic Council [NEC]) centered on whether to insist on five major changes to the Draft Final Act ("Dunkel text"): standard of review for dispute settlement panels; circumvention; sunset; standing for unions; and cumulation.

1. *Standard of review.* The issue was whether WTO panels should act in a de novo or appellate role when considering dumping cases, that is, whether the Dunkel text should be reopened to explicitly circumscribe the ability of WTO panels to reweigh factual evidence and offer their own interpretation of whether national decisions were consistent with a given country's GATT obligations. On the one hand was the argument that WTO panels constitute an important brake on protectionist actions by national authorities. On the other hand was the argument that WTO panels might "dismantle our trade laws."

2. *Sunset.* Under then-existing law, a dumping order was terminated only when Commerce found no dumping in three successive annual reviews. In practice, this meant that most antidumping actions dragged on in perpetuity. In the Dunkel text, antidumping duties would end after five years unless the domestic industry could show that it would be injured by resumed dumping. The question was whether the burden of proof should be placed on the party found to be dumping in the first place or on the party seeking continued trade protection.

3. *Cumulation.* Most countries add together imports from different sources when they make an injury determination. The Dunkel text had no explicit provision on cumulation. The issue was whether to reopen the text to make this explicit.

4. *Circumvention.* The anticircumvention provision in the Dunkel text was designed to deter the shifting of sources by a multinational firm from one country

---

5. It is ironic that Commerce and the U.S. trade representative (USTR) were reportedly discussing noncleared drafts with congressional staff at the same time.

to another after an antidumping measure was imposed by not requiring a new investigation for each country. The question was whether to strengthen the language.

5. *Standing for unions.* The concern was whether unions can file antidumping petitions. While the Dunkel text did not address the issue of standing for labor unions, it expressly allowed governments to permit anyone to be an interested party. As in the case of cumulation, the debate centered on whether to reopen the text to clarify the right of unions to bring an antidumping case.

In preparation for small, deputies-level (generally undersecretaries or their designees) discussions of these issues, the USTR announced that its representatives had consulted with the Department of Commerce, the International Trade Commission, the staff of the House Ways and Means and Senate Finance Committees, and "the trade bar" in order to arrive at positions that could successfully be "sold" to the trade bar and to Congress.[6]

Among the materials prepared by the USTR for the launching of the U.S. strategy toward antidumping in the Uruguay Round on 28 September, there was no attempt to evaluate the substantive effect of the approach being considered on the U.S. economy or any discussion of the tactical option of energizing exporter and MNC groups to weigh in with their own points of view. When discussion papers attempting such an evaluation and suggesting such a tactic had been circulated informally in the preceding months, they had been personally squashed by the NEC's senior trade practitioner for fear they would be leaked; the rationale was that mobilizing forces to counter the antidumping lobby would merely inflame the latter.

The survey that was undertaken of the parties enumerated above indicated that standard of review was "the number one issue on everyone's list." The USTR reported that there was serious concern that panels would reweigh factual evidence and impose their own interpretation of the agreements, rather than deferring to the original determination by investigating authorities. Arguing on behalf of protecting the integrity of U.S. trade law, a position with a sturdy prosovereignty ring, the USTR urged that circumscribing this standard of review, either in the antidumping text or in the Integrated Dispute Settlement text, should become the first on the short list of "must haves" in negotiating a brokered text.

The USTR recommended that the United States seek changes in the Dunkel text in the other four areas as well, recognizing, however, that the United States was "isolated" on these issues among most of the rest of the GATT members and at the end of the day might have to settle for less. The Commerce Department and the new National Economic Council (ostensibly established as an

---

6. From the earliest interagency meetings, *the trade bar* was used exclusively to refer to the petitioners' bar, i.e., those representing industries seeking protection through the antidumping laws.

honest broker for all points of view) firmly sided with the USTR's recommendations.

Other parts of the administration were consistently antiprotectionist. The Council of Economic Advisers (CEA), for example, adopted its traditional position supporting liberalized trade. The Treasury Department and the State Department, however, abandoned their historical roles on this issue. Their behavior defied the conventional bureaucratic policies dictum, "Where you sit is where you stand." The Treasury Department, traditionally stalwart in favor of freer trade, did not play an active role on Uruguay Round issues, except for financial services. The State Department, also traditionally on the side of freer trade, was split: the undersecretary of state for economic affairs, however, consistently decided in favor of those in her department who supported a "strong defense of our trade laws." The Office of Management and Budget (OMB) and Justice generally supported the CEA position, but the NEC frequently excluded the OMB from key meetings (the OMB would be excluded from one, not invited in response to staff-level requests to the next, reinvited to the next only when a senior OMB official intervened, and excluded from the next, necessitating a chip-expending process for OMB subofficials vis-à-vis their bosses, which they had to conserve for deployment on multiple important issues). And Justice was shut out completely despite considerable expertise on trade laws.

As for outside pressures, the USTR reported that "the industries supporting strong U.S. trade laws remain highly agitated." Those representing exporting interests, on the other hand, remain "virtually silent." The only nonprotectionist group whose views are documented at all in the discussions was ECAT (the Emergency Committee for American Trade, a group of approximately fifty of the most international U.S. corporations), repeatedly cited as the exception to what is referred to as the "consensus."

The NEC/USTR-led strategy included an explicit plan to share U.S. government intentions with those who use the antidumping laws for protection, for example, "quietly advising the trade bar" on how the administration intended to handle what the USTR called "margin-protecting" issues (provisions that otherwise might reduce dumping margins when compared with current U.S. practice) and attempting to "sell draft language" on standard of review to the trade bar.

6.4.2   The Geneva Endgame

During the early debates on the administration's antidumping strategy in September and October, the undersecretary of commerce for international trade, the political appointee with organizational responsibility within the executive branch for carrying out the antidumping laws, had not yet been confirmed; by mid-November, as the Uruguay Round endgame in Geneva approached, he was. His first action as part of the Uruguay Round negotiating team in Washington was to make a special request for an "urgent meeting" of the deputies at which the U.S. position on the five issues already identified as critical would be toughened—in particular, standard of review, so that GATT panels cannot "dismantle our trade laws bit-by-bit"; sunset, so that the burden of terminating an order restraining imports be borne by the parties who created the problem, the exporters (in the case in mind, of course, non-U.S. exporters); and cumulation, so that de minimis thresholds be based on share of imports, not share of total consumption. Only in this way could the "broad attack" on U.S. law represented by the Dunkel text be countered. In addition, he proposed a list of other changes in rules governing start-up costs, constructed value, and average prices.

The senior officials in the U.S. delegation in Geneva were from the USTR and the Commerce Department. Other agencies were represented by much lower ranks. In private "confessionals" with Director General Sutherland as well as public statements, the changes in the Dunkel draft on antidumping were listed as the "number one priority," once the dispute over the Blair House agreement on agriculture was settled. The priority placed on changing the anti-dumping text might be expected to have reduced U.S. bargaining power on other issues, such as enhanced market access, better intellectual property rights protection, and/or liberalization of trade in financial services. U.S. negotiators claim, however, that there was no opportunity cost for other trade issues from placing such high priority on the antidumping changes.[7]

This high priority on the part of the U.S. delegation, in the face of strong international opposition, did not lead the U.S. antidumping interest groups to relax their pressures. On the contrary, they managed to mobilize senior congressional representatives, including the chair of the Senate Finance Committee and the House majority leader, to fly over to join the lobbying effort in Geneva.

The group most directly advocating the position of exporters and MNCs, ECAT, went to Geneva with only junior members of Congress supporting their position. Not only was this side outnumbered and outranked, but it became the target of personal attack. After pushing for a sunset clause that made it easy to terminate an antidumping order after five years, a senior lawyer on the ECAT team was accused by colleagues from the Washington trade law community of working to undermine what would be (absent sunset) a stream of ongoing cases.[8]

The outcome in Geneva included eight of the eleven changes demanded by the United States. These included circumscribing the powers of WTO panels via limits on the standard of review and making explicit the standing of labor

---

7. Horlick and Shea (1995, n. 59) note that a contrary view is expressed by others, including Japan's chief negotiator.

8. Since antidumping cases generate more respondents than petitioners, there is no reason a priori to believe that the trade law community is biased toward protection. On the other hand, there may be reason to believe that there is a vested interest among trade lawyers in keeping the anti-dumping process itself continuing.

unions to bring antidumping cases. In addition, procedural rules were altered in a way that would change the results of previous cases, such as the change in negligibility. This change was made because the steel industry would have been more successful at the International Trade Commission (ITC) in the spring 1993 steel cases under the new criterion than under the old one. The principal victory for the more liberal side was the sunset provision under which antidumping orders are terminated after five years unless there is a finding that renewed injury would result.

6.4.3   The Struggle over Implementing Legislation

Once the Geneva agreement was reached, the process of turning that agreement into legislative language to be approved by the Congress began. Problems were expected primarily in four areas, involving sovereignty and the World Trade Organization (in particular, its dispute settlement procedures), provision for renewed fast-track authority, parts of the subsidies agreement, and antidumping. Within antidumping, the debate centered on seven main issues (along with hundreds of "little" ones): "compensation," awarding any antidumping collected to successful petitioners; "duty as a cost," adding antidumping duties to the estimate of the exporter's cost (thereby doubling any antidumping duties levied); "captive production," excluding domestic production used internally for further processing when computing import penetration and examining industry financial performance for injury determination;[9] "averaging in reviews," comparing average foreign market prices to individual domestic prices;[10] "exporter's sales price," adjusting the exporter's price when sales occur through a U.S. affiliate of the foreign exporter;[11] "short supply," suspending antidumping duties if the domestic industry was unable to supply domestic users with sufficient quantity and quality;[12] and "start-up," adjusting production and sales costs of a new product during its start-up period.[13]

The implementing legislation was subject to "fast-track" legislative rules

9. This proposal was spurred by the assessment that several of the ITC's findings of "no injury" in the steel cases (especially those involving hot-rolled steel) decided in 1993 would have gone the other way had "captive production" been excluded.

10. This reflects standard Commerce Department practice prior to the Uruguay Round legislation and imparts an upward bias to calculated dumping margins unless all prices are identical. The Uruguay Round antidumping code prohibits this practice in investigations. U.S. negotiators argued that the code is silent on the procedure to be used in subsequent reviews.

11. This proposal would expand dumping margins on goods sold to U.S. affiliates of foreign MNCs by mandating that the affiliate's profits and selling costs be deducted from the price at which the good was first sold to an unrelated party. No similar adjustment would be made to the prices in the exporting country.

12. Computer manufacturers (Apple, Compaq, Digital, Hewlett-Packard, and IBM) in particular supported this provision, in part in response to the flat panel display case of 1991. They were joined by the Precision Metalforming Association (a group of steel users), Caterpillar, and Michelin. The Energy Industry Group supported the provision because of concerns of shortages of large-diameter steel pipe.

13. The Uruguay Round antidumping code requires that these costs be adjusted to reflect the costs at the end of the start-up period. Two aspects of this requirement were the subject of contro-

that prohibit amendments once the legislation is formally submitted and require that the entire package be voted up or down. But it is misleading to think of "fast track" as a process that prevents congressional changes to the legislation proposed by the administration. Instead, any changes need to be made before the legislation is *formally* submitted. The administration's draft legislation (itself the product of negotiations with the representatives of key committees and their staffs) is first informally submitted to the relevant committees.[14] The committees then hold "mock markup" sessions and reconcile the House and Senate versions in a "mock conference" to produce a congressional version of the package. Only then does the executive formally submit the legislation under fast-track rules.

Although fast-track procedures do not prevent the Congress from influencing the legislative package, they do, of course, affect the relative power of those involved in the implementing legislation. Amendments from the floor of Congress are prohibited, thus concentrating congressional power entirely in the relevant committees. And the administration, which submits the final legislation, can decide which of the changes proposed by the Congress to accept and which to reject subject to the constraint that the package (and possibly other parts of their legislative agenda) be successful.

A second set of legislative rules—the "pay-as-you-go" budget rules adopted as part of the Budget Enforcement Act of 1990—created a potential obstacle to achieving congressional approval of the implementing legislation. The tariff reductions would lead to revenue losses estimated by the Congressional Budget Office at $12 billion over five years and $28 billion over ten years. Under House rules, the five-year revenue losses needed to be offset by other revenues or by spending cuts. Under Senate rules, the legislation would need to offset the ten-year losses unless a sixty-vote waiver was obtained. Since the administration was prepared only to propose offsets for the projected revenue losses during the first five years, the legislation required a sixty-vote majority in the Senate. This budget offset requirement added to potential opposition to the legislation, and the requirement of a supermajority provided added leverage to those seeking to extract concessions in return for supporting the legislation.

As soon as the agreement was reached in Geneva, domestic users of the antidumping laws began to attack the agreement as weakening or dismantling U.S. trade laws. This attack was led by representatives of the integrated steel producers and the semiconductor industry, two groups that had found the antidumping laws helpful in the past and that had lobbied for changes in the Dun-

versy. On one side, petitioners, led by the Semiconductor Industry Association, were pushing for as early an end for the start-up period as possible and for the adjustment to be limited to fixed production costs. On the other side, a group of multinationals led by the computer manufacturers was pushing for setting the end of start-up at six months after normal production levels were achieved and for all start-up costs (production and marketing) to be included in the adjustment.

14. These were the House Ways and Means Committee and the Senate Finance Committee for antidumping and for most of the remaining legislation. A total of eight committees in the House alone claimed jurisdiction over some piece of the legislation.

kel text. In January 1994, Representative Ralph Regula (R-OH), vice chair of the congressional steel caucus, proposed fifty changes to U.S. antidumping and countervailing duty laws. Senator Ernest Hollings (D-SC) renewed proposals to change the calculation of the exporter's sales price (ESP) when imports are made through a related party. Hollings had been unsuccessful in adding these proposals to the 1988 trade bill but pressed the administration to include them and other margin-increasing changes in the implementing legislation.

The administration's efforts on the implementing legislation were again coordinated by an NEC-led group. Negotiations with the Congress were the responsibility of the trade representative's office, joined by the Department of Commerce on antidumping and countervailing duty issues. The focus of the NEC-led group was on getting the agreement through Congress. Because the task was to determine "what package can be sold to Congress," the USTR, which was charged with congressional relations, was in a position of providing judgments as to what could be sold. Consequently, as both the judge of what could be sold and the agent coordinating the negotiation with Congress, the USTR effectively controlled the process.

The administration outlined its approach in a series of memos to the House Ways and Means Committee beginning in March. In particular, they chose not to embrace several of the proposals being pushed by petitioners, including provisions for compensation, tighter anticircumvention rules, and instructions that the International Trade Commission ignore "captive production" in its injury determinations. They also chose not to include a "short-supply" provision that was sought by a group of multinationals and energy firms. The administration's outline for the implementing legislation left some ambiguity about "duty as a cost" and the treatment of ESP. It proposed that Commerce continue with its practice of comparing U.S. prices of specific transactions to averages of foreign prices in computing dumping margins during reviews.

A "lawyers group" consisting of staff from the trade representative's office and the Department of Commerce was formed to draft legislative language.[15] The staff-level group charged with drafting the legislation had enormous power to make small but important changes to the antidumping laws. Even those aspects characterized as containing broader, policy-level issues were composed of highly technical pieces in what is a byzantine set of laws, regulations, and practices. Evaluating those policy-level issues required expertise in U.S. trade laws that made it difficult for those in the NEC-led deputies group who were not trade lawyers to influence the process. More generally, exercising effective control over the legislative language from the deputies' level was largely impossible because of the mind-numbing level of detail, the extraordinary number of provisions, and the fact that the language was withheld from

---

15. Adopting the Geneva agreement verbatim was not possible. The agreement is ambiguous in a number of places, is silent in others, and permits but does not require some practices. This group conducted drafting sessions in close cooperation with the majority staff of the Ways and Means Committee.

staff outside of Commerce and the USTR until the summer.[16] Thus, the staff-level group drafting the legislation had the ability to tilt the language in the direction sought by petitioners, and it did so in several important ways.

In the first half of April, Representatives Norman Mineta (D-CA) and Ralph Regula (R-OH), the chairs of the House Democratic and Republican task forces on the GATT, introduced a bill containing implementing legislation for antidumping and countervailing duties. Although slightly pared down from Regula's earlier efforts, the bill still reflected the changes sought by petitioners. Regula characterized the bill as an attempt to influence the administration's proposals for the implementing legislation, pointing to "some differences within the Administration on how restrictive" the antidumping parts of the implementing legislation would be (Regula was quoted in *Inside U.S. Trade,* 15 April 1994, 6).

The first complete compilation of the administration's proposals for the implementing legislation was presented to the Ways and Means Committee for the 16 June executive session and the 20 June public session of the trade subcommittee. The administration's proposal did not contain several of the most visible provisions sought by petitioners (duty as a cost, circumvention, captive production, or compensation). Nor did it contain the short-supply provision sought by several large multinationals and computer manufacturers.

The treatment of costs during a "start-up" phase of production became an increasingly visible issue during the spring. The administration's initial proposal was fairly close to the petitioners' position. The end of the start-up period was set as no later than the beginning of normal production levels, and only fixed production costs were to be adjusted. Changing this proposal then became one of the key goals of those lobbying for less restrictive provisions in the implementing legislation.

Almost immediately after the administration set out its proposals for the Ways and Means trade subcommittee, a bipartisan group of ten members of the Ways and Means Committee (six Democrats and four Republicans) led by Sander Levin (D-MI) and Amo Houghton (R-NY) charged that the administration's proposals would fail to preserve U.S. trade laws and listed twelve changes that they would seek. The list included the familiar issues of duty as a cost, compensation, captive production, and anticircumvention as well as an early end to the start-up period and a weaker injury standard.[17]

The Ways and Means Committee marked up the antidumping legislation on

---

16. The sheer number of small or subtle ways in which the draft legislation tilted in the direction of petitioners presented problems for oversight at a higher level outside Commerce. It is difficult to justify deputy-level focus on minutiae, and choosing a few of the most important ones is problematic. As one experienced trade lawyer explained, it is impossible for an outsider to know from a simple reading of the text which cases or how many cases will turn on a particular choice of words.

17. The group also pressed for a change in the countervailing duty (CVD) laws that would reverse a 7 June 1994 Court of International Trade decision concerning privatized industries. In two steel cases, the court overturned the Commerce Department's practice of allowing past subsidies to "travel" to the new owners of a privatized firm. The court ruled that no countervailable

20 July, passing an en bloc amendment that included several concessions to the Levin-Houghton group, and rejecting the computer MNC's short-supply amendment.[18] The Levin-Houghton group won partial victories on captive production, duty absorption, anticircumvention, and countervailing duties (CVDs) on privatized firms. On captive production, this markup directed the ITC to "focus primarily on the merchant market for the upstream product" to determine market share and financial performance. Although a duty as a cost provision was not adopted, the ITC was instructed to consider duty absorption when conducting sunset reviews and required that, within two years of an antidumping order being issued, Commerce assess the extent of duty absorption.[19]

Not all the en bloc amendments favored petitioners. The end of the start-up period was set "at" (rather than "no later than") the beginning of commercial production levels, and the resulting adjustment had to include "all production costs" (as opposed to "fixed costs" only). Also, the averaging of prices in administrative reviews was limited to one month.

The antidumping issue that proved to be the most controversial in the Senate, the calculation of the ESP between related parties, was contained in the "chairman's mark" that was presented to the committee for the markup. Senate Finance Committee Chairman Moynihan included language that provided for profits as well as selling costs to be deducted from the price from the first sale to an unrelated party. This provision, which had been championed by Ernest Hollings (D-SC), would inflate dumping margins by an estimated 7 percentage points or more (Lawrence 1994). The administration's proposal (which was approved by the House) provided for a more neutral procedure that would take the sales price from the first sale to an unrelated party and then make adjustments in order to compare that price to the price in the exporter's home market at a comparable level of trade.

---

subsidy survived an "arm's-length" transaction when either an entire enterprise or a division of a subsidized enterprise is privatized. The Levin-Houghton group expressed its desire to "clarify" the law by codifying Commerce's overturned practice. The administration opposed the Levin-Houghton amendments but expressed willingness to "work with the trade subcommittee staff to discuss the concerns of the integrated steel producers" on captive production and said that they would "continue to consider" the issue of CVDs and privatized firms. (The quote is from a memo from the USTR general counsel to acting trade subcommittee chairman Matsui.)

18. The short-supply amendment was rejected by a vote of twenty-three to fifteen, surprising the large computer company and MNC supporters who, earlier in the week, had expected it to pass. The assistant secretary of commerce for import administration voiced strong opposition to the amendment. Chairmen Gibbons and Matsui also opposed the amendment.

19. The assistant secretary of commerce for import administration reportedly told the committee that, if duty absorption were taking place, it would "lead us to find an ever higher duty" (quoted in *Inside U.S. Trade,* 22 July 1994, 21). The en bloc amendment also states that a change in ownership of a firm or a division of the firm "does not, by itself require the administering authority to find that past countervailable subsidies received by the firm no longer continue to be countervailable." Although this amendment was pushed primarily by the integrated steel producers, it was reportedly also supported by Representative Jim McDermott (D-WA) because of Boeing's concerns about the treatment of subsidies to Aerospatiale, one of the partner companies in Airbus, should it be privatized (*Inside U.S. Trade,* 22 July 1994, 22).

On 28 July, the Finance Committee adopted a set of twenty-six en bloc amendments, including the Hollings ESP proposal that was in the chairman's mark and three amendments similar to those adopted by the House. Price averaging in administrative reviews was restricted to one month, and language on captive production, pushed by Senators Rockefeller (D-WV) and Hatch (R-UT), and on the effect of privatization on countervailing duties similar, but not identical, to the House language was adopted. In addition, an amendment pushed by Senators Rockefeller and Danforth to restrict "diversionary dumping" was included in the en bloc amendments.[20]

The House and Senate versions of the implementing legislation then proceeded to conference, where the conferees needed to deal simultaneously with several contentious issues and with the calendar as well. The House and Senate conferees reached agreement on 20 September, although a few controversial issues were left to the administration.[21] A House compromise on fast-track authority did not survive the conference, and fast-track renewal had to await separate legislation. The conference reached a compromise on the treatment of ESP that provided for the deduction of profits in computing the exporter's sales price (thereby inflating dumping margins), as advocated by Hollings and others, but also included language that may result in more frequent "level of trade" adjustments by Commerce. The conference adopted the start-up language in the House version of the legislation, with the result that the start-up period was to end when commercial production levels were achieved and both fixed and variable production costs were to be adjusted. The Senate language on "diversionary dumping" was also adopted.[22]

20. According to its proponents, the amendment was aimed at preventing hot-rolled steel that was under a dumping order from being shipped to another country, where it would be transformed to cold-rolled steel and then shipped to the United States not subject to a dumping order.

21. A change in a rule of origin for textiles and apparel—the country of origin was changed to the country where the object was assembled rather than the country where the fabric was cut—was included in both the House and the Senate versions of the legislation, but the Senate version delayed implementation for five years. A delay of eighteen months (until 1 July 1996) was included in the legislation the administration submitted.

22. The concessions on ESP and textile rules of origin notwithstanding, on 28 September Hollings announced that the Commerce Committee would use the full forty-five days to consider the legislation that fast-track rules allow. The president then asked the Senate to stay in session until a vote could be taken, and a vote was scheduled for 1 December. Once the legislation was formally submitted, the remaining question was whether the required sixty votes would be achieved in the Senate. Minority Leader Dole (R-KS) threw up a number of obstacles during the fall. He implied that he was conditioning his support on, among other things, a capital gains tax cut, assurances that farm programs would not be "singled out" in future budget cuts, and the creation of a commission to examine the decisions of the dispute settlement mechanisms of the WTO. He also requested specific commitments for wheat and oilseed producers. An agreement between the administration and Senator Dole providing for the creation of the Dispute Settlement Review Commission to scrutinize decisions that go against the United States was announced on 23 November. That agreement cleared the way for Senate approval of the legislation. The House approved the legislation by a bipartisan majority of 288-146 on 29 November. On 1 December, the Senate voted sixty-eight to thirty-two to waive the budget rule and then voted seventy-six to twenty-four to approve the legislation. Senator Hollings was not among those voting in favor of the legislation.

6.4.4 The Dynamics of Trade Policy Formation on Antidumping

The preceding sections suggest five conclusions about the dynamics of trade policy formation on antidumping.

First, the policy decision-making structure was largely dominated by members of the trade bar practitioner community, owing in part to the structure of senior-level appointments and in part to the detailed and specialized nature of the subject. This community stretched across the executive and Congress and, whether being solicitous of the demands of petitioners or attempting to constrain the latter's demands at the margin, conducted itself so as deliberately to exclude more liberal outsiders (in the executive or Congress) as much as possible. The few key players who did not come from the trade bar community, such as the undersecretary of commerce for international trade, emerged from the Senate confirmation process thoroughly imbued with an appreciation of the need to cater to the antidumping petitioners' lobby.

Second, reinforcing the strength derived from the technical and specialized nature of the debate, the trade law practitioner community enjoyed the considerable advantage that comes from having captured the rhetorical high ground in characterizing debate on the antidumping issue. *Strengthening our trade laws* became the standard code for awarding protection via antidumping; *weakening our trade laws* became the standard characterization for policy efforts designed to help consumers and exporters. Indeed, *the trade bar* came to be synonymous with the petitioners' lobby. This victory in the Orwellian struggle over use of language reinforced the ability of the trade bar practitioner community to maintain control over the process by handicapping the ability of more liberal participants to enlist the support of senior policy makers elsewhere in the administration.

Third, the policy determination process did not start from an assessment or a debate about what was in the broadest national interest and then proceed to bend policy toward reality from there (initial efforts to proceed in this way were effectively squashed). In fact, except as maverick actions on the part of the more liberal policy players, working from the fringes, there was no attempt on the part of the principal negotiators (the USTR and Commerce) to "round up" countervailing forces or seek out allies to provide some balance against the special interest demands of petitioners. The tactical strategy was to mollify and appease the more protectionist forces, with the hope of thereby keeping their opposition and criticism within some reasonable bounds. In the process, the idea that more restrictive antidumping legislation was the "price" that needed to be paid to obtain congressional approval of the full Uruguay Round package went from received wisdom to a self-fulfilling prophecy.

Fourth, in this contest, the protectionist interests organized their own forces vigorously and well, with an offensive that set the agenda of debate. From the earliest days of determining appointments in the new administration, through lopsided representation on the ground in Geneva, to the final construction of implementing legislation, they mobilized strong supporters from both sides of the aisle, while the administration, at best, played at damage control.

Fifth, those production-oriented interest groups wanting a more liberal outcome (like exporters and MNCs) were never represented on as high a level or with the same expenditure of resources and energy as their counterparts from the ranks of petitioners. Individuals or organizations representing consumers or the economy at large were virtually nonexistent. Companies that stood to benefit from a more liberal approach or to be hurt by the more protectionist options tended to concentrate their efforts on a few relatively narrow issues of particular concern (like short supply or start-up costs).

To provide a fuller perspective on the policy-making process, however, there is an additional dimension that emerges from examining an initiative to revise the antidumping treatment of exports from economies in transition.

6.4.5   The Economies-in-Transition Initiative: High Politics versus Low Politics

During the debate over implementing legislation, there was a major mini-struggle over the antidumping treatment of the economies in transition (EITs) that sheds important light on the relation between "high politics" (national security, central political relations) and "low politics" (economic policy outcomes, especially domestic economic outcomes).

Since early in the Clinton administration, the National Security Council (NSC), State Department, Defense Department, and Council of Economic Advisers had been urging that trade (backed by foreign investment) would have to replace aid in fueling market-led growth and reform in Eastern Europe and the former Soviet Union. This prospect was essentially stymied by the biased treatment accorded EITs on antidumping. What was needed, therefore, was a new method of treating exports from EITs that would be more foreign investor/export friendly.

To remedy this, the administration's senior strategist for Russia and the former Soviet Union set up an NSC-NEC interagency group with instructions to devise options for remedying the situation. At his direction, the group was to be chaired by the undersecretary of commerce for international trade, with the rationale that no solution could be found that was not supported by the Department of Commerce. (In one subsequent interagency meeting, an assistant secretary of state previously from the ranks of "the trade bar" broadened this rationale by asserting that the debate on antidumping policy should be limited to those who had actual experience in the preparation of antidumping cases, in response to which a non–"trade bar" official muttered that it was fortunate that the assistant secretary of state for human rights, who investigates torture cases, did not interrupt interagency proceedings with a comparable demand.)

The first conclusion, unanimously supported, was that administrative reform was not a realistic option since a long record of precedents would allow petitioners to challenge administration of existing laws that were less favorable to their claims successfully in court.

Turning to legislative reforms, the initial option to receive wide support was the so-called Heinz amendment, which would shift antidumping cases from a cost to a price test.[23] EIT exporters would not be found to be dumping as long as they sold at the price of major free market producers. This was vetoed by the assistant secretary of commerce with the argument that the shift to a price test not only undermined the viability of using it but was likely to arouse widespread alarm in the trade bar because of the precedent it might set for broader antidumping reform.

A second option was to shift to reform of 406(D), the safeguard provisions concerning imports from nonmarket economies. This would replace antidumping coverage with a new Section 406 treatment for EITs. The initiative contained a series of hard-fought-out compromises. The injury test that was devised ("a cause of serious injury") lay between the easy-to-meet antidumping standard and the harder-to-meet current 406 standard. Injury would be restricted to imports into the United States, instead of a Commerce proposal that Russian exports anywhere in the world could be used as evidence to protect U.S. industries. A remedy would be mandatory, but the president would have discretion about what type of remedy. The scope of remedy would be to "address" the injury, not to "remedy" the injury (i.e., would not have to compensate 100 percent).

The downside to this "406 reform" route was that the domestic industry seeking protection simply would have only to go once to the ITC to find injury and get relief: thus, 406 reform would become one-stop shopping for protection. The prevailing antidumping practice requires one stop at the ITC for a "preliminary" finding, one stop at the ITC for "final" finding, and one stop at Commerce—or three stops plus international effort to accumulate surrogate data. The cost would drop by two-thirds, from $400,000–$500,000 in an antidumping case to approximately $150,000–$200,000 for a 406(D) case. In sum, the (small) uncertainty of protection would be eliminated and the cost of acquiring it cut by two-thirds, providing much easier access to a much broader array of petitioners.

Worse, under both 406 "reform" and current antidumping law, the outcome in the vast majority of cases would be a VRA (voluntary restraint agreement) negotiated government to government, thus putting the Russian government (and others) right back in the center of developing an industrial policy for the new EIT export sector via case-by-case managed trade.

Even this modest reform, the administration's congressional strategists calculated, would require high-level effort to convince Senate Finance and House

---

23. For background on options on exports from nonmarket economies and economies in transition, see Horlick and Shuman (1984).

Ways and Means committee members to accept on geopolitical grounds. Instead, however, the principal coordinator of policy toward Russia and other Commonwealth of Independent State (CIS) countries within the administration delegated the task of selling the proposal to the assistant secretary of state for economic and business affairs (who told his colleagues that he did not intend to spend any chips on it); the NSC delegated it to the NEC, the USTR, and Commerce; and the Department of Defense (DOD) remained preoccupied with other matters.

As a result, the EIT proposal was introduced very late and, according to staff members on both committees, not vigorously pushed or convincingly explained by those assigned the task at the deputies level (cf. *Inside U.S. Trade,* 22 July 1994, 11–12); according to one of the participants, their behavior constituted a modern-day version of "the treason of the clerks." The cycle was extremely difficult to break: when those in favor of the EIT initiative managed to have calls to the Senate Finance Committee and the House Ways and Means Committee put on the calendar of the deputy secretary of state, for example, he delegated the task to the assistant secretary, who in reality was one of the "clerks," because the latter was more familiar with the details and better known to committee staff.

The only principal from the administration to weigh in, at the last minute, to try to salvage the initiative was the vice president. With an urgent personal phone call, he managed to get it included in Chairman Moynihan's "mark," but the proposal was rejected by the Senate Finance Committee when Senator Hatch moved to strike it from the legislation.

6.5   Testing the Models of the U.S. Trade Policy Process

Evidence from the antidumping parts of the Uruguay Round has its limitations. Clearly, one case study cannot be used to evaluate models of trade policy formation under all circumstances.

Perhaps the outcome on antidumping was, for example, simply the price the country had to pay to get the Uruguay Round completed. Destler reports that USTR Strauss viewed the more protectionist antidumping procedures embodied in the 1979 Trade Agreements Act as a "tolerable price to pay" for the support of the integrated steel producers and their supporters in Congress and characterizes USTR Kantor as viewing defense of U.S. antidumping laws as essential to his and the administration's "reputation for toughness and hence its credibility for pushing trade expansion" in the Congress (Destler 1995, 149, 241).

But surely this begs the question. Opposition to the U.S. position on antidumping was extremely strong and widespread, especially among the Asian trading partners, who themselves were holding out on financial services, industrial market access (e.g., glass and zero-for-zeros in copper, wood products, and chemicals), and agriculture. So the issue was what kind of a grand bargain could be struck—a liberalizing grand bargain, in which the United States put antidumping on the table to elicit more generous offers from others, or a restrictive grand bargain, in which the United States "toughed it out" on antidumping and others reciprocated in areas of special interest to them.

Perhaps the outcome was, alternatively, merely the result of a tactical error of oversolicitousness on the part of the core group of negotiators. Perhaps the outcome may eventually appear to reflect, in part, the familiar revolving-door phenomenon in Washington.[24]

There is, however, a general trend of which this antidumping case is a major part, namely, the greater ease with which import-competing firms have been able to obtain administered protection, over the past two decades, a trend that runs counter to the thrust of overall trade liberalization. It may be particularly useful, therefore, to assess the fit between the most common models of trade policy formation and the Uruguay Round antidumping case, with an eye toward future trade negotiations on issues whose structural characteristics resemble those examined here.

6.5.1 An Institutional Structure for the Executive to Save Congress from Itself

The principal explanation for trade liberalization since the Great Depression, an institutional split between the legislative and the executive branches of government, with the former looking to the latter for ways to save itself from its own worse instincts (or simply to get narrow constituencies off its back), finds no support in the case of antidumping. Congressional proponents of more restrictive antidumping laws were decidedly activist. They lobbied the USTR and Commerce repeatedly on antidumping and exacted pledges in the confirmation hearings of political appointees. Prominent congressional supporters of more restrictive antidumping laws traveled to Geneva to watch over the Uruguay Round endgame. House and Senate trade committees both played energetic roles in turning the implementing legislation in a more protectionist direction. The intensity of the struggle over antidumping policy was not an isolated episode; it was reminiscent of the NAFTA battle, which passed with a narrow majority and created an acrimonious split in the Democratic Party. The administration did not want to risk a bruising intraparty battle with the Uruguay Round legislation, especially with the administration's health care legislation making its way through the Senate Finance and House Ways and Means Committees at the same time and with midterm elections looming.[25]

---

24. It will be impossible to give an impartial assessment of the revolving-door process for some time. Once U.S. trade negotiators have left office, they are barred from representing foreign exporters; they are not barred from working for domestic firms, to help orchestrate their trade strategy in Washington and Geneva, so long as they do not directly lobby their former agencies for a period of one year. (Also, many of the key players who have taken part in determining policy on antidumping policy do not technically qualify as "trade negotiators.")

25. Congressional activism in antidumping policy is not new. Baldwin and Moore (1991), e.g., characterize it as the best example of congressional efforts over the past thirty years to assert a dominant role in trade policy. They point to efforts not only to change the antidumping law but also

Members of Congress were not just active in a general sense during the process but engaged in constituent service. They sought changes in the rules that can be readily traced to the interests of particular constituents—frequently in an effort to reverse previous decisions that had gone against a constituent.[26] Although Congress did not engage in line-by-line tariff setting, there was little doubt about the consequences of the rule changes that were sought (higher dumping margins and more frequent injury determinations) and who would benefit from the changes.[27]

Congressional advocates of more restrictive antidumping laws also exerted influence over the executive branch through staff-level appointments. For example, congressional staff members moved to key posts in the new administration with the backing of their former employers. Together with the pressures exerted through the confirmation process on more senior appointees, members of Congress were able to help shape the legislation.

Was the success of congressional backers of restrictive antidumping laws due to a lack of strong administration pressure that would have served as a counterweight? Once back from Geneva, the administration initially did set out to present implementing legislation that was generally faithful to the Geneva agreement. Even here, however, the interests of import-competing industries were accommodated to some extent by provisions allowed under the

---

to influence regulations and procedures and to influence the "nature of the personnel appointed to political positions" in Commerce. Destler (1995) acknowledges a history of congressional activism in antidumping that contrasts with Congress's usual practice of delegating line-by-line tariff setting to the Executive.

26. For example, the change in the negligibility threshold or the captive production clause would have changed the ITC's ruling of no injury in several of the 1993 steel cases.

27. Douglas Nelson (1989) offers an ingenious method to explain the split between congressional protectionism and executive liberalism while supporting the thesis of what he calls "executive dominance of trade policy." He argues that administered protection (antidumping, countervailing duty, and escape clause) alters the role of the legislative branch from engaging in a distributional struggle in which Congress awards individual industries special favors to pursuing what Theodore Lowi calls a "regulatory issue," defining the rules under which all firms/industries have access to protectionism on the same terms. This transformation undermines the logrolling dynamics of protectionist coalitions and allows the congressional dynamic to remain fundamentally protectionist without derailing the executive's push for liberalization (which Nelson ascribes to the determination of key decision makers, especially in the State Department, to use international trade policy as an instrument of national security policy). "In exchange for guarantees that no significant sectors of the population would suffer sustained injury, the executive branch was given the power to pursue a sustained policy of trade liberalization."

The antidumping case examined here, however, shows congressional representatives intervening on behalf of individual industries (steel and semiconductors, e.g.) to put in place both a broad antidumping regime and particular rules of implementation that will benefit their constituents quite specifically, to the detriment of other major sectors of the economy (e.g., exporters and domestic users of imported steel and semiconductors). Nelson's (1989) idea that antidumping regulations act as a kind of safety net for the economy as a whole (the functional equivalent of an escape clause or an adjustment assistance program), whose presence confers permission to the executive to liberalize goods and services across the board, does not fit the facts as well as the simpler notion of a particularly well-organized and tenacious special interest group maneuvering to get its way at the expense of other sectors and holding their benefits hostage until its interests could be satisfied (or its power negated).

agreement (e.g., by continuing to compare average prices to individual prices in reviews). Moreover, there was ongoing ambiguity about how firmly the administration intended to hold the line against protectionist modifications. USTR Kantor made statements that suggested that the administration might be flexible on ESP and on captive production. In addition, there were leaks to the press to the effect that the administration was "split" or "not firm" in its announced antidumping positions. These reports were no doubt accurate to some extent. Historically, the executive has not been unified on antidumping. Indeed, Congress pressured the executive to transfer antidumping responsibility from the Treasury Department to the Commerce Department because of the contrasting perspectives embedded in the two institutions. But public disclosure of these splits had the effect of strengthening the hand of import-competing interests and weakening the position of those in the administration seeking to resist congressional pressures.

Overall, to fit the policy-formation process on antidumping, this save-Congress-from-itself model would have to be turned not only on its head but also inside out: former practitioners from the ranks of the petitioners' trade bar and from congressional staffs entered the administration to act as custodians against more liberal tendencies operating there. Their interaction with the Congress inflated the value of antidumping as an issue and turned the argument that it was a deal breaker into a self-fulfilling prophecy.

Looking toward the "new trade agenda" on trade and the environment, trade and labor standards, and trade and competition policy, how realistic will it be to expect that one will find a Congress that wants the executive to brush aside its supposed demands and take the higher road toward trade liberalization that the members themselves in their secret heart of hearts really do favor as the preferred outcome?

6.5.2   MNC and Exporter Clout to Expand Market Access Abroad

There is a major mystery why the big U.S. exporters and MNCs did not use their influence to offset the antidumping protectionists (but, rather, in some prominent cases, most notably the semiconductor industry, actually supported them). Indeed, their behavior did not even meet the Yoffie/Milner "strategic trade model" test of making access to the U.S. market contingent on greater reciprocal access abroad. Instead, they permitted a worldwide regime to be codified that would restrict exports among major production centers and restrain global sourcing networks. Why were they the dog that did not bark?

Although they generally have an interest in liberalized antidumping laws, most large exporters and MNCs have a number of other trade policy objectives. The intensity of their interest in antidumping does not match that of frequent antidumping law users for whom administered protection is the central objective in trade policy. And relative intensity of interest is important in Congress. The high priority of antidumping to petitioners (like the integrated steel producers) is mirrored in the high priority of antidumping to those in Congress who push their agenda. When putting together a sizable piece of legislation, even leaders who generally support more liberal trade want to make problems go away. Neutralizing the effect of those who feel strongly about an issue requires effort and political capital that have an opportunity cost, contributing to the idea that doing the right thing on antidumping is a political loser.

In general, large U.S. exporters and MNCs did not match the intensity of interest of the petitioners because they were saving their chips for even more important items for themselves in the Uruguay Round negotiations than antidumping. The representations of prominent international companies for whom antidumping policy was a potential concern directed the bulk of their lobbying efforts toward areas of greater salience for their corporations, such as zero-for-zero tariff cuts in their industries, IPR (intellectual property rights) protection, or government procurement. When they did weigh in, they tended to focus on provisions within the antidumping legislation that would affect their interests as importers of intermediate goods. The Computer and Business Equipment Manufacturers Association (CBEMA), for example, concentrated its antidumping lobbying on narrow subissues like short supply (to facilitate imports of flat panel displays) or start-up costs.

At the same time, they had to conserve their political influence for deployment in other directions altogether; in particular, they had to expend resources to support renewal of most-favored nation (MFN) status for China that could otherwise have gone into lobbying on the implementing legislation. They simply could not match the single-issue intensity on antidumping of, for example, the integrated steel producers. The lack of CEO-level pressure on members of Congress from exporters and MNCs was mentioned repeatedly on Capitol Hill during the late spring as a reason for the lesser exporter/MNC effect on the antidumping legislation.

Contributing to less intense interest in more liberal antidumping laws is the possibility that the interests of some U.S. exporters and MNCs may be ambiguous when it comes to antidumping laws. The U.S. market remains a large one for U.S. exporters and for the MNC community. For some firms, the prospect of using the antidumping laws to attain greater protection in the U.S. market may be attractive even if it might mean that they will be the subject of antidumping actions in foreign markets. And, even if they are the subject of antidumping actions abroad, antidumping laws can act as anticompetitive devices that set price floors and enforce collusive behavior and might raise their profits in some export markets.[28]

In future trade negotiations, how likely might it be that the exporter and MNC community can be more greatly energized to offset the twin clout of

---

28. Staiger and Wolak (1991) present a model in which antidumping laws facilitate collusive behavior during periods of slack demand when enforcement is especially difficult. Staiger and Wolak (1994a, 1994b) present evidence consistent with the use of antidumping petitions as a device to enforce collusive behavior. Messerlin (1990) argues that this is important in the European Union chemicals industry.

domestic protectionists and single-interest groups concerned about the environment, labor, and "inside the border" sovereignty issues?

6.5.3 The Broader Political and Economic Interests of the American Hegemon (Even a Declining Hegemon)

The antidumping case points the trend line in a direction opposite to what these models of system maintenance and realpolitik predict. The United States did not play the role of hegemonic leader, or "benevolent despot" in Kindleberger's characterization, guiding and forcing the international economic system in the direction of liberalization of the antidumping regime. Quite the opposite, it guided and forced the international economic system to accept a more restrictive global antidumping regime.

Nor did the United States play the role of the declining hegemon, calibrating its strategy to produce an outcome that would give greatest relative gains to the United States. Because the United States has been the most frequent target of antidumping cases worldwide, the antidumping outcome will hurt U.S. exporters more than it will foreign exporters.[29] Instead of producing greater relative gains for the United States (per the realpolitik school of Walz and Mastanduno) or greater reciprocity of market access for U.S.-based multinationals (the Yoffie/Milner strategic trade qualification), the reverse will be true.

What is noteworthy is the ease with which the "high politics" community was marginalized, not just on the broad issue of antidumping, but even on the specific issue of treatment of products from economies in transition, the success of whose reforms was characterized as the highest foreign policy priority of the administration during this period of policy struggle. (This case therefore offers a dramatic reversal of Prestowitz's [1988] assertion that trade issues find themselves subordinated to the diplomatic needs of the national security community.)

To be sure, the antidumping debate had arcane elements that could be exploited by the protectionist side in the government. Senior players on foreign policy issues declined to weigh in on the struggle over trade reform for economies in transition because they were uncomfortable debating the intricacies of injury standards or constructed costs, even though the most ardent defender of antidumping (the Commerce Department) admitted in writing that the current system was hopelessly biased against EIT exports and could not be repaired by anything short of new legislation.[30]

---

29. Between 1989 and 1993, U.S. exporters were targeted by more antidumping cases than were exporters from any other country. Moreover, the use of antidumping laws is growing. As recently as 1990, about two dozen countries had antidumping laws. More than forty do now, and several others are likely to adopt such laws in the near future.

30. The director of the policy planning staff at the State Department (a lawyer) ultimately abandoned the trench warfare over the tests for injury and causation with the assistant secretary for economics (a trade lawyer), even while instructing the staff to continue to highlight U.S. support for market access for Eastern Europe and Russia as a priority in the speeches of the secretary of state.

Other senior players did weigh in, and then faded away, preoccupied with other issues. Early in the EIT debate, the undersecretary of defense (later deputy secretary of defense) stormed into an NEC deputies meeting to which the DOD had not been invited, was immediately given the floor, and declared how strategically important it was for the United States to change its treatment of exports from the former Soviet Union. The NEC deputies nodded in agreement, invited the DOD principal deputy assistant secretary (who was professionally very knowledgeable about antidumping issues) to the next few meetings, and then dropped him from the list when he consistently failed to show up while working on the administration's flat panel display initiative.

In coming years, is there greater plausibility that the "high politics" community of security officials in the U.S. government will be *more* able, or *less* able, to hold the "low politics" agenda of domestic interests and enthusiasms in check?

6.6   Implications for Future Trade Policy Making: A "Paradigm Shift" in the Making?

How does the antidumping case study look from the perspective of the comparative literature on policy making in the United States? As one looks to the "new trade agenda" of the future, might there be a need for a paradigm shift in how the trade policy-formation process can best be conceptualized?

Trade policy cannot be explained by economic models of a government seeking to maximize the welfare of its residents. It is difficult to explain either the extent of protection or its structure with models of a benevolent, welfare-maximizing government. While the trade policy process deflects pressures toward general closure, it nevertheless still repeatedly produces suboptimal and nonmajoritarian outcomes. Attempts to model the politics of trade policy with individuals voting their rational self-interest have given way to models that focus on the role of rent-seeking interest groups with disproportional influence via campaign finance when collective goods conditions constrain effective action on the part of the beneficiaries of trade liberalization.[31] More recent work derives an electoral equilibrium in which each political party acts as if it were maximizing a weighted sum of the aggregate welfares of (informed) voters and members of interest groups, trading off extra campaign contributions obtained by catering to the interest groups' demands against the votes that the resulting actions might cost them (Grossman and Helpman 1994).

The comparative literature on public policy making adds a further dimension by focusing less on electoral politics per se and more on the conditions surrounding agenda setting, decision making, and policy implementation. The antidumping case illustrates how important this policy-formation dimension

---

31. Baldwin (1985) and Krueger (1993) survey the development in the economics literature of the political economy of commercial policy. Krueger (1995) examines the political economy of commercial policy in a number of industries.

can be for understanding protectionist outcomes. This dimension is likely to be all the more prominent in the struggle over the "new agenda" trade issues.

This comparative literature on public policy formation yields three rather somber insights.

First, collective-goods problems are prominent in understanding not only who does not take an active part in policy struggles but also who does take an active part. In the face of relative passivity on the part of many who are widely dispersed and only mildly affected by a particular policy outcome, there is a propensity to find the terms of the debate, the posing of alternatives, the tactics of maneuver, and the selection of policy makers to be dominated by "volunteers," who differ from the general public in their zeal and commitment to single issues and in their unwillingness to compromise easily for a more generally accepted definition of the common good.

The literature that analyzes this phenomenon tries to explain perverse outcomes in electoral campaigns (why do the primaries produce candidates and candidate positions at variance with what is desired by the majority of the electorate?), in budget debates (why is a particular category like social security sacrosanct?), and in controversial issue debates (why was the majority-supported Equal Rights Amendment defeated? why is the minority-supported pro life position so often a litmus test?) (cf. Mansbridge 1986).

In the antidumping case, owing to the domination of the Orwellian debate by the protectionists, there was a certain element of "true believer" zealotry about the need to defend the integrity and sovereignty of U.S. policy against the "unfair" practices of outsiders. In the "new agenda," the proponents of the protectionist side of the debate are likely to find it easy to capture the rhetorical high ground and motivate dedicated efforts on the part of those who feel strongly about the environment, labor standards, or sovereign control over domestic issues like competition policy.[32] In contrast to antidumping, the environmental and labor agendas on trade have genuine substantive reasons to appeal to supporters as well as serving as cover for protectionists.

In short, the collective goods problem is likely to show up on the "new agenda" trade issues with doubly perverse consequences, generating single-interest true believers from within the hard-to-mobilize general public plus concentrated special interests from within the easy-to-mobilize sectors threatened by trade liberalization, both on the side of greater protection.

Second, the comparative literature points out a tendency to form "networks" of like-minded supporters across agency boundaries, carefully vetted in the confirmation process, who combine expertise and determination in pursuing their objectives and excluding outsiders, in a policy-making milieu that has become more decentralized and fragmented over the past several decades.

---

32. The rhetorical high ground is surprisingly important. Destler and Odell (1987, 73) found that activity in opposition to trade restrictions was "significantly lighter or absent" in cases "where charges of unfairness were . . . prominent."

In the past, the most prominent power structure that perpetuated outcomes favorable to specific interests was the mechanism christened the "iron triangle" consisting of congressional committee chairs, well-financed lobbies, and well-placed bureaucrats. This has fit well with the conventional conception of rent-seeking behavior. Now that two decades of congressional "reform" have cut back the power of committee chairs while proliferating the numbers of committees and subcommittees themselves and political appointees have replaced career civil servants more widely in policy-making positions within the executive, the newer methodology in the political science literature is to show how special interests have narrowed their demands and created "networks" of committed supporters throughout a much more complex governmental environment than existed in the earlier era (Heclo 1978; Browne and Paik 1993).[33]

The study of U.S. agricultural policy, for example, once relied heavily on the use of the "iron triangle" metaphor. As agricultural issues have been apportioned in a Congress and an executive that is more decentralized, with overlapping jurisdictions for aspects of farming that pertain to the environment, conservation, energy, consumer protection, and international competition as well as agricultural production, the tracing of painstakingly placed networks of supporters and sympathizers has become more prominent in explaining outcomes (Browne and Paik 1993).

In the antidumping case, presided over by the watchful eye of the congressional confirmation process, the deployment of a set of decidedly nonneutral policy players across agency lines made the prospects for participating in interagency debate on antidumping issues, let alone wresting control of the outcome from the "network," exceedingly difficult and unlikely. In the "new agenda," the networks arrayed against trade liberalization (to extend the previous argument) will be *double strength,* combining single-issue "true believers" with opportunistic protectionists. The new trade issues community of environmentalists and labor representatives cum threatened industry interests will be ready and eager to field a team of spirited and determined veteran practitioners in the policy-formation process; the freer trade community is less likely to be similarly prepared or energized. As a consequence, the appointments process is likely to constitute a microcosm of this collective-goods problem: high-level political appointments matter, and true believers will ally with concentrated vested interests to get sympathetic and reliable individuals in place for the battles to come. One might predict, therefore, that the appointments process

---

33. The literature on "iron triangles" and "networks" has important implications for the analysis of rent-seeking behavior. Models of the latter tend to assume that protectionists have to mobilize and expend enough resources to affect aggregate electoral outcomes. But, clearly, this is too high a hurdle. Instead, special interests seeking protection have to dispense just enough rents to nurture an iron triangle of congressional committees, related agencies, and affected industries or, perhaps even less, to maintain a network of committed activists just strong enough to logroll or back scratch successfully on behalf of their sponsors. In short, a little bit of rents may be able to go a long way.

itself will be vulnerable to "capture" in the way that the antidumping case illustrates.

Third, far from finding Congress deliberately ceding control over policy outcomes to the executive in the interest of protecting the broader "national interest," the comparative literature on policy formation shows determined efforts by Congress to create structures and processes that are deliberately designed to insulate policy outcomes from the broader "national interest" test.

Three cases highlighted in the comparative literature, for example, are the Occupational Safety and Health Administration (OSHA), the Environmental Protection Agency (EPA), and the Consumer Product Safety Commission (CPSC) (Moe 1989). Their formal structures vary greatly: OSHA is carefully buried within a presumably friendly agency, the Labor Department; the CPSC is an autonomous regulatory commission, a form strongly desired by consumer advocates despite (or perhaps because of) their observation over the years of the vulnerability of commissions to capture; the EPA is an independent agency with a mandate theoretically covering the entire economy and society. But, in each case, their supporters created them precisely to give them insulation from and superiority over efforts to make their actions mesh with broader conceptions of the public good (Chubb and Peterson 1989). Their supporters have established them to serve particular interests, undeterred by future congresses or presidents with a different agenda.

The antidumping case clearly falls into this subgroup of structures and processes that is difficult to harness and control on behalf of the greatest good for the greatest number, with the ITC an independent agency and the Commerce bureaucracy forming a quasi-independent apparatus, bolstered by administrative procedures and judicial rulings. Even a president must expend large amounts of capital to bring about change. The same is likely to be true on "new agenda" issues.

Moreover, on any issue that is at all technical, where there are contrasting opinions that are not the most blatant traditional protectionism (i.e., not so blatant and simple as to set off 1930s-analogy alarm bells), the high politics community, inattentive and busy with other serious national security issues, is quite vulnerable to being marginalized, at least until faits accomplis are accomplis.

As a consequence, therefore, in contrast to a stylized division between the executive and the Congress, with the former staunchly upholding trade liberalization with the tacit approval of the latter, there will likely be intimate links created with executive-congressional appointees advocating protectionist measures and turning market-opening possibilities into deal breakers whenever they are pursued. Analytically, the notion of a congressional-executive split, with the executive pursuing the broader common interest and offsetting the protectionist impulses of the Congress, is likely to vanish as a useful model for much of the trade policy-formation process.

This might well suggest considerable pessimism about making much trade-expanding progress on the "new agenda," unless proliberalization forces, including the MNC and big exporter community, can be mobilized and energized as an effective counterweight to more market-closing pressure groups in the formation of trade policy.

References

Arnold, Bruce. 1994. How the GATT affects U.S. antidumping and countervailing-duty policy. Washington, D.C.: Congressional Budget Office.

Baldwin, Robert E. 1985. *The political economy of U.S. import policy.* Cambridge, Mass.: MIT Press.

Baldwin, Robert E., and Michael O. Moore. 1991. Political aspects of the administration of the trade remedy laws. In *Down in the dumps: Administration of the unfair trade laws,* ed. Richard Boltuck and Robert Litan. Washington, D.C.: Brookings.

Boltuck, Richard, and Robert E. Litan, eds. 1991. *Down in the dumps: Administration of the unfair trade laws.* Washington, D.C.: Brookings.

Browne, William P., and Won K. Paik. 1993. Beyond the domain: Recasting network politics in the postreform Congress. *American Journal of Political Science* 37, no. 4 (November): 1054–79.

Chubb, John E., and Paul E. Peterson, eds. 1989. *Can the government govern?* Washington, D.C.: Brookings.

Coates, Daniel E., and Rodney D. Ludema. 1994. Unilateral tariff reduction as leadership in the political economy of trade negotiations. Working paper. Georgetown University.

Cohen, Stephen D. 1988. *The making of U.S. international economic policy.* 2d ed. New York: Praeger.

Destler, I. M. 1995. *American trade politics.* 3d ed. Washington, D.C.: Institute for International Economics, with the Twentieth Century Fund.

Destler I. M., John S. Odell, and Kimberly Ann Elliott. 1987. *Anti-protection: Changing forces in United States trade politics.* Policy Analyses in International Economics 21. Washington, D.C.: Institute for International Economics.

Goldstein, Judith. 1986. The political economy of trade: Institutions of protection. *American Political Science Review* 80, no. 1: 161–84.

———. 1988. Ideas, institutions and American trade policy. *International Organization* 42, no. 1: 179–217.

Grossman, Gene M., and Elhanan Helpman. 1994. Protection for sale. *American Economic Review* 84: 833–50.

Heclo, Hugh. 1978. Issue networks and the executive establishment. In *The new American political system,* ed. Anthony King. Washington, D.C.: American Enterprise Institute.

Horlick, Gary N., and Eleanor C. Shea. 1995. The World Trade Organization antidumping agreement. *Journal of World Trade* 29, no. 1 (February): 5–31.

Horlick, Gary N., and Shannon S. Shuman. 1984. Nonmarket economy trade and U.S. antidumping/countervailing duty laws. *International Lawyer* 18, no. 4 (Fall): 307–40.

Hufbauer, Gary Clyde. 1989. *The free trade debate.* Reports of the Twentieth Century Fund Task Force on the Future of American Trade Policy, Background paper. New York: Priority Press.

Kindleberger, Charles P. 1973. *The world in depression, 1929–1939.* Berkeley: University of California Press.

————. 1986. Hierarchy versus inertial cooperation. *International Organization* 40: 841–47.

Krueger, Anne O. 1993. The political economy of U.S. protection in theory and in practice. In *Trade, welfare, and economic policies,* ed. Horst Herberg and Ngo Van Long. Ann Arbor: University of Michigan Press.

————. 1995. *Political economy of trade protection.* Chicago: University of Chicago Press.

Lawrence, Robert Z. 1994. The dangers of the ESP amendment. Working paper. Harvard University.

Mansbridge, Jane J. 1986. *How we lost the ERA.* Chicago: University of Chicago Press.

Mastanduno, Michael. 1991. Do relative gains matter: America's response to Japanese industrial policy. *International Security* 16, no. 1 (Summer): 73–113.

McKeown, Timothy J. 1984. Firms and tariff change: Explaining the demand for protection. *World Politics* 36, no. 2: 215–33.

Messerlin, Patrick A. 1990. Anti-dumping regulations or pro-cartel law? The EC chemical cases. *World Economy* 13: 465–92.

Milner, Helen. 1988. *Resisting protectionism: Global industries and the politics of international trade.* Princeton, N.J.: Princeton University Press.

Milner, Helen, and David B. Yoffie. 1989. Strategic trade policy and corporate trade demands. *International Organization* 43, no. 2 (Spring): 239–73.

Moe, Terry M. 1989. The politics of bureaucratic structure. In *Can the government govern,* ed. John E. Chubb and Paul E. Peterson. Washington, D.C.: Brookings.

Nelson, Douglas. 1989. Domestic political preconditions of U.S. trade policy: Liberal structure and protectionist dynamics. *Journal of Public Policy* 9: 83–108.

Olson, Mancur. 1965. *The logic of collective action: Public goods and the theory of groups.* Cambridge, Mass.: Harvard University Press.

Pastor, Robert. 1980. *Congress and the politics of U.S. foreign economic policy, 1929–1976.* Berkeley and Los Angeles: University of California Press.

Prestowitz, Clyde. 1988. *Trading places: How we allowed Japan to take the lead.* New York: Basic.

Schattschneider, E. E. 1935. *Politics, pressures and the tariff.* New York: Prentice-Hall.

Staiger, Robert W., and Frank A. Wolak. 1991. Strategic use of AD law to enforce tacit international collusion. Working paper. Stanford University.

————. 1994a. Measuring industry-specific protection: Antidumping in the United States. *Brookings Papers on Economic Activity: Microeconomics,* 51–103.

————. 1994b. The trade effects of antidumping investigations: Theory and evidence. In *Analytical and negotiating issues in the global trading system,* ed. Alan V. Deardorff and Robert M. Stern. Ann Arbor: University of Michigan Press.

Walz, Kenneth N. 1979. *The theory of international politics.* New York: Random House.

7 The Trade Effects of U.S. Antidumping Actions

Thomas J. Prusa

Even though tariff rates fell throughout the late 1970s and 1980s, there is growing consensus that the overall level of protection in the United States rose during this period. For instance, Bhagwati (1988, 43) states, "The downward trend in trade restrictions resulting from declining tariffs was rudely interrupted in the mid-1970s," and Nivola (1993) points out that between 1975 and 1985 the volume of U.S. import trade affected by some form of trade barriers doubled. In fact, from a historical perspective, what is surprising is not that the long postwar period of trade liberalization was interrupted (at least temporarily) but that the era of trade liberalization lasted so long.[1]

Rather, what is unusual about the recent rise in protectionism is the form that it has taken. In earlier years, increased demand for protection was met with comprehensive tariff bills. By contrast, the recent rise in protection is almost entirely due to administered protection and nontariff barriers such as voluntary export restraints (VERs), which differ in several important ways from traditional tariff protection. First of all, the modern tools of protection are typically more subtle and less transparent than tariffs, falling in the grey area between GATT-consistent and GATT-inconsistent protection. This ambiguity explains why the modern tools are so popular since it allows countries considerable discretion over when and how to implement these policies. Is a health standard that outlaws the sale of beef from cattle injected with growth hormones truly based on concern for public safety, or is it simply an attempt

Thomas J. Prusa is associate professor of economics at Rutgers University and a faculty research fellow of the National Bureau of Economic Research.

The author is indebted to Rob Feenstra for assistance in constructing the data set and to Bob Staiger and the seminar participants at the NBER conference for their helpful comments.

1. For most of U.S. history, periods of trade liberalization were quite short-lived, typically lasting only five or six years (Taussig 1931).

191

to reduce the amount of imported beef? Are budget cuts that significantly reduce the staff at customs offices a sincere effort to manage the federal deficit or a veiled attempt to raise the cost of exporting into the U.S. market? Is an industry's fall in profits and sales due to increasingly efficient foreign competitors, or is this injury due to dumped imports?

A second key characteristic—and the one that is the focus of this paper—is that the modern instruments are usually not comprehensive. Protection via VERs and the unfair trade statutes is product and country specific. For instance, the 1981 automobile VER with Japan neither restricted automobiles from South Korea nor (initially) restricted light trucks or utility vehicles from Japan. One might expect that the restriction on Japanese automobiles would lead to an increase in the imports of Japanese trucks and utility vehicles and South Korean automobiles.[2] Similarly, an antidumping (AD) duty levied on carbon steel pipes from France is not levied on carbon steel pipes from Germany. One would expect that an antidumping duty levied on a single source would cause exports from the named country (i.e., France) to fall and those from nonnamed countries to increase.

The goal of this paper is to begin to address the issue of how the country-specific nature of AD protection affects its use and effectiveness. I find evidence that AD protection induces substantial trade diversion from named to nonnamed countries. There is also evidence that, the larger the estimated duty, the larger the amount of diversion. Because the magnitude of import diversion is found to be quite large, the results also suggest that AD duties are less restrictive than the domestic industry might expect. Nonetheless, AD duties are valuable since trade is restrained by more in cases resulting in duties than in cases that are rejected. More generally, AD actions are valuable since they induce substantial increases in import prices—by both named and nonnamed countries.

The paper will proceed as follows. In section 7.1, I provide background on the rise of U.S. AD activity and discuss related research. In section 7.2, I present data on the trade effects of AD actions, with particular emphasis on the magnitude of import diversion from named to nonnamed countries. Given that I find import diversion to be substantial, the aggressive U.S. use of AD law has a peculiar side effect—countries that are active in the categories under investigation (but not named) will benefit from the AD sanctions on rivals. In other words, the diversion of imports implies that domestic producers are not the only firms that benefit from an AD action. Countries such as South Korea and Brazil, both of which are frequently named in AD petitions, may nevertheless be net beneficiaries of AD actions since they also gain from sanctions on other countries. This issue of which countries have experienced the most contraction of trade and which have experienced the most expansion as a result

---

2. For analyses of the VER on Japanese automobiles, see Feenstra (1984, 1987) and Dinopoulos and Kreinin (1988).

of U.S. AD actions is discussed in section 7.3. A few concluding comments are made in section 7.4.

7.1 Background

7.1.1 The Rise of AD Law

During the 1980s, there were more cases filed under AD law (almost five hundred) than under all the other trade statutes combined (Baldwin and Steagall 1994; Hansen and Prusa 1995). AD law, however, is far from an overnight sensation. In fact, AD law is one of the oldest of U.S. trade statutes. The emergence of AD law as the preeminent trade statute is the result of many revisions and amendments over the years; the vast majority of the amendments were geared toward expanding its applicability and increasing the likelihood of an AD case resulting in duties. Prior to 1958, for instance, AD actions were extremely rare. Then, in 1958, Congress amended the rules governing the way in which the dumping margin was calculated, and petition filings increased: about twenty to twenty-five petitions were filed per year between 1958 and 1973; however, the rejection rate was quite high (on average, only two or three cases per year would result in duties). In 1974, AD law was again significantly amended: the definition of dumping was broadened to include sales below cost, and strict time limits on the length of the investigation were imposed. Following the 1974 amendments, AD filings jumped by 50 percent. Despite these changes, the rejection rate remained around 85 percent.

Frustrated by the lack of protection afforded by the law, industries lobbied Congress to make the law more likely to result in duties. These lobbying efforts were manifested in the Trade Agreement Act of 1979, which contained numerous significant changes to AD law. Among them, the power to investigate less than fair value was transferred from the Department of Treasury to the Department of Commerce, use of "best information available" was approved, and time limits on cases were shortened. As a result of these amendments, the use of AD law exploded. During the years following these amendments, AD filings surged, averaging forty-five to fifty cases per year, and the rejection rate dropped to about 50 percent.

The point of this historical background is to emphasize that AD is a malleable, frequently amended statute. AD law is now the most widely used trade statute primarily because congressional amendments have made the statute far more applicable than it was in the 1960s and 1970s. The kinds of pricing behavior that are sanctionable under AD have changed over the years. And, importantly, usually these changes are in response to complaints from U.S. industries who find the current implementation of the law unsatisfactory. One would expect, then, that the country-specific nature of AD protection would be a prime target for change. However, GATT guidelines prevent Congress from amending AD law to apply to imports from all sources.

A more creative solution was needed, and the "cumulation" amendment contained in the Trade and Tariff Act of 1984 is a significant step in the direction of making AD protection more comprehensive. The cumulation provision requires the International Trade Commission (ITC) to cumulate imports when a trade dispute involves imports from multiple sources. Without cumulation, imports are evaluated on a country-by-country basis when determining injury; when cumulation is applied, the ITC aggregates all "like" imports from all countries under investigation and assesses the combined effect on the domestic industry.

When Congress was debating whether to mandate cumulation, the issue of diversion was never mentioned. Rather, the stated reason for the amendment was that the source of the dumped or subsidized imports was irrelevant. What mattered was that the cumulated volume was injurious. This argument in favor of cumulation has been referred to as the "hammering effect" since, according to industries and their representatives, "a domestic industry that suffers material injury by reason of 100,000 tons of unfairly traded imports from a single country is injured to the same degree by 20,000 tons of unfairly traded imports from each of five different countries" (Suder 1983, 470–71). The main goal of mandated cumulation was to reduce the rejection rate at the ITC. Hansen and Prusa (in press) find that this has indeed been the result; they estimate that cumulation increases the probability of an affirmative injury determination by 20-30 percent and has changed the ITC's decision (from negative to affirmative) for about one-third of cumulated cases.

Cumulation may also have important implications for import diversion. For instance, if (i) cumulation increases the number of multiple petition filings and (ii) the greater the number of countries named in the petition, the less significant will be the import diversion, then cumulation will effectively make AD law more comprehensive. The first part of the hypothesis is clearly correct since, during the years following mandated cumulation, there has been a 50 percent increase in multiple petition filings. The second part of the hypothesis is an issue we will want to examine in this paper (i.e., Is diversion less important when more countries are named?).

7.1.2 Related Research

The popularity of AD law has spurred a large body of literature, both theoretical and empirical, but none has focused specifically on the issue of diversion. The theoretical research on AD law has focused on its strategic and incentive effects.[3] Broadly speaking, the empirical literature on AD law can be divided into two groups. One line of research is based on Baldwin's (1985)

---

3. Depending on the precise model specification, AD law can induce a rich variety of strategic effects. For example, in Anderson (1992), the threat of an AD duty induces foreign firms to behave more competitively, while, in Staiger and Wolak (1991), Leidy (1993), and Prusa (1994), AD law can facilitate collusion. Fischer (1992) points out that the nature of the strategic competition influences how AD law affects competition.

seminal work on the determinants of administered protection.[4] Another group of papers empirically estimates the effects of antidumping cases.[5] However, a shortcoming of virtually all the empirical papers is that estimates are based on aggregated data, typically four-digit Standard Industrial Classification (SIC) industry data. For example, Lichtenberg and Tan (1994) estimate the effects of AD cases, but their estimates are for all SIC-level imports (i.e., from all source countries). Given that AD protection is country specific, their aggregated approach will not measure the important trade creation and diversion that are a fundamental characteristic of AD protection.

An important exception is Krupp and Pollard (1992), which examines the effects of AD actions in the chemical industry using monthly Tariff Schedules of the United States Annotated (TSUSA) level import data. Krupp and Pollard's use of disaggregated data allows them to examine the effect of AD actions on the chemical industry. However, since they collect disaggregated data for only a single industry, they cannot address the general issue of diversion.

Staiger and Wolak (1994) also control for the aggregation issue caused by using SIC-level data by normalizing SIC-level imports with the number of TSUSA codes under investigation in each SIC category. Staiger and Wolak estimate trade effects of AD investigation, with particular emphasis on the filing and investigation effects. Even though their estimates are based on SIC data, Staiger and Wolak are still able to find evidence of import diversion and in general find that the restraint on overall imports is about one-third to half as much as on imports from the named country.

7.2   The Trade Effects of AD Actions

7.2.1   The Data

In order to examine the trade effects of AD cases, time-series trade data for each AD case needed to be constructed. To do this, I collected the line-item tariff codes named for each of the 428 AD petitions filed between 1980 and 1988. The product codes and the estimated AD duties are found the *Federal Register* notices accompanying each determination made by the Department of Commerce and the ITC.

Until 1988, products were usually identified by their seven-digit TSUSA code. In a significant number of cases, the products were identified by their five-digit TSUSA code. Because of this difference, and in order to reduce the number of missing values due to the numerous changes in the TSUSA codes, I aggregated all seven-digit codes to their five-digit equivalent. In 1989, the

4. Moore (1992), Baldwin and Steagall (1994), and Hansen and Prusa (in press) all focus on the determination of International Trade Commission decisions. A large number of other related papers are cited therein.

5. Work in this area includes Finger, Hall, and Nelson (1982), Harrison (1991), and Hartigan, Kamma, and Perry (1989).

United States adopted the Harmonized Tariff Schedule (HTS). Therefore, in order to extend the time series beyond 1988, the TSUSA codes were concorded with their corresponding HTS codes. Once the TSUSA codes were collected, import trade data for those products under investigation were extracted from the Commerce Department's annual import trade data by source country. Imports were deflated using the GNP price deflator. Time series for the products involved in each case were constructed from 1978 to 1993.

Other work has shown that settled cases can have a significant effect on trade (Prusa 1992; Staiger and Wolak 1994). However, to narrow the analysis, I chose to exclude settled cases in the present analysis and thus compare import diversion in cases that are rejected with diversion in those that result in duties. After dropping cases where only incomplete data series could be constructed, the data set is composed of 109 rejected cases and 126 cases where duties were levied.[6]

The diversity of AD cases complicates matters since trade volume in some cases amounts to only a few million dollars while in others the trade volume is in the hundreds of millions of dollars. To control for these vast differences, I plot all variables as percentage changes relative to their value in the year the petition was filed (year t_0).[7] The year following the petition is denoted t_1, the year after that t_2, etc. Except under unusual circumstances, the case must be decided within one year, so, during year t_1, imports are being investigated.

7.2.2   Filing Behavior: A Look at the Countries Investigated

The set of countries subject to AD investigations between 1980 and 1988 is comprehensive: over fifty countries representing all major U.S. trading partners were subject to investigation. The bulk of cases were against developed countries and the export-oriented growth countries such as South Korea and Taiwan, but countries as small as Trinidad and Tobago, Bangladesh, and Iran were also subject to AD investigations. In table 7.1, the countries most frequently named in AD petitions are listed. As is readily apparent, the countries at the top of the list constitute virtually all important U.S. trading partners.

In addition, I include the percentage of each country's cases resulting in duties. Between 1980 and 1988, about one-third of AD petitions resulted in duties, one-third resulted in settlements, and one-third were rejected. In general, the countries appearing in this table are representative of the general incidence of duties. In the final column, I give information about the number of cases where the listed country was active in an import market that was subject to an AD investigation but where that country was not named. For instance,

---

6. Incomplete data series can arise if a product's TSUSA code changes (with the result that only partial time series could be constructed) or the TSUSA-HTS concordance is unsatisfactory.

7. I also adjusted the trends for macroeconomic trends by measuring relative to changes in overall merchandise trade. The results are qualitatively the same as those presented here and are available on request.

Table 7.1   **Countries Most Frequently Named in AD Investigations**

Country	No. of Cases Named	% of Cases Resulting in Duties	No. of Cases Exporting to U.S. but Not Named
Japan	52	33	112
Taiwan	26	46	115
West Germany	25	56	122
Italy	25	40	139
Canada	24	50	142
Brazil	23	30	108
South Korea	23	39	109
France	21	38	136
United Kingdom	17	47	145
Belgium	16	44	131
People's Republic of China	16	31	94
Spain	14	21	115
Venezuela	11	27	61

Japanese industries were named as alleged dumpers in fifty-two cases, of which seventeen (33 percent) resulted in duties. In 112 other AD cases, Japan exported to the U.S. market but was not the country subject to investigation. As I discuss in section 7.3, in these cases, Japanese firms potentially stood to benefit from U.S. AD actions. If AD duties are levied, some other country (a rival) would be subject to duties, thereby giving Japanese firms an opportunity to expand their sales in the U.S. market.

7.2.3   Named Country Imports

The first issue is the effect of AD actions on imports from the named country. In figure 7.1, I present changes in the value of imports. The trends look as one would have expected. On average, when duties are levied, trade from the named country is restricted, especially in comparison to when the case is rejected. In year t_1, import trade from the named country (when duties are levied) was 9 percent less than it was in t_0 and 16 percent less than import trade from named countries in rejected cases. In year t_2, import trade from the named country (when duties are levied) was 25 percent less than trade in rejected cases. While these numbers suggest that AD duties have a substantial effect on trade, at least from the named country, it should be noted that the largest restriction appears to occur in the very short run. By t_2, trade from the named country (when duties are levied) is already rebounding, and by t_3, trade exceeds its prepetition level.

The size of the duty plays a key role in how restrictive an AD case is. In figure 7.1 I also compare those cases that are subject to duties in the top quartile (i.e., duties greater than 36 percent) with those subject to duties in the bottom quartile (i.e., cases with positive duties, but less than 7 percent). For

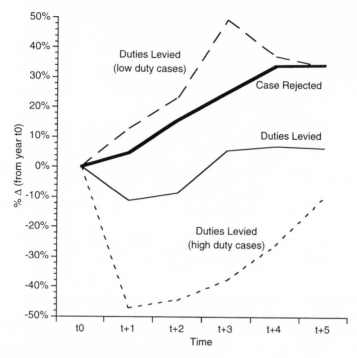

Fig. 7.1 Value of imports (named country)

these two sets of cases, the restrictive effect of AD actions is more marked. For instance, we find that import trade from the named country falls by 47 percent during the first year for countries subject to very high AD duties. By contrast, cases subject to small duties apparently experience no perceptible decline in import trade—and, in fact, imports *grow* by almost 10 percent during the first year following the petition.

While it seems surprising that named imports would grow when duties are levied, this result highlights a unique characteristic of AD protection. If an AD duty is levied and the named country raises its U.S. market price by the full amount of the duty (holding home market prices constant), the assigned duty will never in fact have to be paid. In this case, the AD duty serves to create a price floor for the named country's products. This characteristic likely is part of the explanation for why small duties might be beneficial for the named country. The other key reason is the fact that firms competing noncooperatively typically find that competition forces them to cut their price and that, if they could somehow reduce the incentive to undercut their rivals, they would benefit from higher prices. Since AD duties are essentially government-mandated price floors, and since small duties will raise the named country's AD-distorted price only slightly higher than the original prices, it might easily be the case

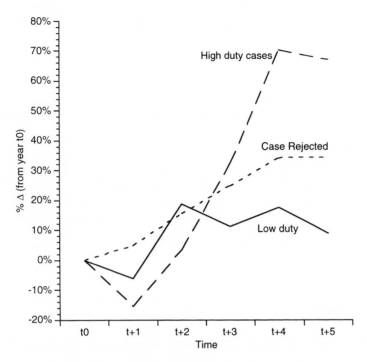

Fig. 7.2 Value of imports (named country), case rejected

that the primary effect of AD duties is the creation of desirable coordination benefits.

It is also instructive to look at imports from named countries in high- and low-duty cases when duties are *not* levied. In figure 7.2, I depict trade patterns for rejected AD cases. What is interesting is that, even when duties are never levied, imports often fall during the investigation. For instance, in cases where high duties are threatened (but ultimately rejected), trade from the named country falls by almost 20 percent during the investigation. This finding is consistent with Staiger and Wolak's (1994) finding that there is a substantial "investigation" effect to an AD petition. It is not surprising that the investigation effect is most apparent for high-duty cases. This effect stems from the fact that, once the Commerce Department makes its preliminary duty calculation, duties are collected (as a bond) pending the final outcome of the investigation. If the case is ultimately rejected, the bond is returned. But, during the investigation, the required bonding creates considerable uncertainty as to the true price of the goods. Once the case is resolved, the uncertainty is resolved, and the investigation effect disappears: imports from named countries (especially those in high-duty cases) rebound sharply.

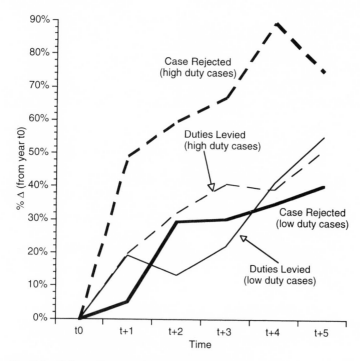

Fig. 7.3   **Value of imports (nonnamed countries)**

7.2.4   Imports from Nonnamed Countries

Even though successful AD actions restrict imports from the named country, the countries that are not subject to the investigation can offset this restraint by increasing their sales to the United States. This potential diversionary effect of AD actions is, indeed, observed. In figure 7.3, the value of imports from non-named countries is depicted. The diversion of trade is large, not only when duties are levied, but also when the case is rejected. In fact, surprisingly, we find that diversion is even more substantial when duties are not levied.

On average, imports from nonnamed countries grow by 22 percent in year t_1. In addition, we find that the diversion is greater for high-duty cases than for low-duty cases. This pattern makes sense given that, in figures 7.1 and 7.2, we saw that the AD actions have a more substantial effect on the named country's imports in high-duty cases than in low-duty cases. For cases where high duties are imposed, nonnamed countries increase their imports 30 percent by year t_2 and 40 percent by year t_3. Diversion is still substantial when low duties are levied, averaging 15-20 percent during each of the first three years following the petition.

In figure 7.4, I again depict imports from nonnamed countries when duties are levied, but here I control for the number of countries named in the petition. As should be expected, diversion is more substantial when only a single coun-

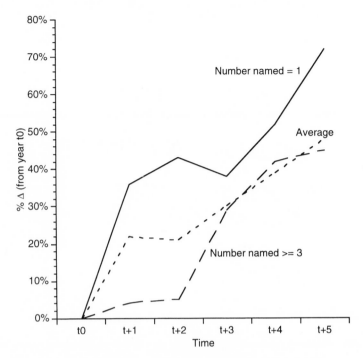

Fig. 7.4   Value of imports (nonnamed countries), duties levied

try is named. In the first year following a petition, nonnamed imports grew by 35 percent when a single country was named, as compared to 4 percent growth when three or more countries are named. This pattern in the amount of diversion persists throughout the years following the case.

7.2.5   Overall Imports

In figure 7.5, the effect on imports (in the investigated product categories) from all source countries is depicted. Two trends emerge. First, the trade effect of AD actions is far less substantial for overall imports than for imports from the named country. For instance, in year t_1, imports from the named country fall by 11 percent when duties are levied. At the same time (year t_1), however, overall imports increase by 15 percent. In year t_2, imports from the named country are still down 9 percent, but overall imports increase by 11 percent. Interestingly, a similar pattern emerges for cases that are rejected. For example, imports from the named country increase by 5 percent in year t_1, but overall imports increase by 19 percent. Clearly, the ability of nonnamed countries to increase imports destined for the United States softens the restrictions imposed by AD duties. Second, diversion does not imply that AD duties have no effect on overall import trade. Overall import growth for cases where duties are levied is about 5–10 percentage points less than for rejected cases during the first

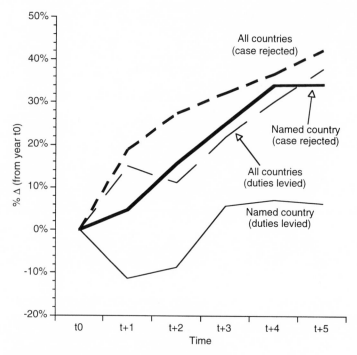

Fig. 7.5   Value of imports (named vs. total)

few years following the AD petition. Taken together, these results indicate that attempts to understand the effect of AD actions will surely fail if one looks only at the effects on import trade from the named country. While AD duties do reduce overall import growth, the effect is more muted than the reduction in imports from the named country.

In figure 7.6, I focus only on cases where duties are levied and again examine imports from all source countries. But the difference here is that I control for the number of countries named in the petition. In figure 7.4, we saw that there is less diversion when three or more countries were named. By contrast, here we see that, overall, imports are not so systematically affected by the number of named countries. During the first two years following the filing, petitions with at least three named countries do appear to have very little import growth, but thereafter overall imports grow more rapidly than in petitions with only a single country. While it is not clear why this is the case, it does reinforce the notion that looking only at the effect of AD on the named country will surely be misleading.

7.2.6   The Effect on Unit Values and Quantities

Underlying the changes in imports are changes in prices (unit values) and quantities. In figure 7.7, the effect of AD actions on unit values (as charged by the named country) is depicted. The results are precisely what one would ex-

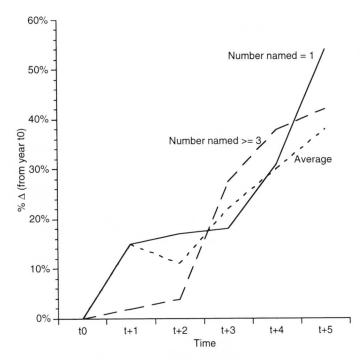

Fig. 7.6 **Value of imports (total), duties levied**

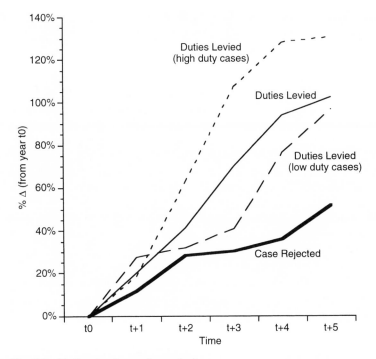

Fig. 7.7 **Unit value (named country)**

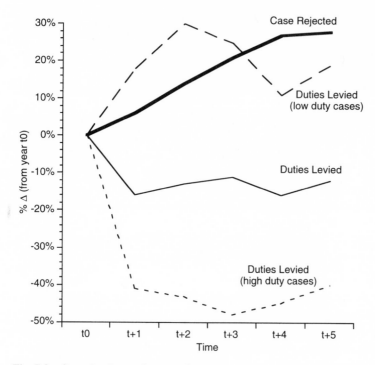

Fig. 7.8   Quantity (named country)

pect. Unit values rise more for cases resulting in duties than for cases that are rejected. For instance, by year t_3, unit values have risen more than twice as much when duties are levied as when they are not. In addition, unit values rise more quickly for cases with high duties than for cases with low duties. For instance, by year t_3, unit values for cases with the highest duties have risen by more than 100 percent since the case was filed; by contrast, in the same period of time, unit values for cases with the lowest duties have risen by about 40 percent.

Figure 7.8 depicts the quantity effect of AD duties. Again, the results are exactly what one would expect to find. We see that quantities fall by more (i) when duties are levied than when the case is rejected and (ii) when high duties are levied than when low duties are levied.

Combining the results depicted in figures 7.3, 7.7, and 7.8, we have a set of patterns that are consistent with the conjecture that AD cases that result in low duties serve as a facilitating practice. Cases with low duties still experience import growth, rising prices, and increasing quantity of sales. Recall that *low-duty cases* are defined as having AD duties less than 7 percent. Remember also that, unlike tariffs, the named country can avoid paying AD duties if it raises its U.S. prices by the full duty amount. A mandated price floor that is only a small amount greater than current prices could easily allow the foreign firm to

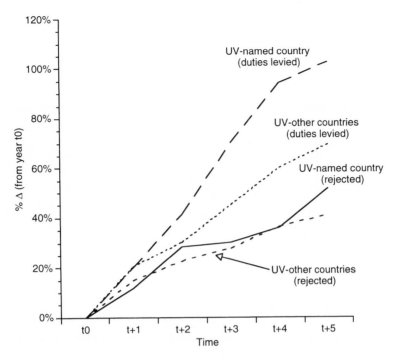

Fig. 7.9   Unit value (named vs. nonnamed)

price more like a Stackelberg leader. It is reasonable to believe that the U.S. industry benefits from higher prices by foreign firms, and, therefore, in this scenario, the AD provides coordination benefits for the rivals.

In a typical model of strategic interaction, other firms in the market respond to price increases by one party. We would expect to observe such strategic interactions in response to AD-induced price changes. In figure 7.9, I depict the unit values for the named country and also for nonnamed countries. (For each case, the nonnamed country's unit value was calculated using a weighted average of the individual countries' imports.)

The results again are clearly consistent with what would be predicted by theory: as the named country's unit values increase, the nonnamed countries' unit values increase, but in general by a somewhat smaller amount (60–70 percent of the named country's change). This trend is found both when cases are rejected and when cases result in duties. This is consistent with the notion that price effects of AD investigation cascade to nonnamed countries. In this respect, AD law is quite effective. The price increases induced by an AD action spur price increases by other foreign rivals.

Finally, in figure 7.10, the effect of duties on unit values is depicted, controlling for the number of countries named in the petition. Certainly, in the short

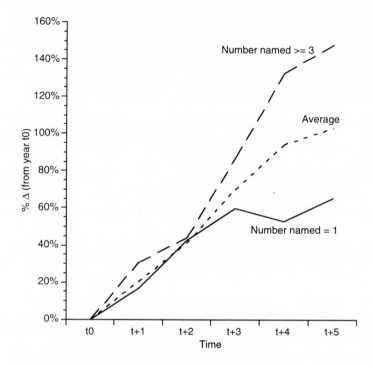

Fig. 7.10   Unit value (named country), duties levied

run, it appears that the number of named countries does not significantly affect the price increases induced by duties. However, in the longer run (greater than three years), it does appear to matter.

7.2.7   Estimation Results

In table 7.2, I present OLS regression results for named imports, nonnamed imports, and overall imports. The basic specification is

$$\ln x_{i, t_j} = \alpha + \beta_0 \ln x_{i,t-1} + \beta_1 \ln(x_{i, t-1}/x_{i, t-2}) + \beta_2 \text{NumNamed}_i$$
$$+ \beta_3 \ln \text{Duty}_i + \beta_4(\text{Dec}_i \ln \text{Duty}_i) + \beta_5 t_j + \beta_6(t_j \text{Dec}_i)$$
$$+ \beta_7 \text{Year}_{t_j}, \quad j = 0, \ldots, 5.$$

The variable x_{i,t_j} denotes imports for case i at time t_j, where t_0 corresponds to the year the petition was filed, t_1 to the period of investigation, and $t_2 \ldots t_5$ are the years following the outcome. The variable Duty_i denotes the size of the duty.[8] Given the discussion above, we might expect the number of countries

---

8. Recall that, even if a case is ultimately rejected, a duty level is estimated by the Commerce Department. Until the final ITC injury determination, duties are collected (as a bond) pending the final outcome of the investigation. If the case is ultimately rejected, the bond is returned.

named (NumNamed$_i$) to have an effect ($= 1$ when three or more countries are named). The variable Dec$_i$ is a decision dummy ($= 1$ if duties are levied). Calendar year dummies (Year$_{ij}$) are included in the estimation to control for macroeconomic trends.

A number of the general trends depicted in the figures also emerge from the regressions. Consider first the effect on imports from the named country. The estimated duty effect is negative and significant. The restriction when duties are levied ($-0.158 = -0.055 - 0.103$) is about three times as large as the restriction stemming from the investigation effect alone (-0.055). Results from an alternative specification where a dummy variable is used to capture the duty effect are also reported. In this specification, the restrictions from low and high duties are estimated (relative to moderate duties). Notice that low duties appear to have little effect on import trade, especially if the case does not result in duties. This result is consistent with the notion that the main effect of small AD duties is beneficial coordination. On the other hand, high duties have a large negative effect on imports, especially when duties are levied. Second, note that, in both specifications, the effect of an AD investigation is quite long-lived. The time effects are negative and quite large, although most are insignificantly estimated.

The results for nonnamed imports help characterize the amount of import diversion. Broadly speaking, the results are consistent with the trends depicted in the figures. We find, for instance, that diversion is greater for cases that are rejected (the time-decision cross-effect coefficients are all negative). We also find that, the larger the duties, the more diversion there is, especially for rejected cases. Interestingly, we find that, after controlling for other effects, diversion seems to increase in the number of countries named, a result that bears further study in future work.

The results for overall imports suggest that import diversion mitigates most, if not all, of the effect of AD actions on the value of imports. For instance, note that overall imports increase in cases where no duties are levied. The time-effect dummies are all positive. However, overall imports do fall for cases that result in duties: the estimated decision-duties and decision-time cross-effects are all positive. On net, AD duties do cause overall imports to fall, but the restriction is far less than the restriction to named country imports.

7.3   Net Country Effects of U.S. AD Actions

Interestingly, the import diversion induced by AD actions implies that many foreign countries benefit from aggressive U.S. use of AD law. On average, it seems reasonable to believe that countries that are named will tend to lose from AD actions while those that are not named will in general benefit. Thus, although the countries listed in table 7.1 were all frequently subject to AD investigations, they were also active in many product categories where some other country was subject to AD investigation. Paradoxically, the main bene-

Table 7.2   OLS Estimates

Variable	Named Imports		Nonnamed Imports		Overall Imports	
Constant	1.797	1.448	.521	.605	1.046	1.111
	(.315)***	(.312)***	(.179)**	(.174)***	(.202)***	(.198)***
Ln(value in $t-1$)	.899	.908	.942	.945	.921	.922
	(.018)***	(.017)***	(.009)***	(.009)***	(.011)***	(.010)***
%Δ value between $t-1$ and $t-2$	.155	.166	.264	.267	.107	.110
	(.037)***	(.036)***	(.027)***	(.026)***	(.016)***	(.016)***
Number named $\geq$ 3 (dummy)	.139	0.01	.120	.132	.097	.103
	(.082)*	(.079)	(.046)**	(.044)**	(.045)**	(.044)**
Size of duty						
Ln(Duty)	−.055		.076		.051	
	(.031)*		(.016)***		(.016)***	
Low duty (dummy)		−.004		−.120		−.146
		(.121)		(.066)*		(.065)**
High duty (dummy)		−.133		.229		.068
		(.129)		(.070)**		(.068)
Cross-effect: Duty × decision						
Ln(Duty), affirmative	−.103		−0.019		−.036	
	(.040)**		(.022)		(.021)*	
Low duty, affirmative (dummy)		.181		.116		.115
		(.157)		(.086)		(.083)
High duty, affirmative (dummy)		−.227		−.098		−.105
		(.162)		(.089)		(.086)

Years following AD petition (dummies)						
t + 1	−.433	−.274	.074	.094	.022	.067
	(.161)**	(.153)*	(.088)	(.083)	(.086)	(.081)
t + 2	−.366	−.212	.166	.191	.111	.159
	(.161)**	(.153)	(.089)*	(.083)**	(.087)	(.081)*
t + 3	−.266	−.104	.207	.232	.099	.150
	(.162)	(.153)	(.090)**	(.084)**	(.087)	(.082)*
t + 4	−.224	−.064	.267	.286	.181	.227
	(.162)	(.153)	(.091)**	(.085)***	(.087)**	(.082)***
t + 5	−.261	−.099	.246	.267	.187	.232
	(.165)	(.156)	(.092)**	(.086)**	(.088)**	(.083)***
Cross-effect: Years × decision						
t + 1 × affirmative	.239	−.051	−.065	−.077	.010	−.050
	(.198)	(.180)	(.109)	(.099)	(.105)	(.095)
t + 2 × affirmative	.002	−.277	−.182	.211	−.142	−.211
	(.198)	(.181)	(.109)	(.099)**	(.106)	(.096)**
t + 3 × affirmative	−.023	−.316	−.115	−.153	−.032	−.110
	(.199)	(.181)*	(.112)	(.102)	(.108)	(.097)
t + 4 × affirmative	−.096	−.388	−.093	−.126	−.040	−.113
	(.201)	(.183)**	(.113)	(.104)	(.108)	(.099)
t + 5 × affirmative	−.033	−.327	−.017	−.051	−.005	−.077
	(.203)	(.187)*	(.114)	(.105)	(.109)	(.100)
Adjusted R^2	0.758	0.753	0.927	0.931	0.912	0.918
Number of observations	1,164	1,214	1,157	1,207	1,195	1,245

Note: Standard errors are given in parentheses. Calendar year dummies are estimated but not reported. ***, **, and * indicate significance at 1, 5, and 10 percent, respectively.

factors of AD duties may not be the U.S. complainant but rather the other countries competing in the U.S. market. If import diversion were complete and the price effects small, the U.S. industry that spent hundreds of thousands of dollars (if not millions) assembling the forms, mobilizing disparate firms to provide information, lobbying congressmen, and incurring all the other sundry expenses associated with filing a petition might receive little or no gain.

Using the estimates reported in table 7.2, we can measure the effect of AD duties. In particular, when a country is named, we can estimate the value of imports with the duty and also what imports would have been if duties had never been levied. The difference is the effect of AD duties for the named country in that case. If we sum the trade effects over all cases where a country was named, a measure of the AD duties-induced trade contraction can be constructed.

Similarly, using the estimates on nonnamed imports, we can estimate the value of nonnamed imports with the duty and also what nonnamed imports would have been had duties never been levied. The difference is the effect of AD duties for the nonnamed country. Summing over all nonnamed countries would yield the total diversion for that case. If we sum the trade diversion over all cases where a country was not named (but was actively exporting to the United States), a measure of the AD duties-induced trade expansion can be constructed.

In table 7.3, I report the results from performing such calculations using the changes in imports between t_0 and t_1 as the measure of the trade effect. Clearly, this measure does not capture all trade effects of AD actions since it does not control for what trade patterns would have been without any AD activity, but it nonetheless highlights the idea that the distortions caused by AD law can be either a blessing or a curse.[9]

In the upper part of the table, I list the countries that have suffered the greatest trade contraction when named in U.S. AD actions (and subject to duties). Japan, the most frequently named country, easily tops the list as the country whose trade has fallen the most as a result of U.S. AD duties (total estimated losses of $7.6 billion). Note, however, that I estimate that Japan's exports to the United States increase by more than $5 billion, yielding a net trade contraction of about $2 billion. The other countries on the list all suffer sizable import losses (when named), but far less than Japan. It is interesting to note that all the remaining countries, except Iran, are estimated to have a net gain in trade with the United States despite their losses in cases where duties were levied. Of particular interest is the fact that Canada is estimated to be a net gainer from AD duties. Given the highly visible nature of many Canadian-U.S. AD disputes, this is somewhat surprising. However, it does serve as a reminder that politics rather than economics is often more important in explaining the tensions created by a trade suit.

---

9. In addition, the calculation does not include any trade distortions from those cases that were settled.

Table 7.3   **Effect of U.S. Antidumping Activity**

	When Named		When Not Named		Net Effect:
	$\%\ \Delta$, t_0 and t_1	Δ Imports, t_0 and t_1 ($millions)	$\%\ \Delta$, t_0 and t_1	Δ Imports, t_0 and t_1 ($millions)	Δ Imports, t_0 and t_1 ($millions)
Countries with the largest trade contraction (when named):					
Japan	−20.37	−7,654	13.46	5,356	−2,298
Brazil	−13.43	−201	17.99	17,962	17,762
Italy	−13.48	−184	18.31	19,514	19,331
South Korea	−8.01	−117	17.62	19,442	19,326
France	−8.07	−109	17.94	20,959	20,850
United Kingdom	−11.56	−69	18.31	21,539	21,470
Taiwan	−5.41	−65	17.29	20,469	20,404
Canada	−6.31	−47	18.98	21,230	21,183
Soviet Union	−25.42	−44	5.42	5,767	5,723
Iran	−62.52	−23	.11	19	−5
People's Republic of China	−14.33	−23	9.46	11,062	11,039
Countries with the largest trade expansion (when not named):					
Belgium	−6.14	−1	18.12	23,110	23,109
Netherlands	−13.99	−4	18.05	23,088	23,084
Austria	. . .	. . .	18.25	22,798	22,798
Switzerland	. . .	. . .	17.88	22,783	22,783
Australia	−26.00	−2	17.92	22,558	22,556
Spain	−8.56	−14	17.98	22,370	22,356
Denmark	. . .	. . .	17.84	22,220	22,220
Mexico	2.74	4	17.91	21,745	21,749
United Kingdom	−11.56	−69	18.31	21,539	21,470
Hong Kong	3.33	3	17.87	21,533	21,536

In the bottom part of the table, I list the ten countries that experience the greatest trade expansion as a result of U.S. AD actions. All the countries on this list are estimated to experience a net gain of over $20 billion as a result of duties being levied on other countries.

7.4   Concluding Comments

Overall, the evidence presented in this paper suggests that the protection offered by AD law is significantly offset by the ability of alternative foreign suppliers to increase their shipments destined for the United States. Even though imports from named countries are restricted, especially for those cases with high duties, most of the protective effect of AD duties is offset by the increased trading activity of nonnamed countries.

The results also suggest that the country-specific nature of AD protection is an important factor both in explaining the surge in AD actions during the 1980s and in evaluating the protective effect of AD actions. In conjunction with previous work on the effect of the cumulation amendment (Hansen and Prusa in press), the results in the paper are consistent with the view that the surge in

AD filings during the 1980s is a strategic attempt to compensate for the limited nature of AD protection and is not evidence of an increase in injurious pricing by foreign competitors.

The fact that almost three hundred AD cases have been filed during the first half of the 1990s leaves little doubt that U.S. firms will continue to use AD law frequently to reduce import competition. The results in this paper suggest that, unless the popularity of multiple petition filings increases the overall share of imports investigated, the other foreign suppliers will mitigate the losses caused by AD protection.

References

Anderson, James E. 1992. Domino dumping, I: Competitive exporters. *American Economic Review* 82 (March): 65–83.

Baldwin, Robert E. 1985. *The political economy of U.S. import policy.* Cambridge, Mass.: MIT Press.

Baldwin, Robert E., and Jeffrey W. Steagall. 1994. An analysis of ITC decisions in antidumping, countervailing duty and safeguard cases. *Weltwirtschaftliches Archiv* 130, no. 2:290–308.

Bhagwati, Jagdish. 1988. *Protectionism.* Cambridge, Mass.: MIT Press.

Dinopoulos, E., and M. Kreinin. 1988. Effects of the U.S.-Japan VER on European prices and on U.S. welfare. *Review of Economics and Statistics* 70, no. 3 (August):484–91.

Feenstra, R. 1984. Voluntary export restraint in U.S. autos, 1980–81: Quality, employment, and welfare effects. In *The structure and evolution of recent U.S. trade policy,* ed. R. E. Baldwin. Chicago: University of Chicago Press.

———. 1987. Gains from trade in differentiated products: Japanese compact trucks. In *Empirical methods for international trade,* ed. R. Feenstra. Cambridge, Mass.: MIT Press.

Finger, J. Michael, H. K. Hall, and D. R. Nelson. 1982. The political economy of administered protection. *American Economic Review* 78, no. 3 (June): 452–66.

Fischer, Ronald D. 1992. Endogenous probability of protection and firm behavior. *Journal of International Economics* 32:149–63.

Hansen, Wendy L., and Thomas J. Prusa. 1995. The road most taken: The rise of Title VII protection. *World Economy* 18, no. 2 (March): 295–313.

———. In press. Cumulation and ITC decision-making: The sum of the parts is greater than the whole. *Economic Inquiry.*

Harrison, Ann. 1991. The new trade protection: Price effects of antidumping and countervailing duty measures in the United States. Working paper. Washington, D.C.: World Bank.

Hartigan, James C., Sreenivas Kamma, and Phillip R. Perry. 1989. The injury determination category and the value of relief from dumping. *Review of Economics and Statistics* 71 (February): 183–86.

Krupp, Corinne M., and Patricia S. Pollard. 1992. Market responses to antidumping laws: Some evidence from the U.S. chemical industry. Michigan State University. Typescript.

Leidy, Michael P. 1993. Quid pro quo restraint and spurious injury: Subsidies and the prospect of CVDs. In *Analytical and negotiating issues in the global trading system,* ed. Alan Deardorff and Robert Stern. Ann Arbor: University of Michigan Press.

Lichtenberg, Frank, and Hong Tan. 1994. An industry level analysis of import relief petitions filed by U.S. manufacturers, 1958–85. In *Troubled industries in the United States and Japan.* New York: St. Martin's.

Moore, Michael. 1992. Rules or politics? An empirical analysis of ITC antidumping decisions. *Economic Inquiry* 30, no. 3 (July): 449–66.

Nivola, Pietro S. 1993. *Regulating unfair trade.* Washington, D.C.: Brookings.

Prusa, Thomas J. 1992. Why are so many antidumping petitions withdrawn? *Journal of International Economics* 33: 1–20.

———. 1994. Pricing behavior in the presence of antidumping law. *Journal of Economic Integration* 9, no. 2:260–89.

Staiger, Robert W., and Frank A. Wolak. 1991. Strategic use of antidumping law to enforce tacit international collusion. Stanford University. Typescript.

———. 1994. Measuring industry-specific protection: Antidumping in the United States. *Brookings Papers on Economic Activity: Microeconomics,* 51–118.

Suder, Jonathan T. 1983. Cumulation of imports in antidumping and countervailing duty investigations. *George Washington Journal of International Law and Economics* 17:463–87.

Taussig, Frank. 1931. *A tariff history of the United States.* 8th ed. New York: A. M. Kelley.

8   Determinants and Effectiveness of "Aggressively Unilateral" U.S. Trade Actions

Kimberly Ann Elliott and J. David Richardson

"Aggressively unilateral" is what America's trading partners call actions under Section 301 of the Trade Act of 1974. The provisions themselves are more than twenty years old; the epithet is of more recent vintage. A helpful analog for those not familiar with the provisions is to labor relations; initiatives under Section 301 are similar to grievance proceedings under a collective-bargaining agreement.[1] Certain aspects are similar to litigation.[2] There have been roughly one hundred formal 301 proceedings since 1974, at least thirty others that were discouraged or withdrawn at an early stage, and an unknown number that were considered, rumored, or fantasized!

Our main interest is in the determinants of various types of resolution and irresolution of 301 actions, from the perspective of negotiators and their constituents. Our main contributions are to apply familiar statistical methods to detect and size up these determinants and then to report the robustness of the results. These statistical approaches extend and complement the exhaustive historical and case-study evaluations of Bayard and Elliott (1994).[3] We also update that study, adding fifteen cases to the seventy-two considered there.

One important conclusion of our work is that the Bayard-Elliott findings are

Kimberly Ann Elliott is a research fellow at the Institute for International Economics. J. David Richardson is a visiting fellow at the Institute for International Economics, professor of economics in the Maxwell School at Syracuse University, and a research associate of the National Bureau of Economic Research.

Earlier drafts of this paper were significantly improved by seminar participants' comments at Purdue and Syracuse Universities and the University of Delaware. The authors are especially appreciative of those received from Robert E. Baldwin, Debra S. Dwyer, Christopher Dumler, Kenneth Koford, and Marcus Noland.

1. On the economics of grievance, see Lewin and Peterson (1988).

2. For a recent example of the economics of litigation, see Hughes and Snyder (1995).

3. See also similar evaluations of Section 301 by Low (1993), Ryan (1995), and Sykes (1992). Hudec (1990) is a broader treatment.

still relevant for the updated and expanded sample of cases. Our statistical approach illuminates and confirms their evaluations but does not change them qualitatively.

Our most important conclusions, ceteris paribus, are the following: (1) Successful resolution of 301 cases is associated with high dependence on the United States and "low reciprocity" toward it. *High dependence* is measured by a target country's share of GNP that is exports to the United States. *Reciprocity* is measured by the U.S. merchandise trade balance with the target country. (2) Section 301 cases about practices that make unfair distinctions at the border for merchandise are far more successful than those about nonborder practices and services trade.

By contrast, we also note the following:

- There is little difference in the distribution of outcomes between cases involving taxes (other than tariffs) and subsidies and those involving less transparent regulatory and nontax practices or between cases involving traditional trade concerns and those involving less well-established "new issues" (services trade and intellectual property protection).
- There is little difference in resolution rates, or in the correlates of successful resolution, between agricultural and nonagricultural cases.
- There is weak evidence, however, of lower resolution rates among "bullied" trading partners, those singled out for a disproportionate share of Section 301 actions over a three-year interval.
- There is no evidence that "big" cases are resolved successfully more often or that the correlates of "success" rates differ between big cases and smaller ones.
- There is no evidence that explicit, public threats, including the publications of retaliation "hit lists," enhance the successful resolution of 301 negotiations.
- There is weak evidence, however, of higher resolution rates among cases that the U.S. trade representative's office was able to bring on its own initiative (rather than a petitioner's) after 1985.
- There is little evidence that Section 301 actions have become more (or less) successful over their full twenty-year history, despite legislative and administrative refinements that were aimed at making them more effective. Success rates were, however, markedly lower in the early 1980s and markedly higher in the mid-1980s, in roughly offsetting ways. This pattern has several observationally equivalent interpretations.

We do not try to estimate the economic consequences of 301 actions or their welfare effects, either for the United States or for the world trading regime. To do so would require a significant commitment to new data construction. Instead, we focus on measures of negotiating success or failure and on what variables influence them.

Our measures of negotiating success or failure are founded on petitions and public statements, which list the various issues leading to grievance, and on follow-up reports from the U.S. trade representative's office that evaluate adherence with respect to these various issues. In our approach, we distinguish four classes of resolution and irresolution of Section 301 cases on the basis of counting issues covered by agreements and ex post implementation. We also take a quantitative approach to those 301 cases where it is reasonable; in these cases, we try to explain the amount of trade recaptured.

At the margins of our qualitative classes, of course, judgment is required. Such judgments are necessarily in the eye of the beholder. We actually employ a mix of subjective judgment and expert opinion in evaluating cases on the margins of our objective categories; thus, our dependent variable is more accurately a consensus variable than a subjective one.[4]

Moreover, our approach can be applied easily by anyone with a different set of marginal judgments about types of success and failure, and their results can be compared to ours.[5] Finally, explaining perceived success and failure is an important task. These are the perceptions that shape *political* support for Section 301 as well as opposition to it and recommendations to revise it. In that spirit, our measurement of success is objective and politically sensitive, not merely subjective.

In light of our conclusions, we close the paper with a discussion of the degrees of success to be expected for alternative options to Section 301 for U.S. trade grievances.

8.1 Background

In broad terms, Section 301 authorizes the president of the United States, or the U.S. trade representative (USTR), to take action against "unreasonable, unjustifiable, or discriminatory" practices of foreign trading partners that impinge on U.S. commerce. Such actions begin with consultations, often involve formal negotiations, and can be enforced by sanctions. There have been a number of legislative and administrative changes in Section 301 over the years.

---

4. We took seriously the judgments of the parties involved in Section 301 cases, solicited through extensive interviews conducted by Bayard and Elliott (1994). Consequently, to the best of our ability, we are explaining the success and failure of 301 actions in the eyes of those with the largest political stake, whether as supporters or critics. Our judgments at the margins are not fundamentally different from those made in using surveys to code categories such as "in" or "out of" the labor force, "head of household" or not, etc.

5. To illustrate the value of that, suppose that both we and they find that explicit, public threats do not enhance 301 success. Then that conclusion is made more robust to the natural accusation that it was due to the vagaries of subjective classification. We, in fact, examine the sensitivity of our results to several of the most controversial single-case evaluations.

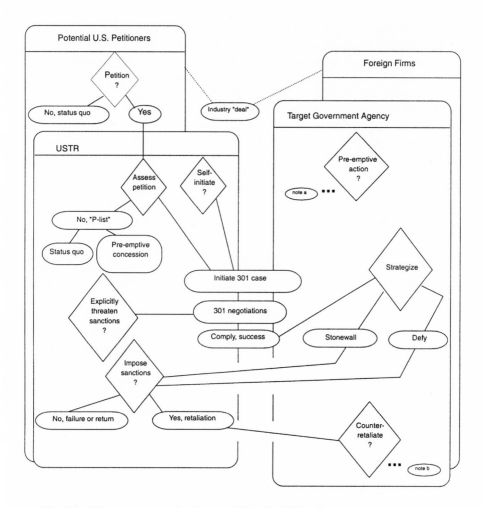

Fig. 8.1 The structure and sequence of Section 301 actions

Note: Diamonds = decisions; Ovals = outcomes.

[a]Such action can involve informal consultation between U.S. negotiators and target-country negotiators even before a decision on the petition is made. Three options are available to the target country. Preemptive concessions can encourage the petitioner to withdraw the petition or the USTR to reject it (some so-called p-list cases). Either stonewalling or defiance in the informal consultation could lead the USTR to accept the petition and to initiate a 301 case.

[b]In the event of U.S. retaliation, the target country once again can comply, defy, or stonewall. In the latter cases, it may also counterretaliate (the EC has counterretaliated in two cases, the linked disputes over pasta and citrus in 1985–86 and the enlargement dispute following the accession of Spain and Portugal in 1986 [although both the retaliation and the counterretaliation in the latter case were symbolic, nonbinding quotas], and Canada in one, the beer war in 1992–93), at which point the USTR is faced with a decision to escalate its retaliation (although this has never occurred in practice), reopen negotiations, or simply stand on the standoff.

Some of these changes expanded its definition of U.S. commerce to non-trade-related services, investment, and intellectual property. Others made its deadlines and procedures less—or more—discretionary (e.g., in 1984, the U.S. trade representative was explicitly authorized to initiate 301 cases even without a petition from a private-sector plaintiff). And still others created "Special" 301 procedures for violations of intellectual property rights and "Super" 301 provisions for egregiously unfair practices by chronically unfair trading partners (trade partners with an attitude or maybe an addiction). Understanding how a Section 301 case proceeds can be facilitated by examining figure 8.1, a stylization to which we return below for purposes of econometric specification.

Section 301 proceedings have been extremely controversial among our trading partners, especially since procedural changes made during the 1980s promoted their more aggressive use and removed elements of presidential discretion. Some supporters, echoing Hudec (1990) (and ignoring his nuances), have seen 301 as a weapon of constructive vigilantism, and others have been quietly happy to enjoy its fruits.[6] Critics have declared the fruit rotten, reacting with outrage at what they see to be a bullying tool of "aggressive unilateralism." These critics supported the new World Trade Organization (WTO) dispute settlement mechanisms as a discipline on U.S. recourse to the 301 procedures.

Among Americans, Section 301 is popular, appealing to our commitment to equal opportunity and fair play—for ourselves, of course, in this case. Support for 301 remains strong, as a contingent arsenal, at least until WTO substitutes prove themselves effective and fair, and certainly for issues and countries not covered by WTO rules.

Especially among supporters, there is an important unspoken assumption. It is that 301 procedures generally work. That is, negotiating goals are usually realized and in predictable ways. Even some critics make the same assumption, arguing that 301 actions really do force target countries to reduce entry barriers or cease restrictive practices. Yet, in the eighty-seven cases we analyze, almost half (forty-two) end in degrees of failure by our measures.[7] Furthermore, the correlates of success and failure are not always what commentators have expected. In the popular view, by contrast, the presumption of success is often undiscriminating, as if occasional failure were just a matter of animal spirits, one of those things.

Our methods in this paper allow us to be more discriminating than this, both about the chances of success and about what conditions enhance them.

---

6. Most 301-inspired concessions are made available to *all* a target country's trading partners, not just to the United States.

7. This is not an unexpected outcome according to the theory of litigation (see Lewin and Peterson 1988). "Plaintiff" and "defendant" will often tend to agree that the odds of either winning are roughly fifty-fifty. If the perceived odds of the plaintiff winning are less than that, then the plaintiff will tend not to bring the case; if they are greater, then the defendant will settle "out of court" before the case is brought. Differences in perception, harassment, or demonstration motives cause variation around this fifty-fifty presumption but do not shift it systematically. We are indebted to Kenneth Koford for drawing our attention to this parallel literature.

8.2   The Bayard-Elliott Approach and Ours

Bayard and Elliott (1994) is a comprehensive evaluation of seventy-two Section 301 cases, with in-depth case studies of nine of them. Relying principally on historical assessments and tabular and cross-tabular displays, Bayard and Elliott drew the following conclusions:

- Section 301 was a reasonably effective tool of U.S. trade policy in the mid- and late 1980s.
- Super 301 (created in the Omnibus Trade and Competitiveness Act of 1988), aimed at egregiously unfair partners and practices, was no more effective than "regular" 301 in this period.
- Section 301 did not trigger major trade wars, nor did agreements under 301 typically result in trade diversion.
- But neither did 301 produce large gains for U.S. exporters in most cases.

Bayard and Elliott (1994, 86–90) also experimented briefly with some of the statistical methods that we use in this paper, in particular, the binomial probit approaches. We extend and reconsider this part of the Bayard-Elliott work. Specifically, we

- adopt binomial probit and tobit and multinomial logit approaches to reevaluate their assessments while also extending and updating their data set from seventy-two Section 301 cases (observations) to eighty-seven (the cases that we add are summarized in table 8.1 and discussed in greater detail in the appendix);[8]
- revisit several of their hypotheses (e.g., that legislative changes to make Section 301 more effective during the 1980s actually had this effect);
- expand their measure of success to a four-part gradation and add to (and subtract from) their catalog of success-failure determinants;
- identify, isolate, and discuss the most anomalous Section 301 cases, which are observations with large and chronic residuals in our approach;
- examine the specification and residuals for evidence that the "size" of a case makes a difference (e.g., because of heteroskedasticity); and
- more precisely define the marginal efficacy of discretionary determinants (e.g., whether explicit, public threats enhance negotiating success) and when the marginal effects of various determinants are interdependent (e.g., whether threats "work better" with European target countries than with others).

---

8. Summaries like those in the appendix for the seventy-two cases in Bayard and Elliott (1994) are available from the authors.

Table 8.1   **Observations Added to Bayard and Elliott Data Sample (Section 301 cases and petitions)**

Case No.	Target	Period of Case[a]	Type of Product	Actual Value of U.S. Exports to the Target[b]	GATT Panel Established?	GATT Panel Ruled?	Negotiating Objective Achieved?	Degree of Trade Liberalization Resulting from 301[c]
Formal investigations								
38	Taiwan	10/25/82–12/19/83	Manufactured (footwear)	Negligible	N.A.	N.A.	No basis for allegations of unfair trade barriers found in investigation, but president directed USTR to pursue Taiwanese offers to lower tariffs and provide marketing assistance to U.S. exporters	Very modest
83	European Community	11/28/90–10/93	Agriculture related (meatpacking)	Approx. $30 million (based on data in USTR files)	No[d]	No	Partially; two sides agreed to use "equivalency" principle in applying meatpacking plant standards to imported meat and meat products	Modest
88[e]	China	10/10/91–10/92	General market access (QRs, licensing, technical barriers, and lack of transparency in import regulations)	Approx. $2 billion, based on USTR retaliation threat	N.A.	N.A.	Partially; although problems in implementation have occurred, China has largely met deadlines for removing specific nontariff barriers	Probably modest thus far, but potentially significant if fully implemented

(continued)

Table 8.1 (continued)

Case No.	Target	Period of Case[a]	Type of Product	Actual Value of U.S. Exports to the Target[b]	GATT Panel Established?	GATT Panel Ruled?	Negotiating Objective Achieved?	Degree of Trade Liberalization Resulting from 301[c]
89[e]	Taiwan	4/29/92–6/5/92	IP (copyright)	$370 million (USTR estimate)	N.A.	N.A.	Partially, although passage and adequate enforcement of necessary legislation took another 18 months	Probably modest, although it also depends on the level of offsetting investment in Chinese pirate plants
91[e]	Brazil	5/28/93–2/25/94	IP	$800 million (industry estimate of losses)	N.A.	N.A.	Nominally, since Brazilian congress has yet to pass either the patent or the copyright bills by the promised deadlines (15 June 1994 and 1 January 1995, respectively)	None to date
93[e]	Japan	10/1/94–6/28/95	Manufactured (auto parts)	$7.5 billion (based on planned retaliation)	No[f]	No	Nominally, given modest results and likelihood of recurrence	Small at best
98	Canada	12/23/94–6/22/95	Service (country music cable TV station)	$130 million (based on planned retaliation)	N.A.	N.A.	Partially, since U.S. firm had to sign joint venture agreement to get back into market, but with two Canadian firms with potentially triple the customer base	Modest

Negotiations resulting from petitions not formally investigated

SROK	Korea, "non–Super 301" negotiation	1989	Goods, services, and FDI	Not calculable	N.A.	N.A.	Nominally because agreements not enforced	Little or none
SROC	Taiwan "non–Super 301" negotiation	1989	Goods, services, IP	Not calculable	N.A.	N.A.	Nominally because promises not fulfilled	Modest at best
P-7	Korea	9/10/85–10/25/85	Manufactured/service (entry and distribution of films and videos)	Approx. $10 million	No	No	Nominally, because case recurred (see P-28)	Little or none
P-11 & 16	Japan	4/11/86–5/29/86; 1/16/87–3/2/87	Service (legal services)	Unknown	N.A.	N.A.	Partially, foreign lawyers allowed to practice but with extensive restrictions	Modest
P-18	Chile	2/22/88–4/7/88	IP	Approx. $15 million (industry estimate of losses)	N.A.	N.A.	Largely, Chile adopted improved patent law with only slight delays from promised deadlines; Chile remains on the lowest level Special 301 watch list, but there have been no recorded complaints about enforcement, only demands for additional protection, e.g., for pipeline products	Modest

(continued)

Table 8.1 (continued)

Case No.	Target	Period of Case[a]	Type of Product	Actual Value of U.S. Exports to the Target[b]	GATT Panel Established?	GATT Panel Ruled?	Negotiating Objective Achieved?	Degree of Trade Liberalization Resulting from 301[c]
P-23	Korea	9/15/88–10/28/88	Manufactured (films)	Approx. $10 million (industry estimate of losses)	N.A.	N.A.	Partially, since complaints after this point focus primarily on piracy, not access and distribution	Modest
P-26	Japan	3/5/90–4/18/90	Manufactured (amorphous metal transformer cores)	Small	N.A.	N.A.	Partially, since Japanese utilities purchased transformers as promised for field testing and Allied Signal has not complained publicly about implementation	Small at best
P-28	Taiwan	12/3/90–1/11/91	Manufactured (distilled spirits)	Small	N.A.	N.A.	Partially, since Taiwan lifted ban on imported distilled spirits, although high taxes and other restrictions remain	Small at best

Note: N.A. = not applicable; QR = quantitative restriction; IP = intellectual property; FDI = foreign direct investment.

[a]The first date is when the petition was filed; the end date is either when the petition was withdrawn or a formal case was terminated, suspended, or otherwise concluded.

[a]Unless otherwise indicated, the figures represent the value of U.S. exports to the target country after the case was concluded. The trade gain (in successful cases) or loss (in failures) would typically be a much lower figure, and, in cases involving homogeneous products, the *net* gain or loss might be close to zero. The overstatement of actual loss is even greater in the cases involving export subsidies that affect third markets; in those cases, the smaller of U.S. or target-country exports to the world are provided, even though it is likely that U.S. exports compete with subsidized exports from other countries in only some of its markets. The export figures provided are intended to give only a general idea—an order of magnitude—of the potential stakes involved and of the importance of trade in the sector to the U.S. economy; in other words, these data are meant only to distinguish "big" cases from "small" ones.

[b]Negative if retaliation imposed with no other resolution; none if there was no resolution or if other measures substituted for targeted practice or policy; modest if practice modified but not eliminated; significant if practice eliminated or if there is a credible commitment to phase it out.

[c]After the European Community twice blocked U.S. demands at GATT council meetings, a decision was finally made to establish a dispute settlement panel in an earlier iteration of this case (301-60). An agreement was reached between U.S. and European negotiators before the panel could be appointed. This case was filed when that agreement failed to hold.

[d]Case self-initiated.

[e]The USTR did notify the World Trade Organization that it was considering filing a complaint charging that Japanese practices "nullified and impaired" expected U.S. benefits under the agreement.

8.3   Econometric Specification and Conceptual Issues

Figure 8.1 above describes Section 301 procedures and actors visually. There are as many as four important groups of actors: private U.S. petitioners, the office of the U.S. trade representative, its foreign counterpart, and private foreign "offenders." There are also, of course, other government agencies that are sometimes involved and occasionally private agents that compete with a petitioner's business.[9]

There are also several possible procedures for "resolving" a case. The most common that we can observe is the sequence of formal petition, consultations and negotiations, and outcome (either agreement, sanctions without agreement, or standoff). USTR records and news accounts also allow us to observe a limited number of "preemptive settlements," in which a trading partner makes concessions adequate to lead to a cessation of formal 301 procedures (we added eight such cases to Bayard and Elliott's sample). We cannot, however, observe two kinds of would-be cases. One is deterrent cases, cases whose potential credibility is so strong that trading-partner actors change actions privately to avoid even the beginnings of a 301 petition. The second is wishful-thinking cases, cases not brought because one or another determinant/ correlate of outcomes makes success very unlikely.[10] The inability to observe these types of cases creates classic selection bias in our procedures. But it is hard to know their net bias. Unobserved would-be cases include both virtual successes and virtual failures. It is also hard to use standard corrections for selection bias since we had no information at all on "unbrought" cases.

The combination of multiple actors and multiple procedures also makes econometric specification troublesome. No single agent's behavior (or group of agents' behavior) is present in every case. Nor is the sequence of environments leading to resolution or irresolution common to each observed case: sometimes it is threat followed by response; sometimes it is petition, "cooperative" negotiation, and then outcome; sometimes negotiations are punctuated by clear "noncooperative" breakdown.

Nevertheless, the same sorts of problems confront descriptive and historical analysis of Section 301 actions, so "loose" specification by itself is not sufficient to abjure our statistical approach. But it does make us more than usually cautious about our results.

In our qualitative approach, we provide a four-part consensus assessment of the degree of negotiating resolution in each Section 301 case, using USTR records, media accounts, and expert interviews, as outlined above. We distin-

---

9. Polaroid, e.g., lobbied for involvement in Kodak's Section 301 case.

10. For example, Bayard's and Elliott's variables include a measure of a target country's reputation for swift, strong *counterretaliation* against U.S. sanctions. The threat of counterretaliation could easily cause cases against *those* target countries not to be brought at all, rather than leading to failure among cases that *are* brought, as they assume in their probit analysis, where they find its influence insignificantly different from zero.

guish cases that ended in the following outcomes: no agreement at all; an agreement on paper that was never implemented or later reversed; an agreement on some, but not all, of the issues under petition; and substantial agreement on all issues. We call these categories *clear failure, marginal failure, partial success,* and *clear success,* respectively. We updated and extended the Bayard-Elliott (1994) sample to eighty-seven cases, adding fifteen cases described in the appendix and table 8.1 above, where it is also possible to see how these assessments are formed. For our eighty-seven cases, the sample size in each of the four groups above is, respectively, twelve, thirty, thirty-four, and eleven.

Determining the correlates of qualitative groupings like ours is one of the principal uses of binomial and multinomial probit, logit, and related approaches. We pursued a binomial probit approach[11] to a success-failure aggregation of the four outcomes from Section 301 cases and a multinomial logit approach to the four-way grouping.[12] For the binomial approach, we treated cases in the first two groups as "failures" and cases in the second two groups as "successes." The binomial probit approach is essentially to fit a nonlinear regression[13] that generates an estimated "probability" of success ($y = 1$) or failure ($y = 0$) from a set of independent variables. The multinomial logit approach is essentially a nonlinear regression that generates estimated "probabilities" that an observation falls into one particular group relative to another, from a set of independent variables correlated with the classification mechanism. When the classification mechanism creates an ordinal ranking of outcome groups, as ours does, an "ordered" multinomial approach also gives boundary points for the estimated probabilities.

We also experimented with a quantitative tobit approach to outcomes of 301 negotiations defined as the amount of trade recaptured. In considering the independent determinants of Section 301 outcomes, we started with the same guidance as Bayard and Elliott (1994, 79–85), based on McMillan (1990). McMillan suggests variables having to do with benefits and costs of compliance or defiance in the target country, and, given those, the net benefit of resolution in the particular case to the United States, plus *perceptions* of the same benefits and costs, perceptions that are shaped largely by negotiating tactics.

To anticipate our results, we find some evidence for the first through a variable measuring a target country's dependence on the U.S. market and hence

11. Binomial logit approaches tend to produce very similar results to binomial probit approaches for samples like ours with balanced extremes, not heavily unbalanced toward either failure groups or success. See, e.g., the discussion in Greene (1993, 638).

12. Baldwin and Steagall (1994), Mutti and Yeung (in press), and Hansen and Prusa (1995) are recent binomial probit approaches to U.S. political-economic decision making as regards trade remedies. In their cases, unlike ours, there is a single dominant U.S. agency whose behavior is being explained. Appendix C of Destler, Odell, and Elliott (1987) is a multinomial logit approach to political activism against border protectionism.

13. The functional form is a cumulative normal probability density function (PDF) in the case of probits and cumulative logistic PDF in the case of logits.

vulnerability to U.S. trade sanctions. But we find no evidence that the U.S. "stakes" in a case, as measured here, mattered to its successful resolution, either qualitatively or quantitatively, and only weak or little evidence that tactics like threats and accentuated pressures made a difference. In fact, our base specification includes two strong correlates that seemed less important to us ex ante than those above: (1) a rough measure of the level of overall "reciprocity," specifically, the aggregate merchandise trade balance of the United States with the target country; and (2) whether the case concerned the "usual suspects," specifically, unfair border practices that blocked merchandise access (in which case it was far more likely to be successful), or some other, newer issue (e.g., practices toward services trade or intellectual property protection), or more narrowly "domestic" practice (e.g., regulatory access barriers).

8.4   Qualitative Results

Our multinomial approaches showed that it was almost impossible to distinguish between clear and marginal failures using the independent variables that we had available. By contrast, cases that partially or largely succeeded could be distinguished both from each other and from the failures on the basis of similar variables (correlates). Therefore, we start below with our results on determinants of (binomial) "success" and "failure," then show how the same variables help forecast clear versus partial successes. The following section describes our attempts to measure and explain Section 301 success quantitatively.

Our results showed a fairly consistent pattern across alternative specifications and robustness checks. Some variables that we expected to be strong determinants of Section 301 outcomes seemed not to be; others that we thought to be less important turned out to be quite strong and omnipresent. We start with results from our so-called base specification, with its most promising variations. We then describe the "dogs that didn't bark"—the patterns that did not emerge. Finally, we summarize several robustness checks and our analysis of "chronic" residuals—the cases that our base-specification correlates always get wrong. Tables 8.2 and 8.3 define and statistically describe the variables involved in variations on our base specification.

8.4.1   Success or Failure? Results from the Probit Approach

Table 8.4 summarizes results from our base specification. Three determinants seemed to predict success and failure well regardless of what else we added: the target's exports to the United States as a share of its GNP (TXDEP2), the U.S. merchandise trade balance with the target (TBAL),[14] and a dummy variable taking on the value one when the case involved a border

---

14. The large numerical size of the TBAL variable does not distort the results, as reported in our discussion below of residuals and heteroskedasticity.

Table 8.2   **Variable Definitions**

A. Dependent variables

SUCCESS	0 if there is no agreement; 1 if an initially "successful" outcome is later reversed or an agreement inadequately implemented; 2 if there is partial achievement of negotiating goals; 3 if negotiating goals are largely achieved. Used in multinomial logits.
OPENING	0 if SUCCESS = 0 or 1; 1 if SUCCESS = 2 or 3. Used in binomial probits.

B. Independent variables

TXDEP2	Target country's exports to the United States as a percentage of GNP.
TBAL	U.S. trade balance with the target country.
BORDER	1 if there is a border measure affecting goods (import and export quotas and tariffs), 0 otherwise.
INITIATE	1 if the case is initiated by USTR, 0 otherwise.
BULLY	Number of cases started against the particular target country in question as a proportion of all cases started during years t, $t - 1$, and $t - 2$. (The number of cases in 1973 [pre-301] and 1974 was set = 0.)

barrier to U.S. merchandise exports (BORDER). We interpret these, respectively, as measures of target vulnerability to U.S. sanctions, crude reciprocity in trade relations,[15] and the simplicity, familiarity, and/or legitimacy of the issue. As the coefficients suggest, 301 successes are more likely the greater is target vulnerability, the less reciprocal its trade posture appears to be, and the more the case concerns simple, familiar border barriers to traded merchandise, where the perceived legitimacy of U.S. complaints is greater. Column 4 records estimated partial derivatives of the probability of success with respect to each determinant,[16] at (approximately) sample means of the variables. The entry for TXDEP2 (1.951), for example, suggests that 301 cases are roughly 13.5

15. Although there is little economic reason to consider the trade balance a measure of reciprocity, politicians and negotiators often do. Nothing that we tried as a more satisfactory economic measure was at all correlated with 301 outcomes. For an approach to all unilateral U.S. trade actions between 1990 and 1994, not just Section 301 actions, that also finds a significant role for the bilateral trade balance as an explanatory variable for U.S. attention to trade disputes, see Noland (1995).

16. Since the probit function is nonlinear, estimated coefficients cannot be interpreted as partial derivatives.

Table 8.3   **Summary Statistics**

	All Cases		"Successful" Cases		"Failed" Cases	
	Mean	SD	Mean	SD	Mean	SD
OPENING	.517		1.000		.000	
TXDEP2	.065	.069	.082	.080	.047	.051
TBAL	−10,009.652	17,476.801	−15,474.556	18,517.581	−4,154.398	14,310.341
BORDER	.310		.444		.167	
INITIATE	.264		.333		.190	
BULLY	.173	.218	.132	.188	.205	.250

Table 8.4   **Binomial Probit for Success-Failure: Base Specification**

Independent Variables	Coefficient	SE	t-Statistic	Partial Derivatives[a]
Constant	−.891	.254	−3.504	−.354
TXDEP2	4.907	2.324	2.111	1.951
TBAL	−.000031	.000009	−3.268	−.000012
BORDER	1.119	.346	3.237	.445
Percentage of cases correctly predicted		72.41		
Maximum likelihood estimates:				
Log likelihood		−47.16		
Restricted log likelihood (slopes = 0)		−60.25		

[a]Partial derivatives of the probability of success with respect to each determinate at (approximately) sample means of the variables. For sample means, see table 8.2.

percent more likely to succeed against a target country with one standard deviation (0.069 from table 8.2) more vulnerability than the mean target (0.069 × 1.951 = 0.135). The column 4 entry for BORDER is notable. The probability of success for a 301 case involving a border barrier to merchandise trade is roughly 44 percent larger than for other kinds of barriers, a quite large differential.

Table 8.5 unpacks the base specification in a cross-tabular format to reveal two negative conclusions, about interactions and tactics.[17] The first is that there is no significant evidence of multiplicative (interaction) effects between the three base determinants. This can be seen in the left-hand panel of the table. Target vulnerability works roughly in the same way to enhance success whether the trade (im)balance is "high," "medium," or "low."[18] And trade imbalance works the same whether target vulnerability is high, medium, or low.

17. These are results from regressions that are not summarized in the tables. We had thought perhaps that success ratios would be especially high in cases where there was both heavy vulnerability and little reciprocity—more than the sum of their effects might have suggested. We had also thought that explicit, public threats enhanced USTR credibility. Neither could be shown.

18. In this context, a "high" trade balance signals a large deficit for the United States.

Table 8.5   Cross-Tabular Analysis of Success-Failure, Base Specification, with Detail[a]

| | Target Dependence | | | | | | | |
| | All Observations | | | | Only Observations with Explicit Threat[b] | | | |
U.S. Bilateral Trade Balance	High	Medium	Low	Total	High	Medium	Low	Total
High:								
B	0	3/3	2/2	5/5	0	2/2	2/2	4/4
NB	0	7/8	1/2	8/10	0	5/6	1/2	6/8
Medium:								
B	6/7	3/4	2/2	11/13	1/1	1/2	1/1	3/4
NB	9/14	2/8	1/7	12/29	5/8	1/4	1/5	7/17
Low:								
B	0	0	4/9	4/9	0	0	1/2	1/2
NB	0	1/3	4/18	5/21	0	0/1	2/7	2/8
Total:								
B	6/7	6/7	8/13	20/27	1/1	3/4	4/5	8/10
NB	9/14	10/19	6/27	25/60	5/8	6/11	4/14	15/33

Note: B = border measure; NB = nonborder trade barrier. For target dependence (target-country exports to the United States as a percentage of the target-country GNP), high = greater than 10 percent, medium = 3–10 percent, and low = less than 3 percent. For the U.S. bilateral trade balance (in dollars), high = greater than −20 billion, medium = from −1 to −19 billion, and low = less than −1 billion.

[a]Each cell shows the number of successes as a proportion of the total number of cases in that category.

[b]Includes only cases "self-initiated" by the USTR plus those in which the USTR or the president issued a formal determination of unfairness with a deadline for taking action or published a hit list of potential retaliation targets.

The likely success of border cases appears in almost every cell. The second conclusion is that cases in which the USTR shows special tactical resolve, such as making explicit, public threats, including "hit lists" of goods to be sanctioned if the target is uncooperative, are no more successful than any other cases. This can be seen in the right-hand panel of the table, which isolates only the thirty-three cases for which this was true. Their covariation through the cells of the table is merely a scaled-down version of that in the left-hand panel for all the cases. In fact, we were never able to find significant evidence that tactical public threats of any kind made any difference, even when they seemed quite credible; they may merely have stiffened target resistance.

Table 8.6 records results for several variations on the base specification. The first adds a dummy variable for those cases that the USTR "self-initiates" without petition. These have a higher chance of success—roughly 24 percent, according to the partial derivative—but the coefficient is significant at only a 10 percent level. The second variation adds a "bullying" variable instead. This variable measures the frequency over a three-year interval that a given target country was hit with 301 cases relative to other target countries. There is weak evidence of diminishing returns from concentrated cases against any single target country, but the coefficient is significant only at the 27 percent level. A 10 percent increase in a target's share of cases during any three-year interval reduces the chances of success by roughly 4 percent, according to the partial derivative, an effect that does not seem especially large. The third variation adds both the self-initiate dummy and the "bullying" variable. Results for the first are little affected, but the "bullying" variable declines still further in size and significance.

Table 8.7 lists the "chronic residuals" for the binomial probits, cases that are mispredicted across virtually all variations.[19] Some of these mispredictions seem innocuous, albeit "chronic"—specifically, those with predicted [Prob $y = 1$] close to 0.50; they were all "close calls" for the regression. Others seems more serious. There is little temporal pattern, in particular, no tendency for more recent cases to fail more often, say, because of completion of the Uruguay Round (but the Japanese automobile case, case 93, may be a single-residual harbinger, according to some commentators). There is no discernible pattern with respect to any measure of the size or importance of a case or a trading partner.

In fact, one of the surprising negative conclusions is that the hypothesis of homoskedasticity of the residuals could not be rejected in any case we tried (we tested for it with respect to both the trade balance and a measure of the alleged size of the trade under dispute). That is, the various regressions suggest that both "big" and "small" cases are governed by the same correlates, with little need for scaling of observations to take account of "size." Indeed, this result seemed so surprising that we pursued it further, using a tobit approach

---

19. Including some not summarized explicitly in the text.

Table 8.6   Binomial Probit for Success-Failure: Alternative Specifications

Independent Variables	With "Self-Initiate" Dummy				With "Bullying" Measure				With "Self-Initiate" Dummy and "Bullying" Measure			
	Coeff.	SE	t-Statistic	Partial Derivatives[a]	Coeff.	SE	t-Statistic	Partial Derivatives[a]	Coeff.	SE	t-Statistic	Partial Derivatives[a]
Constant	-1.076	.282	-3.813	-.428	-.634	.340	-1.863	-.252	-.853	.374	-2.284	-.340
TXDEP2	5.333	2.397	2.225	2.121	4.240	2.373	1.786	1.686	4.744	2.456	1.932	1.887
TBAL	-.000026	.000010	-2.780	-.000011	-.000030	.000009	-3.139	-.000012	-.000026	.000010	-2.718	-.000010
BORDER	1.228	.354	3.465	.488	1.186	.358	3.313	.472	1.279	.366	3.50	.509
INITIATE	.605	.364	1.662	.241					.559	.367	1.522	.223
BULY					-1.056	.951	-1.110	-.420	-.860	.967	-.890	-.342
Percentage of cases correctly predicted	73.56				72.41				73.56			
Maximum likelihood estimates:												
Log likelihood	-45.75				-46.53				-45.35			
Restricted log likelihood (slopes = 0)	-60.25				-60.25				-60.25			

[a]Partial derivatives of the probability of success with respect to each determinate at (approximately) sample means of the variables. For sample means, see table 8.2.

Table 8.7   Binomial Probit for Success-Failure: Chronic Outliers

Case No.	Year Case Resolved	Target Country	Issue	Type of Barrier	Base Specification	Residuals (Probly = 1) from Base Specification with:		
						INITIATE	BULLY	INITIATE and BULLY
Observed failures/predicted successes:								
24	1982	Argentina	Export ban on hides	Border	.624	.598	.653	.626
34	1982	Canada	Investment incentives for machinery	Nonborder	.609	.544	.623	.559
41	1985	Portugal	Restrictions on oilseed imports	Border	.638	.614	.724	.689
48	1991	Japan	Semiconductor market access	Nonborder	.711	.585	.725	.608
72	1990	Thailand	Ban on cigarette imports	Border	.731	.712	.803	.776
80	1992	Canada	Provincial restrictions on beer	Nonborder	.671	.612	.699	.640
93	1995	Japan	Market access for autos and parts etc.	Nonborder	.890	.919	.875	.907
P-7	1985	Korea	Market access for foreign films	Border	.844	.835	.842	.834
SROC	1989	Taiwan	Super 301 negotiations	Nonborder	.611	.545	.648	.581
Observed successes/predicted failures:								
3	1980	EC	Variable levies on egg products	Border	.401	.401	.266	.290
25	1987	EC	Pasta export subsidies	Nonborder	.459	.356	.365	.292
40	1985	Brazil	Export subsidies for soybeans	Nonborder	.270	.212	.304	.241
44	1989	Argentina	Restrictions on air courier services	Nonborder	.217	.169	.251	.196
49	1989	Brazil	Informatics policy	Nonborder	.242	.387	.267	.400
53	1988	Argentina	Export subsidies for soybeans	Nonborder	.207	.160	.258	.199
71	1989	Argentina	Subsidies for canned fruit	Nonborder	.203	.345	.213	.343
83	1992	EC	Meatpacking standards	Nonborder	.148	.116	.170	.134
P-18	1988	Chile	Patent protection	Nonborder	.294	.242	.350	.288

to the subsample of observations for which we had a reliable measure of the trade lost from the allegedly unfair practice abroad.[20] This approach is described below in section 8.5.

We also experimented with the sensitivity of our results to success-failure reclassification of some of the more controversial cases (since the margins of the basic classifications *are* judgmental). The estimated coefficients were quite robust to changing the verdict on both the semiconductor case (48) and the automobile case (93), although, of course, that took care of those two residuals.

Other surprising conclusions from the binomial probits involved expected patterns that did not emerge. In addition to those discussed above, we could find no evidence that the probability of success was influenced by the amount of trade or other business "at stake" in the case. (Although target-country resistance may be high in such cases because the same value is "at risk" in their eyes, properly controlling for the target's benefits and costs of compliance should have left this variable reflecting the U.S. stakes only). We could find no evidence that the probability of success was influenced by whether the case was transparent, involving reasonably clear taxes and subsidies or more opaque barriers, or whether the case involved the complex "new issues" of services and intellectual property or more familiar traditional barriers. We could also find no evidence that the probability of success was influenced by the difference between agricultural or nonagricultural cases or by time in general. As for the latter, recent cases that were not in Bayard's and Elliott's data but that have been added to ours did not change their conclusions using their specifications.

One time-related conclusion, however, can be taken either negatively or positively. Time dummies that isolate the early 1980s from the period from 1985 to 1988 show markedly higher success rates in the latter period and markedly lower success rates in the former, ceteris paribus.[21] Bayard and Elliott relate the higher mid-1980s success to legislative and administrative changes aimed at signaling a new "get-tough" stance. The effects of the two dummies are almost exactly offsetting, however, so that an alternative explanation is the change in trade policy personnel and style between the first and the second Reagan administrations without any necessarily lasting consequence.

8.4.2 Shadings of Success and Failure: Results from the Multinomial Logit Approach

We also experimented with explaining the richer four-way breakdown of the cases into clear and partial successes and failures.

Table 8.8 summarizes the results of two variations of unordered multinomial

---

20. Many cases had no measure at all of the trade under dispute, usually when they involved a large number of disparate practices affecting many different American exports. Case 88 against multiple Chinese access restrictions is one example.

21. See Bayard and Elliott (1994, 86–90), whose configuration of time dummies can be reinterpreted as in the text.

Table 8.8   **Unordered Multinomial Logit for Clear and Marginal Shades of Success and Failure (clear failure = omitted category)**

Independent Variables	Base Specification			With "Self-Initiate" Dummy		
	Coeff.	SE	t-Statistic	Coeff.	SE	t-Statistic
Marginal failure:						
Constant	.753	.494	1.525	.958	.556	1.724
TXDEP2	−.246	7.423	−.033	−.902	7.550	−.119
TBAL	−.000051	.000040	−1.270	−.000057	.000042	−1.360
BORDER	.311	.957	.325	.193	.971	.199
INITIATE				−.803	.877	−.915
Marginal success:						
Constant	−.506	.587	−.863	−.548	.664	−.826
TXDEP2	8.035	7.188	1.118	7.909	7.267	1.088
TBAL	−.000092	.000041	−2.243	−.000092	.000043	−2.148
BORDER	1.820	.954	1.907	1.856	.978	1.899
INITIATE				.177	.889	.199
Clear success:						
Constant	−2.150	.898	−2.393	−3.215	1.253	−2.565
TXDEP2	3.784	8.521	.444	5.548	8.612	.644
TBAL	−.000106	.000043	−2.445000	−.000104	.000045	−2.291
BORDER	3.001	1.122	2.674	3.731	1.287	2.900
INITIATE				1.641	1.197	1.370
Percentage of cases correctly predicted:						
Clear failures		8.33			8.33	
Marginal failures		73.33			70.00	
Marginal successes		73.53			67.65	
Clear successes		9.09			18.18	
Maximum likelihood estimates:						
Log likelihood		−94.31			−91.17	
Restricted log likelihood (slopes = 0)		−110.41			−110.41	

logits with clear failures as the omitted category. The coefficients should be read relative to clear failure; thus, the first four coefficients in table 8.8 record the determinants of the probability of a case being a marginal failure instead of a clear failure. These coefficients are largely insignificant, indicating that the determinants do not allow us to distinguish between clear and marginal failures. But the next four coefficients record the determinants of the probability of a case being a marginal success instead of a clear failure, the last four a clear success instead of a clear failure. Trade dependence (vulnerability) loses its significance here, but the trade balance (reciprocity) and the border dummy are quite significant, and self-initiation is marginally significant.[22] Their coef-

22. In variations with BULLY, its coefficients were never even marginally significant.

ficients are larger in the case of clear successes than in the case of marginal successes, implying that they also contribute in the familiar way to *degrees* of success as well as its likelihood.[23] Nevertheless, the multinomial logit runs clearly underpredict the extremes of the actual distribution, both clear successes and clear failures.

8.5   Quantitative Results

We also experimented with a quantitative counterpart to our multinomial logit approach. For the thirty-six (of eighty-seven) cases in which we could reasonably measure the trade at stake in the dispute,[24] we estimated the amount of trade "reclaimed" by the Section 301 procedure.[25] That amount was zero in cases of clear failures and all the trade under dispute in cases of clear successes. We then ran tobit specifications on base and alternative specifications similar to those in the qualitative results above. Results were in general quite mixed. They were very similar to the qualitative multinomial logits when the trade reclaimed was expressed as a percentage of the historical level of trade in similar goods *and* when three very large percentage outliers (for cases 57, 64, and 65) were omitted. In all other tobit runs, overall explanatory power was very low.

8.6   Policy Considerations

Bayard and Elliott (1994) concluded that Section 301 was unlikely to be as effective in the future as it had been in the previous decade. The sources of disputes are becoming less tractable, and its use will be constrained by the new World Trade Organization, which embodies an alternative, multilateral grievance mechanism that was shaped to match U.S. preferences. That conclusion is buttressed both by results reported here and by recent events. This study finds that the apparent upward trend in post-1985 Section 301 effectiveness largely disappears if the Reagan administration peaks and valleys are controlled for. And a *National Journal* postmortem on the U.S.-Japan automobile dispute concluded, "One clear lesson is that section 301 . . . is no longer a fearsome weapon" (Stokes 1995, 2098). The article also quoted an aide to the Democratic House leadership as saying that "Section 301 has been doomed to a quiet death." That may be too strong, but the recent spat over automobiles

---

23. We also tried ordered multinomial logits corresponding to table 8.8. The general pattern of results is very similar, although the coefficient on the self-initiate dummy grew in significance.

24. See n. 20 above.

25. Procedures and details are available from the authors.

and automobile parts (one of our "chronic residuals") and the dispute with the European Union (EU) over its banana regime highlight another difficulty not seriously considered by Bayard and Elliott or, indeed, by Mickey Kantor: the paucity of feasible WTO-legal sanctions that can be used as negotiating leverage in cases not covered by WTO rules.[26]

Recent cases provide other indicators of the future. One possibility is that Section 301 will be supplemented and then supplanted by the WTO's new alternative grievance mechanism.[27] The recent dispute (301-95) over Korean shelf-life standards for sausages and other meat, for example, suggests that even the threat of asking for formal WTO intervention can provide significant leverage. In that case, Korean and American negotiators reached an acceptable compromise within days of a deadline that U.S. negotiators had set for requesting establishment of a WTO dispute settlement panel.[28]

But, conversely, Bayard and Elliott (1994) predicted that U.S. threats would become weaker if a dispute involved issues covered by the WTO, yet the United States failed to follow WTO dispute settlement procedures or threatened to retaliate by withdrawing WTO-covered concessions (e.g., bound tariffs). Although U.S. negotiators considered filing a "nonviolation nullification and impairment" complaint in the WTO during the recent dispute over Japanese practices in the automobile sector (301-93), the core of that case involved competition policy issues not covered by WTO rules. U.S. negotiators apparently were unwilling to impose blatantly illegal sanctions against Japan—raising bound tariffs to prohibitive levels on imported Japanese luxury automobiles—and, when Japanese negotiators called their bluff, they blinked.

Bayard and Elliott correspondingly predicted that the effectiveness of U.S. threats would be unchanged if disputes involved issues not covered by the WTO or nonmembers *and* the United States did not withdraw WTO-covered concessions. But it has apparently been more difficult than supposed to identify WTO-legal sanctions that might make effective threats in areas where WTO rules do not apply. In testimony before the Senate commerce committee

26. In the language of game theory, this is described as a contraction of the "threat set"—the set of outcomes that can be unilaterally assured and implies diminished effectiveness of these "grievance bilaterals."

27. As of late 1995, eight Section 301 investigations had been launched since the research for *Reciprocity and Retaliation* (Bayard and Elliott 1994) was completed. Five of those cases involve nonborder issues where successful outcomes have been both less frequent and less predictable in the past: one each involving intellectual property issues (China, 301-92), services (Canadian cable television, 301-98), and technical regulatory barriers (Korean health regulations for meat, 301-95) and two alleging anticompetitive practices in Japan (automobiles and parts, 301-93, and photographic film and paper, 301-99). The other three investigations, targeting the European Union, Colombia, and Costa Rica, all involve implementation of the EU's import preference scheme for bananas from former colonial areas.

28. The desire of the Korean negotiators to put the acrimonious dispute behind them before President Kim Young Sam's state visit to Washington at the end of July apparently provided additional leverage (see *Inside U.S. Trade,* 14 July 1995; and *Journal of Commerce,* 21 July 1995, 10A).

in June 1994, USTR Kantor listed several areas that might yield WTO-legal sanctions. But the list is not very long, and in many cases it is not relevant to important trading partners:

- taking action in the maritime sector under the authority of the Federal Maritime Commission;
- denying telecommunications and/or banking licenses;
- placing conditions on foreign aid;
- putting limits on science and technology cooperation agreements; and
- denying certain visas (*International Trade Reporter,* 22 June 1994, 979).

Services like shipping, communications, and banking seem an attractive retaliation option because there are few or no WTO constraints in many sectors and because many tradable services remain relatively heavily regulated. This means that there will often be both administrative authority and tools available to the government to intervene. But the same things that make services attractive for retaliation make counterretaliation easier and, if desired, less transparent to any but the affected target. In the recent banana case, for example, negotiators reportedly considered, among other things, imposing a fee on entry into U.S. ports of EU-owned or -flagged ships but backed off, in part, because they—and the U.S. industry—feared counterretaliation against U.S. shippers (*Inside U.S. Trade,* 17 February 1995, 1).

There are further problems with developing countries. In the short and medium run, retaliation in service sectors is not likely to be at all effective against them because they do not yet have competitive tradable services. Other items on the Kantor list may not be of sufficient value to target countries to induce them to open their markets in important sectors. Termination, reduction, or suspension of benefits under the Generalized System of Preferences (GSP) has been used as a sanction in the past in intellectual property cases, but legislative authority for that program lapsed in mid-1995 and, even if restored by Congress, will be of diminishing value because of country graduations, product restrictions, and declining preference margins as the Uruguay Round tariff concessions are phased in.

In sum, American retaliatory threats under Section 301 may be more constrained than initially realized when the WTO was signed. Shortly before the deadline for taking action in the EU banana case, and apparently having failed to come up with other viable retaliation hit-list candidates, the Clinton administration belatedly decided to take the case to the WTO.[29] The *Journal of Com-*

---

29. The USTR had not earlier taken this case to the WTO because its jurisdiction with respect to the American complaint is somewhat murky. The private plaintiff is a U.S.-based firm, Chiquita, that ships, markets, and distributes Latin American bananas in the EU, but there is no direct trade between the United States and the EU involved. In a case brought by several adversely affected

merce (28 September 1995, 3A) reported that "the decision . . . is a tacit admission that the United States retains little leverage in imposing its will in trade matters outside of the newly powerful WTO."

In U.S. history, vigilantism was ultimately displaced by a more effective system of justice. Bayard and Elliott (1994) consider a strategic alternative to Section 301 that they call "aggressive multilateralism" (using the WTO to settle disputes where possible) and "creative minilateralism" (negotiations with like-minded trading partners to write rules in areas not covered by the international rules). In cases covered by WTO rules, they argue, the United States can retaliate once authorized to do so, just as under Section 301, but that power will probably be rarely needed under the strengthened dispute settlement procedures. In other cases, retaliation against WTO-covered trade risks precipitating a shoot-out that nobody wins. Their discussion seems prescient in the wake of the U.S.-Japan automobile dispute. It may be an auspicious time for the self-appointed marshall to retire.

Appendix
Recent Cases and Issues in Expanding the Bayard-Elliott Database

The Bayard and Elliott (1994) database of Section 301 cases included seventy-two of the ninety-one investigations opened as of that time.[30] One aim of the present analysis was to update and extend the database where possible. This was done in three ways: (1) by reviewing the nineteen Section 301 cases excluded by Bayard and Elliott; (2) by adding Section 301 cases resolved since that research was completed; (3) and by adding cases from the "p-list" of Section 301 petitions filed but not formally accepted by the USTR. Our assessments of the fifteen cases added are summarized in table 8.1 above.

1. Bayard and Elliott omitted several cases where the USTR concluded that the practice cited in the complaint was not actionable, either because the practice was not unreasonable under the statute's meaning or because it did not injure U.S. commercial interests. Following further review, one of those cases was restored to the database used here. Case 301-38 involved alleged Taiwanese subsidies for footwear exporters and restrictions on imports. In his formal

---

Latin American producers, an earlier GATT panel ruled in 1993 that the EU regime violated several GATT articles. The EU blocked adoption of the report, yet reached agreements with most of the major Latin American producers to lessen the injury, and asked for a WTO waiver for its African, Caribbean, and Pacific preference program (*Inside U.S. Trade,* 9 September 1994, 13).

30. For an explanation of which cases were excluded and why, see Bayard and Elliott (1994, 59, n. 3).

determination in that case, President Reagan found that Taiwan's practices were not unreasonable, but he also directed the U.S. trade representative to pursue offers from Taiwan to lower its tariffs on footwear and to provide marketing assistance to U.S. exporters, indicating that the 301 investigation induced some concessions, however modest (Bayard and Elliott 1994, 410–11).

2. Four other cases were excluded because they had not been resolved long enough for the authors to feel confident in making judgments about the outcomes. All those cases have been added to the data used here: 301-83, regarding EU standards for meatpacking facilities; 301-88, which resulted in the memorandum of understanding on access to the Chinese market; and 301-89 and 301-91, regarding protection of intellectual property rights in Taiwan and Brazil, respectively.

Two other cases resolved in the past year have also been added to the database. Although the results are still hotly debated, the recent U.S.-Japan automobile and automobile parts agreement (case 301-93) has been included because it strikes us as a marginal achievement at best, especially given the bluff and bluster surrounding the negotiations. Moreover, given the ongoing disagreement among negotiators about what exactly was agreed, the case seems almost certain to be reopened at some point, which would classify it as a marginal failure. Nevertheless, given the controversy, we tested the sensitivity of the results to variations in this judgment.

The other recent case added (301-98) is the dispute arising from Canada's decision to revoke the license of a U.S.-owned country music cable station operating there. That case was resolved through a joint venture agreement between the American cable company and the Canadian firm that replaced it. The agreement apparently was acceptable to both parties, but the terms also seem to have been influenced by the potential threat of Section 301 sanctions, making it, in our view, a partial success for U.S. negotiators.

3. Finally, we have added eight cases where the threat of a Section 301 investigation being opened appears to have provided leverage to U.S. negotiators. As of the beginning of 1995, twenty-eight Section 301 petitions had been filed but not formally accepted by the USTR between 1980 and 1990, the so-called p-list cases. Only rarely does the USTR openly reject petitions.[31] Most often, petitions are withdrawn just before the forty-five-day deadline for acceptance or rejection by the USTR. In many of these cases, it is simply not known whether the petitioner was persuaded to withdraw its complaint to avoid the embarrassment of rejection or whether a resolution was achieved through quiet diplomacy. In six cases, however, through press reports, the USTR's annual National Trade Estimates reports, and other sources, we concluded that there

---

31. It did formally reject two petitions from the Rice Millers Association when it determined that multilateral negotiations under the Uruguay Round would be a more effective means of opening Japan's market.

was evidence that the USTR had used the threat of a 301 investigation as negotiating leverage and that sufficient information about the outcomes in those episodes existed to include them here. The cases are briefly summarized in table 8.1 above.

We have also added the agreements negotiated with Korea and Taiwan in 1989 under threat of Super 301 designation. In these cases, public comments were requested by the USTR as to what countries or practices should be chosen for Super 301 priority designation. Although no formal petitions were filed in this process, the number and tenor of complaints received, and press reports speculating about likely targets, convinced Korea and Taiwan to negotiate preemptively. Thus, we treat these cases as akin to the other episodes when countries named in Section 301 petitions chose to negotiate in order to avoid a formal 301 investigation.

References

Baldwin, Robert E., and Jeffrey W. Steagall. 1994. An analysis of US international trade commission decisions in antidumping, countervailing duty, and safeguard cases. Discussion Paper no. 990. London: Centre for Economic Policy Research, July.

Bayard, Thomas O., and Kimberly Ann Elliott. 1994. *Reciprocity and retaliation in U.S. trade policy.* Washington, D.C.: Institute for International Economics.

Destler, I. M., John S. Odell, and Kimberly Ann Elliott. 1987. *Anti-protection: Changing forces in American politics.* Policy Analysis no. 21. Washington, D.C.: Institute for International Economics, September.

Greene, William H. 1993. *Econometric analysis.* New York: Macmillan.

Hansen, Wendy L., and Thomas J. Prusa. 1995. Cumulation on ITC decisionmaking: The sum of the parts is greater than the whole. Working Paper no. 5062. Cambridge, Mass.: National Bureau of Economic Research, March.

Hudec, Robert E. 1990. Thinking about the new Section 301: Beyond good and evil. In *Aggressive unilateralism: America's 301 trade policy and the world trading system,* ed. Jagdish Bhagwati and Hugh T. Patrick. Ann Arbor: University of Michigan Press.

Hughes, James W., and Edward A. Snyder. 1995. Litigation and settlement under the English and American rules: Theory and evidence. *Journal of Law and Economics* 38 (April): 225–50.

Lewin, David, and Richard Peterson. 1988. *The modern grievance procedure in the United States.* Greenwood, Conn.: Quorum.

Low, Patrick. 1993. *Trading free: The GATT and US trade policy.* New York: Twentieth Century Fund Press.

McMillan, John. 1990. Strategic bargaining and Section 301. *Economics and Politics* 2 (Spring): 45–58. Reprinted in *Aggressive unilateralism: America's 301 trade policy and the world trading system,* ed. Jagdish Bhagwati and Hugh T. Patrick (Ann Arbor: University of Michigan Press).

Mutti, John, and Bernard Yeung. In press. Section 337 and the protection of intellectual property in the United States: The impact on investment in intangibles. In *Quiet pioneering: Robert M. Stern and his international economic legacy,* ed. Keith Maskus,

Peter Hooper, Edward Leamer, and J. David Richardson. Ann Arbor: University of Michigan Press.

Noland, Marcus. 1995. Chasing phantoms: The political economy of USTR. Washington, D.C.: Institute for International Economics. Typescript.

Ryan, Michael P. 1995. USTR's implementation of 301 policy in the Pacific. *International Studies Quarterly* 39:333–50.

Stokes, Bruce. 1995. Collision course. *National Journal,* 19 August, 2098–2101.

Sykes, Alan O. 1992. Constructive unilateral threats in international commercial relations: The limited case for section 301. *Law and Policy in International Business* 23 (June): 263–330.

III Industry- and Country-Specific Policies

9   Whither Flat Panel Displays?

Kala Krishna and Marie Thursby

In April 1994, the Clinton administration announced a $597 million policy initiative to encourage U.S. companies to invest in the research and development (R&D) as well as the large-scale production of flat panel displays (FPDs). Semiconductors have become a standard part of many manufactured products, and flat panel displays are seen as having a similar potential. In the near future, however, computers are likely to account for more than half of FPD demand. Recommended support for the National Flat Panel Display Initiative included $318 million for core research and development, $50 million for a manufacturing test bed, $199 million for R&D linked to volume production, and $20 million for procurement incentives. Among the initiative's goals is the creation of a U.S.-based industry capable of achieving a 15 percent share of the world FPD market by the year 2000 (Flamm 1994).

The initiative has been highly controversial (see Barfield 1994, 1995; Flamm 1994, 1995; Miller 1995; and Mowery 1995). While the Department of Defense (DOD) claims that domestic production of FPDs is critical for national security, critics label the initiative as misguided industrial policy. Citing surveillance experiences from Desert Storm and the growing importance of digital technologies, DOD officials argue that effective use of advanced information technologies will determine the winners of future military conflicts. Visual dis-

Kala Krishna is professor of economics at the Pennsylvania State University and a research associate of the National Bureau of Economic Research. Marie Thursby is the Burton D. Morgan Professor of International Policy and Management at Purdue University and a research associate of the National Bureau of Economic Research.

The authors are grateful to K. C. Fung for suggesting flat panels as a case study and for assistance with data collection. Krishna is grateful for research support from the National Science Foundation under grant FBR9–9320825, and Thursby gratefully acknowledges support from the Purdue Technology Transfer Initiative. The paper benefited from excellent research assistance by Suddhasatwa Roy and useful discussions with Robert Feenstra, David Mentley, Theresa Proenza, and Jerry Thursby. Each is thanked without implication.

plays are seen as a critical factor in this regard. Moreover, relative to cathode ray tube displays, FPDs are reliable, lightweight, and energy efficient. Thus, the DOD justifies the need for policy by citing limited U.S. capacity to produce FPDs and the apparent refusal of Japanese companies to tailor FPDs to DOD specifications (U.S. Department of Defense 1994).

Critics of the initiative argue that U.S. military demand for FPDs could be met easily by several small to medium-size plants, an increase in capacity much less than that required to capture 15 percent of the world market (Barfield 1994, 1995; Mentley 1994). DOD estimates of future military demand for FPDs are fifteen thousand annually from 1995 to 1999 and twenty-five thousand annually from 2000 to 2009 (U.S. Department of Defense 1994, III-14). Thus, even DOD estimates place defense needs for FPDs far below the initiative's goal of 15 percent of the world market. It is not surprising, then, that the initiative is considered by some to be thinly disguised industrial policy. In addition, it is also argued that the size of the initiative is too small for it to make much of a difference.

Viewed as such, a question of interest becomes whether the initiative will lead to an increase in output and whether these firms will earn economic rents.[1] Although this question has not been directly addressed, Mentley's market projections suggest that the initiative's output effects per se will be small relative to its goal. He claims that a 15 percent market share for U.S. companies would require an investment of $3 billion rather than the planned $600 million. Mentley's projected rates of return for active matrix liquid crystal displays also suggest relatively low profit margins beginning in 1995 (Mentley 1995).[2]

Another point of controversy is whether the initiative is consistent with post–Uruguay Round subsidy codes. Since R&D support under the initiative is limited to 50 percent of project cost, DOD officials argue that it is well within the 75 percent cap for subsidies for specific industrial research. Critics, such as Barfield, argue that the incentives for volume production are beyond precompetitive support and that the procurement incentives directly violate the new GATT codes. There are, however, exceptions to these rules for defense.

In this paper, we consider a related set of issues, namely, the effect of subsidies for core R&D and of subsidies targeted to high-volume production. We do this in the context of a model that we feel captures the importance of investment in capacity, as well as yield-improving R&D, in the flat panel industry. In this model, firms with higher yields, ceteris paribus, invest in more capacity than those with lower yields. This leads to higher capacity and output for high-yield firms. The model has the property that all firms that remain in the industry ultimately have the same yield, that is, in the steady state. Thus, firms with an initial advantage in terms of yields tend to remain ahead for a while, after

---

1. Of course, an important issue here is whether profit increases and/or spillover effects are sufficient to increase national welfare.

2. Lower profit margins are a result, in part, of increased world capacity with the recent entry by Korean firms (Pollack 1995).

which laggards catch up. However, note that this gives firms with higher initial yields a stream of quasi rents, which the laggards do not enjoy. Such characteristics are thought to apply to industries such as FPDs and semiconductors.

Relevant industry characteristics are discussed in section 9.1, and a simple, stylized model is presented in section 9.2. In section 9.3, we examine the fit between the cost structure postulated in the model and data on manufacturing costs for color thin-film transistor liquid crystal displays (TFTLCDs). Policy simulations are presented in section 9.4. We first look at a *permanent* 25 percent subsidy on capacity acquisition versus at 25 percent subsidy on yield-improving R&D. Our results suggest that capacity subsidies have the unfortunate effect of decreasing incentives for R&D.[3] This, in turn, leads the targeted firm to have lower steady-state yields with capacity subsidies than with either R&D subsidies or in the absence of policy.

We then compare the effects of a *one-shot* fixed expenditure by the government on capacity and R&D subsidies. This gives us an idea of the difference in leverage provided by the two instruments since the subsidies are specified as a *given dollar amount*. We find that this type of subsidy has a positive impact effect on the net R&D and capacity expenditure by firms when the subsidy is for R&D but not when it is a capacity subsidy! In our model, R&D subsidies tend to provide more leverage than capacity subsidies. Directions for future work are discussed in section 9.5.

9.1 The Industry

The flat panel industry provides an interesting case study, quite apart from the DOD initiative. It is a highly concentrated industry, in which survival depends on continual investment in both product and process R&D. Much like other high-technology electronics products, in the flat panel industry there are a variety of rival technologies undergoing development. Successful development of one technology does not guarantee profits for long because new technologies and new generations of old technologies are constantly being developed.

There are a multitude of interesting characteristics of the industry, and it is impossible to develop one model that captures all of them. Our model captures the idea that continual innovation is needed to reap profits. If a firm does not improve its yield, it falls behind. As the yields of its competitors rise, market price declines, eventually wiping out the lagging firm's profits, at which point

---

3. Care should be taken in relating the complex and difficult-to-implement DOD proposals to the simpler policies discussed here. According to U.S. Department of Defense (1994, I-9), "Selected companies committed to new investments in volume production facilities for current generation products would be eligible to receive R&D support for next generation products and manufacturing processes, commensurate with the level of commitment demonstrated to volume production." This makes the subsidy conditional on capacity acquisition, with the result that it can be interpreted as, in part, a capacity subsidy.

it exits. In focusing on the role of yield-improving innovation, we take several shortcuts. We assume that firms are concerned only with the current cycle of production, capacity acquisition, and R&D. They do not look forward to anticipate the effect of their behavior today on future cycles. We choose to do this because uncertainty about the future is high in this industry, making standard dynamic approaches ill suited for modeling it. In the interest of simplicity, we also neglect other features such as adjustment costs even though they are important in the industry. Capacity costs are likely to have a high sunk component leading to irreversibilities and adjustment costs. Adjustment costs of this kind create "hysteresis," and therefore history matters. This creates situations where a temporary policy or shock can have permanent effects by causing what looks like a regime change (see, e.g., Baldwin and Krugman 1989).

We abstract from several other factors, which, while important in the industry, have been studied elsewhere. Thus, including these factors would add little that is not already well understood. For example, some of the yield improvement observed in the industry is likely to result from learning by doing. Models of learning by doing are well studied in the literature. In a trade context, Baldwin and Krugman (1988) model the semiconductor industry in this manner. One result from such models is that firms produce more than they would if they equated marginal revenue and cost since they take into account the reduction in future costs implied by an additional unit of current output. In such contexts, capacity subsidies are in effect also R&D subsidies, making these models ill suited for answering the kind of questions we ask. That is, in learning-by-doing models, stark differences between R&D and capacity subsidies cannot be detected. We also assume that there are no spillovers in R&D. Such spillovers occur when a yield improvement by one firm accrues, at least partially, to other firms. Again, it is well understood[4] that spillovers of this kind reduce the ability to internalize the effects of R&D and hence tend to reduce the incentive to do R&D.

9.1.1   FPD Technologies

As shown in table 9.1, liquid crystal displays (LCDs) are the major type of display in today's market, constituting 87 percent of the commercial market. In these displays, light is emitted when voltage is applied to liquid crystals enclosed between the two sheets of glass (substrates) that make up the display.[5] Active matrix LCDs (AMLCDs), which control the polarization of these crystals by use of silicon transistors, are considered the dominant technology for high-information displays. The primary use of AMLCDs is as color screens for laptop computers. Passive matrix LCDs (PMLCDs) control light emission by use of metal horizontal and vertical electrodes on the two sheets of glass. PMLCDs are more commonly used than AMLCDs, but they have slower re-

---

4. For an analysis of R&D spillovers in an international trade context, see Jensen and Thursby (1987).

5. For a detailed description of each of the FPD technologies, see U.S. Department of Defense (1994, chap. 2).

Table 9.1   **Commercial FPD Sales**

	1993	2000[a]		1993	2000[a]
Total value (in $ billions)	6.5	20			
By technology (%):			By application (%):		
Nonemissive (LCD):	87	89	Computer	61	67
AMLCD	29	55	Consumer	12	14
Other	58	34	Business	9	5
Emissive:			Industrial	12	8
Plasma	4	4	Transportation	6	6
Electroluminescent	1	2			
Other	8	5			

Sources: U.S. Department of Defense (1994, figs. 2-1, 2-7, 3-1, 3-2); Stanford Resources (1994).
[a]Projections.

sponse times and tend to be less bright (U.S. Department of Defense 1994). Hence, as noted in the table, the DOD predicts an increase in the importance of AMLCDs relative to PMLCDs.

One problem with LCDs is that, even with redundant transistors at each pixel, some pixels fail to operate, with resulting quality problems in the display. LCDs are produced under the same clean-room conditions as semiconductors, and displays that contain defective pixels risk being discarded. This means that quality-control problems increase dramatically as the screen size increases, and therefore the potential of LCDs for large-screen applications is limited. Moreover, LCD producers engage in R&D to develop new generations of equipment that are capable of producing higher yields, that is, portion of production that is acceptable in terms of defective pixels.

Three alternatives to LCDs are plasma displays (PDPs), electroluminescent displays (ELDs), and field emission displays (FEDs). These displays differ from LCDs in that they produce their own light. PDPs generate light by applying voltage to an inert gas enclosed between the two sheets of glass, while ELDs and FEDs stimulate phosphors to emit light. Notice that these displays constituted only 5 percent of the market in 1993, and U.S. Department of Defense (1994) predicted that emissive displays will remain a small part of the commercial market in 2000. However, in August 1995, a number of companies announced progress toward development and production of PDPs and FEDs (Edmondson and Gross 1995; Patton and Rawsthorn 1995). Fujitsu, Matsushita, Sony, and NEC unveiled working prototypes of large-screen PDPs (up to forty-two inches), and Fujitsu announced plans to produce ten thousand units a month by October 1996. PDPs are considered to have the greatest potential for low-cost, large television screens.[6]

6. Notice in table 9.1 that the primary application of FPDs has been computers, with the consumer market representing only 12 percent of demand. While the DOD predicts a small consumer market in 2000, the evolution of cheaper large-scale FPDs is likely to increase the consumer market dramatically.

9.1.2   Market Shares in FPDs

As with VCRs, the technologies leading to FPDs were developed in the labs of U.S. electronics companies, but the industry is now dominated by Japanese companies.[7] For example, early technologies for FPDs were developed in research labs at RCA, Westinghouse, and IBM in the 1960s and 1970s. Engineers in RCA's Sarnoff Lab developed LCD technology with the goal of developing a television screen "flat enough to hang on a wall" (U.S. Department of Defense 1994, chap. 6). Peter Brody, of Westinghouse, developed the cadmium selenide AMLCD technology underlying the majority of today's AMLCDs. Although these technologies were at the prototype stage, neither RCA nor Westinghouse pursued commercial development of FPDs. RCA switched from LCD to cathode ray research in the 1970s, while Westinghouse dropped its project in 1979. In the 1970s, IBM pursued plasma technologies for computers and business applications, but, in 1984, it switched R&D efforts to LCD technologies. In the late 1980s, IBM and Toshiba formed Display Technologies, Inc. (DTI), a joint venture for the development and high-volume production of LCDs in Japan. None of these companies invested in manufacturing capacity in the United States.[8]

In contrast, companies such as Sharp and NEC actively pursued development and production of FPDs. Both companies stood to benefit from their experience with the types of clean-room conditions and continual process improvements important in semiconductors. Sharp successfully applied FPD technology to handheld calculators in the 1970s, and in the 1980s it became a leader in color TFTLCDs. In 1993, Sharp was the world's largest producer of FPDs, with its sales constituting 44 percent of the world market. NEC and DTI were the next largest producers, with sales constituting 35 percent of the market (U.S. Department of Defense 1994, chap. 4).

In total, approximately fifty companies manufacture FPDs. As noted in table 9.2, Japanese companies accounted for over 90 percent of the LCD market in 1993. Seven Japanese companies accounted for 98 percent of the AMLCD market. In 1993, the only volume producer of AMLCDs in the United States was Optical Imaging Systems, which primarily sold displays for avionics applications. If one views IBM's joint venture, DTI, as a Japanese company, the only markets in which U.S. companies are large players are the PDP and ELD

7. The patent underlying virtually all VCR technologies was obtained by Ampex Corp., a U.S. company, in the late 1950s. Although Ampex successfully commercialized a videotape recorder for broadcast use, the first companies to commercialize a consumer product were Sony, JVC, and Matsushita. This occurred despite early efforts by RCA to develop a consumer video recorder and a joint venture by Ampex and Toshiba for the same purpose. For an analysis that focuses on the role of government policy in VCR development, see Tyson (1992). In contrast, Rosenbloom and Cusumano (1987) take the view that the evolution of the industry is due primarily to different management styles of the companies involved.

8. For an account of other efforts by U.S., European, and Japanese companies, see U.S. Department of Defense (1994, chap. 6).

Table 9.2   **1993 Market Shares by Country (%)**

	LCD	AMLCD	Plasma	Electroluminescent
Japan	92	98	68	47
United States	1	1	19	50
Other	7	1	13	3

Sources: U.S. Department of Defense (1994, figs. 4-1, 4-2, and table 4-1); Stanford Resources (1994).

markets. The fact that these markets constitute only 5 percent of the total value of LCDs (table 9.1 above) is one aspect of the DOD's justification for the flat panel policy initiative.

Several U.S. companies are conducting R&D on FPDs, in part as a response to the DOD initiative. Optical Imaging Systems was awarded an Advanced Research Projects Agency (ARPA) contract to construct a new AMLCD plant, and it is involved in a joint venture with Apple to develop displays for computer applications. Additionally, a consortium formed by AT&T, Standish Industries, and Xerox received a DOD award to develop a manufacturing test bed. Various other R&D projects are ongoing at Motorola, Raytheon, Sarnoff Labs, and Texas Instruments.

9.2   A Simple Model

In this section, we develop a simple model that we feel captures several important features of the flat panel display industry. First, we feel that the timing structure needs to recognize that output is easier to change than capacity, which in turn is easier to change than yield. We therefore assume that, in what we call the short run, both capacity and yield are fixed. In what we call the medium run, capacity is variable, and, in the long run, yield can be chosen. Of course, in the steady state of such a model, long-run and short-run yields must be equal.

Second, we feel that, in the short run, with capacity and yield as given, firms behave competitively and take price as given. Thus, their only decision is whether to produce to capacity.[9] If profits are nonnegative, firms produce; and, if profits are negative, firms do not produce. However, in the medium run, they choose capacity. In making this decision, they take into account the fact that capacity affects output and hence profit. This results in a capacity choice equilibrium resembling a Cournot-Nash equilibrium. In the long run, firms choose R&D expenditure, which affects their yields, and hence their capacity

---

9. The clever reader will immediately think of a counterexample where the last firm's capacity, if used entirely, results in negative profits but, if not used at all, results in a price higher than short-run marginal cost. It is argued below that this case will never arise. The argument consists of showing that capacity choices of this kind are never made.

choice, as well as output. Notice that we abstract from R&D to develop new types of FPDs, with the result that the only R&D is for process improvement.

Third, firms with a high yield find it easier to attain a given yield higher than their existing one than do firms with lower yields. However, any improvement in yields is costly. It is also assumed that there are positive costs of any improvement in yields, no matter how infinitesimal. The latter assumption permits convergence of the yields to a finite level in some steady states.

We wish to use the model to answer questions about the evolution of industry capacity. If, for example, a given number of firms start off with different yields, what should we expect for their capacity and yield paths over time? Do firms that have better yields invest more or less in R&D? Do firms with better yields stay ahead in terms of yields? If there is entry into the industry, will profits be eroded to zero? Does the final profile of an industry depend on the initial profile? How?

By examining these questions, we hope to shed light on the effect of policies designed to encourage investment in R&D and in production facilities. We find that firms with higher yields, ceteris paribus, invest in more capacity than those with lower yields. Since firms produce up to capacity, this implies more output by these firms. Higher outputs, in turn, increase the benefits from investments in R&D to raise yields. As our simulation results show, this conflagration of forces plays a role in the effects of capacity and R&D subsidies. While capacity subsidies initially lead to increased capacity and hence investment in yields, at the margin they reduce the benefit from yield-increasing R&D. As shown in section 9.3, this can lead to steady-state yields that are lower than what would occur without the capacity subsidies. In contrast, subsidies to R&D promote higher steady-state yields.

9.2.1   The Short Run

Assume that there are N firms in the industry. Each firm i has a capacity of S^i and a yield of y^i. The production process can be thought of as being composed of two steps. In order to have one viable unit of production at the end of the first stage, $1/y^i$ units need to be started at a cost of c_1 per unit started. This corresponds to the idea that only y^i percent of the FPDs are usable since panels have to be discarded if any pixels are defective. Following this, further stages of production must be performed on the viable unit at a cost of c_2 per unit. Thus, the total cost of q^i units of produced output in the short run for a firm with yield y^i and capacity S^i is

$$(1) \qquad TC^i_{sr}(q^i, y^i, S^i) = \left(\frac{c_1}{y^i} + c_2\right)q^i \text{ for } q^i \leq S^i$$

$$= \infty \text{ for } q^i > S^i.$$

Such firms have a short-run marginal cost of $MC^i_{sr} = c_1/y^i + c_2$. Profits are thus

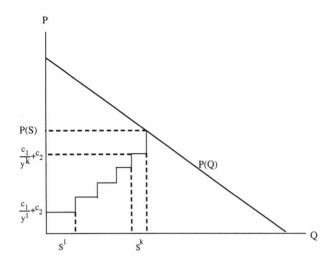

Fig. 9.1   Short-run equilibrium

$$(2) \qquad \Pi^i_{sr}(q^i, y^i, S^i) = P\!\left(\sum_{j=1}^{k} q^j\right)\!q^i - \left(\frac{c_1}{y^i} + c_2\right)\!q^i \text{ for } q^i \le S^i$$
$$= -\infty \text{ for } q^i > S^i.$$

The supply curve for the industry is as depicted in figure 9.1. As firms behave competitively, each firm supplies its entire capacity if price exceeds its marginal cost. This permits us to replace q^i with S^i whenever a firm makes positive profits. It also results in the step-function form of supply depicted. Firms take the intersection of demand and supply as the given price, and they maximize their profits accordingly in the short run. As drawn, firms with lower indices have higher yields and correspondingly lower marginal costs. Only firms with indices less than $k + 1$ supply as drawn in figure 9.1.

9.2.2   The Medium Run

In the short run, firms take their capacities as given as well as their yields. In the medium run, they take only their yields as given, and they choose capacities. The cost of an additional unit of capacity is F^i, but a firm that has a yield of y^i will incur a cost of $(F^i/y^i)q^i$ to get an output of q^i. Of course, firms realize that their choice of capacity affects the price in the market and incorporate such considerations in their decision making. Each firm, therefore, chooses its capacity, S^i, to maximize its medium-run profits, which along with its first-order condition are given below:

$$(3) \qquad \Pi^i_{mr}(y^i, S^i, S^{-i}) = P\!\left(\sum_{j=1}^{k} S^j\right)\!S^i - \left(\frac{c_1}{y^i} + c_2\right)\!S^i - \frac{F^i}{y^i}S^i,$$

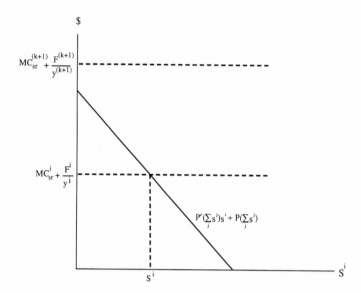

Fig. 9.2   Medium-run equilibrium

$$(4) \qquad \frac{\partial \Pi^i_{mr}(y^i, S^i, S^{-i})}{\partial S^i} = P'\left(\sum_{j=1}^{k} S^j\right) S^i + P\left(\sum_{j=1}^{k} S^j\right) - \left(\frac{c_1}{y^i} + c_2\right)$$
$$- \frac{F^i}{y^i} = 0.$$

Figure 9.2 depicts the capacity choice that solves (4). Note that, if a firm chooses to invest in capacity, its profits in the short run must be *strictly positive*.[10] Hence, firms will choose to produce all their capacity in the short run.

As all firms choose their capacities in this manner, the solution to this system looks like a Cournot-Nash equilibrium. The equilibrium levels of S^i are denoted by $S^i(y^1, y^2, \ldots, y^N)$ for $i = 1, \ldots, N$. Notice that firms with higher yields will choose higher capacity levels, as one would expect.

9.2.3   The Long Run

In the long run, firms choose their yield levels realizing how this affects the outcome in the short and medium runs. The cost to a firm with yield y^i_0 of raising its yield to level y^i is denoted by $R^i(y^i_0, y^i)$. We will assume that this takes a particular functional form given by

$$(5) \qquad R^i(y^i_0, y^i) = z(y^i - y^i_0) + \theta(y^i - y^i_0)^2.$$

---

10. If $P(\sum_{j=1}^{k} S^j) - c_1/y^i - c_2 = 0$, then the lowest-yield firm may produce less than its full capacity. It is easily shown that the medium-run equilibrium rules out capacity choices that will not be used in the short run.

Note that this functional form has the property that even small improvements in yield are costly and that larger improvements become progressively more costly.

Thus, in the long run, firm i wishes to maximize its long-run profits given by

$$(6) \quad \Pi^i_{lr}[y^i, S^i(\cdot), S^{-i}(\cdot)] = P\left[\sum_{j=1}^{k} S^j(\cdot)\right]S^i(\cdot) - \left(\frac{c_1}{y^i} + c_2\right)S^i(\cdot)$$
$$- \frac{F}{y^i}S^i(\cdot) - z(y^i - y^i_0) - \theta(y^i - y^i_0)^2.$$

The first-order condition, after using the envelope theorem, gives

$$(7) \quad \frac{c_1}{(y^i)^2}S^i(\cdot) + \frac{F}{(y^i)^2}S^i(\cdot) - R'(\cdot) + P'(\cdot)S^i(\cdot)\sum_{j \ne i}\frac{dS^j(y^1, \ldots, y^n)}{dy^i} = 0.$$

In addition to the long-run first-order condition given above, we need a steady-state condition for each firm. In the steady state, the yield chosen by each firm must equal its initial yield. The steady-state condition for each firm, therefore, consists of equation (7), where $R'(\cdot)$ is evaluated at $y^i = y^i_0$.

9.3   Costs and Yields

In this section, we examine data for costs of production at various yields to get an idea of the importance of yield differences in the industry. Cost data are from Stanford Resources (Mentley and Castellano 1994; Stanford Resources 1994). They refer to a portion of the AMLCD market, namely, color TFTLCDs produced in 1994.

In the short run, recall that each firm produces up to capacity, as long as its short-run costs fall short of price, with costs given by $(c_1/y^i + c_2)S^i$ if their yield is y^i. Mentley and Castellano report unit costs for final output levels (q^i) between 60,000 and 960,000 panels per year and yields between .1 and .9. These unit-cost data include variable costs such as materials, supplies, and equipment as well as direct and indirect labor employed in producing color TFTLCDs. They also include capital investment cost in the form of depreciation.[11] For our analysis of short-run cost, we compute the unit cost net of depreciation. On the basis of these data (net of depreciation), the following regression was estimated to give us estimates of c_1 and c_2:

$$(8) \qquad\qquad TC^i = \tilde{c}_1\frac{q^i}{y^i} + \tilde{c}_2 q^i + \varepsilon$$

11. Mentley and Castellano report high- and low-cost figures for unit costs and depreciation. The regressions reported here are based on their high-cost figures. Regression results using low costs are similar to those reported here and are available from the authors. For procedures used to compute the unit-cost data, see Mentley and Castellano (1994). Their depreciation figures are based on straight-line depreciation over five years.

Table 9.3   **Cost Regressions**

	Dependent	
Independent	Total Variable Cost	Total Fixed Cost
q/y	47.12	51.82
	(7.03)	(.21)
q	554.13	
	(29.09)	
R^2	.93	.99
No. of observations	45	45

Source: Mentley and Castellano (1994).

Note: Standard errors are given in parentheses.

Coefficient estimates and standard errors are reported in table 9.3. The form seems to fit the data well, with an R^2 of .93.

Note that a two-stage cost structure is embodied in this cost function. A fraction y of the starts are nondefective at the end of the first stage. The cost of the first-stage application is c_1. Thus, to get one unit past the first stage, $1/y$ units are needed as starts with a cost of c_1/y per nondefective unit at the end of the first stage. At the second stage, the cost is c_2 per unit that goes in. Our estimates suggest that variable cost levels rise sharply with reductions in yield, especially at low-yield levels.

Our specification of medium-run costs also depends on yields. That is, $TC_{mr}^i = (c_1/y^i + c_2)S^i - (F^i/y^i)S^i$, where the last term reflects capacity acquisition cost. As noted above, Stanford Resources also reports data for capacity cost in the form of depreciation. Since these data are reported for final output levels between 60,000 and 960,000 panels per year and yields between .1 and .9, we can examine the importance of yields in medium-run cost. We estimate a regression of the form

$$(9) \qquad \text{TFC}^i = \tilde{F}\frac{S^i}{y^i} + \varepsilon$$

As noted in table 9.3, our estimate of $\tilde{F}$ is 51.82, and the R^2 is .99.[12] Thus depreciation on flow capacity costs and hence also plant costs depend on yield.

Taking both estimates into account, it appears that plants with yields of 30 percent or more are viable at 1994 prices. That is, with a yield of 30 percent, variable costs are about $710 per unit, and capacity costs are approximately $170, while the December 1994 price was around $1,000. With a 20 percent yield, variable costs are about $790 per unit, and capacity costs are about $260 per unit. In our model, a firm with this yield would show negative medium-run profits at the 1994 price.

12. Such a high R^2 makes us suspect that the capacity cost data, in particular, come from accounting procedures that replicate our model.

9.4   Simulation Results

In this section, we focus on policy experiments in a simple two-firm version of our model. We do this for several reasons. First, while the cost equations in our model show a good fit with the data, other data and/or elasticity estimates needed to calibrate the model are not publicly available. Second, the model's equilibrium conditions, especially those for long-run equilibrium given by (6) and (7), are highly nonlinear. This makes it difficult to solve the system analytically with many asymmetric firms. We therefore simulate a simple two-firm system to obtain some insights into policy issues.

We focus on two policy experiments. In the first, we look at the effects of a *25 percent permanent subsidy* to R&D or to capacity acquisition. In the second, we look at the effects of a given *one-time subsidy* on either R&D or capacity. In both experiments, we show how the results depend on the degree of asymmetry between the firms.

The model is the same as in the previous sections. For simplicity, we assume a linear form for the market demand curve, which is parameterized as

$$(10) \qquad P\left(\sum_{j=1}^{2} S^j\right) = a - b\left(\sum_{j=1}^{2} S^j\right).$$

Short-run profits are given by (2), medium-run profits by (3), and long-run profits by (6). In each of the simulations, we look at the evolution toward the steady state of key endogenous variables, including yields, capacity, price, and profits. Our purpose in carrying out these simulations is to help understand the possible consequences of proposed subsidies to R&D and to volume production in the flat panel industry. Will subsidies to capacity acquisition help or hinder the long-run competitiveness of the targeted firm? Are such subsidies likely to raise or reduce welfare?

9.4.1   A 25 Percent Subsidy

We first consider the case of two identical firms. We trace the behavior of the simulated market over time under three scenarios. The first is that of no policy. The second is that of a 25 percent subsidy on capacity for one firm, call it firm A, so that F is reduced by 25 percent for firm A alone. The third is that of a 25 percent subsidy on R&D expenditure, which corresponds to a 25 percent reduction in z and θ for firm A. We then repeat the above three simulations for the asymmetric case where firm A has a lower yield than firm B. This allows us to examine the effects of an initial disadvantage on the results of the policy experiments.

In each case, the parameters we use are as follows. The slope of the inverse demand curve, b, and its intercept, a, are set at $b = 1$ and $a = 37$. The marginal costs in the short run are given by $(c_1/y^i + c_2)$ for firm $i = A, B$. We set $c_1 = c_2 = 1$. In the symmetric case, both firms have the same yield of .5, and therefore $y^A = y^B = .5$. In the asymmetric case, $y^A = .4$, and $y^B = .5$. The cost of obtaining a unit of capacity is F and is common to both firms. We set $F = 2$ throughout. The cost parameters in yield-increasing R&D are z and θ, and these are common to both firms and set at $z = 120$ and $\theta = 1,000$.

The Symmetric Case

In the symmetric case, given yields of .5 each, both firms choose a capacity of 10. The market price to start with is 17, short-run marginal cost of each firm is 3, and short-run profits are 140 each. Capacity costs are 40 per unit, and medium-run profits are 100. We run the system through thirty iterations. At each iteration, yields rise, capacity rises, profits rise, and price falls. Yields rise to .583, which is close to the steady-state level of .586. Capacity rises to 10.28, while price falls to 16.43. On the other hand, expenditure on yield-improving R&D falls dramatically to .06 from a starting value of 2.12.

When we reduce the cost of capacity acquisition by 25 percent to firm A, the immediate response in the first iteration is an increase in the chosen capacity to 10.67. In response to this, B's capacity choice is to keep capacity slightly below 10. In addition, A invests less in yield-improving R&D than before and has a lower yield as a consequence! While B invests more than A, its investment in R&D also falls from that with no policy in response to A's reduction in R&D. Initially, A invests 1.12, and B invests 1.85. Both these numbers are below those that would occur in the absence of policy.

The impact effect of the subsidy is to raise A's gross profits and lower B's. Over time, A's profits rise but then begin to fall, while B's rise throughout. The reason for this is that a capacity subsidy (which reduces F) encourages capacity investment, as is evident from (4). However, incentives to do R&D are also *diminished* by the subsidy on capacity costs. The reason is apparent from the first-order condition given in (7). This equation can be thought of as choosing y_i on the part of firm i to equate the marginal benefit of yield-improving R&D,

$$\left[\frac{c_1}{(y^i)^2} S^i(\cdot) + \frac{F^i}{(y^i)^2} S^i(\cdot) + P'(\cdot)S^i(\cdot) \sum_{j \neq i} \frac{dS^j(y^1, \ldots, y^n)}{dy^i} \right],$$

with its marginal cost, $R'(\cdot)$. If the problem is well behaved, we can think of the marginal benefit as decreasing in y^i. The marginal cost is increasing in y^i for our specification, starting from any given initial yield. Recall that a capacity subsidy reduces F by 25 percent. This shifts the marginal benefit curve of doing yield-reducing R&D inward, reducing the chosen yield.

In contrast, a subsidy to R&D reduces $R'(\cdot)$ by 25 percent in (7). This shifts the marginal cost of yield-reducing R&D down and out, raising the chosen level of y^i. This in turn *reduces* the marginal cost of a unit of capacity as seen in (4), and this raises capacity acquisition in the medium run.

At the end of thirty iterations, A has a yield of .544, while B has a yield of .579, both of which are *less* than that without policy! A's capacity exceeds that of B (10.68 vs. 10.08), and price falls to 16.25. R&D expenditure falls to .002

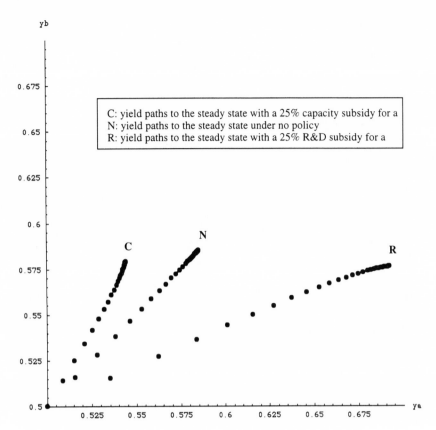

Fig. 9.3   Yield paths to the steady state in the symmetric case with $y_0^A = .5$ and $y_0^B = .5$

for A and .013 for B, both of which are lower than they would be without the policy. Profits in the short run initially go to 142.6 for firm A and 133.8 for firm B as a direct consequence of the higher capacity induced by the subsidy. After thirty iterations, short-run profits go to 143.2 and 136.2, respectively.

In contrast, an R&D subsidy of 25 percent results in an impact effect that almost doubles A's R&D expenditure, which goes to 4.07, while B's goes to 2.06. Both firms' R&D expenditures fall steadily over time to .03 and .005, respectively, after thirty iterations. Firm A's capacity rises steadily over time to 10.8, while B's stays at about 10. Yields also rise steadily to .692 and .576 for A and B, respectively. A's short-run profits rise throughout, while B's fall throughout, ending up at 148.7 and 134.2, respectively, after thirty iterations. Price falls to 16.15 at the end of thirty iterations.

It is perhaps easiest to compare the effects of the three policies on yields by looking at figure 9.3. Each point is an iterative value of yields for A and B. Yields are always increasing. In the first iterations, there are large changes in

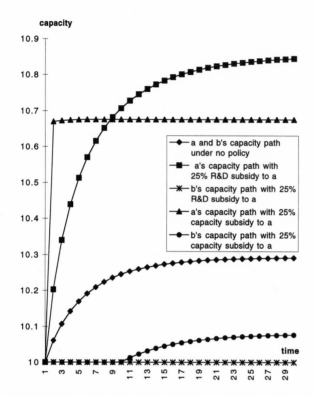

**Fig. 9.4   Capacity paths to the steady state in the symmetric case with $y_0^A = .5$
and $y_0^B = .5$**

yields, but these get smaller over time, as depicted by the dots moving closer
together as yields rise. The R curve, which gives the yields with the R&D
subsidy, always lies to the right of the N curve, which depicts the yields with
no policy. The C curve always lies to the left of the N curve. Thus, while B
reaches roughly the same yield across the three scenarios, A's yields vary considerably, being lowest in the capacity subsidy case and highest in the R&D
subsidy case. Figures 9.4 and 9.5 depict the capacity and short-run profit paths
as a function of time for the two firms across the three scenarios.

The Asymmetric Case

While the simulations above provide useful insights, it is important to ask
about the extent to which they are modified by firm A being at an initial disadvantage. To cast some light on this, we repeated our simulations for starting
values of yields of .4 for A and .5 for B. Without any policy, A's initial disadvantage is slowly overcome. A invests significantly more in R&D than B, and
the two firms arrive at the symmetric steady state as before. When a capacity
subsidy of 25 percent is given, the same kinds of effects are obtained as in the
symmetric case. While A's investment in R&D remains above B's, it falls be-

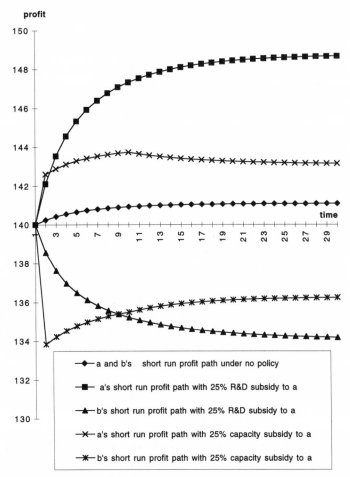

**Fig. 9.5   Short-run profit paths to the steady state in the symmetric case
with $y_0^A = .5$ and $y_0^B = .5$**

cause of the subsidy. However, even after thirty iterations, the yield of firm A
remains below that of firm B, .543 versus .579! In contrast, with an R&D
subsidy, A's yields surpass those of B after only seven iterations. By the end of
thirty iterations, the yields are at .691 and .576, respectively.

Thus, asymmetries in the initial yields only seem to magnify the differences
in the two policies. With initial asymmetries, firm A needs to invest heavily in
R&D to catch up with firm B. A capacity subsidy reduces the incentive to do
R&D, and, as a result, A's yield remains below B's. By contrast, an R&D subsidy enhances the incentives to do R&D, and A's yield, short-run profits, and
capacity overtake B's in a small number of periods. The behavior of yields in
the asymmetric case is depicted in figure 9.6. Again, each point is an iterative
value of yields for A and B. Yields are always increasing, and, at first, there are

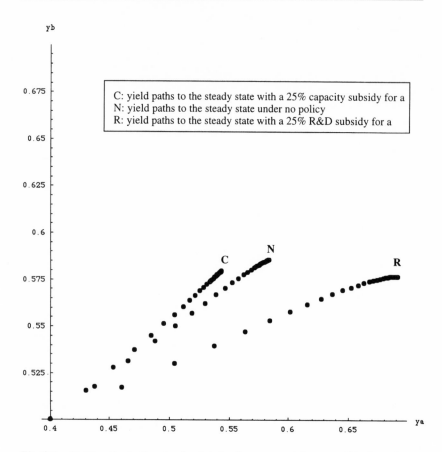

Fig. 9.6   Yield paths to the steady state in the asymmetric case with $y_0^A = .4$ and $y_0^B = .5$

large changes in yield, but these get smaller over time, as depicted by the dots moving closer together as yields rise. The R curve, which gives yields with the R&D subsidy, always lies to the right of the N curve, which depicts the yield with no policy. The C curve always lies to the left of the N curve. Again, while B reaches roughly the same yield across the three scenarios, A's yields vary considerably, being lowest in the capacity subsidy scenario and highest in the R&D subsidy scenario. Figures 9.7 and 9.8 depict the capacity and short-run profit paths as a function of time for the two firms across the three scenarios in the asymmetric case.

9.4.2   A Given Subsidy Expenditure

The results so far suggest that R&D subsidies seem to be more effective than capacity subsidies. The reason is that an R&D subsidy raises yields, which in turn effectively reduces the cost of a unit of capacity and encourages capac-

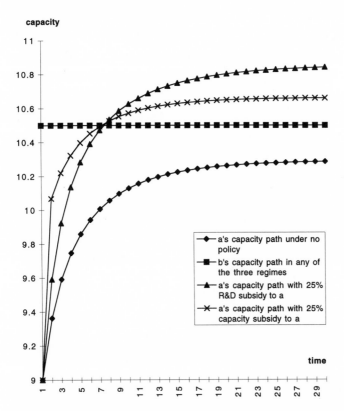

Fig. 9.7   Capacity paths to the steady state in the asymmetric case with $y_0^A = .4$ and $y_0^B = .5$

ity acquisition, while a subsidy on capacity raises the incentive to do capacity acquisition but reduces the incentive to do yield-improving R&D.

The simulations so far compare a given permanent (25 percent) subsidy on R&D with one on capacity. They do not compare the effects of a given, one-shot expenditure on the two kinds of subsidies, which is, of course, the relevant comparison for the allocation of given funds to alternative policies. Such a simulation would also address another criticism of the DOD initiative: namely, that it is *too small* to produce the desired effect. It is obvious that a dollar spent on R&D or capacity subsidies need not result in exactly a dollar increase in gross expenditure. It could result in more than a dollar increase in gross expenditure, in which case net expenditure (expenditure net of the subsidy) rises, or it could result in less than a dollar increase in gross expenditure, in which case net expenditure falls!

First, note that, in our earlier simulations, yields and capacity stabilize as the steady state is reached, with the result that R&D and capacity expenditures fall over time. If we simulate the effects of a one-time subsidy, the immediate

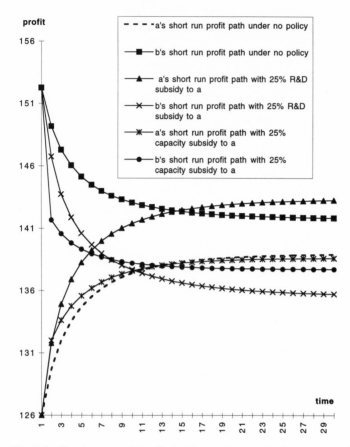

Fig. 9.8   Short-run profit paths to the steady state in the asymmetric case with $y_0^A = .4$ and $y_0^B = .5$

effect will be to raise the gross level of the targeted variable above its no-policy path, but, when the subsidy is removed in the next period, these higher levels cannot be sustained. In the model that we use, there is no effect of a one-shot policy on the steady state. However, this does not mean that these policies have no effect: the path to steady state is very different under the two policies.

Figure 9.9 plots the *net* effect of a $1.00 subsidy (applied as the equivalent ad valorem level) when applied to R&D and to capacity in the symmetric case. The dashed line in the figure plots the difference between the targeted firm's R&D expenditure (net of the government subsidy) when it receives a one-shot dollar subsidy for R&D and its R&D expenditure without policy. The cross-hatched line plots the difference in the firm's capacity expenditure (net of the subsidy) with and without this R&D subsidy. The solid and dotted lines have the same interpretations when the policy is a one-shot subsidy for capacity

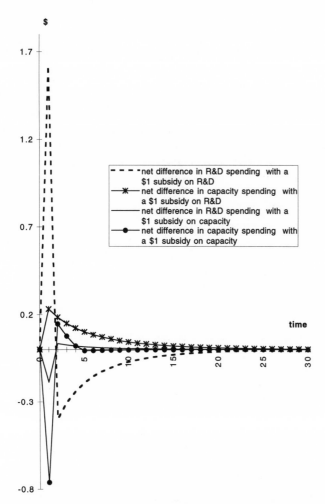

Fig. 9.9   Net effects of $1.00 subsidies for the symmetric case with $y_0^A = .5$ and $y_0^B = .5$

acquisition. We focus on these plots since the path of yields and capacity can be inferred from them.

A dollar spent on R&D results in an immediate increase in *gross* expenditure on R&D of about $2.62, and therefore net expenditure rises by about $1.62, as shown in figure 9.9. Of course, in the following period, expenditure on R&D falls below that with no policy. However, this reduction is only about .4, with the result that the impact effect dominates. This results in the path of yields lying above the no-policy path. Moreover, the impact effect of the R&D subsidy on capacity expenditure is to raise it above its no-policy path, as shown in figure 9.9. This is because, as discussed earlier, higher yields reduce the cost of investing in capacity and so result in a greater incentive to invest in capacity. Thus, capacity also lies above its no-policy path in this case.

In contrast, a dollar spent on a capacity subsidy results in an impact effect of a net reduction in expenditure on capacity acquisition of about −.76! In other words, gross expenditure rises by only .24 as there is crowding out of private expenditure by the government subsidy. In addition, expenditure on R&D falls as a capacity subsidy reduces the incentive to invest in R&D, as argued earlier. In subsequent periods, there is a small positive effect on R&D and capacity expenditures relative to the no-policy path, which fades out over time, with the capacity expenditure becoming negative in some later periods.

Figure 9.10 plots the *net* effect of a $1.00 subsidy (applied as the equivalent ad valorem level) when applied to R&D and to capacity in the asymmetric case with firm A's yield reduced from .5 to .3. The four curves have the same interpretation as in figure 9.9 above.[13] First, note that a dollar spent on R&D results in an immediate increase in *gross* expenditure on R&D of only $1.68, and therefore net expenditure rises by about $0.68, as shown by the dashed line in the figure. To understand this, recall that, with asymmetric firms, if the laggard (firm A) does not drop out, it spends more on R&D than the firm that is ahead in order to catch up. With a convex R&D cost function, the more R&D that is done, the more expensive is further R&D. This, plus the fact that steady states are independent of initial conditions as long as the firms remain in the market, makes a given dollar subsidy on R&D translate into a smaller equivalent percentage in the asymmetric case (as compared to the symmetric one). While both factors reduce the effectiveness of R&D subsidies in the asymmetric case, the qualitative conclusions drawn in the symmetric case remain. As before, capacity acquisition is encouraged by the R&D subsidy, and, in subsequent periods, R&D expenditure falls below that with no subsidy at all.

A capacity subsidy of a dollar initially reduces and then raises R&D expenditure. Net expenditure on capacity falls by about .61 as the gross expenditure rises by only .39. In contrast to the symmetric case, however, expenditure on capacity does not rise above the no-policy level in subsequent periods. These simulations thus suggest that R&D subsidies dominate capacity subsidies if the aim is to raise yields and capacity. They also suggest that R&D subsidies have greater leverage in the symmetric case as they have a larger net impact effect under these circumstances.

9.5 Concluding Remarks

The public debate on flat panels has focused largely on whether the Clinton administration initiative is clever promotion of dual use technology or straightforward industrial policy. In contrast, we examine whether subsidies to promote volume production ($199 million of the initiative) or R&D subsidies

---

13. The intermediate case where firm A's yield is .4 shows effects similar to these.

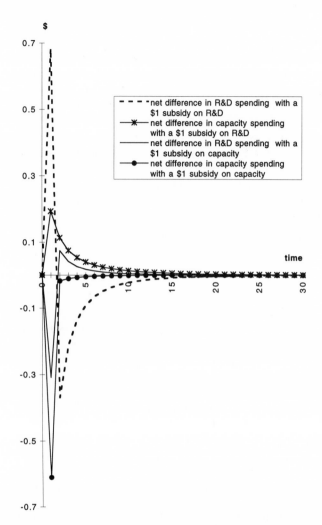

**Fig. 9.10   Net effects of $1.00 subsidies for the asymmetric case with $y_0^A = .3$
and $y_0^B = .5$**

($318 million of the initiative) are more effective. Our results suggest that
R&D subsidies provide the government more leverage in supporting an industry. In the context of our model, subsidies for capacity can, in fact, backfire
because they reduce a firm's incentive to invest in yield-improving R&D. As
always, these results should be interpreted in the context of the model and its
exclusions. For example, the inclusion of learning by doing would make our
distinction between R&D and capacity subsidies less clear. Perhaps the most
interesting revision would be to see how the inclusion of forward-looking behavior by firms would affect our results with and without policy.

Our model can be used to examine other issues, such as the effects of entry. The effect of entry is important for the flat panel industry, not only with respect to entry of U.S. firms, but also with respect to recently announced capacity increases of Korean firms (Pollack 1995). It is entirely possible that profits are not eroded to zero by entry because entrants use technologies with lower yields than incumbent firms that have done the necessary R&D to maintain higher yields.[14]

An additional issue of interest is how the initial configuration of firms' capacities and yields determines final industry configuration. Indeed, we suspect that firms that enter early can remain and earn profits later on when new entry is not viable! These issues, as well the effect of R&D or capacity subsidies on the final configuration of firms and the minimum size of subsidies necessary to accomplish particular goals, are left for future work.

References

Baldwin, Richard, and Paul Krugman. 1988. Market access and international competition: A simulation study of 16K random access memory. In *Empirical methods for international trade,* ed. Robert Feenstra. Cambridge, Mass.: MIT Press.
———. 1989. Persistent trade effects of large exchange rate shocks. *Quarterly Journal of Economics* 104:635–54.
Barfield, Claude E. 1994. Flat panel displays: A second look. *Issues in Science and Technology* 11, no. 2 (Winter): 21–25.
———. 1995. Flat-panel initiative: A bad idea. *Issues in Science and Technology* 11, no. 3 (Spring): 9–12.
Edmondson, Gail, and Neil Gross. 1995. The grand alliance in flat panels. *Business Week,* 28 August, 73.
Flamm, Kenneth S. 1994. Flat-panel displays: Catalyzing a U.S. industry. *Issues in Science and Technology* 11, no. 3 (Fall): 28–32.
———. 1995. In defense of the flat-panel display initiative. *Issues in Science and Technology* 11, no. 1 (Spring): 22–25.
Jensen, Richard, and Marie Thursby. 1987. A decision theoretic model of innovation, technology transfer, and trade. *Review of Economic Studies* 54:631–47.
Mentley, David E. 1994. Flat panel displays for military airplanes. *International Display Report* (Mountain View, Calif.: SEMI Newsletter Service), 15 July.
———. 1995. Financial analysis of the TFT industry. *International Display Report* (Mountain View, Calif.: SEMI Newsletter Service), 13 June.
Mentley, David E., and J. A. Castellano. 1994. *Flat panel display manufacturing cost: A comparative analysis.* 2d ed. San Jose, Calif.: Stanford Resources.
Miller, Debra L. 1995. Forum: Flat-panel displays. *Issues in Science and Technology* 11, no. 3 (Spring): 5–6.
Mowery, David C. 1995. Forum: Flat-panel displays. *Issues in Science and Technology* 11, no. 3 (Spring): 5.

14. Hence, new firms have disincentives for entry. Incumbent firms realize that raising capacity will reduce price, and this results in their voluntarily limiting their capacity. Thus, it is likely that, despite firms choosing output competitively, profits are nonzero owing to quasi rents that arise.

Patton, Robert, and Alice Rawsthorn. 1995. A wall-hanging wonder. *Financial Times,* 1 September, 8.

Pollack, Andrew. 1995. Japanese face glut of computer screens. *New York Times,* 29 May, A39.

Rosenbloom, Richard S., and Michael A. Cusumano. 1987. Technological pioneering and competitive advantage: The birth of the VCR industry. *California Management Review* 29, no. 4:51–76.

Stanford Resources. 1994. World average selling prices TFT-LCDs used in portable computers. In *The proceedings of the 11th annual flat information display conference and exhibition.* San Jose, Calif.: Stanford Resources.

Tyson, Laura D'Andrea. 1992. *Who's bashing whom: Trade conflict in high-technology industries.* Washington, D.C.: Institute for International Economics.

U.S. Department of Defense. 1994. *Building U.S. capabilities in flat panel displays: Final report.* Washington, D.C.

10   Causes and Consequences of the Export Enhancement Program for Wheat

Pinelopi Koujianou Goldberg and Michael M. Knetter

Trade has played a major role in U.S. agriculture throughout the twentieth century. The share of annual U.S. wheat production that was exported rose from approximately 25 percent at the beginning of the century to 60 percent by the beginning of the 1980s. The federal government has supported agricultural production in general, and exports in particular, with several programs. The export programs aim to achieve three basic goals: maintain appropriate surplus levels of agricultural commodities, increase foreign demand for U.S. products, and support humanitarian causes. Export programs have taken four basic forms: export subsidies (in kind or in cash) that have allowed domestic prices to exceed world prices and countered subsidization by U.S. competitors; export credit and credit guarantee programs that have assisted countries with foreign exchange difficulties; food aid programs, directed toward countries suffering from hunger; and nonprice promotion programs that have attempted to increase foreign demand for U.S. products. The focus of this paper is on the effects of the most recent export subsidization program, known as the Export Enhancement Program (EEP). Since the primary commodity sold under this program iş wheat (wheat sales account for approximately 80 percent of total EEP sales), we concentrate our analysis on the wheat market.

The EEP was established by the secretary of agriculture in the spring of 1985 in reaction to the continuing decline in U.S. agricultural exports and the increase in government stocks of grain. The program is considered a success by the U.S. Department of Agriculture (USDA) and the majority of research-

Pinelopi Koujianou Goldberg is assistant professor of economics at Princeton University and a faculty research fellow of the National Bureau of Economic Research. Michael M. Knetter is associate professor of economics at Dartmouth College and a faculty research fellow of the National Bureau of Economic Research.

The authors thank Edward Allen, Steve Haley, Howard Leathers, and Jim Werden for many helpful discussions and help with the data. Rachel Levy and Amy Schneeberger provided research assistance. The responsibility for any errors is of course the authors' own.

ers. This evaluation is based on two facts. First, coincident with the implementation of EEP legislation, U.S. wheat exports have increased significantly. Second, the majority of existing studies on the effects of the EEP find positive, albeit small, effects of the program on exports, revenues, and domestic prices. The method employed in such studies is almost exclusively that of simulation.[1] The wheat market is modeled in detail, and the equilibrium conditions for the world market are derived; next, the equilibrium is computed under alternative scenarios concerning the relevant policy variables. Comparing the outcomes corresponding to scenarios with and without the EEP provides an estimate of the effects of the program. Simulation studies typically consider one year at a time; owing to the reference to different years and the sensitivity of the results to modeling assumptions and functional forms, a comparison of results across studies is often difficult. The analysis is complicated by the complexity of farm programs; the EEP was introduced in conjunction with other changes in basic farm support.

In this paper, we employ a different method to analyze the effect of a variety of factors on the world wheat market and U.S. producers. Rather than relying on simulation analysis, we explore time-series data for the period 1970–94 to investigate the relation between export performance, subsidies, and other factors. Our analysis will attempt to address the following questions: (1) How important are relative cost changes in explaining the performance of U.S. wheat producers prior to the EEP program? (2) Which was primarily responsible for the decline in U.S. production and export shares in the world wheat market in the early 1980s—relative cost changes or European subsidization? (3) Do U.S. policies toward wheat, such as price guarantees, have detectable effects on the behavior of wheat growers? (4) How important are policy changes and relative cost changes in explaining the recovery of production and exports after 1985?

The remainder of the paper is organized as follows. In section 10.1, we provide an overview of the U.S. wheat market and the EEP and summarize the results of the literature to date on the effects of the program; we conclude this section by describing our own approach. In section 10.2, we describe the data used in the empirical analysis. Section 10.3 reports and interprets the results, and section 10.4 concludes.

10.1   Overview of the Export Enhancement Program

10.1.1   The U.S. Wheat Market

Understanding the determinants of domestic supply and demand is a prerequisite for studying exports in any market. Domestic demand comprises two

---

1. Examples of such studies include Anania, Bohman, and Carter (1992), Brooks, Devadoss, and Myers (1990), Seitzinger and Paarlberg (1989a, 1989b, 1990), and Haley (1989).

major components: private demand and demand for stocks. Private demand is fairly stable and predictable since policy reduces price fluctuations through the holding of stocks. Stocks are held both commercially (known as "free" stocks) and by the federal government. Government stockholding is a major tool of U.S. agricultural policy. The Commodity Credit Corporation (CCC) buys wheat from farmers participating in price-support programs at a specified price called the loan rate, in whatever quantities necessary to cause the market price to rise to the loan rate. Thus, the loan rate becomes a floor on U.S. prices. In periods when market prices exceed loan rates, accumulation of government stocks is low. If private market prices would tend below the loan rate, on the other hand, farmers would have incentive to sell to the CCC until market prices equaled the loan rate, leading to rapid growth in government stocks. In addition to the loan rate, the government uses target prices to support farm income; farmers receive deficiency payments equal to the difference between the target price and the maximum of the loan rate and market price.

The domestic supply of wheat is the product of acreage planted and yield per acre. The acreage devoted to wheat will generally depend on wheat market conditions in recent years and overall farm policy variables. During the 1980s, farmers participating in agricultural support programs were subject to requirements that limited the acreage for wheat growing. While a high loan rate might encourage production, the fact that participation in the program is conditional on acreage restrictions makes the connection between loan rates and acreage uncertain. It will depend on the set-aside requirements that are associated with any particular loan rate. It is possible that high loan rates encourage participation in the program, which then imposes sufficiently stringent set-asides that acreage declines with the loan rate. Although yield is partially determined by exogenous factors such as weather conditions and soil quality, it may also be influenced by behavior; when market conditions are favorable, owing to strong export demand, farmers can partly overcome the effect of acreage restrictions on production by using resources more intensively to increase yield.

The description given above of the U.S. wheat market demonstrates the channels through which domestic policy instruments influence exports. A high loan rate, for example, increases market price, inducing an increase in domestic production, provided that acreage restrictions are not too strong. But higher loan rates, and thus domestic prices, can make exports to world markets less desirable. The excess of domestic supply over private domestic demand is more likely to be absorbed by a rise in government stocks. As a result, one would generally expect loan rates to be positively related to production volume (for a given acreage at least) and government stocks and inversely related to exports. Since the value of the dollar dictates the relative cost advantage of U.S. producers on the world market, it, too, should influence acreage, production, and export decisions. All else equal, a weak dollar implies a higher dollar price on the world wheat market and greater incentive to plant, produce, and export wheat.

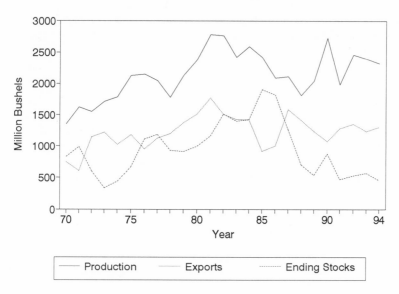

Fig. 10.1   U.S. wheat, 1970–94: Production, exports, and ending stocks
Source: World Wheat Situation and Outlook Yearbook.

10.1.2   Historical Background

The EEP was enacted during a period of financial distress for farmers, characterized by declining land values, a significant loss of export markets and farm income, and a growing surplus of government stocks. Figure 10.1 depicts wheat production, exports, and government stocks for the period 1970–94; while exports were relatively stable during the early 1970s and soared during the second part of that decade, they started faltering in 1981; between crop years 1981–82 and 1985–86, the export volume fell from 1,771 to 909 million bushels. During the same period, government stocks increased steadily to reach a peak level of 1,905 million bushels in 1985.

Several factors contributed to these developments. On the domestic side, high legislated loan rate levels for wheat (fig. 10.2) increased the incentive to sell to the CCC. On the international side, the strong appreciation of the dollar in the early 1980s eroded the competitiveness of U.S. wheat exports relative to foreign-produced wheat. Figure 10.3 depicts three alternative, weighted-average real exchange rate indices for wheat markets, one against the currencies of the major importing countries (Japan, Brazil, Morocco, Nigeria, Egypt, India, etc.), one against the currencies of the major wheat competitors (Canada, Argentina, Australia, and the European Community), and a combined index that measures the value of the dollar in the overall world agricultural trade market.[2] All three indices increased sharply between 1980 and 1985. Together,

---

2. These trade-weighted indices are constructed as follows. First, the current exchange rate for each country (in units per dollar) is adjusted by taking the ratio of the same-period CPI in the

Fig. 10.2   U.S. wheat, 1970–94: Market price, loan rate, and target price
Source: World Wheat Situation and Outlook Yearbook.

the high loan rates and strong dollar shifted sales away from export markets and toward government stocks.

Other factors held responsible for the situation in the export markets were the debt problems and slow income growth in many importing countries and the extensive subsidization of wheat exports by the European Community (EC). The EC subsidies took the form of export restitutions paid to exporters to compensate for any difference between the world market price for wheat and an internal price floor. Under the Common Agricultural Policy (CAP), intervention prices—the prices guaranteed on EC sales—are set. Quantities not consumed domestically are sold in the international markets at going world prices. The difference between the world price and the EC intervention price is the export restitution. Thanks in part to the extensive subsidization, the EC switched from being a net importer of wheat until 1974 to becoming a major U.S. competitor in the world wheat markets in the 1980s. In addition, the exchange rate swings that worked against U.S. exports worked in favor of European producers.

Against this background, the Food Security Act of 1985, which outlined the farm policy for crop years 1986–90, set out to reduce government stocks and

---

United States to that of the country in question. Then, the percentage change from the base period (1980) is multiplied by a weight. The geometric mean of these changes constitutes the real weighted exchange rate index. The weights used in the construction of the three indices are the average dollar shares of U.S. exports from 1983 to 1985 for the customer-based index, the world less U.S. shares in wheat exports for the competitor-based index, and U.S. market shares for the combined index.

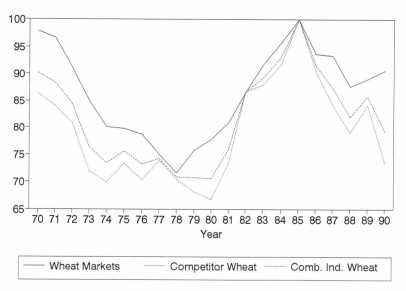

Fig. 10.3   Exchange rate indices: Weighted average, annual, 1970–90
Source: World Wheat Situation and Outlook Yearbook.

improve the situation in the export markets through a series of measures. A reduction in the loan rates was aimed at lowering U.S. prices for wheat, making the United States more competitive in the export markets while reducing the growth in government stocks. To maintain farm income support, target prices were frozen at the 1985 level for crop year 1986–87 and slowly declined afterward. To make exports more competitive, the EEP was established and designed in such a way as to simultaneously contribute to the reduction of government stocks. Under the original design of the program, government-owned surplus commodities were to be paid as bonuses to exporters to allow them to lower the prices of U.S. agricultural products in specific markets. By 1989, however, the government stocks were reduced to such a level that payment in kind was no longer feasible, and cash subsidies replaced the old system. The EEP was further designed as a targeted subsidization program; the targeted markets were ones where U.S. competitors, the European Community in particular, heavily subsidized their exports.

The EEP was initially codified as a three-year export subsidy program; during this time frame, a total of $2 billion worth of surplus commodities was to be made available to exporters as bonuses. Later, the overall amount of bonuses was limited to a maximum of $1.5 billion. In 1987, however, the USDA announced that the program would continue once the authorized $1.5 billion was exhausted. In fact, the Omnibus Trade and Competitiveness Act of 1988 authorized an additional $1 billion in commodities, raising the ceiling to $2.5 billion. By the end of 1990, approximately $2.9 billion had been allocated to subsidize U.S. agricultural exports. The 1990 Farm Bill established minimum expenditures of $500 million per year for 1991–95. An additional $1 billion would be available if GATT negotiations failed or if no agreement were reached by 1992.

10.1.3   Criteria for the EEP

The Foreign Agricultural Service (FAS) of the USDA, which administers the program, specified four criteria for evaluating sales under the EEP. These were as follows:

1. *Additionality.* Sales under the EEP should increase agricultural exports above the level that would have occurred in the absence of the program.

2. *Targeting.* The EEP is not a global export program; subsidies are to be targeted to markets that the EC heavily subsidizes. This is an important feature of the EEP since it implies that marginal exports are unlikely to be eligible for subsidies.

3. *Budget neutrality.* Budget outlays should not increase beyond what they would have been in the absence of the program. The original design of the EEP as an in-kind subsidy program served this purpose directly as no cash payments were made to exporters; on the contrary, the government saved on the storage costs of the surplus commodities. In later years, even though cash payments replaced in-kind bonuses, the EEP can be viewed as a substitute to domestic support payments; by increasing export sales and thus supporting higher wheat market prices, the program reduces the amount of deficiency payments to farmers.

4. *Cost effectiveness.* The last criterion is rather vague as it specifies that EEP sales should result in a net gain to the overall economy. It has been a subject of intense debate in the literature under which conditions export subsidies increase national welfare (for an overview, see Anania, Bohman, and Carter 1992); but the U.S. wheat market does not fit the theoretical framework of any of the models that provide a justification for such subsidies.

In late 1989, the FAS reformulated the guidelines for approval of EEP sales to emphasize the EEP's trade policy objectives: further the U.S. negotiating strategy in the Uruguay Round by countering competitors' unfair trade practices, and develop, maintain, and expand markets for U.S. agricultural products.

10.1.4   Implementation of the EEP

The USDA uses a flexible multistage process to determine and award subsidies to exporting firms. First, the FAS receives and reviews proposals from USDA specialists, members of the U.S. agricultural community, and foreign governments before selecting countries and commodities to target. An approved proposal is announced as an initiative, specifying the targeted country, the commodity, and the maximum quantity (e.g., 300,000 metric tons) that can be sold under the EEP.

Next, the FAS uses information based on market intelligence reports to set minimum acceptable sale prices and maximum bonuses. The minimum price is one that is competitive with the prices of alternative suppliers. The FAS also estimates the U.S. domestic price plus freight and handling to a particular destination. The difference between the minimum price and the U.S. price represents the maximum acceptable bonus. To promote competition among exporting firms, neither minimum prices nor maximum bonuses are announced publicly.

After the initiative is announced, U.S. exporting firms compete for sales in the foreign markets through an FAS-administered bidding process. In particular, exporters negotiate with the targeted country to determine the quality, quantity, and price of wheat that they will deliver. This information is submitted as a bid to the FAS. If the price specified in the bid is lower than the minimum acceptable price set by the FAS, the bid is rejected. If the price is higher, the FAS compares the bonus amount to the maximum acceptable bonus. If the exporter's bonus is higher, the bid is rejected. A rejected bid can be revised and resubmitted. If the bid passes both the price and the bonus tests, the FAS compares its bonus amount to the bonus amounts of all acceptable bids received and awards the subsidies in ascending order of bonuses until the approved quantity is filled.

Firms with successful bids export and receive EEP subsidies. Until 1989, these subsidies took the form of commodity certificates with value equal to the per-unit bonus times the amount of wheat sold to the targeted country. Exporting firms could exchange the certificates for an equivalent value of surplus commodities in government storage or sell them. After 1989, the commodity certificates were replaced by cash subsidies.

10.1.5   Activity under the EEP

As mentioned above, the main commodity sold under the EEP is wheat; other commodities include barley (7 percent of total EEP sales), wheat flour, sorghum, rice, poultry, dairy cattle, and eggs.

In the first year of the program (May–September 1985), four North African countries (Algeria, Egypt, Morocco, and Yemen) were targeted. Over the next four fiscal years, the number of countries grew to sixty-five. No additional countries have been targeted since 1988. The major recipients are the Soviet Union (27 percent of total EEP sales), China (19 percent), and Algeria, Egypt, and Morocco (a combined 28 percent). The other sixty countries account for the remaining 26 percent of EEP wheat sales. It is interesting to note that the two major recipients (the Soviet Union and China) were originally excluded from the EEP. Both countries reacted to the exclusion by refusing to buy U.S.

wheat; as a result, the U.S. market shares dropped from 34 percent in 1984 to 8 percent in 1985 and 1 percent in 1986 in China and from 22 percent in 1984 to 1 percent in 1985 and 5 percent in 1986 in the Soviet Union. The decline in market shares was reversed in 1987, when both countries became eligible for the EEP. Critics of the EEP view these particular episodes in China and the Soviet Union as evidence that the United States lacks market power in the world wheat market and that it cannot therefore act as a price-discriminating monopolist (see Anania, Bohman, and Carter 1992). The inability to price discriminate reduces the likelihood that U.S. welfare is increased by subsidizing exports.

EEP subsidy levels (average bonus as a percentage of average sales price) vary substantially by commodity, country, and year. For wheat, the average subsidy level over the entire period the EEP has been in effect is about 27 percent; the year 1987 is associated with the highest subsidies (43 percent). A comparison across countries shows that the Soviet Union and other Eastern European countries successfully negotiated the higher per-ton subsidies, followed by North Africa and China. Latin American and Middle Eastern countries received lower than average subsidies. In general, subsidy levels have been higher for the countries in which the EC has been more competitive.

Since the implementation of the EEP, U.S. wheat exports have increased significantly; the fastest growth occurred between 1985 and 1988, when exports went from twenty-five to forty-three metric tons (see also fig. 10.1 above). EEP sales during this period accounted for approximately 50 percent of total U.S. wheat exports, but, as with subsidy levels, there was substantial variation across years and countries. The maximum EEP share was reached in 1987, when the EEP accounted for approximately 74 percent of wheat exports. Of course, this does not imply that, without the EEP, U.S. exports would have been minimal; it is an open question whether, despite its stated objective of additionality, the EEP merely displaced commercial exports.

Around seventy-five firms have sold and delivered commodity certificates under the program. Many of these firms are foreign owned but have been incorporated for business in the United States. The four largest exporters (Cargill, Continental Grain, Louis Dreyfus, and Artfer) account for 65 percent of total EEP bonuses received, each receiving over $100 million in bonuses.

10.1.6 Evaluation of the EEP

As previously mentioned, policy makers consider the EEP a success. This assessment is based on the fact that, after the introduction of the EEP, U.S. wheat exports started increasing, suggesting that the additionality criterion was being met, while government stocks started dropping, suggesting that budget neutrality and cost effectiveness were being satisfied as well. By 1990, the stocks were reduced to the lowest level since the mid-1970s; the concern about how to reduce the wheat surpluses has given way to the question of optimal stock size.

The academic community, however, has been more skeptical in its evaluation of the EEP. On the theoretical side, it is not obvious that additionality will be met since subsidies will be inframarginal owing to the targeted nature of the program. Critics also point out that the wheat export increase coincides with several favorable developments in the international markets, and isolating the contribution of the EEP is therefore difficult. Some of the factors suspected of having increased wheat exports independent of the program were the low yields in export-competing countries because of the drought, the depreciation of the U.S. dollar, the low loan rate legislated in 1985, and the large increase in demand by the Soviet Union and China. To isolate the effects of the EEP, economists have constructed detailed models of the world wheat market and simulated the effects of alternative policy scenarios. As usual with this type of analysis, the results depend on the particular assumptions that the research is willing to make about the behavior of the economic agents and the functional forms.

One of the most important assumptions in this context concerns the response of the other export-competing nations, the EC in particular, to the EEP. According to the USDA Economic Research Service, EC export restitutions for wheat grew from $365 million in 1985 to $1.8 billion in 1988. This increase supports the presumption that, in conjunction with the dollar depreciation against the ECU and the lower loan rates, the EEP forced the European Community to lower its export prices. It is, however, an open question whether EC restitutions were targeted to specific countries to counter EEP bonuses or whether they were extended globally to achieve domestic EC goals (see Haley 1989).

The evaluation criteria for the EEP are closely related to the FAS guidelines for EEP sales approval. In particular, researchers have been interested in assessing whether the program successfully targeted heavily subsidized markets and in computing the program's effects on domestic prices, export volume, and export revenues. While the majority of researchers agree that the EEP successfully targeted countries where the European Community had aggressively subsidized its wheat exports, Anania, Bohman, and Carter (1992) view the Soviet Union and China episodes as evidence that the targets were partially determined by the market power of some large-purchasing countries rather than the European Community's unfair trade practices. In addition, they claim that, because of the European Community's response to U.S. subsidies, it was other exporters and not the European Community that lost market share as a result of the EEP; in China, for example, the expansion of the U.S. market share in 1987 and 1988 occurred at the expense of Australia and Canada.

The USDA has meanwhile been more concerned with the question of whether value-added products are better targets for EEP sales than bulk commodities. Most EEP sales have been targeted to basic grains; some argue that processed commodities are good candidates for the EEP since the European Community subsidizes both bulk and processed foods. The EEP effects on domestic prices are of special interest since an explicit goal of the EEP has been budget neutrality; had domestic prices declined as a result of the EEP, higher deficiency payments to the farmers would have been necessary, increasing the cost of the program. In general, the effect on domestic prices depends on two factors. An EEP-induced increase in demand for U.S. exports tends to increase domestic prices; on the other hand, the release of EEP bonus commodities from government storage has a dampening effect on domestic prices. Most researchers found that—at least for the years 1985–87—the EEP had a positive, although modest, effect on domestic prices. The exact magnitude of the price effects depends on assumptions about how aggressively the European Community subsidized its exports in response to the EEP. Haley (1989), for example, estimates that assuming that in the absence of the EEP the European Community would have uniformly subsidized its exports at $90.00 per metric ton implies a U.S. domestic price increase of 7 percent. If, however, one assumes that the European Community had targeted specific markets independent of the EEP, the effect of the program on domestic prices is much larger: over 22 percent. These results are in sharp contrast with Anania, Bohman, and Carter (1992), who simulated price effects for the year 1988; they find that, because of the release of commodity surpluses from government stocks, domestic prices in the United States went down during that year; as a result, the budgetary cost of deficiency payments increased.

With respect to export volume and revenues, most studies find that wheat exports rose because of the EEP; the additionality of the program is estimated between 2 and 30 percent, with the highest increases concentrated in the years 1986–87. It is generally agreed that the EEP displaced to some extent unsubsidized commercial sales to certain countries; competing exporters displaced from markets subsidized through the EEP moved into other untargeted markets where the United States used to be a major supplier. Because of the simultaneous increase of U.S. market prices and export volume, gross export revenues rose as a result of the EEP; the effect on net revenues, however, is less clear. The latter are computed by subtracting the economic cost of the bonuses awarded to exporters under the EEP from the gross revenues. For the period 1985–89, this cost is equal to the value of the surplus commodities in the government stocks minus the storage cost the government would have incurred had these products not been used in the EEP. Using this cost measure, it is estimated that the EEP led to a slight increase in revenues of about 1 percent.

A current issue of special interest is whether the EEP has encouraged U.S. trading partners to negotiate. The United States has used the EEP as a negotiating tool in the GATT negotiations, offering to eliminate the program if other countries cut their export subsidies. Although the expansion of EEP sales has coincided with progress in the Uruguay Round, it is unclear precisely what role the EEP has played in the trade negotiations.

In summary, most existing studies find that the EEP had small but positive effects on exports and domestic prices. It is interesting to note that all the work cited above refers to the period 1985–88; little is known about the EEP effects in subsequent years. But 1985–88 represents exactly the years that coincide with a sharp depreciation of the dollar and a decrease in loan rates. It is thus an interesting question to what extent the decline in U.S. exports in the early 1980s was caused by the relatively high value of the dollar as opposed to the EC subsidization and whether U.S. subsidies played a significant role in increasing U.S. exports beyond the level to which these would have risen as a result of exchange rate changes. The following sections address these questions by relating acreage, production, and export shares of U.S. wheat producers to exchange rates, loan rates, and subsidies for various time periods. Before moving to estimation, we next discuss the data used in our analysis.

10.2   Data

One attractive aspect of studying the market for wheat is that the USDA and other national and international organizations track agricultural production and marketing in great detail. Consequently, there is a wide array of data sources from which to choose.

The analyses that follow rely on two different data sources. The first is the *World Wheat Situation and Outlook Yearbook.* In particular, we used annual data from this publication to construct measures of the U.S. and other competing countries' shares of world wheat acreage, production, and exports. This publication also provides data on U.S. market prices, support prices, and ending stocks held by the federal government. We focus on the period 1970–93 for most of our work, with careful attention paid to the pre- and post-EEP subperiods. Additional information on subsidization in the United States and other competing countries was obtained from *Estimates of Producer and Consumer Subsidy Equivalents.* Subsidy data are available for only a limited number of years in different countries, usually 1983–92. These data are used to evaluate the success of the EEP and other policy instruments in influencing the level of U.S. wheat production and exports.

The second of our data sources is destination-specific data on the value and quantity of wheat exports provided by a statistical office of the USDA Economic Research Service (ERS). These are annual data from the period 1975–94. We use these data to assess the effect of the EEP on U.S. prices relative to prices in export markets.

10.3   Empirical Evidence

This section of the paper describes how we use the data to shed some light on several important questions concerning the EEP and other government support instruments, such as the loan rate. As mentioned in section 10.1, previous research on these questions has relied on simulations of models of the world wheat market. Since it is difficult to compare and evaluate such models owing to the myriad assumptions that underlie them, these models have not produced a consensus view on the effect of the EEP. Our aim is to see what the data suggest about the effect of agricultural policies. We make no attempt to estimate a structural model of behavior since we lack sufficient information on participation and set-aside rates for the wheat programs. We will instead estimate reduced-form equations that include some key policy and market variables. We will explore the stability of these reduced forms to ensure that our results are not too fragile to draw conclusions from the data.

Our first objective is to determine how relative cost changes and policy measures affected the behavior of the U.S. share of total wheat acreage, production, and exports. We choose to focus on shares of the so-called competitor group (defined as Argentina, Australia, Canada, the European Community, and the United States) totals, as opposed to physical quantities of output. Focusing on competitor group shares allows us to abstract from the effect of world demand shocks and supply shocks emanating from producers outside the competitor group on the physical quantity measures observed for the group.

Wheat growers are probably best viewed as making sequential decisions regarding (1) how much acreage to plant, (2) how intensively to cultivate the planted acreage, and (3) how to allocate output between domestic and export markets, where domestic markets include the option of selling to the government at the loan rate if private market prices would be lower than the loan rate. Decisions should be a function of policy variables, such as loan rates and set-aside requirements, and relative costs of production. Since exchange rate fluctuations constitute shifts in relative costs of production, they will be our main proxy for market conditions faced by U.S. exporters in the international wheat market.

Timing issues complicate our analysis. At each stage, more relevant information is revealed to producers. For example, the exchange rate prevailing when the export versus domestic sales decision must be made is not known at the time of the acreage and production decisions. In fact, it is likely that wheat production decisions might respond to the previous period's relative cost and demand conditions rather than the conditions that prevail at harvest time. The conditions at harvest time will influence the export decision only. Dynamic links may also arise because policy responds to the behavior of stocks, which in turn are affected by market conditions prevailing in the previous period.

Simple OLS exploration of the acreage and production shares confirms the importance of market conditions and, to a lesser extent, government policies on outcomes. Table 10.1 reports the results of an OLS regression of U.S. acreage share on a constant, acreage in the prior period, the (log of the) lagged real exchange rate index of the U.S. dollar relative to the competitor group (using weights for group members provided by the USDA in construction of its index), and the (log of the real) loan rate. Changes in the real exchange rate have

Table 10.1   **U.S. Wheat Acreage Share Regression, 1971–93**

	Coefficient	SE	*t*-Statistic
Constant	8.30799	2.40536	3.45395
ACUSSHR(−1)	.507102	.144802	3.50203
RXCOMP(−1)	−5.36061	2.41292	−2.22163
LRLOANRT	−.496470	.781046	−.635647
Dependent variable		ACUSSHR	
No. of observations		23	
SD of dependent variable		1.62514	
SE of regression		1.21214	
R^2		.519547	
Durbin-Watson statistic		1.97892	

a direct effect on the common currency relative costs of the competitor group vis-à-vis the United States. An increase in the index (a real appreciation of the dollar) will increase U.S. relative costs.

The results show that acreage is indeed significantly influenced by the real exchange rate but is insensitive to the loan rate for the period 1971–93. Since the dependent variable is in share percentage points and the exchange rate is in logs, the estimated coefficient implies that a 10 percent appreciation of the dollar will lead to a reduction in U.S. acreage share of 0.5 percentage points in the following wheat year. A similar regression using the contemporaneous exchange rate produced insignificant results. This is not surprising since the relevant choices are made before the contemporaneous exchange rate is known. The lack of a significant relation between loan rates and acreage probably reflects the fact that higher loan rates coincide with larger set-aside requirements. In the absence of such a relation, one would expect high loan rates to encourage more acreage.[3]

Table 10.2 reports the analogous regression for the U.S. production share.[4] The results are very similar with respect to the effect of exchange rates on production. The estimated coefficient on the exchange rate implies that a 10 percent real dollar appreciation leads to a reduction in the U.S. share of group production of 0.8 percentage points. Production is also significantly, positively related to loan rates. The estimated model implies that a 10 percent increase in the loan rate leads to a 0.4 percentage point increase in the U.S. share of competitor group production. The fact that loan rates are positively related to production, but not to acreage, suggests that the production effect of loan rates

3. We tested to see whether lagged stocks were helpful in explaining acreage. They were highly correlated with lagged exchange rates, but neither variable was significant when both were included in the model. Since the model fit best with exchange rates instead of stocks, we report that specification.

4. Including lagged production has almost no effect on the model, so we left it out in the interest of parsimony.

Table 10.2   **U.S. Wheat Production Share Regression, 1971–93**

	Coefficient	SE	*t*-Statistic
Constant	18.6095	.410900	45.2895
RXCOMP(−1)	−7.60734	3.78993	−2.00725
LRLOANRT	4.27263	1.24511	3.43152
Dependent variable		PUSSHR	
No. of observations		23	
SD of dependent variable		2.58332	
SE of regression		1.93358	
R^2		.490697	
Durbin-Watson statistic		1.96472	

Table 10.3   **U.S. Wheat Export Share Regression, 1970–93**

	Coefficient	SE	*t*-Statistic
Constant	37.7959	.895404	42.2110
RXCOMP	−29.9157	8.32227	−3.59466
LRLOANRT	11.5216	2.71300	4.24680
Dependent variable		XUSSHR	
No. of observations		24	
SD of dependent variable		6.52075	
SE of regression		4.33095	
R^2		.597225	
Durbin-Watson statistic		1.96635	

works through yields. Farmers can apparently offset some of the acreage set-aside requirements to take advantage of higher loan rates.

Table 10.3 shows the results for the analogous equation using U.S. export share as the dependent variable. The exchange rate used here is the contemporaneous exchange rate rather than the lagged exchange rate used in the acreage and production equations. The current exchange rate determines the relative benefit of export sales versus sales to the CCC. Table 10.3 shows that exchange rates and loan rates together explain a great deal of variation in the U.S. export share over the period 1970–93, with an R^2 value of .60. Each of the regressors is statistically significant at the 1 percent level. The exchange rate coefficient implies that a 10 percent appreciation of the dollar leads to a 3 percentage point reduction in the U.S. export share. Meanwhile, a 10 percent increase in the loan rate leads to a 1.2 percentage point increase in U.S. export shares. The link between loan rates and exports is likely to be quite complex. High loan rates stimulate production, and high production periods are also likely to be high export periods, for given values of the exchange rate. Later in the paper, we explore this linkage in more detail using an instrumental variables procedure.

Table 10.4   **U.S. Wheat Stocks Regression, 1970–93**

	Coefficient	SE	t-Statistic
Constant	27,330.8	1,670.43	16.3616
RXCOMP	68,062.8	15,525.7	4.38389
LRLOANRT	14,762.4	5,061.25	2.91674
Dependent variable		ESTUSMT	
No. of observations		24	
SD of dependent variable		11,741.9	
SE of regression		8,079.62	
R^2		.567686	
Durbin-Watson statistic		.836020	

Table 10.5   **U.S. Wheat Export Share Regression, 1970–85**

	Coefficient	SE	t-Statistic
Constant	40.8789	1.69523	24.1141
RXCOMP	−35.1576	8.59186	−4.09197
LRLOANRT	−6.27077	8.35666	−.750392
Dependent variable		XUSSHR	
No. of observations		16	
SD of dependent variable		5.70066	
SE of regression		4.03979	
R^2		.564770	
Durbin-Watson statistic		2.15520	

Table 10.4 reports the behavior of U.S. government wheat stocks in relation to exchange rates and loan rates. Not surprisingly, both variables are statistically significant. Either an appreciation of the dollar or an increase in the loan rate will lead to an increase in government stocks of wheat by making sales to the CCC more attractive relative to export sales.

Tables 10.1–10.4 all report the results of estimation over the entire period 1970–93. Since the implementation of the EEP and other aspects of the 1985 Farm Bill constituted a major policy shift, it is worth examining the subperiod 1970–85 separately. The results for exports are reported in table 10.5. We find that, in this subperiod, loan rates are unrelated to export shares, with a negative point estimate. This is in sharp contrast to our results in table 10.3 above for the entire period. The effect of exchange rates is even more pronounced in this subperiod, however. A 10 percent real dollar appreciation leads to a 3.5 percentage point reduction in exports according to the estimated coefficients.

An interesting exercise is to use the reduced-form coefficients of table 10.5 to project U.S. wheat export shares for the period 1985–93, in which the EEP was put into effect. There is no reason to think that the behavioral relations that generated these reduced-form coefficients would have remained the same

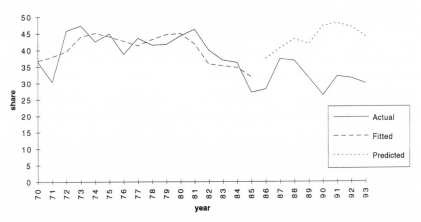

Fig. 10.4   Actual, fitted, and predicted U.S. wheat exports based on OLS over 1970–85 sample
Source: World Wheat Situation and Outlook Yearbook and authors' calculations.

with the implementation of the EEP and the other policy changes that occurred in 1985. Nonetheless, we think of this projection as one type of estimate of how U.S. wheat export shares might have evolved after 1985 as a result of the sharp fall in the value of the dollar had there been no major policy changes in the United States or in other competitor group countries.

The results of this exercise are shown in figure 10.4, which plots the actual, fitted, and predicted shares of U.S. wheat exports from 1970 to 1993. The fitted values are the within-sample estimated values of U.S. export share for the 1970–85 sample period. The predicted shares are obtained by substituting realized values of the exchange rate and the loan rate from the 1986–93 prediction period into the regression relation estimated over the sample period. The first thing to notice about the figure is that actual shares are below predicted shares for every year of the 1986–93 prediction period. Furthermore, the shortfall of actual relative to predicted levels rises dramatically after 1989. One might have expected just the opposite: that, with the implementation of the EEP program, U.S. export shares would increase for given values of the exchange rate and loan rate relative to the pre-EEP period. Since we are projecting on the basis of the pre-EEP relation, it is rather puzzling that actual values consistently fall short of projected values. One interpretation is of course that the EEP and the policy responses of competitor countries to the EEP actually hindered U.S. exports on balance in the period 1986–93. However, it is likely that other changes in farm policy played a role in this breakdown in the relation between export shares, exchange rates, and loan rates.

The results of this regression analysis also underscore the fact that the decline in U.S. exports in the early to mid-1980s was very much in line with the historical relation between the value of the dollar and the U.S. share of competitor group exports. Indeed, inspection of the residuals, represented by the gap

Table 10.6   **U.S. Wheat Export Share Regression, 1970–80**

	Coefficient	SE	t-Statistic
Constant	41.2188	1.93237	21.3307
RXCOMP	−35.9205	15.5964	−2.30313
LRLOANRT	−13.3121	9.55981	−1.39250
Dependent variable		XUSSHR	
No. of observations		11	
SD of dependent variable		4.38326	
SE of regression		4.09306	
R^2		.427456	
Durbin-Watson statistic		2.71456	

between actual and fitted values in figure 10.4, reveals that the model's fitted values for U.S. export shares during the period 1981–84 were less than the actual level of U.S. export shares in each of those years. Only in 1985 did fitted values exceed actual. The fitted values implied a 14 percentage point decline in U.S. export shares from 1980 to 1985 owing to the changes in exchange rates and loan rates. Actual shares declined 17 percentage points over this period. It is not clear that European subsidies could have played a substantial role in the collapse of wheat export markets, above and beyond the effect of exchange rates. They may have magnified the collapse in 1985–86, according to our inspection of the residuals.

A potential criticism of this exercise is that rising European subsidies coincided with the dramatic appreciation of the dollar in the early to mid-1980s. The biggest increases in European subsidies did occur during 1985. Since no subsidy measures are included in the model, the estimated coefficients on the exchange rate may be biased upward owing to the omitted variable, which is causally related to U.S. export share and by chance correlated with the value of the dollar. To check the robustness of our results, we estimated our simple export share equation over the period 1970–80, during which European subsidies were not viewed as a big factor and U.S. wheat export shares were large by historical standards.

The results of estimating the reduced-form export share equation over the period 1970–80 are reported in table 10.6. While the standard errors on the coefficient estimates have increased relative to the results in table 10.5, the exchange rate coefficient remains of similar magnitude and is still statistically significant. Figure 10.5 uses the pre-1981 results to project export shares using realized values of the exchange rate and the loan rate. These predicted values are almost identical to the fitted values obtained when the model was estimated over the period 1970–85. In other words, the relation between exchange rates and export shares over the period 1981–85 appears no different from the relation that prevailed from 1970 to 1980. Consequently, it is hard to

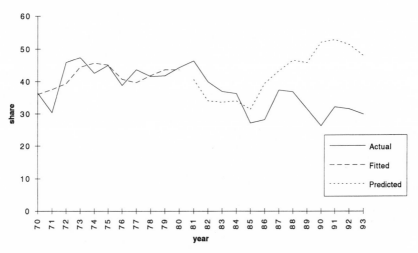

Fig. 10.5   Actual, fitted, and predicted U.S. wheat exports based on OLS over 1970–80 sample
Source: World Wheat Situation and Outlook Yearbook and authors' calculations.

believe that the omission of European subsidies is an important factor in explaining the data over the period 1981–85. Export shares behaved very much in line with what would have been expected given the evolution of common currency relative costs (proxied by the exchange rate) and U.S. government policies.

Data on EC producer subsidy equivalents for wheat were available over the period 1982–89 from the USDA Economic Research Service. This is a very short sample period, but we wanted to further investigate the relative importance of exchange rates and subsidies for this period. Table 10.7 reports the simple regression of export shares on exchange rates only for this eight year period. While this is a very short sample, there was substantial variation in both subsidies and exchange rates over the period. European subsidies rose from just over 3 percent per unit in 1984 to over 50 percent by 1986. The point estimate of the coefficient on the exchange rate remains quite close to the values obtained on the entire sample and the various subsamples considered thus far. It is no longer statistically significant at the 5 percent level owing to the smaller sample size, although the marginal significance level for a one-sided test is only .06. The results obtained when the data on European wheat subsidies are added are reported in table 10.8. Adding the subsidies does almost nothing to the estimated coefficient on the exchange rate or its *t*-value. Meanwhile, the coefficient on the subsidy variable has a *t*-value only slightly greater than one. It seems that, even over this period, exchange rates have a more substantial effect on export shares than subsidies. The huge increase in European subsidies in 1985, from 3.8 percent per unit to 31.1 percent per unit, translates

Table 10.7   **U.S. Wheat Export Share Regression, 1982–89**

	Coefficient	SE	t-Statistic
Constant	38.6034	2.79378	13.8176
RXCOMP(−1)	−39.6450	21.9647	−1.80495
Dependent variable		XUSSHR	
No. of observations		8	
SD of dependent variable		4.70255	
SE of regression		4.08910	
R^2		.351900	
Durbin-Watson statistic		1.04753	

Table 10.8   **U.S. Wheat Export Share Regression with European Subsidy Variable, 1982–89**

	Coefficient	SE	t-Statistic
Constant	40.8149	3.46508	11.7789
PSPECS	−.081783	.077197	−1.05940
RXCOMP	−38.6518	21.7643	−1.77593
Dependent variable		XUSSHR	
No. of observations		8	
SD of dependent variable		4.70255	
SE of regression		4.04804	
R^2		.470708	
Durbin-Watson statistic		1.32271	

into only a slightly more than 2 percentage point decline in the predicted U.S. export share, on the basis of the coefficients in table 10.8. As noted earlier, actual shares declined about 17 percentage points from 1980 to 1985. Thus, our regression results with both subsidies and exchange rates imply that subsidies account for very little of the erosion of U.S. export market shares. European subsidies may explain the larger than predicted drop in U.S. export shares in 1985 but none of the decline before that.

As an intermediate step toward a more structuralist approach to modeling export shares, we also investigated the behavior of export shares conditional on production shares themselves, in addition to exchange rates. If export and production shares are jointly determined, we need to use a two-stage least squares or instrumental variables (IV) procedure. Our earlier work on production shares suggests that lagged exchange rates might be an ideal instrument for this purpose. The IV estimates of the model for the period 1970–85 are reported in table 10.9, while the actual, fitted, and predicted values from the model are shown in figure 10.6. As can be verified from the table or the figure, the IV estimates are nearly identical to the OLS estimates in terms of their

Table 10.9   **U.S. Wheat Export Share Regression Using Instrumental Variables, 1971–85**

	Coefficient	SE	*t*-Statistic
Constant	28.6351	10.9552	2.61384
RXCOMP	−34.4867	7.04317	−4.89648
PUSSHR	.572087	.520660	1.09877
Dependent variable		XUSSHR	
No. of observations		15	
SD of dependent variable		5.80801	
SE of regression		4.07381	
R^2		.578308	
Durbin-Watson statistic		1.85743	

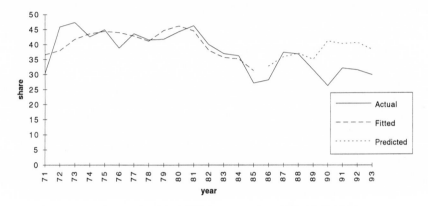

Fig. 10.6   Actual, fitted, and predicted U.S. wheat exports based on IV estimation over 1971–85 sample
Source: World Wheat Situation and Outlook Yearbook and authors' calculations.

implications for the role of exchange rates in explaining the behavior of wheat exports.

All the evidence on export shares points to the same basic conclusion: that the overvaluation of the dollar was primarily responsible for the collapse of U.S. wheat exports from 1981 to 1985. The spike in European subsidies in 1985–86 may have contributed a few percentage points to the decline in U.S. wheat export shares, but the damage had largely been done by that point in time.

What was the effect of the EEP on export shares of U.S. producers? There is nothing in the overall performance of exports to suggest that the EEP and the ensuing subsidy war with the EC left U.S. exporters with a larger share of world markets than would have been obtained without the EEP. For every

Table 10.10   **Relative Wheat Prices during the EEP**

	Coefficient	SE	t-Statistic
Constant	−.831739	.099076	−8.39496
EEPDUM	.206136	.212107	.971845
LRLOANRT	−.271162	.294884	−.919554
Dependent variable		PDIFF	
No. of observations		247	
SD of dependent variable		.817428	
SE of regression		.797199	
R^2		.056614	
Durbin-Watson statistic		1.78274	

model of wheat export shares estimated in this paper, the out-of-sample projections of wheat export shares conditional on realized values of the exchange rate and other factors (such as loan rates and production shares) show that actual exports began to turn down substantially relative to projections after 1988.

This breakdown in the relation between export shares, exchange rates, and loan rates may reflect other aspects of farm policy. In particular, there is some evidence that set-aside requirements became more stringent after 1985: the simple correlation between loan rates and acreage shares switched from being 0.28 over the period 1970–85 to −0.58 in the period 1986–94. This suggests that, while higher loan rates encouraged participation in farm programs, they were combined with tighter restrictions on acreage than had previously been the case. Thus, the decline in export shares may have been the result of policy-driven reductions in U.S. acreage share. Without a detailed structural model and the necessary information on target prices, loan rates, set-asides, and participation rates, we cannot be sure what is driving behavior over this period.

A final question of interest is the effect of the EEP on U.S. wheat prices. Our approach to this issue is to compare the level of U.S. domestic wheat prices with the level of U.S. export prices to different regions in the pre- and post-EEP periods. Wheat export destinations are grouped into thirteen regions, and regional export unit values per bushel are calculated for the period 1975–93 on an annual basis. We then regress a measure of the price difference (U.S. price minus export region price) on a constant, an EEP dummy (which equals one in EEP periods and zero otherwise), and the loan rate (which may influence the relative price of what in the United States). The results for the regression that pools all the export regions into a single regression are given in table 10.10. The point estimate on the EEP dummy suggests that the price differential changed such that relative prices in the United States rose by $0.21 during the EEP period, but the coefficient is not statistically significant. In estimation on a region-by-region basis, the only region where prices fell significantly relative to the United States was North Africa, a huge recipient of

EEP-subsidized wheat. These regression results suggest that the effect of the EEP on U.S. domestic prices was modest.

10.4   Conclusion

This paper has attempted to use regression analysis to study the effect of the Export Enhancement Program on U.S. wheat exports. We find that measures of change in common currency relative costs of the competitor group of exporters have important effects on production, acreage, and export shares as well as government wheat stocks. Policy variables, such as the loan rate, also have important effects on these outcomes in most of our specifications.

The main findings of our analysis are as follows. The decline of U.S. export market shares in wheat during the early and mid-1980s can be attributed primarily to the appreciation of the dollar. In fact, our simple regression model of export market shares as a function of exchange rates and loan rates does quite well at out-of-sample prediction of the evolution of export shares for the period 1981–85. This finding holds up in a number of different specifications of the export share model. Furthermore, results for a small subperiod in which European wheat subsidies per unit are available suggest that the subsidies explain only about 2 percentage points of the 17 percentage point decline in U.S. export market share from 1980 to 1985. It appears inaccurate to blame the collapse of wheat exports on the EC subsidies and, consequently, dubious to attempt to rectify the situation with countervailing subsidies, such as the EEP.

Ironically, shortly after the implementation of the EEP, the dollar underwent a drastic real depreciation. Nonetheless, the EEP program grew substantially over the period we study. This may reflect a more general phenomenon: that one of the costs of exchange rate misalignments might be the adoption of temporary import protection or export promotion programs that are difficult to remove even after the realignment of exchange rates. Had historical relations between the U.S. export share, the dollar, and loan rates prevailed after 1985, U.S. wheat export shares would have recovered almost fully to their 1980 levels by the end of the decade. However, the historical relations no longer appear to hold, which is perhaps a consequence of the EEP, other changes in farm programs, and competitor country subsidies in influencing wheat market behavior. The fact that the EEP is not a subsidy that operates at the margin implies that it is at least plausible that it would have little effect on export shares.

If the EEP was not successful in restoring U.S. exports, at least it did not appear to be very harmful to U.S. consumers. The price of wheat in the United States relative to the average export price from the United States to various regions changed very little after the EEP was implemented. On the other hand, this means that the EEP was not successful in reducing the need for other support measures for farmers.

References

Anania, G., M. Bohman, and C. A. Carter. 1992. United States export subsidies in wheat: Strategic trade policy or expensive beggar-thy-neighbor tactic? *American Journal of Agricultural Economics* 74:534–45.

Brooks, H. G., S. Devadoss, and W. H. Meyers. 1990. The impact of the U.S. wheat export enhancement program on the world wheat market. *Canadian Journal of Agricultural Economics* 38:253–77.

Estimates of producer and consumer subsidity equivalents. Various years. Washington, D.C.: U.S. Department of Agriculture, Economic Research Service.

Haley, S. L. 1989. Evaluation of export enhancement, dollar depreciation, and loan rate reduction for wheat. Staff Report no. AGES 89–6. Washington, D.C.: U.S. Department of Agriculture, Economic Research Service, April.

Seitzinger, A. H., and P. L. Paarlberg. 1989a. The export enhancement program: How has it affected wheat exports? Agriculture Information Bulletin no. 575. Washington, D.C.: U.S. Department of Agriculture, Economic Research Service.

———. 1989b. A simulation model of the U.S. export enhancement program for wheat in the presence of an EC response. *European Review of Agricultural Economics* 16, no. 4:445–62.

———. 1990. A simulation model of the U.S. export enhancement program for wheat. *American Journal of Agricultural Economics* 72:95–103.

World wheat situation and outlook yearbook. Various years. Washington, D.C.: U.S. Department of Agriculture, Economic Research Service.

11 The Effects of Offshore Assembly on Industry Location: Evidence from U.S. Border Cities

Gordon H. Hanson

One of the principal arguments presented against the North American Free Trade Agreement (NAFTA) was that it would encourage domestic manufacturers to shut down their operations in the United States and move them to Mexico. The NAFTA debate was by no means the first time labor unions and other protectionist interests had appealed to such concerns in an attempt to restrict trade between the United States and low-wage countries. The offshore assembly provision (OAP) of the U.S. tariff code has been the focus of repeated debates, with labor consistently arguing for its repeal.[1]

An OAP permits the duty-free return of domestically manufactured components that have been processed in another country. The importing agent is required to pay import duties only on the value added abroad. OAPs do reduce the cost of moving assembly operations abroad—hence the source of labor opposition—but this is by no means the sole effect of offshore assembly on the domestic economy. The existence of transport costs gives domestic components manufacturers an incentive to locate near the foreign assembly plants they supply. If a U.S. producer supplies assembly plants in a particular foreign region, the firm, all else equal, has an incentive to locate its production operations in the U.S. port city or border area that offers the least-cost access to the foreign market. An OAP, then, potentially affects not only the international location of assembly but also the internal location of complementary manufacturing activities in the source country.[2]

Gordon H. Hanson is assistant professor of economics at the University of Texas, Austin, and a faculty research fellow of the National Bureau of Economic Research.

The author thanks James Harrigan and conference participants for helpful comments. Raymond Robertson provided excellent research assistance.

1. For a discussion of labor union opposition to the U.S. OAP, see Grunwald and Flamm (1985), Schoepfle and Perez-Lopez (1988), and Mendez (1993).

2. This possibility may explain labor's coolness toward the argument that an OAP prevents the United States from losing entire industries—components production and assembly—to foreign countries. For a union, there is little difference between a components firm moving to Asia and it moving to a right-to-work state such as Texas.

In this paper, I study the effect of offshore assembly on the location of manufacturing activity in the United States. The locational effects of OAPs have yet to be addressed in the literature. Grossman (1982) develops a theoretical framework that identifies the conditions under which an OAP offers greater protection than a conventional pure-tariff scheme. Finger (1976), Mendez, Murray, and Rousslang (1991), and Mendez (1993) examine the welfare effects of OAPs. All three studies find that, compared to a flat-rate tariff scheme, the U.S. OAP offers a slight to moderate improvement in welfare and redistributes income from domestic assemblers to components producers and consumers. One shortcoming of these analyses is that they aggregate over regions within a country. To the extent that an OAP causes components production in the source country to relocate internally, it may generate interregional distributional effects that are missed at the national level.

An additional motivation for studying the U.S. OAP is that it offers a preview of the effects that NAFTA is likely to have on industry location in the United States.[3] Mexico is one of the largest suppliers of OAP imports to the U.S. economy. Given Mexico's proximity to the United States and its relatively abundant supply of low-wage labor, the country is a natural site in which to locate offshore assembly for the U.S. market. There is little reason to believe that NAFTA will change the current binational pattern of specialization in manufacturing. In the absence of trade barriers, it is likely that the United States will have a comparative advantage in components production and that Mexico will have a comparative advantage in assembly operations. To the extent that transport costs matter for industry location, the U.S.-Mexico border region is likely to become an important production site for the integrated North American market.

The approach I take is to study how the growth of offshore assembly in Mexico has affected the U.S. border economy. I construct a data set of manufacturing activities in U.S. and Mexican border cities using a combination of U.S. and Mexican government sources. The cities on the U.S.-Mexico border form, in many respects, binational metropolitan areas. City pairs such as San Diego–Tijuana and El Paso–Ciudad Juarez are divided by an international boundary, but they engage in extensive trade in goods and labor services. It is in the larger Mexican border cities that most offshore assembly for the U.S. market occurs. This makes U.S. border cities a natural site in which to locate complementary manufacturing activities. The particular question I ask is whether the growth of export assembly plants in Mexican border cities has contributed to the expansion of specific manufacturing activities in neighboring U.S. border cities.[4]

---

3. There have been many studies on how NAFTA will affect resource allocation in the United States, Canada, and Mexico (for a survey, see Brown, Deardorff, and Stern [1992]). Only Henderson (1993) addresses the intranational locational consequences of economic integration.

4. Hanson (1996) examines the effect of U.S.-Mexico integration on the overall pattern of economic activity in the U.S. border region.

The body of the paper has five sections. Section 11.1 discusses U.S. and Mexican trade policies regarding offshore assembly. Section 11.2 describes manufacturing activities in the U.S.-Mexico border region. Section 11.3 presents empirical results. Section 11.4 concludes.

11.1 Offshore Assembly and U.S.-Mexico Trade

There are two categories of goods that qualify for the U.S. OAP. Item 9802.00.60 of the Harmonized Tariff Schedule (HTS) of the United States (formerly item 806.30 of the Tariff Schedule of the United States [TSUS]) permits the duty-free import of metal products that are manufactured in the United States and sent abroad for further processing.[5] Item 9802.00.80 of the HTS (formerly item 807.00 of the TSUS) permits the duty-free entry of inputs that are manufactured in the United States and assembled abroad.[6] To qualify for the 9802.00.80 exemption, the stated requirements are that domestic components may only be subject to assembly and assembly-related activities abroad. Goods imported under item 9802.00.80 account for over 98 percent of total OAP imports in any given year.

Figure 11.1 shows total U.S. OAP imports in levels and as a share of total U.S. imports for the period 1970–90. Between 1980 and 1990, the share of OAP imports in total imports increased from 4.7 to 12.2 percent.[7] OAP imports are concentrated in three product groups: motor vehicles and motor vehicle parts, electronics, and apparel. Table 11.1 shows the share of selected products in total U.S. OAP imports, total dutiable U.S. OAP imports, and total duty-free U.S. OAP imports over the period 1980–90. Duty-free OAP imports represent the value of the final product that can be attributed to U.S.-manufactured parts and components; dutiable OAP imports represent value added abroad. Machinery and equipment, in total, accounted for 88.6 to 92.3 percent of total

5. TSUS item 806.30 incorporated into the tariff code a provision of the Tariff Act of 1930. While the provision was intended to facilitate the manufacturing practices of U.S. steel firms that maintained operations in Canada, there was no apparent desire on the part of Congress to limit the provision to contiguous countries (U.S. International Trade Commission 1988).

6. Item 807.00 was created in 1963 by the U.S. Tariff Commission. It codified into law a 1954 decision by the U.S. Customs Court regarding customs practices established under the Tariff Act of 1930 (U.S. International Trade Commission 1988).

7. OAP imports show a large increase between 1986 and 1987. This is partly the result of firms reclassifying their imports under the OAP in order to avoid paying a custom user fee, which was introduced in December 1986 (U.S. International Trade Commission 1988). There are several tariff provisions that allow firms to import goods duty free, including the Generalized System of Preferences (GSP), the Caribbean Basin Economic Recovery Act (CBERA), the Automotive Products Trade Act (APTA), the Civil Aircraft Agreement, and the U.S.-Israel Free Trade Agreement. In addition, certain goods have a free duty rate under the most-favored-nation (MFN) clause. Firms entering imports under these provisions had until 1986 no incentive to also enter their goods under the OAP. With the imposition of a 0.22 percent ad valorem custom user fee in December 1986, many firms (except those using the GSP or CBERA, which are precluded from using the OAP) have begun entering their imports under the OAP to take advantage of the fact that both the dutiable and the duty-free portions of OAP imports are exempt from the user fee (U.S. International Trade Commission 1988).

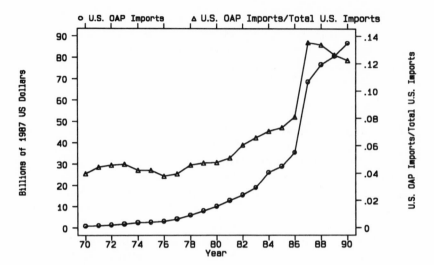

Fig. 11.1   U.S. OAP imports

OAP imports over the period. Motor vehicles are the single largest category of OAP imports, accounting for 59.1 percent of total OAP imports in 1990. The next largest categories are electronic items, including semiconductors and office machines, followed by apparel.

There is considerable variation across products in the U.S. content of OAP imports. Table 11.2 shows duty-free OAP imports and dutiable OAP imports as shares of total OAP imports by product over the period 1980–90. In 1990, the duty-free share of OAP imports—the share of the value of the final product attributable to U.S. parts and components—was 50 percent or higher in apparel, semiconductors, circuit breakers, and electrical conductors but was less than 25 percent in motor vehicles, internal combustion engines, and television receivers.

Mexican trade policy allows domestic and foreign firms to take full advantage of the U.S. OAP. In 1965, Mexico began to permit the creation of export assembly plants under the Border Industrialization Program.[8] The program exempted the plants, known as *maquiladoras,* from value-added taxes, duties on imported inputs, and restrictions on foreign ownership, as long as they exported all their output (Hansen 1981). The tariff exemption was of particular importance prior to Mexico's liberalization of trade in 1985. The combination of the U.S. OAP and Mexico's *maquiladora* program implies that a firm that ships U.S.-manufactured components to a plant in Mexico for assembly and

8. One motivation for the Border Industrialization Program was the end of the Bracero Program (1948–64), which had allowed Mexican nationals to work as agricultural laborers in the United States. The Mexican government was concerned about a sudden influx of returning workers and sought to create employment opportunities for them along the border (Hansen 1981).

Table 11.1   U.S. OAP Imports of Selected Products, 1980–90

	OAP Imports of Product as Share of:		
Product and Year	All OAP Imports	Dutiable Imports	Duty-Free Imports
Apparel, textiles:			
1980	.043	.022	.010
1982	.036	.019	.085
1984	.032	.016	.082
1986	.039	.018	.144
1988	.032	.019	.078
1990	.046	.032	.081
Machinery, equipment:			
1980	.886	.927	.776
1982	.890	.926	.792
1984	.919	.954	.817
1986	.910	.953	.702
1988	.923	.950	.832
1990	.902	.930	.830
Motor vehicle parts:			
1980	.048	.061	.012
1982	.017	.018	.014
1984	.024	.023	.026
1986	.025	.022	.035
1988	.053	.053	.055
1990	.038	.034	.048
Motor vehicles:			
1980	.375	.507	.016
1982	.439	.584	.022
1984	.447	.589	.028
1986	.641	.744	.148
1988	.598	.672	.347
1990	.591	.672	.385
Circuit breakers:			
1980	.012	.007	.027
1982	.014	.009	.031
1984	.013	.007	.033
1986	.013	.005	.046
1988	.010	.005	.027
1990	.023	.007	.063
Electrical conductors:			
1980	.011	.006	.023
1982	.013	.007	.031
1984	.018	.009	.045
1986	.023	.011	.080
1988	.016	.008	.045
1990	.018	.010	.038
Combustion engines:			
1980	.004	.004	.005
1982	.012	.010	.017
1984	.028	.027	.029

(continued)

Table 11.1   (continued)

Product and Year	OAP Imports of Product as Share of:		
	All OAP Imports	Dutiable Imports	Duty-Free Imports
1986	.029	.027	.037
1988	.035	.039	.022
1990	.027	.033	.011
Office machines:			
1980	.044	.044	.045
1982	.042	.041	.044
1984	.064	.069	.052
1986	.017	.016	.024
1988	.035	.036	.033
1990	.028	.028	.025
Semiconductors:			
1980	.176	.089	.413
1982	.170	.084	.417
1984	.161	.084	.388
1986	.015	.008	.047
1988	.059	.035	.142
1990	.065	.040	.127
Television receivers:			
1980	.009	.011	.003
1982	.007	.008	.003
1984	.005	.007	.002
1986	.012	.012	.012
1988	.012	.012	.011
1990	.019	.021	.015

Source: U.S. International Trade Commission, *Imports under Items 806.30 and 807.00 of the Tariff Schedule of the United States* (various editions).

Note: For the period 1980–90, OAP imports are those entered under items 806.30 and 807.00 of TSUSA. The dutiable portion of OAP imports is that equal to the value added by foreign sources; the duty-free portion is that equal to the value of U.S.-made parts and components. All products that follow machinery and equipment in the table belong to that product category.

then reimports the finished good will, between the two countries, pay import duties in the United States only on the value of Mexican labor and raw materials used in the assembly process. Initially, the *maquiladora* provisions were limited to a free-trade zone that occupied a twenty-kilometer strip on the Mexican side of the border with the United States. In 1972, the Mexican government began to allow the creation of *maquiladoras* in most parts of the country, and, in 1988, the government began to allow the plants to sell up to half their output on the domestic market (Schoepfle and Perez-Lopez 1990).

Figure 11.2 shows U.S. OAP imports from Mexico as a share of total U.S. OAP imports for the period 1980–90. For comparison, figure 11.2 also shows the share of total U.S. imports from Mexico. Mexico is the third largest supplier of OAP imports, accounting for 16.99 percent of total U.S. OAP imports

Table 11.2   **Dutiable and Duty-Free Content of OAP Imports, 1980–90**

	Share of OAP Imports of Product That Are:	
Product and Year	Dutiable	Duty Free
All products:		
1980	.740	.260
1990	.723	.277
Apparel, textiles:		
1980	.375	.625
1990	.501	.499
Machinery, equipment:		
1980	.766	.235
1990	.740	.260
Motor vehicle parts:		
1980	.932	.068
1990	.642	.358
Motor vehicles:		
1980	.989	.011
1990	.816	.184
Circuit breakers:		
1980	.417	.583
1990	.227	.773
Electrical conductors:		
1980	.433	.567
1990	.408	.592
Combustion engines:		
1980	.664	.336
1990	.879	.121
Office machines:		
1980	.726	.274
1990	.742	.258
Semiconductors:		
1980	.370	.630
1990	.447	.553
Television receivers:		
1980	.905	.095
1990	.782	.218

Note: See note to table 11.1.

in 1990.[9] Table 11.3 shows Mexico's share of U.S. OAP imports for selected products over the period 1984–90. Compared to the overall pattern of U.S. OAP imports, OAP imports from Mexico are much less concentrated in motor vehicles: Mexico's share of U.S. OAP imports of motor vehicles did not exceed 6 percent over the period. Mexico is the major supplier of U.S. OAP imports

9. The largest suppliers of U.S. OAP imports are Canada and Japan, owing mainly to motor vehicle imports from the two countries. In 1987, Canada and Japan accounted for 31.4 and 21.7 percent of total U.S. OAP imports, respectively. Motor vehicles and motor vehicle parts accounted for 77.1 percent of OAP imports from Canada and 94.1 percent of OAP imports from Japan.

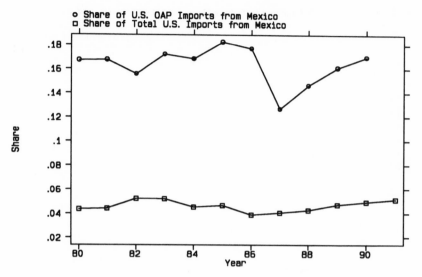

Fig. 11.2   U.S. imports from Mexico

in a number of electronic and electrical products. In 1990, the country accounted for over 80 percent of U.S. OAP imports of electrical conductors, motors and generators, and television receivers and over 30 percent of U.S. OAP imports of motor vehicle parts and circuit breakers. During the 1980s, Mexico became a relatively less important source of U.S. OAP apparel imports.

Export assembly plants in Mexico are overwhelmingly concentrated in states on the country's northern border. Table 11.4 shows employment in *maquiladoras* for border and nonborder states in Mexico over the period 1974–89. There has been a tremendous expansion in offshore assembly over the last two decades. During the sample period, total export assembly employment (in border and nonborder plants combined) in Mexico grew at an average annual rate of 11.3 percent. Within border states, *maquiladoras* are concentrated in a few border cities. In 1989, *maquiladora* employment in the six largest border cities accounted for 66.7 percent of national *maquiladora* employment.[10] One factor that may explain the geographic concentration of export assembly plants within the border region is the existence of industrial parks in certain border cities, which provide water and power services and often rent warehouse space and production facilities (Sklair 1989). Such services are scarce or nonexistent in other parts of the border region.

In its original conceptualization, U.S. and Mexican supporters of the *maquiladora* program envisioned a "twin-plant" production arrangement, in which a plant located in a U.S. border city would manufacturer components and a plant

10. These cities are Tijuana, Mexicali, Ciudad Juarez, Nuevo Laredo, Reynosa, and Matamoros.

Table 11.3   **OAP Imports from Mexico as Share of Total U.S. OAP Imports, 1984–90**

Product and Year	Share of U.S. OAP Imports from Mexico		
	All OAP	Dutiable	Duty Free
Apparel, textiles:			
1984	.319	.198	.388
1986	.326	.198	.401
1988	.238	.151	.310
1990	.236	.134	.337
Machinery, equipment:			
1984	.154	.099	.343
1986	.157	.092	.578
1988	.130	.085	.300
1990	.153	.108	.282
Motor vehicle parts:			
1984	.407	.292	.701
1986	.219	.089	.618
1988	.159	.071	.447
1990	.359	.198	.647
Motor vehicles:			
1984	.008	.003	.286
1986	.036	.021	.398
1988	.039	.029	.105
1990	.058	.042	.128
Circuit breakers:			
1984	.725	.623	.786
1986	.778	.711	.816
1988	.797	.725	.847
1990	.429	.633	.369
Electrical conductors:			
1984	.855	.741	.920
1986	.832	.715	.907
1988	.902	.822	.948
1990	.952	.935	.964
Combustion engines:			
1984	.661	.605	.817
1986	.590	.536	.776
1988	.218	.164	.531
1990	.136	.101	.393
Motors & generators:			
1984	.681	.547	.847
1986	.793	.682	.908
1988	.815	.692	.943
1990	.889	.809	.963
Office machines:			
1984	.131	.078	.343
1986	.057	.045	.096
1988	.141	.112	.246
1990	.161	.115	.290

(continued)

Table 11.3   (continued)

Product and Year	Share of U.S. OAP Imports from Mexico		
	All OAP	Dutiable	Duty Free
Semiconductors:			
1984	.047	.038	.053
1986	.109	.083	.132
1988	.054	.041	.065
1990	.060	.052	.066
Television receivers:			
1984	.386	.410	.114
1986	.779	.752	.894
1988	.902	.883	.971
1990	.924	.912	.966

Note: See note to table 11.1.

located in the neighboring Mexican border city would assemble the components into a finished good (Grunwald and Flamm 1985). A common management team located in the United States would run both plants. Under this scheme, the expansion of assembly production in Mexico would lead directly to the expansion of complementary manufacturing activities in the United States. In the now large literature on the *maquiladora* industry, there is near unanimity that the twin-plant system never materialized. It is well known that *maquiladoras* have expanded rapidly, but there is a general belief that, outside the growth of transport and related services, counterpart development has not occurred on the U.S. side of the border.[11] Curiously, there has been no systematic study of manufacturing activities in U.S. border cities. It is to this issue that I now turn.

11.2   The U.S. Border Economy

While the border region encompasses a vast area, most economic activity, and certainly most manufacturing activity, occurs in a few large cities. For the purposes of this study, I focus on the six largest U.S. border cities and their Mexican counterparts. The U.S.-Mexico border city pairs are the following: San Diego–Tijuana, Imperial County–Mexicali, El Paso–Ciudad Juarez, Laredo–Nuevo Laredo, McAllen-Reynosa, and Brownsville-Matamoros.[12] The first two U.S. urban areas are in California; the second four are in Texas. Data

11. On the perceived failure of the twin-plant scheme, see Grunwald and Flamm (1985), Sklair (1989), and Wilson (1992).

12. The two principal cities opposite Mexicali, Calexico and El Centro, are not large enough to be classified as metropolitan statistical areas (MSAs). Instead, I measure economic activity in these cities using data on Imperial County, California, in which both cities are located.

Table 11.4   **Maquiladora Employment in Mexico, 1974–89**

Year	Mexico Border States		Mexico Nonborder States	
	Employment	Share of Total	Employment	Share of Total
1974	70,929	.934	5,045	.066
1975	61,912	.921	5,302	.079
1976	67,258	.903	7,238	.097
1977	70,494	.899	7,939	.101
1978	82,130	.906	8,574	.095
1979	100,138	.899	11,227	.101
1980	106,208	.888	13,338	.112
1981	116,142	.887	14,831	.113
1982	112,875	.888	14,173	.112
1983	134,086	.889	16,781	.111
1984	175,778	.880	23,906	.120
1985	184,664	.871	27,304	.129
1986	210,635	.843	39,198	.157
1987	249,595	.818	55,658	.182
1988	297,127	.804	72,362	.196
1989	338,516	.788	91,209	.212
Average annual growth rate	.104	. . .	.193	. . .

Source: Mexico National Institute of Statistics, Geography, and Information (INEGI).

Note: Border states refers to states in Mexico that border the United States. The employment share is the share of national *maquiladora* employment. The average annual growth rate is the average annual log change over the period.

on one-digit employment and two-digit earnings for U.S. metropolitan statistical areas (MSAs) are available for the period 1970–90 from the Bureau of Economic Analysis (BEA). Data on earnings, employment, value added, and imported inputs in *maquiladoras* are available for Mexican border cities over the period 1974–89 from the Mexican National Institute for Statistics, Geography, and Information (INEGI).

U.S. border cities have experienced rapid employment growth over the last two decades. Table 11.5 shows employment in private nonfarm activities and in manufacturing for the U.S. border region over the period 1970–90. During the 1970s and, to a lesser extent, the 1980s, California and Texas experienced rapid growth in total employment and in manufacturing employment relative to the nation as a whole. With a few exceptions, employment growth has been even more rapid in the border cities. In the 1980s, while California, Texas, and the rest of the nation had near zero employment growth in manufacturing, manufacturing employment grew at an annual average rate of 3.9 percent in McAllen, 2.4 percent in San Diego, and 1.5 percent in El Paso.

The expansion of manufacturing activities in the border has been concentrated in certain industries. Table 11.6 shows an average annual growth in total

Table 11.5　　　　**Employment in U.S. Border Cities and Border States, 1970–90**

Region and Year	Private, Nonfarm Employment ('000s of workers)		Manufacturing Employment ('000s of workers)	
	Employment	Annual Growth	Employment	Annual Growth
U.S.:				
1970	70,868.2	. . .	19,684.4	. . .
1980	91,121.8	.025	20,776.6	.005
1990	114,610.3	.023	19,755.6	−.005
Texas:				
1970	3,825.2	. . .	755.8	. . .
1980	6,039.1	.046	1,067.8	.035
1990	7,649.8	.024	1,033.7	−.003
Brownsville:				
1970	36.1	. . .	5.0	. . .
1980	63.4	.056	11.8	.086
1990	79.1	.022	12.1	.003
El Paso:				
1970	101.9	. . .	23.9	. . .
1980	156.0	.043	36.4	.042
1990	208.4	.029	42.4	.015
Laredo:				
1970	18.6	. . .	1.1	. . .
1980	30.3	.049	2.1	.064
1990	44.3	.038	1.9	−.013
McAllen:				
1970	36.3	. . .	3.5	. . .
1980	70.5	.067	9.5	.099
1990	103.9	.037	14.0	.039
California:				
1970	6,917.9	. . .	1,594.5	. . .
1980	10,315.8	.040	2,074.1	.026
1990	14,330.9	.033	2,229.4	.007
Imperial:				
1970	18.1	. . .	1.6	. . .
1980	27.7	.043	2.0	.025
1990	37.8	.031	1.6	−.023
San Diego:				
1970	376.6	. . .	67.8	. . .
1980	680.0	.059	112.2	.050
1990	1,106.3	.049	142.3	.024

Source: BEA, Regional Economic Information System.

Note: The cities listed are metropolitan statistical areas, as defined by the BEA (except for Imperial, which is Imperial County, California). MSAs typically encompass groups of cities that form a contiguous urban area. Annual growth refers to the annual average log change in employment over the previous decade.

Table 11.6   **Average Annual Growth in Total Earnings by Manufacturing Industry, 1975–90**

Border City Industry	Average Annual Growth in Total Earnings (log change in total earnings/U.S. PPI)		
	City	State	Nation
Manufacturing:			
Brownsville	.020	.034	.021
El Paso	.034	.034	
Laredo	.027	.034	
McAllen	.069	.034	
Imperial	−.014	.038	
San Diego	.060	.038	
Nondurable goods:			
Brownsvillle	.017	.031	.023
El Paso	.023	.031	
Laredo	.024	.031	
McAllen	.066	.031	
Imperial	−.029	.035	
San Diego	.066	.035	
Apparel:			
Brownsville	.052	−.001	.003
El Paso	.002	−.001	
Laredo	.109	−.001	
McAllen	.081	−.001	
Imperial	−.044	.046	
San Diego	.012	.046	
Durable goods:			
Brownsville	.024	.036	.019
El Paso	.058	.036	
Laredo	.031	.036	
McAllen	.079	.036	
Imperial	.013	.040	
San Diego	.059	.040	
Elec. & electronic equip.:			
Brownsville	.068	.071	.018
El Paso	.198	.071	
Laredo	.094	.071	
McAllen	.162	.071	
Imperial	.158	.028	
San Diego	.075	.028	
Motor vehicles:			
Brownsville	.182	.030	.018
El Paso	.060	.030	
San Diego	.068	.003	

Note: See note to table 11.5.

earnings, deflated by the U.S. PPI, for selected manufacturing industries in U.S. border cities over the period 1975–90. Relative to the United States as a whole, average annual earnings growth in durable goods was more rapid in five of the border cities, and average annual earnings growth in nondurable goods was more rapid in four of the border cities. The most dramatic differences in earnings growth are for the specific industries that account for most offshore assembly: apparel, electric and electronic equipment, and motor vehicles and motor vehicle parts. While average annual real earnings growth in apparel was nearly flat (0.3 percent) for the nation as a whole, it was 5.2 percent in Brownsville, 10.9 percent in Laredo, and 8.1 percent in McAllen. And, while average annual real earnings growth in electric and electronic equipment was 1.8 percent for the United States as a whole, it was over 6 percent in each of the border cities and over 15 percent in El Paso, McAllen, and Imperial County. Owing to disclosure restrictions, earnings data in motor vehicles are available only for Brownsville, El Paso, and San Diego. In each of these cities, average annual real earnings growth was more than 4 percent higher than for the nation as a whole.

The industries in which offshore assembly is concentrated now account for the majority of border manufacturing activity.[13] Table 11.7 shows the share of two-digit earnings in total manufacturing earnings for border cities and states in 1975 and 1990. In 1990, while apparel accounted for 2.8 percent of national manufacturing earnings, it accounted for over 25 percent of manufacturing earnings in Brownsville, El Paso, and McAllen. Similarly, while electrical and electronic equipment accounted for 9.0 percent of national manufacturing earnings, the industry accounted for over 14 percent of earnings in El Paso, Laredo, and San Diego.

Some questions remain regarding the nature of the manufacturing activities located in U.S. border cities. While I argue that these activities represent components production and other activities that are complementary to offshore assembly, it is entirely possible that part or all of border manufacturing is unrelated to export manufacturing in Mexico. Unfortunately, the BEA data do not identify whether manufacturing activities take the form of components production, final goods production, or assembly. Anecdotal evidence, however, suggests that much U.S. border manufacturing represents components production for Mexican *maquiladoras*. Reports in the *Twin Plant News,* a U.S. trade magazine for firms that engage in offshore assembly in Mexico, identify two types of manufacturing activities that predominate in U.S. border cities: plastic injection molding and metal stamping. Both activities are general techniques used to create parts and components for domestic electronic devices and motor ve-

---

13. Food products has historically been the major manufacturing industry in the U.S. border region. In 1975, it accounted for over 20 percent of manufacturing earnings in Brownsville, Laredo, McAllen, and Imperial County. While the industry is still relatively large in McAllen and Imperial County, over the period 1975–90 the industry's share of manufacturing earnings fell from 23.8 to 14.4 percent in Brownsville and from 29.3 to 13.4 percent in Laredo.

Table 11.7   **Regional Industry Shares of Regional Manufacturing Earnings, 1975 and 1990**

Industry and Region	1975	1990
Nondurable goods:		
United States	.371	.382
Texas	.439	.422
Brownsville	.532	.506
El Paso	.692	.570
Laredo	.576	.552
McAllen	.796	.762
California	.304	.290
Imperial	.715	.574
San Diego	.162	.178
Apparel:		
United States	.037	.028
Texas	.044	.026
Brownsville	.155	.251
El Paso	.443	.268
McAllen	.250	.302
California	.031	.034
San Diego	.024	.012
Durable goods:		
United States	.630	.618
Texas	.561	.578
Brownsville	.468	.494
El Paso	.308	.430
Laredo	.424	.448
McAllen	.204	.238
California	.696	.710
Imperial	.285	.427
San Diego	.838	.822
Elec. & electronic equip.:		
United States	.093	.090
Texas	.069	.120
Brownsville	.056	.115
El Paso	.016	.176
Laredo	.052	.142
McAllen	.013	.051
California	.155	.132
San Diego	.127	.160
Motor vehicles:		
United States	.059	.057
Texas	.015	.014
Brownsville	.039	.104
El Paso	.006	.036
California	.021	.012
San Diego	.004	.004

Note: See note to table 11.5.

hicles.[14] Injection-molding and metal-stamping firms appear to be mostly independent suppliers of major automobile companies or name-brand electronics producers. Some of these firms have relocated to the border at the behest of their major buyers.

The data presented in this section are consistent with the hypothesis that the expansion of export assembly activities in Mexican border cities has contributed to an increase in manufacturing activities in U.S. border cities. The expansion of border manufacturing could, however, be due to local labor market conditions, such as low wages arising from an abundant local immigrant labor supply. In the next section, I use more formal techniques to identify the effects of offshore assembly in Mexico on border manufacturing activities in the United States.

11.3   Empirical Results

11.3.1   Model Specification

To study the effects of offshore assembly in Mexico on manufacturing activities in U.S. border cities, I develop a simple model of employment at the city and industry level. As the demand for a city-industry's output expands, the city-industry will increase the amount of labor it employs. Following Hanson (1996), labor demand at the city-industry level can be modeled as a function of sources of demand for city-industry output.

Consider a competitive labor market in which labor demand in city i by industry j at time t is given by the expression

$$(1) \qquad L_{ijt}^D = f(X_{ijt}, W_{ijt})\, e^{\varepsilon_{ijt}},$$

where X_{ijt} is a vector of factors that shift labor demand, W_{ijt} is the wage in city-industry ij, and ε_{ijt} is an unobserved shock to city-industry labor demand that has mean zero and constant variance σ_ε. Let labor supply in the city-industry be given by

$$(2) \qquad L_{ijt}^S = g(\mathrm{AWG}_{ijt}, W_{ijt})\, e^{\mu_{ijt}},$$

where AWG_{ijt} is the alternative wage for workers in the city-industry, and μ_{ijt} represents an unobserved shock to city-industry labor supply that has mean zero and constant variance σ_μ.

From equations (1) and (2), I derive a reduced-form regression equation for equilibrium city-industry employment. I assume that this expression can be written as

---

14. Reports in the *Twin Plant News* state that employment in the El Paso plastic injection molding industry grew by 700 percent between 1981 and 1988 (Roard 1990) and that in 1993 the industry supplied $200 million worth of plastic components to Mexico's offshore assembly industry (Goldsberry 1993). El Paso Community College and the University of Texas at El Paso now offer specialized courses in injection-molding techniques (Pannell 1993).

(3) $$\ln L_{ijt} = \alpha + \gamma \ln \text{AGW}_{ijt} + \ln X_{ijt}\beta + v_{ijt},$$

where α and γ are scalars, β is a vector of parameters, and the error term v_{ijt} is the weighted sum of the labor demand and labor supply shocks. There is also, of course, an analogous reduced-form expression for the equilibrium city-industry wage. Given that there are no data on wages at the two-digit industry level, I restrict my attention to employment.

I identify three variables that shift city-industry labor demand: total personal income in the state in which the MSA is located (SINC_{ijt}), total employment in the national industry (USL_{ijt}), and employment in *maquiladoras* that are located in the Mexican border city that neighbors the U.S. MSA (MAQ_{it}). The first two variables capture domestic demand for output by the city-industry. The third variable, *maquiladora* employment, captures foreign demand for city-industry output. To avoid introducing simultaneity bias into the regression, I measure state personal income excluding the MSA on which the observation is taken and measure national industry employment excluding the state in which the MSA is located.

Incorporating the output-demand variables into equation (3), the estimating equation is

(4) $$\ln L_{ijt} = \alpha + \gamma \ln \text{AWG}_{ijt} + \beta_1 \ln \text{SINC}_{ijt} \\ + \beta_2 \ln \text{USL}_{ijt} + \beta_3 \ln \text{MAQ}_{it} + v_{ijt}.$$

Two measures of the alternative wage are available: the average state manufacturing wage, which I calculate excluding the MSA on which the observation is taken, and the average wage in private nonfarm, nonmanufacturing activities in the MSA.

Unobserved factors may cause employment to vary systematically between border cities or over time. A downturn in the Mexican economy may lead to a sudden influx of Mexican immigrants at all border sites, or the existence of port facilities in one border city may cause it to have higher employment relative to other border cities. To control for idiosyncratic factors that influence city-industry employment, I include dummy variables for the year and city-industry in the regression. Table 11.8 defines the variables and provides summary statistics.

The variable of interest in equation (4) is $\ln \text{MAQ}_{it}$. If the expansion of offshore assembly in a Mexican border city increases the demand for manufacturing goods produced in the neighboring U.S. border city, the estimated coefficient on $\ln \text{MAQ}_{it}$ will be positive. This would indicate that the increase in offshore assembly increases the demand for local cross-border manufacturing goods, which in turn increases the demand for local cross-border manufacturing labor. Given the concentration of offshore assembly in certain industries, the effect of *maquiladora* activities may vary across industries. I allow for this possibility in the estimation.

Table 11.8   **Summary Statstics for Regression Variables**

Variable	Definition	Mean	SD	No. of Obs.
ln L	Log MSA industry earnings/average MSA manufacturing wage (dependent variable)	8.467	1.490	180
ln AWG1	Log average state manufacturing wage outside MSA (deflated by U.S. CPI)	−1.345	.036	180
ln AWG2	Log average MSA wage in private nonfarm, nonmanufacturing activities (delated by U.S. CPI)	−1.970	.111	180
ln SINC	Log state personal income outside MSA (deflated by U.S. PPI)	14.732	.358	180
ln USL	Log national industry earnings/national industry manufacturing wage, outside state in which MSA is located	16.007	.275	180
ln MAQ	Log *maquiladora* value added (converted into dollars and deflated by the U.S. PPI) in the Mexican border city that neighbors the U.S. MSA	−.755	.115	90

Note: Observations for all variables are for the period 1975–89.

11.3.2   Data and Estimation Issues

One problem for the estimation is that, at the two-digit industry level, data are available for total earnings but not for total employment. This does not present an issue for estimating reduced-form coefficients on variables that shift labor demand, given that, as long as labor supply is not backward bending, outward labor-demand shifts increase both earnings and employment. It does, however, present a problem for estimating reduced-form coefficients on variables that shift labor supply. Depending on labor demand elasticities, shifts in the labor supply curve may generate earnings and employment changes of opposite sign. To deal with this issue, I adjust earnings by dividing the variable by the average one-digit manufacturing wage in the MSA.[15]

A second problem is that BEA disclosure restrictions prevent the release of data on industries that contain a single establishment. In the smaller urban areas, such as Laredo and Imperial County, disclosure restrictions apply to over half the twenty two-digit manufacturing industries. A complete set of observations at the two-digit level is available only for San Diego. My approach is to use data aggregated over durable and nondurable manufacturing industries at

---

15. Estimation results using total earnings deflated by the U.S. PPI as the dependent variable are similar to results using earnings divided by the average one-digit wage as the dependent variable.

the MSA level. The BEA publishes complete earnings data on durable-goods and nondurable-goods industries for all the MSAs in my sample. The durable-nondurable distinction remains useful for my purposes, given that, from table 11.6 above, the industries that account for most offshore assembly—electrical and electronic equipment and motor vehicles and motor vehicle parts—also account for most durable-goods manufacturing activity in U.S. border cities. Hence, I expect that the effects of offshore assembly on employment in U.S. border cities will be stronger for durable-goods industries than for nondurable-goods industries.

A final issue for estimation is that the variable ln MAQ_{it} may be correlated with the error term, v_{ijt}. One source of correlation is measurement error. It may be the case that ln MAQ_{it} does not capture all activity in the Mexican border area that creates demand for manufacturing goods produced in the neighboring U.S. border city. Measurement error will tend to bias the coefficient estimate on ln MAQ_{it} toward zero (Griliches 1986). A second source of correlation between ln MAQ_{it} and v_{ijt} is that the allocation of *maquiladora* activities across Mexican border cities may itself be a function of the characteristics of U.S. border cities. It may be desirable to locate assembly plants opposite a U.S. border city that has a large local consumer market or good highways and warehouse facilities. In such a case, the unobserved shocks to U.S. city-industry employment will also affect the level of production in *maquiladoras* located in the neighboring Mexican city. If the level of *maquiladora* activity in a Mexican border city is correlated with employment shocks in the U.S. border city, the OLS coefficient estimate on *maquiladora* activities will be biased.

To correct for measurement error and possible endogeneity bias, I use instrumental variables (IV) estimators. An ideal instrument is one that is correlated with ln MAQ_{it} and uncorrelated with v_{ijt}. If there is no serial correlation in the error term, lagged values of the suspect endogenous variable are valid instruments. The instruments I use are current values of the other explanatory variables and lagged values of ln MAQ_{it}.

11.3.3 Empirical Results

I report OLS and IV estimation results for equation (4). Observations are pooled across MSAs on durable and nondurable manufacturing industries for the period 1974–89. I use two measures of the alternative wage, the state manufacturing wage (outside the MSA) and the MSA average wage in nonmanufacturing activities.

In table 11.9, I report OLS and IV regression results for equation (4), in which I constrain the coefficient on *maquiladora* employment to be equal for durable- and nondurable-goods manufacturing industries. The results are consistent with the hypothesis that growth in offshore assembly in Mexico contributes to the expansion of manufacturing in U.S. border cities. Coefficient estimates on ln MAQ are positive and statistically significant in the 1 percent level

Table 11.9   **U.S. Border-City Manufacturing Employment Estimation Results (standard errors in parentheses)**

| | Estimation Method | | | |
| | OLS | | IV | |
Variable	(1a)	(1b)	(2a)	(2b)
ln AWG1	−1.9878		−2.4398	
	(1.9955)		(2.0390)	
ln AWG2		.3966		.6251
		(.5391)		(.5555)
ln SINC	.9544	.1402	.8929	−.2141
	(.8121)	(.7019)	(.8279)	(.7256)
ln USL	−1.1096	−1.0212	−1.2230	−1.0971
	(.9034)	(.9103)	(.9213)	(.9312)
ln MAQ	.3329**	.3347**	.4794**	.4952**
	(.0629)	(.0636)	(.0792)	(.0809)
Hausman specification test statistic			−3.324**	−3.546**
Adjusted R^2	.984	.984	.983	.985
No. of observations	168	168	168	168

Note: Observations are pooled across durable-goods and nondurable-goods manufacturing industries in six U.S. border urban areas (San Diego, Imperial County, El Paso, Laredo, McAllen, and Brownsville) over the period 1974–89. All regressions include dummy variables for the city-industry and the year, which are not shown. Instruments include the (presumed) exogenous independent variables and the first lag of ln MAQ.

**Indicates significance at the 1 percent level.

in all regressions. The results do not depend on which measure of the alternative wage I use.[16]

The coefficient estimates on ln MAQ in the IV regressions are approximately one-third larger than those in the OLS regressions, which is consistent with the presence of measurement error. To determine whether there is measurement error/endogeneity bias in the regression, I perform a Hausman specification test. I reject the null hypothesis that ln MAQ is uncorrelated with the error term at a 1 percent level of significance. The coefficient estimates from the IV regressions should, then, be viewed as the more reliable.

The data presented in section 11.2 suggest that the growth of offshore assembly in Mexico has contributed to the expansion of specific manufacturing industries in U.S. border cities. These industries—electrical and electronic equipment and motor vehicles and motor vehicle parts—produce durable goods. To determine whether the expansion of offshore assembly in Mexican border cities has had larger effects for durable-goods manufacturing,

16. The very high R^2 statistics in tables 11.9 and in table 11.10 below are due primarily to the city-industry dummy variables. When the city-industry dummies are excluded from the regression, the adjusted R^2 falls to 0.42.

Table 11.10   **Estimation Results with Industry-Varying Coefficients (standard errors in parentheses)**

| | Estimation Method | | | |
| | OLS | | IV | |
Variable	(1a)	(1b)	(2a)	(2b)
ln AWG1	−1.9282		−2.3644	
	(1.8930)		(1.9438)	
ln AWG2		.5138		.7432
		(.5114)		(.5282)
ln SINC	1.0406	.1652	.9825	−.1823
	(.7706)	(.6648)	(.7896)	(.6887)
ln USL	.6233	.7605	.5633	.7583
	(.9574)	(.9648)	(1.0036)	(1.0121)
ln MAQ · DNON	.2200**	.2225**	.3590**	.3757**
	(.0658)	(.0661)	(.0827)	(.0831)
ln MAQ · DDUR	.4328**	.4387**	.5782**	.6006**
	(.0646)	(.0653)	(.0823)	(.0818)
F-statistic on equality of coefficients for ln MAQ	16.47**	16.94**	13.54**	13.98**
Adjusted R^2	.9853	.9853	.9846	.9845
No. of observations	168	168	168	168

Note: All regressions include dummy variables for the city-industry and the year. DNON is a dummy variable indicating nondurable-goods industry; DDUR is a dummy variable indicating durable-goods industry. Instruments include the (presumed) exogenous independent variables and the first lag of ln MAQ.

**Indicates statistical signifance at the 1 percent level.

I allow the coefficient on ln MAQ to vary across durable- and nondurable-goods industries. Table 11.10 reports OLS and IV regression results. I again find that the coefficient estimates on ln MAQ are positive and statistically significant at the 1 percent level in all regressions. There is a striking difference between the results in tables 11.9 and 11.10. The coefficient estimates on ln MAQ for durable-goods industries are nearly twice as large as those for nondurable-goods industries. In the first IV regression (col. 2a), the coefficient estimate on *maquiladora* value added is 0.578 for the durable-goods industry, compared to 0.359 for the nondurable-goods industry. I reject the null hypothesis that the coefficient on ln MAQ is equal for durable- and nondurable-goods industries at a 1 percent level of significance in all regressions.

The estimation results are consistent with the hypothesis that the growth of offshore assembly in Mexico has contributed to the growth of complementary manufacturing activities in U.S. border cities. The quantitative effect of *maquiladora* growth on U.S. border employment implied by the coefficient estimates is substantial. IV estimation results (table 11.10, col. 2a) imply that a 10 percent increase in offshore assembly activities in Mexico leads to a 5.8 percent increase in durable-goods manufacturing and a 3.6 percent increase in nondurable-goods manufacturing in U.S. border cities. These effects are large, considering that offshore assembly along the Mexican border has been growing at a rate of more than 10 percent per year for the last two decades.

11.4   Concluding Remarks

The results of this paper have implications for how the U.S. economy will adjust to NAFTA, conditional on the outcome that NAFTA causes export assembly in Mexico to expand. U.S. border cities are an obvious site in which to locate production of parts and components consumed by Mexican *maquiladoras*. While manufacturing growth in the U.S. border region has been largely overlooked in the discussion surrounding North American economic integration, the data tell a very clear story. As *maquiladoras* in Mexico have expanded over the last two decades, so, too, have complementary manufacturing activities in U.S. border cities. The estimation results provide strong support for the hypothesis that the growth of *maquiladoras* in Mexico increases the demand for manufacturing goods produced in U.S. border cities.

A key question is whether the export assembly industry in Mexico will continue to expand with the implementation of NAFTA. In a purely legalistic sense, NAFTA means the end of the *maquiladora* regime: it eliminates the "in-bond" arrangement, under which Mexican export assembly plants posted a bond for the value of the duties on the inputs they imported from abroad that was later returned to them once the products containing the imported inputs were exported. This does not mean, however, that NAFTA will alter the current pattern of specialization in which Mexican plants assemble goods from U.S.-made components and export the goods to the U.S. market. Curiously, none of the computable general equilibrium models developed to study NAFTA address the effects of trade reform on Mexico's export assembly industry. In an appendix, I use the partial equilibrium framework developed by Grossman (1982) to determine what effect NAFTA will have on the offshore-assembly arrangement—the arrangement in which goods made from U.S. components are assembled in Mexico. While such an approach has obvious limitations, the general thrust of the analysis is sensible.

Given Mexico's low relative wages, it is likely that the country will continue to specialize in the assembly of manufactured goods for the North American market. The more difficult question is which country will produce the components that *maquiladoras* assemble. The pre-NAFTA pattern of trade between the United States and Mexico tells us something about each country's comparative advantage. Prior to NAFTA, many goods, including television receivers, motor vehicle parts, and apparel, that were produced from U.S. components and assembled in Mexico were consumed in both the United States and Mexico. Even with the pre-NAFTA tariff disadvantage in the Mexican market, U.S.-made components were cheaper than Mexican-made components. The abolition of trade barriers should strengthen the comparative advantage of the United States in components production. Of course, such an argument ignores the possibility that NAFTA will change relative prices enough that the United States no longer has a comparative advantage in components production. This is unlikely, however, given that pre-NAFTA tariffs were low for most products. The most likely scenario is that NAFTA will cause Mexican assembly plants and U.S. components producers to expand, in which case one can expect manufacturing activities in the United States to continue to relocate to the U.S. border region.

Appendix

I use the framework in Grossman (1982) to assess the effects of NAFTA on industries that engage in offshore assembly. The analysis considers the pattern of production that would emerge if tariffs were eliminated and pre-NAFTA prices remained constant. Such an exercise ignores the general equilibrium effects of trade reform, but it remains useful as a way to identify who benefits from the lowering of trade barriers, holding constant changes in other industries.

Consider a final good j that is produced in two stages. In stage 1, an intermediate good n is produced, and, in stage 2, the intermediate good is assembled into a final product. One unit of n is required to produce one unit of j. Let $P_j^{i,k}$ be the price of the final good j, where i is the source country for the intermediate good, and k is the country in which assembly occurs. Let P_n^i be the price of good n produced in country i. There are two countries: the United States, indexed by U, and Mexico, indexed by M. Both have tariffs on intermediate and final goods, where t_h^i is the tariff on good h in country i. There are also costs in shipping goods between countries, where s_h is the unit cost of shipping good h from the United States to Mexico, or vice versa.

I assume that all agents are price takers and that identical goods are consumed in the two countries. In practice, there are three possible structures of production: (1) pure U.S. production, (2) intermediate-good production in the United States and assembly in Mexico, and (3) pure Mexican production. The type 2 structure is the offshore assembly arrangement. Arbitrage implies that, in any given market, all types of good j must sell for the same price.

Consider the U.S. market for good j. The U.S. price for a type 2 good is

$$(A1) \qquad P_j^{U,M} + t_j^U \left(P_j^{U,M} - P_n^U - s_n \right) + s_j.$$

The price $P_j^{U,M}$ is the unit cost of producing the good (which includes the cost s_n of transporting the intermediate good from the United States to Mexico for assembly). The final good must be transported from Mexico to the United

States, where a tariff is levied on the value added abroad. In the United States, type 2 goods compete with type 1 goods (e.g., television sets, apparel, motor vehicles). While assembly costs are higher for goods wholly produced in the United States, producers of these goods avoid the transport costs and import duties incurred in offshore assembly. Arbitrage requires that the U.S. price for all types of good j be equal:

(A2) $$P_j^{U,U} = P_j^{U,M} + t_j^U (P_j^{U,M} - P_n^U - s^n) + s_j.$$

In few, if any, of these markets are goods wholly produced in Mexico consumed in the United States. It must then be true that

(A3) $$P_j^{M,M} (1 + t_j^U) + s_j \geq P_j^{U,M} + t_j^U (P_j^{U,M} + P_n^U - s_n) - s_j.$$

The price of goods wholly produced in Mexico, inclusive of tariffs and transport costs, exceeds the price of offshore assembly goods and goods wholly produced in the United States.

Given (A2) and (A3), the effects of eliminating tariffs are ambiguous. Depending on the sign of $P_j^{M,M} - P_j^{U,M}$, NAFTA may or may not cause goods wholly produced in Mexico to be sold in the U.S. market. Pre-NAFTA competition in the Mexican market implies price relations that help resolve this ambiguity. Suppose that Mexico consumes quantities of good j that are wholly domestically produced (e.g., apparel, some motor vehicles). If Mexico also consumes goods wholly produced in the United States, it must be true that

(A4) $$P_j^{M,M} = P_j^{U,U} (1 + t_j^M) + s_j.$$

If, instead or in addition, Mexico consumes offshore assembly goods, it must be true that

(A5) $$P_j^{M,M} = P_j^{U,M} + t_n^M P_n^U.$$

Equation (A5) shows that offshore assembly goods sold in Mexico are required to pay duties on the imported inputs used in production. Equations (A4) and (A5) may hold simultaneously.

Consider the effects of eliminating tariffs in both countries. Take first the case in which, prior to NAFTA, Mexico consumes quantities of good j produced under offshore assembly. At pre-NAFTA prices, equations (A2) and (A5) imply that

(A2′) $$P_j^{U,U} > P_j^{U,M} + s_j,$$

(A5′) $$P_j^{M,M} > P_j^{U,M}.$$

Offshore assembly becomes the least-cost strategy of producing good j for both markets. This would cause U.S. components producers and Mexican assembly plants to expand and Mexican components producers and U.S. assembly plants to contract. Now consider the case where, prior to NAFTA, goods wholly produced in the United States are consumed in Mexico. At pre-NAFTA prices, it is again true that equation (A2′) holds, and, from equation (A4), it is now true that

(A4′)
$$P_j^{M,M} > P_j^{U,U} + s_j.$$

Combining equations (A2′) and (A4′), it is clear that, in this case also, offshore assembly is the least-cost production strategy for both markets. Holding constant changes in other industries, NAFTA causes offshore assembly to expand.

In addition to ignoring general equilibrium effects, the analysis ignores the existence of countries outside NAFTA and the effects of scale economies. The second omission is likely to be the more serious. If production in manufacturing is subject to increasing returns to scale, NAFTA may lead to greater specialization in components production in all three countries. In this event, NAFTA would cause components production to expand in both the United States and Mexico. Even in this case, however, there is still no reason to believe that product assembly in Mexico would contract. As long as Mexico specializes in assembly, U.S. components producers would have an incentive to locate a portion of their activities in the U.S. border region.

References

Brown, D. K., A. V. Deardorff, and R. M. Stern. 1992. North American integration. *Economic Journal* 102:1507–19.

Finger, J. M. 1976. Trade and domestic effects of the offshore assembly provision of the U.S. tariff. *American Economic Review* 66:598–611.

Goldsberry, Clare L. 1993. An editorial perspective. *Twin Plant News,* March, 45.

Griliches, Z. 1986. Economic data issues. In *Handbook of econometrics,* vol. 3, ed. Z. Griliches and M. D. Intriligator. Amsterdam: North-Holland.

Grossman, G. 1982. Offshore assembly provisions and the structure of protection. *Journal of International Economics* 12:301–12.

Grunwald, J., and K. Flamm. 1985. *The global factory: Foreign assembly and international trade.* Washington, D.C.: Brookings.

Hansen, N. 1981. *The border economy: Regional development in the Southwest.* Austin: University of Texas Press.

Hanson, G. 1996. U.S.-Mexico integration and regional economies: Evidence from border-city pairs. Working Paper no. 5425. Cambridge, Mass.: National Bureau of Economic Research.

Henderson, J. V. 1993. Some favorable impacts of a U.S.-Mexico Free Trade Agreement on U.S. urban employment. In *The Mexico-U.S. Free Trade Agreement,* ed. P. Garber. Cambridge, Mass.: MIT Press.

Mendez, J. A. 1993. The welfare effects of repealing the U.S. offshore assembly provision. *Journal of International Economics* 34:1–22.

Mendez, J. A., T. Murray, and D. J. Rousslang. 1991. U.S.-Mexico employment effects of repealing the U.S. offshore assembly provision. *Applied Economics* 23:553–66.

Pannell, Keith H. 1993. Border education: Responding to the converging needs of the region. *Twin Plant News,* March, 38–39.

Roard, Mike. 1990. Advanced technology. *Twin Plant News,* January, 41–42.

Schoepfle, G., and J. Perez-Lopez. 1988. U.S. employment impact of TSUS 806.30 and 807.00 provisions and Mexican maquiladoras: A survey of issues and estimates. Economic Discussion Paper no. 29. Washington, D.C.: U.S. Department of Labor.

———. 1990. Employment implications of export assembly operations in Mexico and the Caribbean Basin. Working Paper no. 16. Washington, D.C.: Commission for the Study of International Migration and Cooperative Economic Development.

Sklair, L. 1989. *Assembling for development: The maquila industry in Mexico and the United States.* New York: Unwin Hyman.

U.S. International Trade Commission. 1988. *Imports under items 806.30 and 807.00 of the tariff schedule of the United States, 1984–87.* Publication no. 2144. Washington, D.C.

Wilson, P. A. 1992. *Exports and local development: Mexico's new maquiladoras.* Austin: University of Texas Press.

12   Market-Access Effects of Trade Liberalization: Evidence from the Canada-U.S. Free Trade Agreement

Keith Head and John Ries

While the Canada-U.S. Free Trade Agreement (FTA) of 1988 received much less attention in the United States than the follow-up agreement that included Mexico, it drew adamant criticism in Canada. The 1988 federal elections were considered a referendum on free trade with the United States. Although the party in favor of the FTA carried a majority, opposition to the agreement persisted. In the early 1990s, critics attributed the alleged loss of 350,000 manufacturing jobs to the elimination of tariffs between the countries. The purpose of this paper is to examine changes in Canadian and U.S. manufacturing industries and relate those changes to the removal of trade barriers. We use a generalized version of Krugman's (1980) trade model to predict the expected change in the relative size of Canada's manufacturing industries resulting from tariff reductions. Since the restrictive version of the theory appears unable to explain the main features of the data, we will also consider extensions of the model that allow for differences in cost and demand structures.

Import protection in Canada dates back to the National Economic Policy of 1878. In an effort to avoid being solely a nation of "hewers of wood and drawers of water," Canada imposed large tariffs on manufacturing imports. One hundred ten years later, successive GATT rounds had reduced average tariffs on goods to 4.5 percent. Nonetheless, the government provided significantly greater protection to a number of industries. The size and proximity of the United States suggested to many that even small tariff changes might have large consequences.

To date, there have been few studies of the actual effects of the FTA, partly

Keith Head and John Ries are assistant professors at the Faculty of Commerce of the University of British Columbia.

The authors thank their discussant, John Helliwell, as well as Tim Hazledine and the participants at the conference for their helpful suggestions and comments. Meng Zhang provided valuable research assistance.

323

since the data have only recently become available. Gaston and Trefler (1994), Hazledine (1994), and Statistics Canada (1993) are recent papers on the topic. These papers, which examine two-digit Standard Industrial Classification (SIC) manufacturing industries, have concentrated on documenting "what happened" without developing formal economic models. The Statistics Canada study finds correlations of -0.8 and -0.7 between initial tariffs and the U.S. and Canadian propensity to import from each other. The strong correlation indicates that liberalization had potentially large effects on North American manufacturing through its effect on import penetration. Gaston and Trefler show that employment changes are positively related to changes in Canadian tariffs (hence, the lowering of Canadian trade barriers reduces output), while Hazledine does not find statistically significant relations between tariff changes and Canadian shipments.

In this paper, we take an alternative route of attempting to link our examination of the change in the relative size of each Canadian industry to the predictions of a specific trade model. We match Census of Manufactures data from the United States and Canada to examine industry changes occurring at the four-digit SIC level. This allows us to examine a large number of relatively disaggregated industries with greater variation in tariffs and other characteristics than those analyzed in the other studies. Before developing the formal model, it seems worth considering several possible accounts of what might be expected to happen to a small country when it liberalizes manufacturing trade with a larger neighbor.

Simple notions of Ricardian comparative advantage would predict that free trade would cause Canada's relative output share to expand in industries where Canadian workers are relatively productive. The problem with applying this theory is that it predicts one-way trade, whereas most North American manufacturing industries exhibit two-way trade. For instance, Canada's largest export industry, automobile-related products, is also its largest import industry.

Table 12.1 depicts several aspects of North American manufacturing trade by major industry group (according to the Canadian two-digit classification system) prior to the FTA. The first data column shows each industry's Grubel-Lloyd (1975) intraindustry trade index. The second column lists the share of each industry's trade in total manufacturing trade between Canada and the United States. The final column shows Canadian exports divided by imports. The table reveals a large amount of two-way trade within industries. Transport equipment, the industry with by far the largest trade share, realizes almost balanced trade. The trade data suggest that we move in the direction of a model that is consistent with intraindustry trade.

Some proponents of freer trade argued that Canada could reduce its trade barriers, obtain efficiency gains, and maintain its North American production shares. The reasoning was that, under protection, Canadian plants produce multiple product lines in order to serve the local market's demand for variety. With free trade, these plants would specialize in particular lines, achieving

Table 12.1	North American Trade in Manufactures, 1985–87		
Industry	IIT (%)	Share (%)	X_C/X_{US}
All manufacturing	96.0	100.0	1.08
Food	99.7	2.4	.99
Beverages	28.0	.5	6.15
Tobacco	92.9	.0	.87
Rubber products	89.1	.9	1.24
Plastic products	74.9	1.1	.60
Leather products	91.1	.1	1.19
Primary textiles	36.6	.5	.22
Textile products	56.4	.3	.39
Clothing	47.8	.3	3.19
Wood	23.0	3.8	7.70
Furniture & fixtures	29.1	1.0	5.86
Paper products	22.3	6.5	7.96
Printing & publishing	57.0	1.2	.40
Primary metals	58.7	7.0	2.41
Fabricated metal products	98.6	3.0	1.03
Machinery	55.9	7.1	.39
Transport equipment	98.8	43.5	1.02
Electrical	64.6	8.7	.48
Nonmetallic mineral products	90.4	1.3	1.21
Refined petroleum & coal products	49.4	2.6	3.05
Chemicals	76.6	5.0	.62
Other manufacturing	53.1	3.2	.36

Source: Authors' calculations based on data from Statistics Canada (1993).

Note: IIT is the Grubel and Lloyd (1975) intraindustry trade index, 2 min $(X_C, X_{US})/(X_C + X_{US})$, where X_C are Canada's exports to the United States and X_{US} are U.S. exports to Canada. "Share" is the portion of total manufacturing trade between Canada and the United States in each industry group.

lower costs through larger production runs. Meanwhile, plants south of the border would specialize as well. Increased trade flows would maintain the level of product variety in both markets. The end result would be less duplication without net shrinkage or loss of product diversity.

Adherents to this sanguine view of the likely effects of free trade pointed to the experience of the automobile industry as a prototype for an across-the-board free trade agreement. In 1965, the United States and Canada eliminated tariffs in automotive-related products. "Safeguards" requiring that Canadian production not drop below 75 percent of Canadian sales for any vehicle producer never posed a binding constraint on the manufacturers. Instead, even as the Big Three rationalized production, Canada's share of North American vehicle assembly rose from 7 percent in 1965 to 15 percent in the early 1980s (U.S.-Canada Automotive Agreement Policy Research Project 1985).

The theory sketched above makes no reference to the market-size asymmetry between the United States and Canada. When trade impediments impose additional costs on exports, firms prefer to locate in the larger country in order to avoid incurring these costs. This incentive gives the large country an inherent advantage attracting firms. Trade liberalization that achieves a truly integrated market would eliminate large countries' size advantage. However, even in the absence of tariffs, impediments to trade will remain. At the very least, there will be transportation costs; moreover, frontier controls, cabotage restrictions, and exchange rate risk may pose significant barriers to trade. This implies that, even after trade liberalization, the small country will have incomplete access to consumers in the larger country. Formal modeling is required to predict the precise effect of tariff reductions in these circumstances, but adjustments certainly involve more than the simple shift in the composition of product lines suggested above.

In section 12.1, we develop a model in which the market-size asymmetry between the United States and Canada tends to promote concentration of production in the larger country. The model predicts that Canada's production share in differentiated product industries will be smaller than Canada's expenditures share unless there are substantial offsetting asymmetries in trade barriers or costs. While bilateral trade liberalization offers firms in the small country greater access to the large market, it will nevertheless tend to reduce the relative size of the small country's differentiated-product industries. Section 12.2 matches industry data from Canadian and U.S. sources and examines whether initial relative size and the changes between 1987 and 1992 conform to the predictions of the monopolistic-competition model. Our main results are the following: (1) Canada's relative shipments declined between 1987 and 1992 in 83 percent of the matched industries. (2) The industries that were large in Canada relative to the United States in 1987 tended to decline the most over the subsequent five years. (3) Regression analysis of the changes in relative size finds significant negative effects of Canadian tariff reductions after including controls for industry sensitivity to the business cycle and exchange rate movements.

12.1   The Monopolistic-Competition Trade Model

We examine the effects of the FTA in the context of the monopolistic-competition trade model developed in Helpman and Krugman (1985). Their model has three main components: constant elasticity preferences over differentiated products, zero-profit entry equilibrium, and trade barriers. We generalize the model in two ways. First, as in Krugman and Hanson (1993), we decompose trade barriers into tariffs and other border costs (all trade impediments that remain after a free trade agreement is implemented). Second, we allow for industry-specific marginal cost differences. This last assumption makes our model a hybrid in which trade arises from both product differentiation and standard comparative advantage.

Total utility is given by $U(u_1, u_2, u_3, \ldots)$ in the home country and $U^*(u_1, u_2,$

u_3, . . .) in the foreign country.[1] Each industry comprises either differentiated products or homogenous goods. The form of each subutility function u_i depends on whether i is a differentiated-products industry or a homogeneous product. Let C_{ij} denote consumption of industry i goods produced by firm j. For homogeneous goods, $u_i = \sum_j C_{ij}$, that is, the consumer cares only about total consumption, not the identity of the manufacturer. In contrast, demand for the output of firm j in differentiated-products industry i is derived from a subutility function with a constant elasticity of substitution between varieties equal to σ_i. We now suppress the i subscript and focus on the determination of equilibrium in a particular differentiated-products industry.

In the monopolistic-competition model, firms specialize in the production of a single good in a single location.[2] Costs consist of a fixed cost, F, and constant marginal costs, c. It is customary to assume that the firm maximizes its profits with respect to a perceived elasticity of demand equal to σ, the elasticity of substitution between varieties, yielding

(1)
$$p = \frac{\sigma c}{\sigma - 1}.$$

Entry occurs until price is driven to average cost. This implies that each firm will produce

(2)
$$q = \frac{(\sigma - 1)F}{c}.$$

Consider representative domestic and foreign firms with costs c and c^*. Relative prices (at the factory door) will be $p/p^* = c/c^*$, whereas relative per-firm outputs will be $q/q^* = c^*/c$. Note that these relations imply that relative industry shipments, $S/S^* \equiv pqn/p^*q^*n^*$, equal the relative number of varieties produced at home and abroad (n/n^*). When labor is the only input and used in fixed proportions (the usual assumption in models of this type), relative employment (L/L^*) will also equal n/n^*.

Trade barriers create wedges between the price paid for locally produced and imported products. Consumers in the home country pay p for home-produced goods and $p^*\tau$ for imports. Similarly, consumers in the foreign country pay p^* for foreign-made goods and $p\tau^*$ for goods they import from the home

1. We focus on bilateral trade between the United States and Canada and, therefore, ignore third-country competition and markets. The small country, Canada, will be referred to as the *home country*. Third countries tend to have small shares of the North American market. Across twenty-two two-digit industries, the U.S. and Canadian share of the combined market is over 90 percent in fifteen cases, over 80 percent in nineteen cases, and over 70 percent in twenty-one cases, with this share being relatively low (48 percent) only in the case of leather.

2. This is a very restrictive assumption since it rules out both multiproduct and multinational enterprises. The investigation of how the effect of trade liberalizations depends on whether firms have multiple plants or products will be left for future research.

country. We decompose total trade impediments into the intrinsic costs of transborder shipments, κ, and ad valorem tariffs, t and t^*:

$$\tau = (1 + \kappa)(1 + t),$$

$$\tau^* = (1 + \kappa)(1 + t^*),$$

where κ includes transborder transaction costs such as freight, insurance, exchange rate hedges, customs documentation, and the threat of antidumping or countervailing duties.[3]

We now turn back to consumer demand to derive the equilibrium distribution of production. Let E and E^* denote the total expenditures at home and in the foreign country on the products in a particular industry. Let x equal the share of home expenditures devoted to home-produced varieties and x^* the share of foreign expenditures on foreign-produced varieties. Total shipments from each country, S and S^*, comprise production for the national market and exports. Using the notation defined above, we obtain

(3) $$S = xE + (1 - x^*)E^*,$$

(4) $$S^* = x^*E^* + (1 - x)E.$$

In the basic monopolistic-competition model, the allocation of expenditures between domestic and imported varieties depends solely on the prices that consumers face. We generalize the model to allow for an asymmetry between domestic and imported varieties in the utility function. Specifically, denoting H and F as the sets of home- and foreign-produced varieties, the subutility function for any industry is

$$u = \left[\sum_{j \in H} (\beta C_j)^{(\sigma-1)/\sigma} + \sum_{j \in F} C_j^{(\sigma-1)/\sigma} \right]^{\sigma/(\sigma-1)},$$

where β measures the degree to which, on average, consumers prefer home-produced varieties ($\beta > 1$) or foreign varieties ($\beta < 1$). A value of β larger than one need not represent nationalistic preferences; rather, it could be viewed as a shortcut for getting at the idea that domestic firms choose to produce product varieties that match domestic tastes.

Utility maximization subject to prices p and p^* yields

(5) $$x = \frac{np^{1-\sigma}}{np^{1-\sigma} + n^*(p^*\tau\beta)^{1-\sigma}},$$

(6) $$x^* = \frac{n^*p^{*1-\sigma}}{n(p\tau^*\beta)^{1-\sigma} + n^*p^{*1-\sigma}}.$$

---

3. McCallum (1995) and Helliwell (1995) have found evidence of very strong effects of national borders on trade volumes. After controlling for distance and economy size, the volume of trade between two Canadian provinces is twenty times larger than the volume of trade between a province and an American state.

Note that any observed domestic expenditure share, x, for given factory prices, p and p^*, can arise either because of high trade impediments, τ, or home bias in preferences, β. Since $\beta\tau$ and $\beta\tau^*$ always appear raised to the power of $1 - \sigma$, results are streamlined somewhat by defining

$$\rho \equiv [\beta(1 + \kappa)(1 + t)]^{1-\sigma}$$

and

$$\rho^* \equiv [\beta(1 + \kappa)(1 + t^*)]^{1-\sigma}.$$

These variables can be interpreted as indicators of "openness" to international trade.

Division by p^* in the numerators and denominators of equations (5) and (6) expresses x and x^* in terms of $(p/p^*)^{\sigma-1}$. Recall that relative prices equal relative marginal costs. Hence, substitution yields $\theta \equiv (c/c^*)^{\sigma-1}$ as an additional determinant of expenditure allocation. Thus, we have reduced x and x^* to functions of ρ, ρ^*, and θ. Substituting these expressions into equations (3) and (4), and solving for relative shipments, we obtain

$$(7) \qquad S/S^* = \frac{\theta[(E/E^*)(1 - \theta\rho) - \rho(\theta - \rho^*)]}{(\theta - \rho^*) - (E/E^*)\rho^*(1 - \theta\rho)}.$$

This equation forms the theoretical basis for our empirical analysis of the relative size of Canadian manufacturing industries and the changes brought about by trade liberalization. Since it is highly nonlinear, we will examine its implications using graphs. We will consider first the case of symmetric costs, preferences, and trade barriers. Thus, the only difference between the two countries is size. By assuming that $c = c^*$, we focus on trade driven entirely by product differentiation. Let α_i and α_i^* equal the share of GDP spent on industry i at home and in the foreign country. Assuming these shares to be constants, $E_i/E_i^* = (\alpha_i/\alpha_i^*)(GDP/GDP^*)$. Hence, if preferences are identical, that is, $\alpha_i = \alpha_i^*$, relative expenditures will equal relative GDP. The assumptions of symmetric costs and preferences allow us to obtain two stark predictions, which are illustrated in figure 12.1.

Figure 12.1 plots relative shipments of the small country as a function of symmetric trade barriers for three different values for the elasticity of substitution. The horizontal line at 0.1 represents relative expenditures since that is the approximate ratio of Canadian to U.S. GDP. Two results stand out. First, relative shipments for the small country lie strictly below its relative GDP. Second, relative size falls as trade impediments decline. The intuition for these results is that, from the point of view of minimizing trade costs, firms want to locate in the large market and pay border costs only on the small share of goods they export to the small market. However, the trade-cost-inflated prices in the small market give at least a few firms the incentive to locate there. A symmetric reduction in trade costs tilts the balance somewhat in favor of the large country.

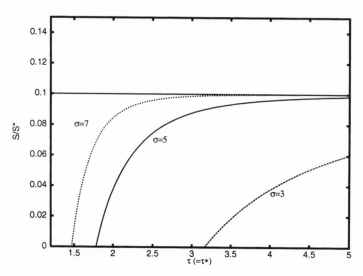

Fig. 12.1   Relative industry size, trade barriers, and the elasticity of substitution

The model predicts that the industry in the small country will disappear altogether if trade costs (including home bias in preferences) become sufficiently small. The figure also shows how the responsiveness of industry output to trade is a function of the elasticity of substitution. Small values of σ correspond to industries where, in equilibrium, economies of scale are more important. The lower the value of σ, the greater is the pressure for the industry to concentrate in the large country.

Figure 12.2 shows the effect of a cost advantage on relative industry size of the small country. Notably, cost advantages possessed by firms in the small country are not always sufficient to offset the market size disadvantage and result in relative output exceeding relative expenditures. When relative costs are 0.70, the small country will enjoy a relatively high industry share, which is magnified by liberalization. However, when the cost advantage is smaller, for a large range of trade impediments, relative size is less than relative expenditures. Moreover, trade liberalization does not necessarily raise relative industry size.[4] However, one clear prediction emerges—when cost advantages yield higher Canadian industry shares than expenditure shares, liberalization causes a relative expansion of the Canadian industry.

The cases discussed thus far consider bilateral reductions of symmetric trade barriers. Since Canada generally had higher levels of protection than the United States in 1987, we need to discuss the effect of liberalization under asymmetric protection. The contour plot in figure 12.3 adds a dimension to the

---

4. The U shape apparent in the curve is noted in Krugman and Hanson (1993).

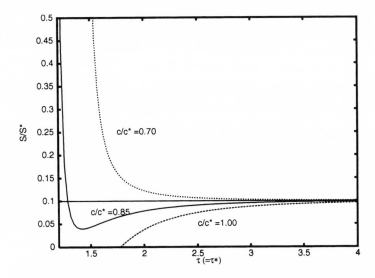

Fig. 12.2   Relative industry size, trade barriers, and relative marginal costs

previous graphic analysis by showing relative industry size as a function of trade barriers in each country. (Here, we revert to the assumption of equal marginal costs.) The contour where relative industry size equals 0.1 represents combinations of τ and τ^* that yield relative industry sizes equal to relative expenditures in the two countries. Combinations below this contour correspond to industry shares for the small country that exceed relative expenditures. This indicates that relatively high small-country industry shares are possible even without a cost advantage. However, levels of protection in the small country must be quite large relative to protection in the big country. In this figure, bilateral liberalization corresponds to movements toward the origin. As the arrow indicates, it is possible for liberalization to increase the relative size of the small country's industry. However, if both countries have the same remaining trade impediments, that is, if free trade corresponds to a position along the diagonal where $\tau = \tau^*$, then tariff reductions are certain to lower small-country industry shares.

To summarize, the model allows for a variety of possible results, but it also offers some general predictions. First, if Canada does not have a cost advantage, a symmetric trade liberalization will reduce Canadian relative industry size. Second, two effects are possible when Canadian industries start out with higher industry shares than relative expenditures. If the high share is a consequence of relatively high Canadian trade barriers, then the removal of the protection will lower the relative size of the Canadian industry. When it is the outcome of a cost advantage, Canada's share should rise. In the next section, we examine the changes that occurred in North American manufacturing to see whether actual changes are consistent with the predictions of the model.

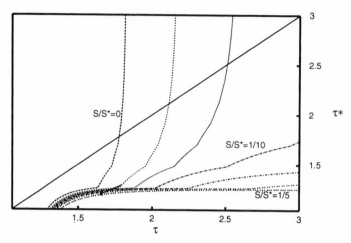

Fig. 12.3   Relative industry size with asymmetric trade costs

12.2   Relative Industry Size before and after the FTA

Canada and the United States use different industry classification systems. In 1991, the two countries developed a correspondence, but, unfortunately, there are many cases where part of a U.S. industry is assigned to one Canadian industry and part to another. In most cases, we were able to use seven-digit product-class data from the U.S. census to apportion U.S. SICs into our constructed industries. For instance, we were able to create a balanced "wine" industry by subtracting the brandy proportion of the U.S. "wine and brandy" industry. In addition, missing Canadian data for certain industries poses a problem. Ultimately, we obtained data and a satisfactory correspondence for 128 industries accounting for 77 percent of Canadian manufacturing shipments and 72 percent of U.S. shipments. Canadian industries are often more aggregated than their U.S. counterparts. Hence, many of our composite industries are similar to three-digit U.S. industries. Complete documentation for the correspondence is available from the authors (Head, Ries, and Zhang 1995).

Table 12.2 lists the ratio of Canadian industry size to U.S. industry size for three measures of size—the value of shipments, employment, and the number of establishments. Close to half the 128 industries we constructed had Canadian relative shipments in excess of Canada's relative GDP in 1987 (0.1004 at the PPP [purchasing power parity] exchange rate).[5] Moreover, contradictory

---

5. Ideally, we would compare relative shipments to industry-level relative expenditures. However, to calculate relative expenditures requires information on production, imports, and exports. It is quite difficult to match trade flows to domestic production for disaggregated industries. However, Statistics Canada information for two-digit SIC industries is available and shows that relative Canadian expenditures range from a low of 0.056 (other manufacturing) to a high of 0.114 (leather and allied products) with the larger machinery, transport equipment, and electrical and electronic productions taking values of 0.095, 0.082, and 0.058.

Table 12.2   **Relative Canadian-U.S. Manufacturing Performance**

	1987			1992		
	Q1	Median	Q3	Q1	Median	Q3
Shipments	.065	.094	.124	.052	.073	.105
Employment	.084	.125	.162	.074	.103	.147
Establishments	.091	.116	.170	.078	.110	.164
Shipments per establishment	.526	.749	1.027	.484	.684	.888
Value added per hour	.520	.664	.850	.533	.694	.825

Source: Authors' calculations based on data from the Canadian and U.S. censuses of manufacturing.

Note: Q1 and Q3 are the upper bounds of the first and third quartiles of the sample consisting of 128 constructed manufacturing industries. We convert to a common currency using the PPP exchange rate of 0.827 in 1987 and 0.845 in 1992.

to the theory, the relative number of establishments does not equal relative shipments. On the contrary, Canadian establishments appear to be systematically smaller than U.S. establishments in the same industry. This fact is inconsistent with the simple monopolistic-competition model.

Relative employment also frequently exceeds Canada's GDP share and generally lies above the shipments share.[6] The median Canadian establishment appears to have about the same number of workers as its U.S. counterpart, but these workers produce substantially less per hour.[7] Workers in Canada appear to generate only two-thirds the value added per hour of U.S. workers in the same industry. Although value added per hour is a crude measure of productivity in that it fails to control for price differences or the levels of other factors of production, these results conform with Baldwin, Gorecki, and McVey's (1986) finding that total factor productivity in Canadian manufacturing industries averaged 0.7 of the productivity in the same U.S. industries. Using PPP exchange rates, median relative productivity increased only a small amount between 1987 and 1992.

While Canada enjoyed 10 percent lower manufacturing wages in 1987, this was not sufficient to offset lower value added per worker. By 1992, owing largely to the stronger Canadian dollar, this wage advantage had disappeared. It seems clear that, if cost advantages are to explain the prevalence of Canadian industries that are larger than one-tenth the size of their American counterparts, input costs other than labor must be responsible. Unfortunately, we lack information about the unit costs of other factors and intermediate goods.

An inspection of table 12.2 reveals that the relative size of Canadian industry

6. The two are highly correlated, however: 0.98 in 1987 and 1992.

7. Using the same data set, John Helliwell found that, in both Canada and the United States, worker value added per employee tended to be lower in high-tariff industries. Helliwell's regression analysis also revealed that industries with more employees per establishment generated more value added per employee, although this result did not extend to relative productivity.

fell from 1987 to 1992. It is well documented that employment in both Canadian and U.S. manufacturing declined over this period (see, e.g., Gaston and Trefler 1994). The fact that the decline was relatively greater in Canada is consistent with a main tenet of the theory—the larger country starts out with an advantage that tends to be reenforced by trade liberalization. We now turn to an examination of whether the theory can explain the outcomes in individual industries.

Consider a scatter diagram that charts changes in industry relative size against initial relative size, with the diagram divided into quadrants by lines corresponding to relative change equal to zero and relative size equal to 0.1 (the relative GDP of Canada). The basic monopolistic-competition theory predicts that, with symmetric costs and trade barriers and expenditure shares equal to GDP shares, all points should lie in the lower-left-hand quadrant; that is, Canadian manufacturing industries should start out small, and then trade liberalization should further reduce their size relative to the corresponding U.S. industries. If Canadian firms enjoy large cost advantages, then we would also expect observations in the upper-right-hand quadrant. That is, if a Canadian industry has a large-enough cost advantage so that its production share exceeds its GDP share, liberalization may cause it to grow larger. The upper-left-hand quadrant is a possibility if the Canadian industry has an intermediate cost advantage and its trajectory corresponds to the U shape depicted in figure 12.2 above. Thus, only a quite specific combination of parameters will put an industry into the upper-left-hand quadrant. Relative size may also exceed 0.1 if Canada has much higher levels of import protection (either from tariffs or asymmetric transport costs). In that case, we expect trade liberalization to reduce Canada's relative size. Hence, the lower-right-hand quadrant is also possible if there are large asymmetries in trade barriers.

Figure 12.4 plots Canadian and U.S. tariffs for each industry in 1987. Tariffs levels are generally small but range as high as 22.7 percent. Since the majority of the points are below the diagonal line, it is clear that Canadian tariffs are generally higher than U.S. tariffs. These tariff asymmetries provide an avenue for the relative size of Canadian industry to exceed relative expenditures. Once protection is removed, then the relative size of these industries should fall, and we could obtain observations in the lower-right-hand quadrant of the hypothetical scatter diagram.

We employ a simulation to investigate more fully our model's predictions of the effect that tariff reductions under the FTA had on relative industry size. The theory tells us that changes in industry size depend on key parameters such as relative production costs and relative trade costs as well as the elasticity of substitution. Unfortunately, while we know tariff reductions, we do not observe other important industry characteristics. The simulation randomly assigns parameter values to industries. In the case of Canadian and U.S. tariffs, the simulation generates t and t^* with the means, standard deviations, and covariance of the actual data (see fig. 12.4). The distributions for the other param-

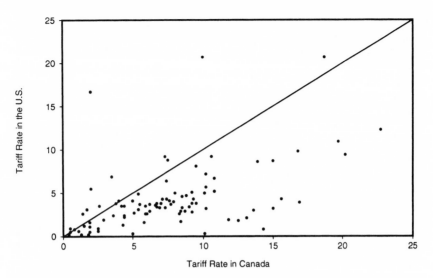

Fig. 12.4   Import tariffs in Canada and the United States in 1987

eters in the model—border costs, home bias, the elasticity of substitution between varieties, and relative marginal costs—are set so as to be reasonable and also to yield an initial distribution of relative size that approximates the 1987 distribution.[8] This assignment allows us to generate relative size before and after the removal of tariffs. Relative size is measured as Canadian shipments divided by U.S. shipments.

The results of the simulation are presented in figure 12.5, which is a scatter diagram divided into the quadrants defined above. Virtually all the points are in either the lower-left- or the upper-right-hand quadrants. The lower-left-hand quandrant corresponds to industries that start out with shipments ratios below 0.1 and decline with the removal of the tariff. These are Canadian industries that do not have a cost advantage vis-à-vis U.S. industries, and liberalization therefore shifts production to the larger country. Points in the upper-right-hand quandrant are industries where Canada has a comparative advantage, and improved access to the U.S. therefore increases Canada's relative production. Interestingly, the simulation shows that tariff asymmetries are not large enough to generate points in the lower-right-hand quadrant. Thus, while in principle Canadian industries can initially be large owing to asymmetric protection and then decline with liberalization, in practice it appears that these asymmetries are not sufficiently high. Overall, the simulations exhibit a positively sloped scattered diagram where relatively large Canadian industries grow and small Canadian industries decline with tariff reductions.

8. Specifically, σ is uniformly distributed between 3 and 7 (the implied markups over marginal costs vary from 14 to 33 percent), c/c^* is uniform between 0.5 and 1.5, and the combined home bias and border cost, $\beta(1 + \kappa)$, varies uniformly between 1.5 and 4.

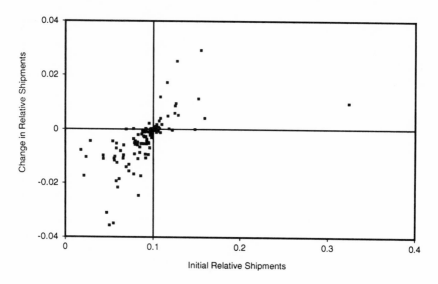

Fig. 12.5   Simulated changes in relative shipments

Figure 12.6 plots the actual data and presents a very different pattern than anticipated. Only industries with initial relative shipments less than 0.5 are included in the diagram. This eliminates just three industries: fur goods, pulp, and newsprint. The last two industries were actually larger than their U.S. counterparts (with relative shipments of 1.1 and 2.3). All three declined sharply in relative size between 1987 and 1992. An examination of the quadrant figure reveals that most of the points lie in the lower two quadrants (106 of 128). Moreover, contrary to our expectations, the diagram suggests that, the larger a Canadian industry was in 1987, the more it tended to shrink relative to its U.S. counterpart.

We may rule out some potential explanations for these features of the data. First, by construction, common business-cycle effects or trends away from manufacturing into services will not affect relative shipments. Similarly, if all North American consumers begin to avoid products made from asbestos or animal furs (two industries in our sample), relative shipments would be unaffected. Second, while Canada's relatively large pre-FTA tariffs seem consistent with the idea that the high-protection industries would start out largest relative to the United States and decline the most, the simulations show that the tariff asymmetries were too small to generate the negative correlation between changes and initial levels. Furthermore, most of the large industries that declined were resource-intensive industries with low Canadian tariffs (newsprint, pulp, nonferrous refining, fish products).

The negative correlation that appears in figure 12.6 does not necessarily imply that relative industry size is converging. As formalized in Quah (1993), even if there is no underlying change in the distribution of some cross section

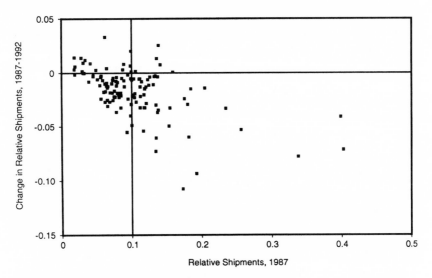

Fig. 12.6 **Actual changes in relative shipments**

of data, we would expect changes to be negatively related to initial levels. The intuition is that, if the parameters that determine relative size are not fixed over time, then the industries that are particularly large at any moment are likely to be ones that were "lucky" that period. Five years later, those favorable circumstances are likely to have receded somewhat. Quah considers the case where each cross-sectional unit has its own distribution from which each time period is a random, independent draw. Under those assumptions, the regression of changes on initial conditions will yield a negative coefficient. An alternative procedure (suggested by our discussant, John Helliwell) consists of regressing changes on the average of initial and final levels, which results in a zero coefficient under the Quah scenario. A positive or negative estimate of the coefficient indicates a rise or fall of the cross-sectional variance.[9] The regression of changes in relative shipments on initial (1987) relative shipments yields a coefficient of -0.20 with standard errors of 0.03. The coefficient declines but remains significantly negative at -0.16 when we replace the 1987 value with the average of 1987 and 1992 relative shipments. Thus, there has been a reduction in the dispersion of relative industry size during the period we study.

Changes in the macroeconomic environment serve as potential explanations for the pattern of changes in relative shipments. First, the Canadian dollar ap-

9. To see why, define y_0^i and y_1^i as the initial and final data for some industry. Each y^i may be drawn from a different distribution as long as draws at different time periods are independent. Let $\Delta y^i = y_1^i - y_0^i$ and $\bar{y}^i = (y_0^i + y_1^i)/2$. A regression of Δy on $\bar{y}$ will yield a coefficient equal to the cross-sectional covariance of Δy and $\bar{y}$ divided by the cross-sectional variance of $\bar{y}$. The covariance term will equal $(V_1 - V_0)/2$, where V_1 and V_0 are the final and initial cross-sectional variances of y_1 and y_0. Thus, an expansion in the cross-sectional variance, $V_1 > V_0$, implies a positive coefficient in the regression.

preciated 11 percent against the U.S. dollar during the period 1987–92 (and by 21 percent from 1986 to 1991), raising the relative cost of production in Canada. In addition, the sample period was characterized by a decline into recession that appears to have been more severe in Canada than in the United States. An interest rate differential emerged in the late 1980s, peaking at 4 percentage points in 1990. In the context of the model, exchange rate appreciation would raise relative marginal costs, c/c^*, whereas a deeper recession or higher interest rates in Canada would tend to lower relative expenditures, E/E^*. While these factors could easily explain relative shipments declines in certain industries, it is not obvious why the largest Canadian industries would experience the biggest declines. It could be the case that industries sensitive to macroeconomic changes simply happened to be relatively large in Canada. It is also possible that the conditions that made Canadian industries large also led to large reductions under adverse macroeconomic conditions.

Exchange rate appreciation raising c/c^* will have the greatest negative effect on industries that have low trade costs or home bias. A cost advantage for Canada translates into high exports and relatively large shipments when import barriers are low. When currency appreciation undermines this cost advantage, exports and relative size decline. Thus, low trade costs may account for observations in the lower-right-hand quadrant. This same logic, however, argues that, when trade costs are low, comparatively disadvantaged Canadian industries would start out small and lose significantly with the appreciation. Thus, rather than a downward slope, differences in trade sensitivity imply an inverted-U pattern in which trade-insensitive industries have shipment ratios roughly equivalent to relative expenditures and are largely unaffected by the appreciation.

Relative expenditures in Canada could be lowered by deeper recession or higher interest rates. If the Canadian and U.S. economies were fully integrated, Canadian producers would be no more affected by declines in Canadian demand than U.S. producers. Thus, the geographic distribution of demand would not affect the distribution of production. Since the North American economy is only partially integrated, declines in E/E^* may account for the reductions in the relative size of Canadian manufacturing industries. There seems to be little a priori reason for the declines in relative expenditure to be largest in the industries with high Canadian relative shipments.[10] Hence, we do not expect the inclusion of macroeconomic sensitivity variables to eliminate the negative size effect. Nevertheless, in assessing the effects of tariffs on relative shipments, we want to control for characteristics of industries that make them likely to be more affected by the business downturn in 1990–92 and the accompanying high Canadian interest rates.

10. Differences between the Canadian and the U.S. share of GDP expended on goods of a particular industry could, however, generate such a result. The industries on which Canadians spend a disproportionate amount would tend to be relatively large and also be the most affected by a decline in Canada's GDP relative to the United States.

Table 12.3   **Changes in Relative Manufacturing Size after the FTA**

	Dependent Variable: $\Delta(S/S^*)$				
	(1)	(2)	(3)	(4)	(5)
Constant	.007	.008	.008	.011[b]	.015[b]
	(.005)	(.005)	(.005)	(.005)	(.006)
Size (S/S^*)	−.174[a]	−.176[a]	−.172[a]	−.177[a]	−.191[a]
	(.032)	(.032)	(.037)	(.036)	(.037)
Canadian tariffs ($|\Delta t_C|$)	−.151[b]	−.12[c]	−.123[c]	−.085	−.122[c]
	(.060)	(.069)	(.071)	(.073)	(.070)
U.S. tariffs ($|\Delta t_{US}|$)		−.095	−.097	−.147	−.165
		(.107)	(.108)	(.110)	(.111)
Openness			−.012	.025	.036
			(.055)	(.059)	(.059)
Cyclical sensitivity				−.07[c]	
				(.039)	
Durable goods					−.009[b]
					(.004)
R^2	.207	.212	.212	.234	.242
Root MSE	.020	.020	.020	.020	.020
No. of observations	125	125	125	125	125

Note: Ordinary least squares regressions with standard errors in parentheses. The superscripts a, b, and c indicate significance in a two-tailed test at the 1, 5, and 10 percent levels. Size is the average of 1987 and 1992 relative shipments.

We now turn to statistical analysis to estimate the strength of the link between trade liberalization and relative manufacturing performance while including controls for changes in macroeconomic conditions. Table 12.3 reports regression estimates of the effects of changes in tariffs and the macroeconomy on changes in the relative size of manufacturing industries.[11] In each specification, we include the average of the industry's 1987 and 1992 relative shipments as a covariate. Its coefficient reflects the tendency of the industry cross-sectional variance to expand or decline after conditioning on other observed characteristics of the industry.

The first two columns show that the removal of both Canadian and U.S. tariffs is associated with lower Canadian relative shipments. When we enter Canadian tariff levels alone, the effect is highly significant. Thus, the elimination of Canadian tariff protection appeared to have led to the relative contraction of Canadian industry. When we include both tariff levels, the Canadian tariff remains significant at the 10 percent confidence level, while the U.S. tariff variable enters with a perverse sign but is not statistically significant.

---

11. The regression sample excludes three extreme observations: fur goods, pulp, and newsprint. These industries were the three largest relative to the United States in 1987 (with relative shipments of 0.76, 1.1, 2.3). They also experienced declines that were an order of magnitude larger than the average for other industries (−0.37, −0.44, and −0.74, compared to −0.02).

The following three columns display results when we add controls for industry sensitivity to exchange rate appreciation and the deeper Canadian recession. "Openness" is calculated as the 1987–92 average of bilateral trade divided by the sum of Canadian and U.S. production in North America. We use it as a proxy for each industry's trade impediments. Open industries are more vulnerable to exchange rate appreciation. Column 3 shows that the variable obtains the expected negative sign, but the estimate is insignificantly different from zero. Thus, we find little evidence that exchange rate appreciation affected the pattern of changes across industries.

Columns 4 and 5 present results incorporating variables representing business-cycle sensitivity. The "cyclical sensitivity" variable employed in the column 4 regression is based on Bloskie's (1991) study of the performance of two-digit industries during the last eight recessions preceeding the one in 1991–92. Bloskie calculated the average percentage drop in output from the last quarter prior to the recession to the last quarter of the recession. The negative coefficient estimate supports the hypothesis that cyclically sensitive industries declined disproportionately in Canada. Somewhat stronger results obtain for an alternative measure of business-cycle sensitivity, "durable goods," which is an indicator variable based on the Statistics Canada classification.[12] Given the relatively high interest rates that prevailed in Canada from 1989 to 1991, it seems likely that durable-goods industries would decline disproportionately in Canada. Column 2 results bear this expectation out; the durable-goods effect is significant at the 5 percent confidence level.

The results appearing in table 12.3 suggest that both Canadian tariff reductions and a deeper Canadian recession share responsibility for the tendency of Canadian industries to decline relative to their U.S. counterparts. The purported gains from opening U.S. markets to Canadian producers receive no support from the regression analysis. U.S. tariffs were generally small, and they also tended to be positively correlated (Spearman rank correlation of 0.6) with Canadian tariffs. Thus, industries that benefited from more access to U.S. markets tended to be industries that experienced even larger reductions in the protection afforded them by Canadian tariffs. Industries that are consistently more cyclical or that produce durable goods declined more during the period 1987–92. Interestingly, the strong negative effect of average relative size remains across all specifications. Thus, the data suggest that the FTA and adverse macroeconomic factors produced a negative shift in the distribution of relative industry size. Meanwhile, the variance of that distribution declined.

12.3 Conclusions

This paper extends a two-country model of intraindustry trade to allow for asymmetries in country size, rates of protection, and production costs. While

---

12. Machinery, electronics, transportation equipment, furniture, metals, and miscellaneous manufactures are all classified as durable goods. Nondurables include paper, textiles, chemicals, food, and beverages.

trade liberalization may generate a large variety of outcomes for the relative size of industries in the two countries, the primary prediction of the model is that market-access considerations encourage production of differentiated products to concentrate in the larger of two trading partners. Using data for 128 matched industries in the United States and Canada for the years 1987 and 1992, we examine what happened over the period that the FTA was implemented.

The data reveal that most Canadian industries experienced relative shipments reductions from 1987 to 1992, a result consistent with the model. Our examination of the distribution of these reductions across industries indicates that they are related to Canadian tariff reductions and the business cycle. Thus, the elimination of Canadian protection and a deeper recession in Canada partly explain the relative decline of Canadian manufacturing over this period. We could not, however, provide evidence that Canadian dollar appreciation harmed specific industries. Moreover, U.S. tariff reductions do not appear to have increased relative output in Canada. Indeed, our regressions consistently yield the wrong sign for U.S. tariffs, although the estimates lack statistical significance.

A striking feature of the data is that Canadian industries that were relatively strong in 1987 did not expand after trade liberalization; rather, they were the ones that suffered the greatest relative declines. Our statistical evidence indicates a convergence in relative size even when we include controls for the tariff changes and sensitivity to macroeconomic influences. The observed tendency of the industry cross section to converge during the period 1987–92 suggests that some underlying source of variation in relative size has become less important. Some possible mechanisms would include convergence in North American factor prices or production technologies. Overall, it appears that trade liberalization explains only a small part of the changes in U.S. and Canadian manufacturing from 1987 to 1992.

References

Baldwin, J., P. Gorecki, and J. McVey. 1986. Canada-U.S. productivity differences in the manufacturing sector: 1970–79. In *Canadian industry in transition,* ed. D. McFetridge. Toronto: University of Toronto Press.

Bloskie, C. 1991. Industry output in recessions. *Canadian Economic Observer* 4:3.1–3.15.

Gaston, N., and D. Trefler. 1994. The role of international trade and trade policy in the labour markets of Canada and the United States. *World Economy* 17:45–62.

Grubel, H., and P. Lloyd. 1975. *Intra-industry trade.* New York: Wiley.

Hazledine, T. 1994. Free trade: What happened? University of Auckland. Mimeo. (Paper prepared for the annual meeting of the Canadian Economics Association.)

Head, K., J. Ries, and M. Zhang. 1995. A correspondence between constructed manufacturing industries, Canadian SICs, United States SICs, and United Nations SITCs. Mimeo.

Helliwell, J. 1995. Do national borders matter for Quebec's trade? Working Paper no. 5215. Cambridge, Mass.: National Bureau of Economic Research.

Helpman, E., and P. R. Krugman. 1985. *Market structure and foreign trade: Increasing returns, imperfect competition, and the international trade.* Cambridge, Mass.: MIT Press.

Krugman, P. 1980. Scale economies, product differentiation, and the pattern of trade. *American Economic Review* 70:950–59.

Krugman, P., and G. Hanson. 1993. Mexico-U.S. free trade and the location of production. In *The Mexico-U.S. Free Trade Agreement,* ed. P. M. Garber. Cambridge, Mass.: MIT Press.

McCallum, J. 1995. National borders matter: Canada-U.S. regional trade patterns. *American Economic Review* 85:615–23.

Quah, D. 1993. Galton's fallacy and tests of the convergence hypothesis. *Scandinavian Journal of Economics* 95:427–43.

Statistics Canada. 1993. *Trade patterns: Canada-United States, the manufacturing industries, 1981–1991.* Catalog no. 65-504E. Ottowa.

U.S.-Canada Automotive Agreement Policy Research Project. 1985. *The U.S.-Canadian Automotive Products Agreement of 1965: An evaluation for its twentieth year.* Policy Research Project Report no. 68. University of Texas, Austin, Lyndon B. Johnson School of Public Affairs.

Contributors

Bruce A. Blonigen
Department of Economics
University of Oregon
435 Prince Lucien Campbell Hall
Eugene, OR 97403

Robert E. Cumby
Department of Economics
Georgetown University
580 Intercultural Center
Washington, DC 20057

Andrew R. Dick
Economic Analysis Group
Antitrust Division
U.S. Department of Justice
600 E St., Suite 10,000
Washington, DC 20530

Kimberly Ann Elliott
Institute for International Economics
11 Dupont Circle
Washington, DC 20036

Robert C. Feenstra
Department of Economics
University of California
Davis, CA 95616

Pinelopi Koujianou Goldberg
Department of Economics
Princeton University
307 Fisher Hall
Princeton, NJ 08544

Gordon H. Hanson
Department of Economics
University of Texas
Austin, TX 78712

Keith Head
Faculty of Commerce
University of British Columbia
2053 Main Mall
Vancouver, BC V6T 1Z2, Canada

Michael M. Knetter
Department of Economics
Dartmouth College
Hanover, NH 03755

Kala Krishna
Department of Economics
401 Kern Graduate Building
The Pennsylvania State University
University Park, PA 16802

James Levinsohn
Department of Economics
University of Michigan
Ann Arbor, MI 48109

Theodore H. Moran
Department of Economics
Georgetown University
580 Intercultural Center
Washington, DC 20057

343

Thomas J. Prusa
Department of Economics
Rutgers University
Hamilton Street
New Brunswick, NJ 08903

J. David Richardson
Department of Economics
347 Eggers Hall
Syracuse University
Syracuse, NY 13244

John Ries
Faculty of Commerce
University of British Columbia
2053 Main Mall
Vancouver, BC V6T 1Z2, Canada

Deborah L. Swenson
Department of Economics
University of California
Davis, CA 95616

Marie Thursby
Department of Economics
Krannert Graduate School of
  Management
Purdue University
West Lafayette, IN 47907

David E. Weinstein
School of Business Administration
University of Michigan
Ann Arbor, MI 48109

Name Index

Subject Index